THREE

An Unfinished Woman
Pentimento
Scoundrel Time

By Lillian Hellman

PLAYS

THE CHILDREN'S HOUR (1934)

DAYS TO COME (1936)

THE LITTLE FOXES (1939)

WATCH ON THE RHINE (1941)

THE SEARCHING WIND (1944)

ANOTHER PART OF THE FOREST (1947)

MONTSERRAT (*An adaptation*, 1950)

THE AUTUMN GARDEN (1951)

THE LARK (*An adaptation*, 1956)

CANDIDE (*An operetta*, 1957)

TOYS IN THE ATTIC (1960)

MY MOTHER, MY FATHER AND ME (*An adaptation*, 1963)

THE COLLECTED PLAYS (1972)

MEMOIRS

AN UNFINISHED WOMAN (1969)

PENTIMENTO (1973)

SCOUNDREL TIME (1976)

THREE (*The collected memoirs, with new
commentaries by the author*, 1979)

EDITOR OF

THE SELECTED LETTERS OF ANTON CHEKHOV (1955)

THE BIG KNOCKOVER: SELECTED STORIES AND SHORT
NOVELS BY DASHIELL HAMMETT (1966)

THREE

An Unfinished Woman
Pentimento
Scoundrel Time

by LILLIAN HELLMAN

with new commentaries by the author

Introduction by RICHARD POIRIER

LITTLE, BROWN AND COMPANY · BOSTON · TORONTO

 with photographs

Portions of *An Unfinished Woman* originally appeared in the
New York Review of Books, The Atlantic, and *Partisan Review.*
The Introduction to *The Big Knockover* copyright © 1965,
1966 by Lillian Hellman. Reprinted from *The Big Knockover:
Selected Stories and Short Novels of Dashiell Hammett,* edited
by Lillian Hellman, by permission of Random House, Inc.

Portions *of Pentimento* originally appeared in *The Atlantic,
Esquire,* and the *New York Review of Books.*

*Published simultaneously in Canada
by Little, Brown & Company (Canada) Limited*

PRINTED IN THE UNITED STATES OF AMERICA

Contents

*Illustrations appear between
pages 166–167 and 646–647.*

INTRODUCTION

by Richard Poirier

WITH the success of *The Children's Hour* in 1934, Lillian Hellman became a celebrated person while still in her late twenties. Even before that, working in the publishing world of Horace Liveright and in the Hollywood of Sam Goldwyn, she had found herself among famous and very powerful people. These, it might have been expected, would be the focus of the essays in recollection that she began in 1969 with *An Unfinished Woman: A Memoir*, and continued with *Pentimento: A Book of Portraits* in 1973, and then with *Scoundrel Time* in 1976, a memoir of the witch-hunting years of the 1950's, with a historical introduction by Garry Wills. But if in the collection of these three books we find a portrait of Dashiell Hammett, the man whose life she shared for over thirty years, there is also the portrait of Helen, the black woman who for a long time tended to her needs and contended with her ways without deigning to admit that she had needs and ways of her own. And if these pages give a more human and often superbly comic dimension to well-known figures like Henry Wallace and Hemingway, Dorothy Parker and Eisenstein, with glimpses of Franklin D. Roosevelt and a sad, lovable Fitzgerald in his late Hollywood days, they also give a degree of immortality to people the reader could know nothing about, like Bethe, a remote cousin sent from Germany to work for a branch of her father's family in New Orleans and eventually to marry a ne'er-do-well relative named Styrie Bowman, one of the grotesquely interesting subsidiary figures in these pages. These books are a gallery of people nearly anonymous, and this is one clue to the beauty and substantiality of Hellman, both in her life and in her writing. She never abstracts herself into any "brightest hour," theatrical, political, or social. Though she has been close to the great and famous in all these areas, her focus on mostly obscure people simply means that they, and not Tallulah Bankhead or Goldwyn, who are among the many fascinating miniatures in this gallery, have meant most to her. It is a choice so free of self-congratulation or pastoral condescension that one carries away feelings that these people — Bethe and Willy and Julia and Arthur Cowan, each of whom has a separate portrait, and such others as her Aunt Jenny or Aunt Hannah, or the people who helped on her farm in Pleasantville, or the aged Caroline Ducky, who had been born into slavery in her mother's family — are all important not because they knew Hellman but, as she would have it, because she was privileged to know them.

This gathering of three books will especially please

any reader who has long suspected that gossip about the famous by the famous, a standard fare of most reminiscences, does not constitute revelation but is rather the evasion of it, and very often an indication that the public life of the writer has long since obliterated the capacity for a private one, for "the daily stuff" that Hellman says is "the real truth." Hellman has no interest in gossip or in celebrities or for that matter in the places where these become a commodity. New York City, Hollywood, London, Rome, and Paris all figure in her life and in these pages. But as with people, so with places, and one is taken often to spots less renowned like New Orleans, Martha's Vineyard, or Cambridge, Massachusetts. On her visits to Spain during the Civil War, she managed to wander about on her own and had her most significant experiences with people she met by chance; during World War II in the Soviet Union she was happiest outside Moscow, visiting the front. It is very possible that she would still be living on a farm in Pleasantville, New York, where she and Dashiell Hammett spent some of the happiest of what were to be thirty-one years together, but which they had to sell in 1952 after Hammett was sent to jail for refusing to name contributors to a Civil Rights Congress bail fund and after Hellman was blacklisted for refusing to play games with the House Un-American Activities Committee: "To hurt innocent people whom I knew many years ago in order to save myself," she told them, "is, to me, inhuman and indecent and dishonorable."

Hellman's sense of place and of people is a strongly Southern one, not simply because much of her childhood was spent in New Orleans but because she intuitively re-

sponded to the intense familial and communal relationships she encountered there. It was in the South that she
learned to like a kind of American cooking, developed a
lifelong love for fishing, a feeling for the land which was
to make her a good farmer. It was there, too, that she first
learned about injustice and exploitation. She did not
learn these as liberal abstractions. She was bound by
blood to people who profited from them, and by an often
greater love to people who were the victims, like the
black woman Sophronia, her wet-nurse and her guide
through childhood and the pains of early adolescence.
As it turned out, Sophronia's habits of mind were very
much those exhibited by Hellman when she appeared before HUAC, though so deep and inward is the obligation that she herself does not seem aware of this specific
manifestation of it. Significant connections of this kind
emerge all the more clearly now that these three books
are in the close proximity of one volume. Thus, the mem-
orable statement before HUAC recorded in *Scoundrel
Time*, in which she expresses her willingness to talk fully
about herself and her unwillingness to talk about other
people, can be seen as perhaps a full flowering of the advice given by Sophronia many, many years before to the
hungry, humiliated child, so angry she had thrown herself from a tree and broken her nose, who had seen her
father get into a taxi with a "faded, sexy, giggly" woman
named Fizzy: "On the way [home] she told me that I
must say nothing about Fizzy to anybody ever, and that
if my nose still hurt in a few days I was only to say that I
had fallen on the street and refuse to answer any questions about how I fell." As a child, she picked up wisdom
that comes, as Yeats would say, "from beggary," from

people like Sophronia and Bethe and Caroline Ducky, and her maiden aunts Jenny and Hannah.

These books are full of travel and its chance adventures, and travel is a good enough metaphor for the special kind of reading experience offered by these pieces. In a manner both exciting and inevitable, the announced or titular subject at any given point becomes for long stretches only the spur to recollections of places and people in the past. A strange place will somehow provoke memories of a familiar one which then becomes, thanks to this new and unexpected conjunction, endowed with an unaccustomed strangeness and life of its own. The writing is given a reverberating and reflective depth by the composure with which Hellman is able simultaneously to present multiple versions of herself. The one who addresses us as the writer of a piece, that is, will recollect an earlier Hellman who is then often described as someone in the very act of recollecting a scene wherein a still earlier version, young woman or child, may be seen. Thus in *An Unfinished Woman* we learn of a night in 1966 at the gloomy National Hotel in Moscow. She has just spent the evening trying to explain to Raya, a dear friend who was her guide and translator during a wartime visit to the USSR, the political difficulties that forced the sale of the Pleasantville farm in 1952. Recollections are given an orchestration that can be called Faulknerian while taking its authority not from him so much as from movements and drifts of mind belonging by instinct to Hellman. These find so brilliant a correspondence in the structure of her sentences that the reader experiences not merely the intimacies of her discernibly human voice but the greater intimacy of being able to feel, in the very movement of the prose, a mind at work on itself. It is as if she were saying that while these are indeed things that happened to me and not to you, you and I are nonetheless both here, in the presence now of this writing, and we share equally in what the language might yield to us:

The memories mounted with the cigarettes and, I guess, with the vodka. They were not bad memories, most of them, and I was not disturbed by them, or so I thought, but I knew that I had taken a whole period of my life and thrown it somewhere, always intending to call for it again, but now that it came time to call, I couldn't remember where I had left it. Did other people do this, drop the past in a used car lot and leave it for so long that one couldn't even remember the name of the road?

The road had to be to the lake in Pleasantville. But at first, I could only remember the last day I had ever walked it. After the moving vans had left the house, I had gone down to the lake remembering that we had left two turtle traps tied to a tree. I climbed up and around to bring in the traps, and then wondered what to do with them, how to ask the storage people to keep turtle traps safe for the future. Then the memory of the turtle traps brought back the first snapping turtles Hammett and I had caught, the nights spent reading about how to make the traps, how to kill the turtles, how to clean them, how to make the soup; and the soup brought back the sausage making and the ham curing, and the planting of a thousand twelve-inch pines that must now be a small forest; and the discovery of the beaver dam, and the boiled skunk cabbage and pickerelweed for dinner, in imitation of American Indians, that had made everybody sick but me; and working late into the night — I had written four plays at the farm and four or five movies — and then running, always with a dog and sometimes four, in the early summer light to the lake for a swim, pretending I was somebody else in some other land, some other century. And then back again to that last day: I had carried the turtle traps back to the house, forgetting, until I got to the tree nursery along the lake road, that I didn't own the house anymore. I stopped there to look at the hundred French lilac trees in the nursery, the rosebushes waiting for the transplant place they would never get, the two extravagant acres of blanched asparagus, and standing there by the road that May afternoon of 1952, I finally realized that I would never have any of this beautiful, hardscrabble land again. Now, in the Moscow room, I was glad it was gone, but sorry that the days of Joseph McCarthy, the persecution of Hammett, my own appearance before the House Un-American Activities Committee, the Hollywood blacklist, had caused it to be gone. There could never be any place like it again because I could never again be that woman who worked from seven in the morning until two or three the next morning and woke rested and hungry for each new day.

One memory excites another memory here, the one gets enveloped in the other and touches on a history nearly mythic, the American Indian, "some other land, some other century." Just when it seems that recollection may degenerate into nostalgia it moves directly to intractable memories of a more recent past, the McCarthy era, and from there to the firm ground of the present, the physical reality of Hellman now. She recovers herself at the end as a woman who, in the moment of writing, and by virtue of the very exercise of writing, discovers that she is no longer her earlier self, no longer someone who could physically do what she is writing about. The act of writing can be said to dispel rather than create the illusion that the past can ever repeat itself.

Hellman has kept that capacity for movement back and forth which she learned as a young child when she shuttled every year between New York and New Orleans, six months in each, surrounded in the one by her mother's family, originally from Alabama, and in the other living with her father's sisters, whose parents had come to New Orleans as part of the German immigration of 1845–1848. Requiring an "adjustment in two very different worlds," this semiannual change "made formal education into a kind of frantic tennis game, sometimes played with children whose strokes had force and brilliance, sometimes with those who could barely hold the racket." In a child so questing and questioning and anxious for love, the unsettling and resettling also nurtured a genius, essential to the kind of writer she was to become, for seeing persons and places relatively and within the complex changes wrought by the passage of time and geographic separations.

Hellman's style is a catalytic medium for registering the shadows of things present and the vividness of things absent. Like Hellman herself, the style is strong and pliant enough to allow all the people with whom she deals the fullest and freest movement as they work out their individual destinies. It is therefore noteworthy — though it must be stressed that Hellman herself never summarizes in this way — that Julia is not the only person she loves who, it seems, is always out of reach, a kind of fugitive. And when not fugitives to a cause, her people can, like Bethe, have a prior commitment to a lover, who happens also to be a fugitive. Or they are in pursuit, like Uncle Willy, of pleasures and wealth that are a reprieve from a silly, cocaine-addicted wife who has taken her part black part Indian chauffeur as a lover, or they may, like Arthur Cowan, be so enslaved to the special disciplines of madness that, except in fits and starts, they can't settle anywhere or with anyone. Or, like

Hammett, they may simply go upstairs when things aren't to their liking and shut the door. There is a kind of emotional range-finding, even in the movement of dialogue, very often on the question or possibilities of loving. Efforts to determine, in relation to any given person, those limits of closeness which are sometimes the precondition of love, can be felt in the exploratory, tentative quality of her conversation with Jimsie, the young man in the title chapter of *Pentimento* whom Hellman befriends while teaching at Harvard. He tells her at dinner some years later that he hopes she will meet the woman he lives with. "You like Carrie?" "She's O.K.," he says. "That's all?" Hellman asks. "Isn't that enough?" "No," she says. "I don't think so." "Not for you," he says. "For me." Her capacity in any given situation or conversation to carry in her head and in her heart analogous moments from the past and, perhaps as a consequence, to allow positions she does not immediately share to have the last word — it is this which helps make a positive virtue of that "indecision and vagueness" which irritated one theatrical director about her. "Indecision and vagueness" is the sure sign of her near total saturation in the always elusive, random, sometimes resistant materials, including the people, about which she writes.

To write out of a saturated mind is altogether different from writing out of a calculating one. By calculation one event can be made to mean many different things, but in Hellman it is as if an event, bathed in the atmosphere of her style, is, as in a dream, indivisibly the source of radiating impressions and experiences. Thus, when she writes a portrait called "Willy" it becomes, by a process too inevitable to have been conscious, a drama of politi-

cal as well as romantic alternatives. Her feelings about
Willy, a compound of emotions left over from adolescent
infatuation and intensified by a strange mingling in the
older woman of pity and desire for oblivion, are by
necessity immersed in other feelings, feelings having to
do with her family as an aspect of the South and of an
older America, with power and exploitation as she became aware of these at the family dinner table, and with
the injustice of socially ordained inferiority visited especially on blacks and on women. By this circuitous route
the story of Willy is also the story of Hammett, the most
powerful man in her life, toward whom she can feel resentment as nearly inarticulate as her love. His was the
unpremeditated injustice of a man who demands his way
in things while denying the woman hers, thereby precipi-
tating complaints which, in Hellman's case, would then
leave her with the burden of feeling guilty for any consequences.

Hellman's conflicted relationships to men of great personal power, "vivid, impetuous, high-living men," as she
calls them at one point, is inseparable from the complexi-
ties of her politics. There is in her a near contradiction
of feeling about the strange, perhaps necessary alliance
of power to unscrupulousness. This may be one reason
why in *Scoundrel Time* she admits to being less angry at
Nixon and McCarthy than at the intellectuals and enter-
tainers who let themselves be used. Abstracted moralism
gave way early on to a rich mixture of fascination and
distaste for the exercises of privilege and power: "I began to think that greed and the cheating that is its usual
companion were comic as well as evil and I began to like
the family dinners with the talk of who did what to

whom." Willy was as often a topic as a participant in these dinners. As a speculator in Central and South American trade, he had been part of the most pugnacious thrusts of American economic imperialism, and if he had not himself killed any "natives," he had almost certainly ordered other people to do so. At the end of "Willy" it is not Hellman but Hammett who insists that Willy should be portrayed as a scoundrel. Perhaps what made the demand so eloquent is that it came from someone who had himself once been offered five thousand dollars to kill a labor union organizer. Hellman does not make this connection, but it is one which this gathering of books now calls attention to, should any reader look retrospectively at "Willy" from the vantage point of *Scoundrel Time*, where we learn something about Hammett's experiences as a Pinkerton agent. It is obvious that Hellman makes the right choice under Hammett's tutelage, but it should also be obvious that if being morally circumspect were all that mattered she would never have been able to write the piece to begin with. The decision not to go away with Willy, that is, does not erase the fascination and affection that brings her vibrant image of him into existence.

One of the remarkable things about Hellman as a writer, in her plays as well as in her prose, is that she works against her own tendencies to be assertive, stabilized, moralistic, and knowing. Her paragraphs are supported not by dogma but by qualifications, by words like "perhaps," "however," by admissions of what she could not remember and of what she is not prepared to say. She is mystified by overly clarified interpretations of her work, as we learn in *Pentimento*, where she describes her pained reaction to the drama critics who raved about *The Little Foxes* without ever helping her to understand why she should feel so uncertain about it. It was based on aspects of her mother's family in which "life had been too big, too muddled for writing." What puzzled her about the responses to the play from audiences and critics was that "I had meant to half mock my own youthful high-class innocence in Alexandra, the young girl in the play; I had meant people to smile at, and to sympathize with, the sad, weak Birdie, certainly I had not meant them to cry; I had meant the audience to recognize some part of themselves in the money-dominated Hubbards; I had not meant people to think of them as villains to whom they had no connection."

After its great success on Broadway, she nonetheless grew "restless, sickish, digging around in the random memories that had been the conscious, semiconscious material of the play," much of which is to be found in these three books. Anyone who has read *The Little Foxes* recently will be aware that the shadings Hellman wanted to put there can indeed be found. But an understanding of her place in American letters depends on our recognizing why she chose to enter on a second career as a writer, turning from plays to prose portraiture and reminiscence. She has achieved a redirection of energies, unprecedented in our literature, from one form into another which, in her conception of it, is so ample and flexible that she does not have to do any restless "digging around" *after* the writing and can instead make this process part of the very substance of the writing itself. The writing, that is, does not so much communicate her already confirmed sense of a place or a person; rather it enacts her own quite tentative explorations of them. It often seems as if she gets to know how she feels about something only by writing about it. Sentences like "I know all that I have written here, or I know it the way I remember it, which, of course, may not be the whole truth," or " 'In these days,' I have written, and will leave here," make us realize that we are faced with a unique kind of writing which will at one moment question the motives, even the authenticity of what was written the moment before. It is a style which manages to capture the "conscious semiconsciousness" which she discovered at a wonderful moment in "Bethe" as she rides home on the streetcar with her aunts and realizes that she had seen between Bethe and Mr. Arneggio her first and wonderful glimpse of adult sexual love.

It is not surprising that she should prefer the sea and its shore, filled with mysterious, submerged fullness of life in constant reciprocation, to more settled and inert bodies of water whose movements are constrained. In the frighteningly calm opening of "Turtle" she describes being caught in the ocean current while swimming alone off a boat in the heavy tides of Martha's Vineyard; she realized she was about to drown and she was "thinking that water had been me, all my life, and this wasn't a bad way to die if only I had sense enough to go quietly and not make myself miserable with struggle." Similarly in the opening paragraphs of "Helen" she discerns connections between her childlike pleasure in "digging and mucking about on the edge of the shore" and "the digging about that occasionally happens when I am asleep." For her, the act of writing is still another way of "digging around" among "random memories" and among the words that now, in the present, might sufficiently embody them. She is not interested in things known ahead of time to be there, like the salt fish hung mischievously on the fishing line of Antony by an aquatic slave of Cleopatra. There is not to be found in these pages those flash revelations by which contemporary writers of biography and autobiography purchase the attention of their readers. In Hellman's books people are so steeped in conjecture that it is impossible to imagine how a "secret" about any one of them, or an isolated revelation, could be of consequence. Cowan is as much a mystery at the end as at the beginning of the portrait about him. Like other people Hellman favors, he exists in contradiction, in erratic movement, and in a casual contempt of ordinary or predictable schedules. His oddity might remind us that one of Hellman's favorite stories is Melville's *Bartleby the Scrivener*. The story can be read as a meditation on the kind of eccentricity condoned and the kind of eccentricity condemned at the center of American economic life, Wall Street. If Cowan displays eccentricity, it is nonetheless of a Dickensian variety, like that of Ginger Nut and Turkey in Melville's story. It poses no threat to anyone at the presumed center, and may even help define its location. (It is not surprising to learn that when Cowan died he might have been on a government mission.) By contrast, Hammett could be eccentric only in a society whose center had in large part lost its claim to legitimacy, and this often secluded and quiet man belongs with Bartleby to the class of nonconformists. Bartleby's famous and thrillingly simple declaration, "I would prefer not to," could be imagined either for Hammett or for Hellman herself. Hellman's discriminations in favor of people not obedient to a center, who move to their own signals however erratic, is of a piece with her declaration in Washington, the center of American political power, that "I cannot and will not cut my conscience to fit this year's fashions."

To elicit a connection between her political actions, her capacity to like Cowan and to love Hammett, and to see all of this as synchronized with her stylistic and narrative movements is but a way of suggesting that we are always referred back to a strong but free-moving individual presence, a spiritual presence, that suffuses the writing at every point and allows nothing to seem isolated or beyond the reach of sympathy. Nothing in these writings comes to an end, in the sense of being conclusive, since there is always some form of "however," the word that even as it closes *An Unfinished Woman* releases us to conjectures that go beyond it. There are no trophies here to be exhibited. And if other people's reputations are not to be used as trophies, neither is the historical act of courage by which she refuses to so use them. She tells us that after the hearings in Washington she did not want immediately to talk to Hammett for fear of saying "even by inference, 'See, I was right and you were wrong.' " In what for others would have been a moment of victory and heady vindication, she doubted even that she had been "right": "Because, of course, I had not been right, if by right one means what one wanted to say, didn't say, and the fact that I got off without being prosecuted didn't prove that I had been right."

She tells us in *Scoundrel Time* what it is she had wanted to say to the committee: "a blunt, damning statement that represented the moral position for my case."

Her reason for not at the time even admitting her inclinations to Abe Fortas, the lawyer, later to be a Supreme Court justice, with whom she conferred, brings into sharp focus a recurrent preoccupation of all three books: "I didn't say any of that to Fortas because I knew I would never be able to say it at all." *Scoundrel Time* is about many things other than Hellman's appearance before HUAC, including the hauntingly beautiful memory of the final parade of deer that marked her last hours at Pleasantville with Hammett and the half-comic spy thriller, focused on her, in Rome and London, but it also resolves a question implicit everywhere else — what at last is an appropriate way to talk about oneself, about others, about that mystery which, for want of a better word, we call "life"? It is a question on which Hemingway has no exclusive rights, and his answer, a style learned from a despair, is too one-dimensional for Hellman, who remarks sadly of Hemingway's friends Gerald and Sara Murphy that "I came to think too much of their lives had been based on style." In particular, Hellman is suspicious of the kind of "brave" or "emphatic" talk she has to listen to when Clifford Odets pounds the table in a restaurant and shouts, "Well, I can tell you what I am going to do before those bastards on the Committee. I am going to show them the face of a radical man and tell them to go fuck themselves." He turned out, of course, to be a cooperative witness. Hellman means to suggest a good deal, therefore, when she tells us that Hammett, "sober, was always a silent man." He was so laconic in his speech, so tough-minded about language, that even as he neared death he would not allow Hellman the keepsake of what is in fact a very restrained sentiment. "Sometimes," she writes, "I would resent the understated or seldom stated side of us and, guessing death wasn't too far away, I would try for something to have afterwards. One day I said, 'We've done fine, haven't we?' He said, 'Fine's too big a word for me. Why don't we just say we've done better than most people?' "

Any serious writer probably addresses some imaginary ideal reader, and it is possible to imagine these writings as addressed, in continuing, loving contention, to the man who wanted always to determine what "we" shall say. There are confirmations everywhere in this collection of his provocative candor, his critical intelligence about people and about writing, his daring risks with a woman of unflappable independence whom he loved more than any other. But with a frequency on which Hellman never comments, these writings bring him into her life as he is in the very act of absenting himself from it, moving himself out of the easy reach of her voice. He makes his presence felt by the threat of denying it (as in the argument about Willy), by dismissive withdrawals (when he retires to his room and doesn't come out for three days when Cowan visits the Vineyard), or by a refusal or inability to understand (as when he will not imagine that Hellman's admiration for Bethe's renegade love affair helped her to accept the difficulties, in the 1930's, of living publicly with a man when you had no intention of marrying him). In that particular instance, Hellman became "so angry that I left the apartment, drove to Montauk on a snowy day, and came back two days later with the grippe." There is a similar moment, especially revealing about the provocative difficulties of talk and of dialogue between Hellman and

Hammett, at the end of the funny, spooky story — really a moral tale — called "Turtle." Astonished by a huge turtle surviving at Pleasantville even after they had severed its head from its body, she wonders aloud to Hammett that "it moved so far. It's that I've never before thought about *life,* if you know what I mean." "No, I don't," he said. Only with Hammett does she ever sound so sophomorically earnest, reporting that she went on to ask, "Well, what is life and stuff like that." So far from being an idle question, it becomes obvious throughout these writings, notably in "Julia," that Hellman is everywhere concerned with the awesome stubbornness of "life," with animal and spiritual "life" as it exceeds the usual rationalistic formulas, including most novelistic ones. Her concern is articulated at a level which makes her remarks in "Turtle" charmingly simple, eager, and, under the pressure of his shrugging response, at once comic and sad.

The inference to be drawn from this is not that Hammett was begrudging of her experience but that he challenged precisely the kinds of submerged continuity which she is always trying to locate, the marvelous inner sense of connectedness, the ability to bring disparate things together, which is one of the most notable accomplishments of these three books, with their subtle yet intense grasp of possible analogies among different places, different people, different times. It is in this sense that the book is written as if for the edification of a lover who "didn't understand what I meant." This is doubtless a frequent, and surely one of the best reasons for writing anything.

Such speculations have to contend, of course, with the still surer evidence that Lillian Hellman is a woman of formidable strength and stubbornness of mind. The stubbornness shines forth as both a literary and a human virtue in the intensity of her loyalties to the essential wholeness of the people she cares about. It comes out in her sifting of probable delusion from possible conjecture, memory from record, a later from an earlier feeling, all of it compelled by her natural deference toward anyone she is writing about. If the title of one of the volumes, *Pentimento,* refers us to painting — the bodying forth through the paint on an old canvas of lines and figures the artist had painted over, "repented" of — then the portraiture in all these books is in its composite effect like something of the Dutch school of Rembrandt. Henry James once remarked of such works that they projected a sense of character markedly different from any produced in "our modern degenerescence," wherein we "analyze and theorize and rub off the bloom of the mystery" of human character. Hellman's deepest loyalty is finally to integrity of being, and the swarm of fine, sometimes conflicting impressions that reflect off one another ultimately resolve themselves into a massive yet flexible image. Her work provides one of those rare instances where the moral value of the style is wholly inseparable from its immense literary worth, where the excitations, the pacing, and the intensifications manage to create in us perceptions about human character that have all but disappeared from contemporary writing.

THREE

An Unfinished Woman
Pentimento
Scoundrel Time

On Reading Again

*A*s most writers differ about the best hours for work,
morning, night, night-day, so they differ about reading
work from the past. My dislike of going back over old
work would not matter to anybody but me, except as it
affects the collection of these three books.

The same turning away from completed work was true
in the theatre. I have never seen a full performance of
any of my plays once they opened, although it was my
habit always to drop by the theatre once a week for perhaps a half hour, to be sure the general performances
were still good and to give myself the pleasure, when a
play was successful, of listening and being part of the
audience. It is a pleasure to be found in no other form of
writing and my guess as to why so many good novelists
have been willing to chance being bad playwrights. During the run of "Watch on the Rhine" there was a small
story that made the rounds of gossip columns and theatre

3

*circles. A few months after the play opened, I was stand-
ing in the back aisle, watching the play, with the head
usher pacing behind me. She told everybody, for a good
many years, that after about ten minutes of watching the
play, I said to her, "Ruthie, what act are they in?"*

*All the obvious reasons for this are possibly true, but
nothing seems to explain the stubbornness of the fight I
make against going back to anything I have written, returning in any form to finished work.*

*Marcel Proust once wrote to a friend, "The eyes of
memory see nothing if we strain them too hard." I don't
believe that to be true, and I would guess, since the letter
was written before his major work was begun, that he
came to find it untrue. In my case, Proust's "nothing," or
almost nothing, comes after the first strain, after the
work is over, performed, published or put aside. Then
the eyes of memory are not strained into nothingness,
but into questions about nothingness. What didn't I see
during the time of work that I now see more clearly?
(Whenever I am aware that this has happened in these
three books I have added comments.) Or what did I see
in the past that I could not now duplicate? Perhaps because the emotions that made it possible are over and are
not recoverable — that should not be, but should not be
has nothing to do with it — or perhaps because the years
blank out even passions. Or maybe just the act of writing
it down, then and then only, turned it into the past, and
nothing can or will bring it back.*

*But in my case, I think it's mainly because I am just
plain nervous: if the work has been good, then maybe I
can never be that good again; if it is no good then I am
no good, and that has to be faced and is painful. In any*

case, even though these three books are made up of memories — selective memories — I have no love for the past, written or remembered. To hell with all that happened once upon a time, I always want to say, when I hear myself or other people tell tales about it: the only hope is to put it aside, most of it, the only hope for the future. I was somebody else, even yesterday, I fool myself into thinking I must make a snail's pace into today.

Having said all that, having just been through all of it by reading these three books, I must say, simply, that I liked them. I have reservations, of course, many of them, and when I have, I have tried to say so in the comments. I did not make changes in the books, although I was often tempted, because alteration seemed a kind of cheating. If I don't like all that I was, or all that I wrote, I would equally dislike tampering on the basis that I am now wiser. I do not think I am. Maybe I always guessed that, but I knew it clearly only a few years ago from a young-ish woman whose name I cannot remember, if indeed I ever heard it.

But the seeds of doubt were, of course, there long before the lady spoke to me. In looking about me, in looking at me, I have long believed that few people grow wiser with the years. Most of us know more, may have learned a great deal, but I have found very few who have come out with what we are told, in our younger years, will be the wisdom of age. Writers, for example, learn skill, learn how to handle material, how to make fewer mistakes, how to write better: nice things, but seldom much more wisdom than they showed in their early books. And when an attempt, an honorable attempt, is made to gather it all together, which is what the search for wisdom must be about, as in the writings of the talented Graham Greene, it often settles into weary sadness, and resignation is not necessarily wise. Perhaps those who deal in the basic sciences come out with wisdom: an experiment succeeds and thus proves; half succeeds and knowledge must be carried further; fails, and all must be put together again.

"Practice," for artists, is something else. (And not to be sneezed at.) I first heard the use of it as a substitute for wisdom from the unpleasant-looking youngish woman at a London cocktail party. For ten years she had been the paid companion-secretary to a distinguished woman, Mrs. Smith, who happened to be a lesbian, had died a few years before, and had been semi-senile and then senile for many years before that. I had once been invited to dinner by Mrs. Smith in her good days, and during our taxi ride to the restaurant she made a very minor pass at me. In an odd fit of middle-aged girlishness which would not have happened with a man, I was so worried about hurting her feelings that as the taxi reached the restaurant, I made so awkward an exit that I fell out of the taxi and cut my knee. (I still, these many years later, have an ugly, dark scar.) For the last five senile years of her life, Mrs. Smith, when we would meet, would refer to the accident of so many years before as if it had happened last week or the night before, and tell a room of people that it was not a question of "bravery," my going through dinner in bleeding pain, "bravery" was the least, it was a question of "courtesy," the purest example she had ever known.

Now, at the London cocktail party, Mrs. Smith's former secretary came to sit next to me.

Her first words were, "I hope your knee has fully healed."

There was such open mockery in the voice that I was surprised into saying, "Most minor cuts heal after, what, maybe sixteen, eighteen years."

"Minor cuts? Then why did you act so brave?"

"I didn't. I didn't act brave at all. I was ashamed of myself."

"For what?"

I am sorry to say that in the face of this open antagonism, I told her the truth of my foolish embarrassment.

She was smiling at me when I finished. Then she thanked me and patted my hand.

She said, "Yes. Mrs. Smith always knew why you fell. That was the way she told me the story. And whenever she told me she would laugh very hard, you know the way she did."

I went to think about myself and what I had just been told in an adjacent almost empty room until I saw the young woman standing in the hall, struggling to put a pair of rubbers over her shoes.

Nice. A nice awkward position to find a woman in, so I said, "Mrs. Smith never told you that story, it's out of character. But I really came to tell you that for the first time in life, I think I am a wiser woman than I used to be. I don't care that you lied and don't want to know why."

"I need a job," she said. "I thought maybe —" But when she straightened from the struggle with the overshoes the tone was different. She said, "Wiser? I wouldn't be too sure. Just more practiced about life and mischief."

I laughed. "Wouldn't malice be a better word for what you did?"

"O.K.," she said. "I'll give up mischief if you give up wisdom."

"I'll write you," I said.

And so, I guess, I am writing her. I have been through lists of people I know and of those I've read. (Not quite the same, of course.) And my conclusion brings little comfort. I have known a few people who have grown wiser with time. But most others have only learned to practice better. Most of us stop learning earlier than we think.

I believe that it was not a child's charming exercise-game that made Edmund Wilson learn Russian when he was no longer young and Hungarian when he was in his sixties. He was out to find his own kind of solidity, and solidity for him came from knowledge and not theory; even small knowledge might, just might, make for wisdom. (He would, by the way, have been the last to have claimed it.) I have the happiest memory of the time when, in his seventies, Wilson discovered the comic strips, found that I had read most of them since childhood, and would persist in questions about the beginnings of Orphan Annie and Warbucks, why they had met and why did he always leave Annie without a dime, of what had led Dick Tracy to get married, where was the bride, etc. For at least a year after that weekend of questions, he would telephone me if a reference to the past in that day's strip puzzled him, and if I couldn't remember, that bewildered and annoyed him. He was, in my definition, not resting on the past for what is called wisdom; he knew that the search had to include as much as one can manage, the discards growing only from the search.

So it is with these books for me now. I have said that, on the whole, they please me. But often parts of them now seem to have been written by a woman I don't know very well. Some of what people have written about them leaves me puzzled: they are not angry books, not nearly angry enough. I know now that I was often in an aimless uproar, but I am sad that some of the good anger has been lost to age, and age loses to energy. Youth often takes good and worthwhile chances — and I am glad I did that — and older people, or people who didn't take the chances, don't like that. One of our missions in life is to wait, often in amusement, to see time, marriage, children, jobs, pressures of comfort and pain turn youth into the curtailed rest of us. Hope, belief in change, the desire for a different future, are seldom analyzed and sorted out; they are oddities to be waited out, knowing sensibly that if we cannot teach worldly patience to a teenager, time and life will usually do it for us. Too many parents count on that, too many teachers are bored with its truth.

What a word is truth. Slippery, tricky, unreliable. I tried in these books to tell the truth. I did not fool with facts. But, of course, that is a shallow definition of the truth. I see now, in rereading, that I kept much from myself, not always, but sometimes. And so sometimes in this edition I have tried to correct that. But I can be sure I still do not see it and never will. That is a common experience for all writers, I think, and I wonder, therefore, whether what I, or they, have to say about past work is worth very much. Judge for yourself, is the only answer.

1978

AN UNFINISHED WOMAN

To Hannah, Dick and Mike

1

I WAS born in New Orleans to Julia Newhouse from Demopolis, Alabama, who had fallen in love and stayed in love with Max Hellman, whose parents had come to New Orleans in the German 1845–1848 immigration to give birth to him and his two sisters. My mother's family, long before I was born, had moved from Demopolis to Cincinnati and then to New Orleans, both desirable cities, I guess, for three marriageable girls.

But I first remember them in a large New York apartment: my two young and very pretty aunts; their taciturn, tight-faced brother; and the silent, powerful, severe woman, Sophie Newhouse, who was their mother, my grandmother. Her children, her servants, all of her relatives except her brother Jake were frightened of her, and so was I. Even as a small child I disliked myself for the fear and showed off against it.

The Newhouse apartment held the upper-middle-class

trappings, in touch of things and in spirit of people, that never manage to be truly stylish. Heavy weather hung over the lovely oval rooms. True, there were parties for my aunts, but the parties, to a peeping child in the servants' hall, seemed so muted that I was long convinced that on fancy occasions grown people moved their lips without making sounds. In the days after the party one would hear exciting stories about the new suitors, but the suitors were never quite good enough and the parties were, obviously, not good enough for those who might have been. Then there were the Sunday dinners with great-uncles and aunts sometimes in attendance, full of open ill will about who had the most money, or who spent it too lavishly, who would inherit what, which had bought what rug that would last forever, who what jewel she would best have been without. It was a corporation meeting, with my grandmother unexpectedly in the position of vice-chairman. The chairman was her brother Jake, the only human being to whom I ever saw her defer. Early, I told myself that was because he was richer than she was, and did something called managing her money. But that was too simple: he was a man of great force, given, as she was given, to breaking the spirit of people for the pleasure of the exercise. But he was also witty and rather worldly, seeing his own financial machinations as natural not only to his but to the country's benefit, and seeing that as comic. (I had only one real contact with my Uncle Jake: when I graduated from school at fifteen, he gave me a ring that I took to a 59th Street hock shop, got twenty-five dollars, and bought books. I went immediately to tell him what I'd done, deciding, I think, that day that the break had to come. He stared at me for a long time, and then he laughed and said the words I later used in *The Little Foxes*: "So you've got spirit after all. Most of the rest of them are made of sugar water.")

But that New York apartment where we visited several times a week, the summer cottage where we went for a visit each year as the poor daughter and granddaughter, made me into an angry child and forever caused in me a wild extravagance mixed with respect for money and those who have it. The respectful periods were full of self-hatred and during them I always made my worst mistakes. But after *The Little Foxes* was written and put away, this conflict was to grow less important, as indeed, the picture of my mother's family was to grow dim and almost fade away.

It was not unnatural that my first love went to my father's family. He and his two sisters were free, generous, funny. But as I made my mother's family all one color, I made my father's family too remarkable, and then turned both extreme judgments against my mother.

In fact, she was a sweet eccentric, the only middle-class woman I have ever known who had not rejected the middle class — that would have been an act of will — but had skipped it altogether. She liked a simple life and simple people, and would have been happier, I think, if she had stayed in the backlands of Alabama riding wild on the horses she so often talked about, not so lifelong lonely for the black men and women who had taught her the only religion she ever knew. I didn't know what she was saying when she moved her lips in a Baptist church or a Catholic cathedral or, less often, in a synagogue, but it was obvious that God could be found anywhere, because several times a week we would stop in a church, any church, and she seemed to be at home in all of them.

But simple natures can also be complex, and that is difficult for a child, who wants all grown people to be sharply one thing or another. I was puzzled and irritated by the passivity of my mother as it mixed with an unmovable stubbornness. (My father had not been considered a proper husband for a rich and pretty girl, but my mother's deep fear of her mother did not override her deep love for my father, although the same fear kept my two aunts from ever marrying and my uncle from marrying until after his mother's death.)

Mama seemed to do only what my father wanted, and yet we lived the way my mother wanted us to live. She deeply wanted to keep my father and to please him, but no amount of protest from him could alter the strange quirks that Freud already knew about. Windows, doors and stoves haunted her and she would often stand before them for as long as half an hour, or leaving the house, would insist upon returning to it while we waited for her in any weather. And sad, middle-aged ladies would be brought home from a casual meeting on a park bench to fill the living room with woe: plain tales of sickness, or poverty, or loneliness in the afternoon often led to their staying on for dinner with my bored father.

I remember a time when our apartment was being painted and the week it was supposed to take stretched into three because one of the two painters, a small, sickly man with an Italian accent, soon found that my mother was a sympathetic listener. He would, in duty, climb the ladder at nine in the morning, but by eleven he was sitting on the sofa with the tale of the bride who died in child-birth, the child still in Italy, his mother who ailed and half starved in Tuscany, the nights in New York where he knew nobody to eat with or talk to. After lunch, cooked by our bad-tempered Irish lady, and served to him by my mother to hide the bad temper, he would climb the ladder again and paint for a few hours while my mother urged him to stop work and go for a nice day in the sun-shine. Once, toward the end of the long job — the other painter never returned after the first few days — I came home carrying books from the library, annoyed to find the painter in my favorite chair. As I stood in the door-way, frowning at my mother, the painter said, "Your girl. How old?"

"Fifteen," said my mother.

"In Italy, not young, fifteen. She is healthy?"

"Very healthy," said my mother. "Her generation has larger feet than we did."

"I think about it," said the painter. "I let you know."

I knew my mother didn't understand what he meant because she smiled and nodded in the way she always did when her mind had wandered, but I was angry and told my father about it at dinner. He laughed and I left the table, but later he told my mother that the painter was not to come to the house again. A few years later when I brought home for dinner an aimless, handsome young man who got roaring drunk and insisted upon climbing down the building from our eighth-floor apart-ment, my father, watching him from the window, said, "Perhaps we should try to find that Italian house paint-er." My mother was dead for five years before I knew that I had loved her very much.

My mother's childbearing had been dangerously botched by a fashionable doctor in New Orleans, and forever after she stood in fear of going through it again, and so I was an only child. (Twenty-one years later, when I was married and pregnant, she was as frightened for me, and unashamedly happy when I lost the child.) I was thirty-four years old, after two successful plays, and fourteen or fifteen years of heavy drinking in a nature that wasn't comfortable with anarchy, when a doctor told me about the lifelong troubles of an only child. Most certainly I needed a doctor to reveal for me the violence and disorder of my life, but I had always known about the powers of an only child. I was not meaner or more ungenerous or more unkind than other children, but I was off balance in a world where I knew my grand importance to two other people who certainly loved me for myself, but who also liked to use me against each other. I don't think they knew they did that, because most of it was affectionate teasing between them, but somehow I knew early that my father's jokes about how much my mother's family liked money, how her mother had crippled her own children, my grandmother's desire to think of him — and me — as strange vagabonds of no property value, was more than teasing. He wished to win me to his side, and he did. He was a handsome man, witty, high-tempered, proud, and — although I guessed very young I was not to be certain until much later — with a number of other women in his life. Thus his attacks on Mama's family were not always for the reasons claimed.

When I was about six years old my father lost my mother's large dowry. We moved to New York and were shabby poor until my father finally settled for a life as a successful traveling salesman. It was in those years that we went back to New Orleans to stay with my father's sisters for six months each year. I was thus moved from school in New York to school in New Orleans without care for the season or the quality of the school. This constant need for adjustment in two very different worlds made formal education into a kind of frantic tennis game, sometimes played with children whose strokes had force and brilliance, sometimes with those who could barely hold the racket. Possibly it is the reason I never did well in school or in college, and why I wanted to be left alone to read by myself. I had found, very early, that any other test found me bounding with ease and grace over one fence to fall on my face as I ran towards the next.

2

T<small>HERE</small> was a heavy fig tree on the lawn where the house turned the corner into the side street, and to the front and sides of the fig tree were three live oaks that hid the fig from my aunts' boardinghouse. I suppose I was eight or nine before I discovered the pleasures of the fig tree, and although I have lived in many houses since then, including a few I made for myself, I still think of it as my first and most beloved home.

I learned early, in our strange life of living half in New York and half in New Orleans, that I made my New Orleans teachers uncomfortable because I was too far ahead of my schoolmates, and my New York teachers irritable because I was too far behind. But in New Orleans, I found a solution: I skipped school at least once a week and often twice, knowing that nobody cared or would report my absence. On those days I would set out for school done up in polished strapped shoes and a prim hat against what was known as "the climate," carrying my books and a little basket filled with delicious stuff my Aunt Jenny and Carrie, the cook, had made for my school lunch. I would round the corner of the side street, move on toward St. Charles Avenue, and sit on a bench as if I were waiting for a streetcar until the boarders and the neighbors had gone to work or settled down for the post-breakfast rest that all Southern ladies thought necessary. Then I would run back to the fig tree, dodging in and out of bushes to make sure the house had no dangers for me. The fig tree was heavy, solid, comfortable, and I had, through time, convinced myself that it wanted me, missed me when I was absent, and approved all the rigging I had done for the happy days I spent in its arms: I had made a sling to hold the school books, a pulley rope for my lunch basket, a hole for the bottle of afternoon cream-soda pop, a fishing pole and a smelly little bag of elderly bait, a pillow embroidered with a picture of Henry Clay on a horse that I had stolen from Mrs. Stillman, one of my aunts' boarders, and a proper nail to hold my dress and shoes to keep them neat for the return to the house.

It was in that tree that I learned to read, filled with the passions that can only come to the bookish, grasping, very young, bewildered by almost all of what I read, sweating in the attempt to understand a world of adults I fled from in real life but desperately wanted to join in books. (I did not connect the grown men and women in literature with the grown men and women I saw around me. They were, to me, another species.)

It was in the fig tree that I learned that anything alive in water was of enormous excitement to me. True, the water was gutter water and the fishing could hardly be called that: sometimes the things that swam in New Orleans gutters were not pretty, but I didn't know what was pretty and I liked them all. After lunch — the men boarders returned for a large lunch and a siesta — the street would be safe again, with only the noise from Carrie and her helpers in the kitchen, and they could be counted on never to move past the back porch, or the chicken coop. Then I would come down from my tree to sit on the side street gutter with my pole and bait. Often I would catch a crab that had wandered in from the Gulf, more often I would catch my favorite, the crayfish, and sometimes I would, in that safe hour, have at least six of them for my basket. Then, about 2:30, when house and street would stir again, I would go back to my tree for another few hours of reading or dozing or having what I called the ill hour. It is too long ago for me to know why I thought the hour "ill," but certainly I did not mean sick. I think I meant an intimation of sadness, a first recognition that there was so much to understand that one might never find one's way and the first signs, perhaps, that for a nature like mine, the way would not be easy. I cannot be sure that I felt all that then, although I can be sure that it was in the fig tree, a few years later, that I was first puzzled by the conflict which would haunt me, harm me, and benefit me the rest of my life: simply, the stubborn, relentless, driving desire to be alone as it came into conflict with the desire not to be alone when I wanted not to be. I already guessed that other people wouldn't allow that, although, as an only child, I pretended for the rest of my life that they would and must allow it to me.

22

I liked my time in New Orleans much better than I liked our six months apartment life in New York. The life in my aunts' boardinghouse seemed remarkably rich. And what a strange lot my own family was. My aunts Jenny and Hannah were both tall, large women, funny and generous, who coming from a German, cultivated, genteel tradition had found they had to earn a living and earned it without complaint, although Jenny, the prettier and more complex, had frequent outbursts of interesting temper. It was strange, I thought then, that my mother, who so often irritated me, was treated by my aunts as if she were a precious Chinese clay piece from a world they didn't know. And in a sense, that was true: her family was rich, she was small, delicately made and charming — she was a sturdy, brave woman, really, but it took years to teach me that — and because my aunts loved my father very much, they were good to my mother, and protected her from the less wellborn boarders. I don't think they understood — I did, by some kind of child's malice — that my mother enjoyed the boarders and listened to them with the sympathy Jenny couldn't afford. I suppose none of the boarders were of great interest, but I was crazy about what I thought went on behind their doors.

I was conscious that Mr. Stillman, a large, loose, good-looking man, flirted with my mother and sang off key. I knew that a boarder called Collie, a too thin, unhappy looking, no-age man, worked in his uncle's bank and was drunk every night. He was the favorite of the lady boarders, who didn't think he'd live very long. (They were wrong: over twenty years later, on a visit to my retired aunts, I met him in Galatoire's restaurant looking just the same.) And there were two faded, sexy, giggly sisters called Fizzy and Sarah, who pretended to love children and all trees. I once overheard a fight between my mother and father in which she accused him of liking Sarah. I thought that was undignified of my mother and was pleased when my father laughed it off as untrue. He was telling the truth about Sarah: he liked Fizzy, and the day I saw them meet and get into a taxi in front of a restaurant on Jackson Avenue was to stay with me for many years. I was in a black rage, filled with fears I couldn't explain, with pity and contempt for my mother, with an intense desire to follow my father and Fizzy to see whatever it was they might be doing, and to kill them for it. An hour later, I threw myself from the top of the fig tree and broke my nose, although I did not know I had broken a bone and was concerned only with the hideous pain.

I went immediately to Sophronia, who had been my nurse when I was a small child before we moved, or half moved, to New York. She worked now for people who lived in a large house a streetcar ride from ours, and she took care of two little red-haired boys whom I hated with pleasure in my wicked jealousy. Sophronia was the first and most certain love of my life. (Years later, when I was a dangerously rebellious young girl, my father would say that if he had been able to afford Sophronia through the years, I would have been under the only control I ever recognized.) She was a tall, handsome, light tan woman — I still have many pictures of the brooding face — who was for me, as for so many other white Southern children, the one and certain anchor so needed for the young years, so forgotten after that. (It wasn't that way for us: we wrote and met as often as possible until she died when I was in my twenties, and the first salary check I ever earned she returned to me in the form of a gold chain.) The mother of the two red-haired boys didn't like my visits to Sophronia and so I always arrived by the back door.

But Sophronia was not at home on the day of my fall. I sat on her kitchen steps crying and holding my face until the cook sent the upstairs maid to Audubon Park on a search for Sophronia. She came, running, I think for the first time in the majestic movements of her life, waving away the two redheads. She took me to her room and washed my face and prodded my nose and put her hand over my mouth when I screamed. She said we must go immediately to Dr. Fenner, but when I told her that I had thrown myself from the tree, she stopped talking about the doctor, bandaged my face, gave me a pill, put me on her bed and lay down beside me. I told her about my father and Fizzy and fell asleep. When I woke up she said that she'd walk me home. On the way she told me that I must say nothing about Fizzy to anybody ever, and that if my nose still hurt in a few days I was only to say that I had fallen on the street and refuse to answer any questions about how I fell. A block away from my aunts' house we sat down on the steps of the Baptist church. She looked sad and I knew that I had displeased her. I touched her face, which had always been between us a way of saying that I was sorry.

She said, "Don't go through life making trouble for people."

I said, "If I tell you I won't tell about Fizzy, then I won't tell."

She said, "Run home now. Goodbye."

And it was to be goodbye for another year, because I had forgotten that we were to leave for New York two days later, and when I telephoned to tell that to Sophronia the woman she worked for said I wasn't to telephone again. In any case, I soon forgot about Fizzy, and when the bandage came off my nose — it looked different but not different enough — our New York doctor said that it would heal by itself, or whatever was the nonsense they believed in those days about broken bones.

We went back to New Orleans the next year and the years after that until I was sixteen, and they were always the best times of my life. It was Aunt Hannah who took me each Saturday to the movies and then to the French Quarter, where we bought smelly old leather books and she told me how it all had been when she was a girl: about my grandmother — I remembered her — who had been a very tall woman with a lined, severe face and a gentle nature; about my grandfather, dead before I was born, who, in his portrait over the fireplace, looked too serious and distinguished. They had, in a middle-class world, evidently been a strange couple, going their own way with little interest in money or position, loved and respected by their children. "Your grandfather used to say" was a common way to begin a sentence, and although whatever he said had been law, he had allowed my father and aunts their many eccentricities in a time and place that didn't like eccentrics, and to such a degree that not one of his children ever knew they weren't like other people. Hannah, for example, once grew angry — the only time I ever saw her show any temper — when my mother insisted I finish my dinner: she rose and hit the table, and told my mother and the startled boarders that when she was twelve years old she had decided she didn't ever want to eat with people again and so she had taken to sitting on the steps of the front porch and my grandmother, with no comment, had for two years brought her dinner on a tray, and so what was wrong with one dinner I didn't feel like sitting through?

I think both Hannah and Jenny were virgins, but if they were, there were no signs of spinsterhood. They were nice about married people, they were generous to children, and sex was something to have fun about. Jenny had been the consultant to many neighborhood young ladies before their marriage night, or the night of their first lover. One of these girls, a rich ninny, Jenny found irritating and unpleasant. When I was sixteen I came across the two of them in earnest conference on the lawn, and later Jenny told me that the girl had come to consult her about how to avoid pregnancy.

"What did you tell her?"

"I told her to have a glass of ice water right before the sacred act and three sips during it."

When we had finished laughing, I said, "But she'll get pregnant."

"He's marrying her for money, he'll leave her when he gets it. This way at least maybe she'll have a few babies for herself."

And four years later, when I wrote my aunts that I was going to be married, I had back a telegram: FORGET ABOUT THE GLASS OF ICE WATER TIMES HAVE CHANGED.

I think I learned to laugh in that house and to knit and embroider and sew a straight seam and to cook. Each Sunday it was my job to clean the crayfish for the wonderful bisque, and it was Jenny and Carrie, the cook, who taught me to make turtle soup, and how to kill a chicken without ladylike complaints about the horror of dealing death, and how to pluck and cook the wild ducks that were hawked on our street every Sunday morning. I was taught, also, that if you gave, you did it without piety and didn't boast about it. It had been one of my grandfather's laws, in the days when my father and aunts were children, that no poor person who asked for anything was ever to be refused, and his children fulfilled the injunction. New Orleans was a city of many poor people, particularly black people, and the boardinghouse kitchen after the house dinner was, on most nights, a mighty pleasant place: there would often be as many as eight or ten people, black and white, almost always very old or very young, who sat at the table on the kitchen porch while Carrie ordered the kitchen maids and me to bring the steaming platters and the coffeepots.

It was on such a night that I first saw Leah, a light tan girl of about fifteen with red hair and freckles, a flat, ugly face, and a big stomach. I suppose I was about fourteen years old that night, but I remember her very well because she stared at me through her hungry eating. She came again about a week later, and this time Carrie herself took the girl aside and whispered to her, but I don't think the girl answered her because Carrie shrugged and moved away. The next morning, Hannah, who always rose at six to help Jenny before she went to her own office job, screamed outside my bedroom window. Leaning out, I saw Hannah pointing underneath the house and saying softly, "Come out of there."

Slowly the tan-red girl crawled out. Hannah said, "You must not stay under there. It's very wet. Come inside, child, and dry yourself out." From that day on Leah lived somewhere in the house, and a few months later had her baby in the City Hospital. The baby was put out for adoption on Sophronia's advice with a little purse of money from my mother. I never knew what Leah did in the house, because when she helped with the dishes Carrie lost her temper, and when she tried making beds Jenny asked her not to, and once when she was raking leaves for the gardener he yelled, "You ain't in your proper head," so in the end, she took to following me around.

I was, they told me, turning into a handful. Mrs. Stillman said I was wild, Mr. Stillman said that I would, of course, bring pain to my mother and father, and Fizzy said I was just plain disgusting mean. It had been a bad month for me. I had, one night, fallen asleep in the fig tree and, coming down in the morning, refused to tell my mother where I had been. James Denery the Third had hit me very hard in a tug-of-war and I had waited until the next day to hit him over the head with a porcelain coffee pot and then his mother complained to my mother. I had also refused to go back to dancing class.

And I was now spending most of my time with a group from an orphanage down the block. I guess the orphan group was no more attractive than any other, but to be an orphan seemed to me desirable and a self-made piece of independence. In any case, the orphans were more interesting to me than my schoolmates, and if they played rougher they complained less. Frances, a dark beauty of my age, queened it over the others because her father had been killed by the Mafia. Miriam, small and wiry, regularly stole my allowance from the red purse my aunt

29

had given me, and the one time I protested she beat me up. Louis Calda was religious and spoke to me about it. Pancho was dark, sad, and, to me, a poet, because once he said, *"Yo te amo."* I could not sleep a full night after this declaration, and it set up in me forever after both sympathy and irritability with the first sexual stirrings of little girls, so masked, so complex, so foolish as compared with the sex of little boys. It was Louis Calda who took Pancho and me to a Catholic Mass that could have made me a fourteen-year-old convert. But Louis explained that he did not think me worthy, and Pancho, to stop my tears, cut off a piece of his hair with a knife, gave it to me as a gift from royalty, and then shoved me into the gutter. I don't know why I thought this an act of affection, but I did, and went home to open the back of a new wristwatch my father had given me for my birthday and to put the lock of hair in the back. A day later when the watch stopped, my father insisted I give it to him immediately, declaring that the jeweler was unreliable.

It was that night that I disappeared, and that night that Fizzy said I was disgusting mean, and Mr. Stillman said I would forever pain my mother and father, and my father turned on both of them and said he would handle his family affairs himself without comments from strangers. But he said it too late. He had come home very angry with me: the jeweler, after my father's complaints about his unreliability, had found the lock of hair in the back of the watch. What started out to be a mild reproof on my father's part soon turned angry when I wouldn't explain about the hair. (My father was often angry when I was most like him.) He was so angry that he forgot that he was attacking me in front of the Stillmans, my old rival Fizzy, and the delighted Mrs. Dreyfus, a new, rich boarder who only that afternoon had complained about my bad manners. My mother left the room when my father grew angry with me. Hannah, passing through, put up her hand as if to stop my father and then, frightened of the look he gave her, went out to the porch. I sat on the couch, astonished at the pain in my head. I tried to get up from the couch, but one ankle turned and I sat down again, knowing for the first time the rampage that could be caused in me by anger. The room began to have other forms, the people were no longer men and women, my head was not my own. I told myself that my head had gone somewhere and I have little memory of anything after my Aunt Jenny came into the room and said to my father, "Don't you remember?" I have never known what she meant, but I knew that soon after I was moving up the staircase, that I slipped and fell a few steps, that when I woke up hours later in my bed, I found a piece of angel cake — an old love, an old custom — left by my mother on my pillow. The headache was worse and I vomited out of the window. Then I dressed, took my red purse, and walked a long way down St. Charles Avenue. A St. Charles Avenue mansion had on its back lawn a famous doll's-house, an elaborate copy of the mansion itself, built years before for the small daughter of the house. As I passed this showpiece, I saw a policeman and moved swiftly back to the doll palace and crawled inside. If I had known about the fantasies of the frightened, that ridiculous small house would not have been so terrible for me. I was surrounded by ornate, carved reproductions of the

mansion furniture, scaled for children, bisque figurines
in miniature, a working toilet seat of gold leaf in suit-
able size, small draperies of damask with a sign that
said "From the damask of Marie Antoinette," a miniature samovar with small bronze cups, and a tiny Madame Récamier couch on which I spent the night, my
legs on the floor. I must have slept, because I woke
from a nightmare and knocked over a bisque figurine.
The noise frightened me, and since it was now almost
light, in one of those lovely mist mornings of late spring
when every flower in New Orleans seems to melt and
mix with the air, I crawled out. Most of that day I
spent walking, although I had a long session in the
ladies' room of the railroad station. I had four dollars
and two bits, but that wasn't much when you meant it to
last forever and when you knew it would not be easy for
a fourteen-year-old girl to find work in a city where too
many people knew her. Three times I stood in line at the
railroad ticket windows to ask where I could go for four
dollars, but each time the question seemed too dangerous
and I knew no other way of asking it.

Toward evening, I moved to the French Quarter, feeling sad and envious as people went home to dinner. I
bought a few Tootsie Rolls and a half loaf of bread and
went to the St. Louis Cathedral in Jackson Square. (It
was that night that I composed the prayer that was to
become, in the next five years, an obsession, mumbled
over and over through the days and nights: "God forgive
me, Papa forgive me, Mama forgive me, Sophronia,
Jenny, Hannah, and all others, through this time and that
time, in life and in death." When I was nineteen, my
father, who had made several attempts through the years

to find out what my lip movements meant as I repeated the prayer, said, "How much would you take to stop that? Name it and you've got it." I suppose I was sick of the nonsense by that time because I said, "A leather coat and a feather fan," and the next day he bought them for me.) After my loaf of bread, I went looking for a bottle of soda pop and discovered, for the first time, the whore-house section around Bourbon Street. The women were ranged in the doorways of the cribs, making the first early evening offers to sailors, who were the only men in the streets. I wanted to stick around and see how things like that worked, but the second or third time I circled the block, one of the girls called out to me. I couldn't understand the words, but the voice was angry enough to make me run toward the French Market.

The Market was empty except for two old men. One of them called to me as I went past, and I turned to see that he had opened his pants and was shaking what my circle called "his thing." I flew across the street into the coffee stand, forgetting that the owner had known me since I was a small child when my Aunt Jenny would rest from her marketing tour with a cup of fine, strong coffee.

He said, in the patois, *"Que faites, ma 'fant? Je suis fermé."*

I said, *"Rien. My tante attend —* Could I have a doughnut?"

He brought me two doughnuts, saying one was *lagniappe,* but I took my doughnuts outside when he said, *"Mais où est vo' tante à c' heure?"*

I fell asleep with my doughnuts behind a shrub in Jackson Square. The night was damp and hot and through the sleep there were many voices and, much later, there

33

was music from somewhere near the river. When all sounds had ended, I woke, turned my head, and knew I was being watched. Two rats were sitting a few feet from me. I urinated on my dress, crawled backwards to stand up, screamed as I ran up the steps of St. Louis Cathedral and pounded on the doors. I don't know when I stopped screaming or how I got to the railroad station, but I stood against the wall trying to tear off my dress and only knew I was doing it when two women stopped to stare at me. I began to have cramps in my stomach of a kind I had never known before. I went into the ladies' room and sat bent in a chair, whimpering with pain. After a while the cramps stopped, but I had an intimation, when I looked into the mirror, of something happening to me: my face was blotched, and there seemed to be circles and twirls I had never seen before, the straight blonde hair was damp with sweat, and a paste of green from the shrub had made lines on my jaw. I had gotten older.

Sometime during that early morning I half washed my dress, threw away my pants, put cold water on my hair. Later in the morning a cleaning woman appeared, and after a while began to ask questions that frightened me. When she put down her mop and went out of the room, I ran out of the station. I walked, I guess, for many hours, but when I saw a man on Canal Street who worked in Hannah's office, I realized that the sections of New Orleans that were known to me were dangerous for me.

Years before, when I was a small child, Sophronia and I would go to pick up, or try on, pretty embroidered dresses that were made for me by a colored dressmaker called Bibettera. A block up from Bibettera's there had been a large ruin of a house with a sign, ROOMS — CLEAN

— CHEAP, and cheerful people seemed always to be moving in and out of the house. The door of the house was painted a bright pink. I liked that and would discuss with Sophronia why we didn't live in a house with a pink door.

Bibettera was long since dead, so I knew I was safe in this Negro neighborhood. I went up and down the block several times, praying that things would work and I could take my cramps to bed. I knocked on the pink door. It was answered immediately by a small young man.

I said, "Hello." He said nothing.

I said, "I would like to rent a room, please."

He closed the door but I waited, thinking he had gone to get the lady of the house. After a long time, a middle-aged woman put her head out of a second-floor window and said, "What you at?"

I said, "I would like to rent a room, please. My mama is a widow and has gone to work across the river. She gave me money and said to come here until she called for me."

"Who your mama?"

"Er. My mama."

"What you at? Speak out."

"I told you. I have money . . ." But as I tried to open my purse, the voice grew angry.

"This is a nigger house. Get you off. *Vite.*"

I said, in a whisper, "I know. I'm part nigger."

The small young man opened the front door. He was laughing. "You part mischief. Get the hell out of here."

I said, "Please" — and then, "I'm related to Sophronia Mason. She told me to come. Ask her."

Sophronia and her family were respected figures in New Orleans Negro circles, and because I had some vague memory of her stately bow to somebody as she passed this house, I believed they knew her. If they told her about me I would be in trouble, but phones were not usual then in poor neighborhoods, and I had no other place to go.

The woman opened the door. Slowly I went into the hall.

I said, "I won't stay long. I have four dollars and Sophronia will give more if . . ."

The woman pointed up the stairs. She opened the door of a small room. "Washbasin place down the hall. Toilet place behind the kitchen. Two-fifty and no fuss, no bother."

I said, "Yes ma'am, yes ma'am," but as she started to close the door, the young man appeared.

"Where your bag?"

"Bag?"

"Nobody put up here without no bag."

"Oh. You mean the bag with my clothes? It's at the station. I'll go and get it later . . ." I stopped because I knew I was about to say I'm sick, I'm in pain, I'm frightened.

He said, "I say you lie. I say you trouble. I say you get out."

I said, "And I say you shut up."

Years later, I was to understand why the command worked, and to be sorry that it did, but that day I was very happy when he turned and closed the door. I was asleep within minutes.

Toward evening, I went down the stairs, saw nobody,

36

walked a few blocks and bought myself an oyster loaf. But the first bite made me feel sick, so I took my loaf back to the house. This time, as I climbed the steps, there were three women in the parlor, and they stopped talking when they saw me. I went back to sleep immediately, dizzy and nauseated.

I woke to a high, hot sun and my father standing at the foot of the bed staring at the oyster loaf.

He said, "Get up now and get dressed."

I was crying as I said, "Thank you, Papa, but I can't."

From the hall, Sophronia said, "Get along up now. *Vite.* The morning is late."

My father left the room. I dressed and came into the hall carrying my oyster loaf. Sophronia was standing at the head of the stairs. She pointed out, meaning my father was on the street.

I said, "He humiliated me. He did. I won't . . ."

She said, "Get you going or I will never see you whenever again."

I ran past her to the street. I stood with my father until Sophronia joined us, and then we walked slowly, without speaking, to the streetcar line. Sophronia bowed to us, but she refused my father's hand when he attempted to help her into the car. I ran to the car meaning to ask her to take me with her, but the car moved and she raised her hand as if to stop me. My father and I walked again for a long time.

He pointed to a trash can sitting in front of a house. "Please put that oyster loaf in the can."

At Vanalli's restaurant, he took my arm. "Hungry?"

I said, "No, thank you, Papa."

But we went through the door. It was, in those days, a

37

New Orleans custom to have an early black coffee, go to the office, and after a few hours have a large breakfast at a restaurant. Vanalli's was crowded, the headwaiter was so sorry, but after my father took him aside, a very small table was put up for us — too small for my large father, who was accommodating himself to it in a manner most unlike him.

He said, "Jack, my rumpled daughter would like cold crayfish, a nice piece of pompano, a separate bowl of Béarnaise sauce, don't ask me why, French fried potatoes . . ."

I said, "Thank you, Papa, but I am not hungry. I don't want to be here."

My father waved the waiter away and we sat in silence until the crayfish came. My hand reached out instinctively and then drew back.

My father said, "Your mother and I have had an awful time."

I said, "I'm sorry about that. But I don't want to go home, Papa."

He said, angrily, "Yes, you do. But you want me to apologize first. I do apologize but you should not have made me say it."

After a while I mumbled, "God forgive me, Papa forgive me, Mama forgive me, Sophronia, Jenny, Hannah . . ."

"Eat your crayfish."

I ate everything he had ordered and then a small steak. I suppose I had been mumbling throughout my breakfast.

My father said, "You're talking to yourself. I can't hear you. What are you saying?"

"God forgive me, Papa forgive me, Mama forgive me, Sophronia, Jenny . . ."

My father said, "Where do we start your training as the first Jewish nun on Prytania Street?"

When I finished laughing, I liked him again. I said, "Papa, I'll tell you a secret. I've had very bad cramps and I am beginning to bleed. I'm changing life."

He stared at me for a while. Then he said, "Well, it's not the way it's usually described, but it's accurate, I guess. Let's go home now to your mother."

We were never, as long as my mother and father lived, to mention that time again. But it was of great importance to them and I've thought about it all my life. From that day on I knew my power over my parents. That was not to be too important: I was ashamed of it and did not abuse it too much. But I found out something more useful and more dangerous: if you are willing to take the punishment, you are halfway through the battle. That the issue may be trivial, the battle ugly, is another point.

3

My mother had gone to Sophie Newcomb College in New Orleans, and although the experience had left little on the memory except a fire in her dormitory, she felt it was the right place for me. (My aunts Jenny and Hannah could keep an eye on me.) But I had had enough of Southern education and wanted to go to Smith. A few months before the autumn entrance term, when I thought the matter had been settled, my mother and father held out for Goucher on the strange ground that it was closer to New York. But a month before I was to leave for Goucher, my mother became ill and it was obvious that I was meant to stay at home. I do not remember any sharp words about these changes and that in itself is odd, because sharp words came often in those years, but I do remember a feeling of what difference did it make. I knew, without rancor, that my parents were worried about a wild and headstrong girl; and then, too, a defeat for an only child can always be turned into a later victory.

New York University had started its Washington Square branch only a few years before, with an excellent small faculty and high requirements for the students it could put into one unattractive building. I was, of course, not where I wanted to be and I envied those of my friends who were. And yet I knew that in another place I might have been lost, because the old story was still true: I was sometimes more advanced but often less educated than other students and I had little desire to be shown up. And by seventeen, I was openly rebellious against almost everything. I knew that the seeds of the rebellion were scattered and aimless in a nature that was wild to be finished with something-or-other and to find something-else-or-other, and I had sense enough to know that I was overproud, oversensitive, overdaring because I was shy and frightened. Ah, what a case can be made for vanity in the shy. (And what a losing game is self-description in the long ago.)

It was thus in the cards that college would mean very little to me, although one professor opened up a slit into another kind of literature: I began an exciting period of Kant and Hegel, a little, very little, of Karl Marx and Engels. In a time when students didn't leave classes or even skip them very often, I would slip away from a class conducted by a famous editor, annoyed at the glimpses of his well-bred life, and would slam my seat as I left in the middle of a lecture by the famous Alexander Woollcott whenever he paraded the gibe-wit and shabby literary taste of his world. (My bad manners interested Woollcott. He went out of his way, on several occasions, to find me after class and to offer a ride up-town. But the kindness or interest made me resentful and guilty, and I remember a tart exchange about a novel written by a friend of his. Years later, because Woollcott admired Hammett, who did not admire him, I was to meet him again. And after that, when I wrote plays, he was pleasant to me — if saying that I looked like a prow head on a whaling ship is pleasant.)

A good deal of the college day I spent in a Greenwich Village restaurant called Lee Chumley's curled up on a dark bench with a book, or arguing with a brilliant girl called Marie-Louise and her extraordinary, foppish brother, up very often from Princeton, carrying a Paris copy of *Ulysses* when he wasn't carrying Verlaine. (Hal was a handsome, strange young man and we all hoped to be noticed by him. A few years later he married one of our group and a few years after that he killed himself and a male companion in a Zurich hotel room.)

In my junior year, I knew I was wasting time. My mother took me on a long tour to the Midwest and the South, almost as a reward for leaving college. We returned to New York for my nineteenth birthday and the day after I began what was then called an "affair." It was an accident: the young man pressed me into it partly because it satisfied the tinkering malice that has gone through the rest of his life, mostly because it pained his best friend. The few months it lasted did not mean much to me, but I have often asked myself whether I underestimated the damage that so loveless an arrangement made on my future. But my generation did not often deal with the idea of love — we were ashamed of the word, and scornful of the misuse that had been made of it — and

42

I suppose that the cool currency of the time carried me past the pain of finding nastiness in what I had hoped would be a moving adventure.

In the autumn, feeling pleasantly aimless, but knowing that I deeply wanted to work at something, I went to a party and met Julian Messner, the vice-president of Horace Liveright. I had never met a publisher before, never before had a conversation with a serious man much older than myself, and I mistook what was an automatic flirtatious interest for a belief that Julian thought I was intelligent. In any case, by the time the party was over, I had a job.

A job with any publishing house was a plum, but a job with Horace Liveright was a bag of plums. Never before, and possibly never since, has an American publishing house had so great a record. Liveright, Julian, T. R. Smith, Manuel Komroff, and a few even younger men had made a new and brilliant world for books. In the years before I went to work, and in the few years after I left, they discovered, or persuaded over, Faulkner, Freud, Hemingway, O'Neill, Hart Crane, Sherwood Anderson, Dreiser, E. E. Cummings, and many other less talented but remarkable people, all of them attracted by the vivid, impetuous, high-living men who were the editors. It didn't hurt that Horace was handsome and daring, Julian serious and kind, Tom Smith almost erudite with his famous collection of erotica and odd pieces of knowledge that meant nothing but seemed to; that the advances they gave were large and the parties they gave even larger, full of lush girls and good liquor; that the sympathy and attention given to writers, young or old, was more generous than had been known before, possibly more real than has been known since. They were not truly serious men, I guess, nor men of the caliber of Max Perkins, but they had respect for serious writing. Their personal capers, which started out as outrageous and dashing in the fusty world of older publishing houses, became comic and, in time, dangerous and destructive. In the case of Horace himself, the end was sad, broken, undignified. But I was there at a good time and had a good time while I was there.

4

By the time I grew up the fight for the emancipation of women, their rights under the law, in the office, in bed, was stale stuff. My generation didn't think much about the place or the problems of women, were not conscious that the designs we saw around us had so recently been formed that we were still part of the formation. (Five or ten years' difference in age was a greater separation between people in the 1920's, perhaps because the older generation had gone through the war.) The shock of Fitzgerald's flappers was not for us: by the time we were nineteen or twenty we had either slept with a man or pretended that we had. And we were suspicious of the words of love. It was rather taken for granted that you liked one man better than the other and hoped he would marry you, but if that didn't happen you did the best you could and didn't talk about it much. We were, I suppose, pretend cool, and paid for it later on, but our

45

revolt against sentimentality had come, at least, out of distaste for pretense. Of the five girls I knew best, three married for money and said so, and we were not to know then that two of them, in their forties, would crack up under deprivation or boredom.

I was not, therefore, attracted by the lady intellectuals I met at Liveright's. They puzzled me. They talked so much about so little, they were weepy about life and men, and I was too young to be grateful for how much I owed them in the battle of something-or-other in the war for equality. They came through the office door as novelists or poets or artists and, there, I caught only glimpses and heard only gossip. But at parties I saw them in action and felt envy for their worldliness, their talent, their clothes, their age — and bewilderment at their foreign, half-glimpsed problems.

Liveright gave a great many parties. Any writer on a New York visit, any new book, any birthday was an excuse for what he called an A party or a B party. (Liveright was possibly the first publisher to understand that writers care less for dollars than for attention.) The A parties were respectable and high-class chatty. The B parties were drunk, cutup sex stuff and often lasted into another day and night with replacements. I was invited to both the A and B parties, maybe because I was young and thought to be unjudging, maybe for reasons not so good.

The respectable parties were filled with wives, single or divorced ladies, and a few wellborn Lesbians. They chatted about books and Freud. Not many of them had read Freud carefully and so he was considered by some as a metaphysician and by others as a welcome emancipator. And his conclusions about children were considerably misunderstood: I remember one of Maxwell Bodenheim's wives deploring, in Freud's name, the stodgy mind of her very young son who would not admit that when his mama flapped her arms she really rose in the air and soared above the city. She had been cursed, she felt, with a seven-year-old banker type. When she turned to me for agreement, I truly ran across the room feeling younger than her son and more ignorant. But I felt that way most of the time: Edmund Wilson, who met me somewhere in those years, says that I was a shy girl who spoke very little. I like him to say that, but the shyness was a cover for the fear of being shown up.

The B parties were filled with pretty ladies, semi-ins, almost-actresses or newspaper girls, and they slept quite openly with the gentlemen guests, or executives of Liveright's, or the bankers Horace so often had at his parties because he so often needed their money. Some of the ladies had permanent alliances — permanent meant about six months, and semi-permanent meant a few weeks. The B party girls puzzled me as much as the A party ladies and seemed to me no livelier. (If I had known the word square, I would have used it.) I felt that the words of emotion they spoke were not the truth, but then I was not yet old enough to be kind about lost ladies. Whatever step my generation had taken, forward or backward, it was large enough to separate us from people not too much older than ourselves.

Sometimes the parties were given at Horace's apartment, more often they were given at the office. And the office was a wacky joint in a brownstone house on 48th Street. Certain jobs were more clearly defined than others, but even the stenographers and shipping clerks often wandered about reading manuscripts, offering opinions about how to advertise or sell a book, and there was seldom a day without excitement. Some days a "great" new book was found; some days no corner could be found for work because too many writers were in town or had just dropped by; sometimes one of the editors had been in mysterious trouble the night before and everybody went around to his house or hospital to call upon him; on no day could you ever be sure what you would see through a half-open office door, or how long lunch hour would be for Horace and the editors, or who was taking a long nap afterwards. All the men in the office made routine passes at the girls who worked there — one would have had to be hunchbacked to be an exception — and one of the more pleasant memories of my life is the fast sprinting I would do up and down the long staircases to keep from being idly pinched or thrown by a clutching hand on a leg.

But the nicest times came when an efficiency cleanup was ordered. Then for a short time we would look and act like every other office and return from lunch prompt and sober, and work late into the night. I enjoyed the calm and was sorry that such periods never lasted more than a few days.

It was in one of those efficiency periods that I knew there was talk of firing me — I had misplaced an important manuscript, I didn't know how to file, my typing was erratic, my manuscript reports were severe. I would have been fired if I hadn't, that very week, discovered that I was pregnant by the man who, a half year later, I would marry.

A young man called Donald Friede had just been made a partner because Horace needed the money Donald brought into the firm. (He always needed money and often found it by selling part of the business to rich young men.) Donald seemed friendly, more my age, and I was so desperate to find an abortionist that, foolishly, I asked if he knew such a doctor. He found one immediately, swore himself to secrecy, and I made an appointment with the doctor for the following week. The morning following Donald's vow of secrecy, every member of the firm called me into his office to offer money, to ask the name of my child's father, to guess that it was one of them, to make plans and plots for help I didn't want. I was suddenly a kind of showcase. I was angry about that and so, throughout the good-natured questionings, I sat sullen, staring into space, refusing answers, trying not to think about the vicarious, excited snoopiness I knew was mixed with the kindness.

The operation, done without an anesthetic in a Coney Island half-house, with the doctor's mother as assistant, was completed on a Monday evening. I went home, weak and more frightened than I had ever been about anything, and so ignorant that I was awake all night worried that my parents could tell what had happened by just looking at me. On Tuesday morning, feeling sick, but sure that my mother would call a doctor if I said that, I went back to work. Horace called me in to ask how I was and to give me a glass of midmorning champagne; Friede stopped by my desk to ask if I had now decided to reveal the name of the father; Julian Messner asked me out to lunch and bought me a drink that was called a pink-un, and stared at me throughout lunch as if I were a recent arrival from a distant land. We didn't talk much at lunch, but as we walked back to the office he said, gently, "I don't understand what you're about."

I said, "That's all right, Julian," and knew he didn't like the answer.

As we climbed the steps of the brownstone, T. R. Smith yelled, "Julian, tell that ninny to go home to bed. She shouldn't have come to work today. Tell her to get out of here."

I was sure this was his way of firing me, so on my way past his office, I stopped in. I said, "I know I've lost the manuscript, Tom, but I've been nervous and tomorrow I'll find it —"

He said, "What are you made of, Lilly?"

I said, "Pickling spice and nothing nice."

He said, "That kind of talk. I don't understand you kids. Go home."

I said I couldn't, that if I went home too early my mother would be nervous and make a fuss, so I'd go to the movies.

He said, "You look awful. Lie down on the couch. I'll send you in some supper. When you feel better, go home, or go wherever you go."

He went back to the manuscript he was reading, the phone calls he was making, and I went to sleep on the couch.

When I woke up he said, "What's your generation about?"

"I don't know what it's about and I don't know why all of you keep asking questions like that. Everybody here seems angry with me for a reason I don't understand, and I'm angry with Donald for breaking his word."

Smith said, "It isn't that we're angry with you. We're worried about ourselves. We're used to bums and we're used to nice or near nice girls who make speeches and cause a fuss. We're not used to a respectable girl who doesn't make trouble for the man, says she is probably going to marry him anyway, but won't when she's pregnant, doesn't even tell him what day the abortion is —"

"I didn't tell him because it would have made me more nervous."

"How many men have you slept with?"

"Three hundred and thirty-three, Tom, not counting my brothers and uncles who don't much like to be counted."

I came toward his desk, took a deep breath, and no longer cared about being fired. "And it's none of your business. I haven't much liked being everybody's pregnant pet the last few days and all the questions. It's as if all of you were waiting for me to cry or to throw myself from a window or to tell you the man had deserted me and wouldn't I come home with one of you nicer boys —"

He said, "Not me. I don't want you home with me. You're not up my alley. But you're right. Exactly right."

"Funny," I said, "because none of you gives a damn about me."

"Not one damn. They even forgot you were here until this happened. But you acted too calm, wouldn't talk, came to work and so on, so now we realize that you're younger, different than the women we know. There *is* a new generation and nobody here likes to think that. But we'd better catch up on it if we want to publish it. I don't think we're going to like it, but maybe you'd better start telling us about it."

A waiter came into Smith's office, bringing a tray from the speakeasy next door. Smith moved a table in front of me, gave me a drink, and stared at me as I ate all of the good food. I grinned at him and he said, "So?"

I said, "I don't know how to answer you. I don't know about my generation. It's just us. We think we sound better than your ladies, but we don't know even that much because we haven't had time to make theories or maybe even need any."

"What do you think of what you call our ladies?"

I said, "All the talk about love, all the stuff."

"Did you ever read *Flaming Youth?*"

"Certainly not."

"Well, smarty, a lot of people did. We want Sam Adams to do a new book, maybe a sequel. But I think things have changed even in these few years, and I don't think we know, or he knows, what we're talking about. You can help."

I said I wasn't flaming youth, didn't even know what it meant.

"Yes, you do. You're it. Or it to us."

He came and sat by me and patted my hand. "It was I who wanted to fire you. You're not very efficient. But I'll make you a bargain. Get a couple of your bright friends, bring them over to Horace's this Saturday night, let Sam Adams ask all of you a few questions, and you can keep the job. For a while, anyway."

Saturday night my two friends, Marie-Louise and

52

Alice, and I were escorted to Horace's apartment entrance by Alice's two brothers. As flaming youth we'd each had a root beer and a sandwich in a delicatessen. The boys left us at the door with a few bad jokes and the three of us went up to Horace's duplex apartment.

I should have guessed there would be a party, there was a party almost every Saturday night, but I couldn't have guessed how noisy it would be. We stood in the door, knowing nobody, feeling awkward and foolish, until Tom Smith saw us and, crossing the room, motioned us up the stairs. I remember Liveright calling out from his place on the sofa, telling us to come and join him, but Tom hurried us to a kind of small library–guest room, and then, having made a leering examination of my friends, went out, closing the door. None of us talked: we felt like new patients in a hospital ward. In a few minutes Tom came back carrying glasses and a bottle. He was followed by Mr. Adams, who sat down on the couch bed and motioned us to chairs around him.

I would like to say these many years later that I remember his questions. But I don't, and for a good reason: he had already decided on whatever he meant to write and the questions were fitted to his decisions. So most of the time we didn't know what he was talking about.

After a few drinks, Mr. Adams's boredom with us was no longer concealed. (I think he had agreed to meet us only because Smith had insisted upon it. And the hour was late and he wasn't young.) The three of us felt silly and resentful, so when he got down to stuff like "How old were you when you had your first sexual encounter?"

Marie-Louise said she didn't know what encounter meant, kind of, and when Mr. Adams explained that it meant being in bed with a man, she said that in Bombay, where she had been born, things like that didn't take place in a bed. She had been born in Albany, New York, was a virgin until she married two years later, but it was a good thing to say because it put a little fire under Alice and me, who had been acting sulky. I said I had my first encounter in a chicken coop in New Orleans when I was four years old, but Mr. Adams was more interested in Alice, who was a beautiful girl and who could cry any time she felt like it. She was crying now over her first encounter, an imaginary geographer-explorer who had disappeared on what she sometimes called the Niger and sometimes called the Amazon. Marie-Louise, tired of Alice's overlong fantasy, took to singing. She had a pretty voice and she was improvising about her love in Bombay. Mr. Adams liked the singing and asked her if she wanted him to speak to Liveright, who would speak to Otto Kahn, the culture-kick banker, about money for singing lessons. Alice had now left the geographer behind and was trying to tell Mr. Adams that she had had so many encounters that only her priest could remember the details, but she'd make him write them all down for Mr. Adams because her father was a papal count. (Her father was a rich Jew from Detroit and she was already started on the road to Marxism that would lead her, as a student doctor, to be killed in the Vienna riots of 1934.)

The three of us had had too many drinks, were talking at the same time, were laughing too much at nothing. Mr. Adams rose, thanked us, suggested that we all go downstairs and join Horace's party.

But the door wouldn't open. I don't know why it wouldn't open, and although he later denied it, I've always believed that Tom Smith had locked us in and forgotten about us. In any case, there we were. We tried hitting the door, we shouted, we stamped on the floor, but no sounds could overreach the noise of the party below. Mr. Adams finally threw himself against the door with such angry force that he reeled and fell back over a chair, and pushed Alice when she tried to help him up. She stayed on the floor and claimed that it was the first time in all of her many encounters that a man had been mean to her. When she started to cry, Marie-Louise said to cut it, but by now the tears were real and they were soon being nasty to each other.

The only other door in the room led to a bathroom, and when Mr. Adams went in there we had no reason to be curious. (In any case we were too busy: Marie-Louise and Alice were shouting at each other and I was explaining the damage alcohol did to the brain.) When the three of us quieted down, and Alice and Marie-Louise had apologized to one another, we whispered and giggled about the new encounters we were making up for Mr. Adams's return. It took us quite a while to realize that he had been missing for longer than a toilet usually requires. We knocked on the bathroom door, got no reply, consulted, and finally opened the door. There was no sign of him, but the bathroom window was open and sounds were coming from below. We climbed the bathtub ledge to see that Mr. Adams was on a fire escape three flights below us, one story above ground level. He was shouting into a window that faced him, but nobody answered. He took to pounding on the window and then to pushing it. He was sweating and he looked sick. Slowly he walked to the opening of the fire escape, crouched, and began to shake the ladder. But the ladder had rusted through the years and would not budge. Mr. Adams stood erect as if to jump. But he didn't make the jump and he was right: it was a long jump, he was not young, and frustration and anger had turned him clumsy. He slipped and fell the length of the fire escape landing.

Marie-Louise said, "Ssh. He wouldn't want us to see him."

Alice said, "He's going to hurt himself." She pushed us both aside, climbed out the window, going young and rapid down the ladders. Adams didn't see her until she had almost reached him and then, in some kind of panic, or shame, he grabbed her leg and motioned her to go back. Alice kicked his hand and made the long jump to the ground with an athlete's soft, forward motion. Adams shouted something to her we couldn't hear, but we could see that her face changed to anger.

She stepped back to look up at us and called out, "Don't ever have encounters with old gentlemen on fire escapes." Then she disappeared around a corner of the building and in a few minutes Mr. Adams rose from his fire escape and began a slow climb back to our bathroom window.

I said to Marie-Louise, "Take your clothes off, get in the shower, and when he gets here, pop out and offer yourself. I think that's what flaming youth does every Saturday night."

She said, "Don't be mean," and backed me out of the bathroom.

The three of us didn't speak during the half hour it took the janitor and his assistant to take the door off the hinges. We faced a large group of people from the party who treated us as if we were a vaudeville turn put on for their amusement. By the time we got past them and downstairs, Mr. Adams had disappeared and Alice was sitting next to Tom Smith.

I said, "Tom, flaming youth thinks you locked us in and it was a dirty trick."

Tom put his arm around Alice. "This little girl has sense. Some little girls don't have too much. I think we'll fire you tomorrow."

I wasn't fired, but I left a few months later to get married. Mr. Adams never wrote a sequel to *Flaming Youth*, although he did write a book called *The Flagrant Years* about the "beauty market." I don't think that could have been us.

After I was married I would often drop around to the office to see my old friend Louis Kronenberger, who had gone to work there, and sometimes Julian Messner would take me out to lunch. I wanted very much to ask him to give me back my old job, but I guess I knew I wouldn't get it. In any case, I had a feeling that the place was in a decline. Rumors went about that Horace was wasting money producing plays and was drinking too much; and because the depression had now set in, the rich, available young men partners were no longer to be found. Gradually the firm began to disappear, its assets and contracts taken over by a man who had been the head of the shipping room. It was, of course, a sad story, but there were so many sad stories in the early 1930's that I don't re-

member any special pain when I met Horace again in
Hollywood. He had become a producer at Paramount
Pictures: some of the old glamour was there, where his
name was still famous and his recent history not yet
fully understood. But every time I saw him — not many
times, perhaps five or six — I knew, for a simple reason, that the pride was breaking: he would, immediately, cross the room to sit beside me because I alone
in the room was the respectful young girl who had
known him in the great days, and the more he drank
the more we talked of those days, not so many years
before. (He had, as a mistress, a very nice actress, and
was by this time divorced from his wife. The nice actress
was good to him and faithful, and we all took for
granted that he would marry her.)

Then for a long time I didn't see him, and I no longer
can remember whether he was fired from Paramount or
resigned. I saw him again after I was divorced and Hammett and I had moved to New York. About a year after
that, I had a call from him asking me to his wedding
reception the following week. I didn't want to go, although I don't know what instinct dictated that, but
Hammett, who didn't know him very well and didn't like
him very much, unexpectedly insisted that we go.

The reception was given at the apartment of one of
his respectable lady cousins. The room was filled with
people I had never seen before, although an occasional
familiar face would float in and float out. The party
seemed in the managerial hands of two brothers who,
when they weren't kissing the gentlemen guests, were
kissing each other.

I said to one of them, "Where's Horace?"

"Passed out," he shrieked with laughter, "and so has the bride. They had a simply, simply splendid fight."

"She never used to drink," I said.

"Always. Always. How do you know? You never met her."

When we got that straight, it turned out that Horace had not married the nice actress, but another actress, recently met, a dark beauty who appeared in a few minutes, lurching, demanding that somebody find the bridegroom because she wanted an immediate divorce.

I said to Hammett, "Let's get out."

Hammett said, "No. Wait for him, the poor bastard."

And so we sat through the long afternoon and night, neither of us having much to drink, although those were the heavy drinking days. Hammett, sober, was always a silent man, and after a while I couldn't bring myself to even the smallest conversation with the strange men and women in the room. We must have been an odd pair, sitting silent on a big couch as the place emptied, filled again, grew quiet, then noisy with new visitors, the bride screaming "darlings" at some, curses at others, explaining over and over again that the bridegroom had given her a black eye. (Her eyes were beautiful and clear.) Toward midnight, I think I must have dozed, because I remember being surprised to see Hammett on his feet as Horace came through the door. The fine clothes were rumpled, the strong, handsome face was set as if it had been arranged before a mirror. He came directly towards me and I rose to meet him.

Horace said, "You don't have to rise to greet me. Nobody does anymore."

Hammett said, "Don't tell her things like that. I'm having enough trouble keeping her respectful."

It was a good thing to say because it made Horace smile. He said, "I need a drink. Lilly, were you the only one to come today?"

I said that all his old friends and writers had been there — it was not true — but it was late now, and they had gone when they couldn't find him.

He said, "I've been resting. Where's the bride?" When he went to look for her, and Hammett came back with the drink Horace had forgotten about, we decided to go home. On the way down the stairs, voices were suddenly raised, and I recognized Horace angry, and the bride even angrier.

I was never to see him again. But in 1933 one of his former secretaries called to tell me that he was very ill and broke and living alone. She gave me the address, I took five hundred dollars from the bureau where Hammett always left money for me, and took a taxi to the address. But I had the wrong address and had to telephone home to ask Hammett to find the piece of paper on which I had written it.

I said, "I'm taking him five hundred dollars. Is that enough?"

Hammett said, "Enough to make you feel noble. Get yourself in a taxi and come back here. He won't want money from you, have a little sense. Find somebody else to take it to him."

I said, "That's foolish. Why wouldn't he want it from me?"

Hammett said, "O.K., do what you want."

But I went home and called Dick Simon, of Simon and Schuster, who had once worked for Liveright. Simon's secretary said he was out of town, would be back in a week. But three days later Horace died.

5

I HAD left my job at Liveright's to marry Arthur Kober, who was a charming young man working as a theatre press agent and just beginning to write about his friends in the emerging Jewish-American lower middle class world.

We didn't have much money, but we had enough for a pleasant life of reading, afternoon bridge for me, and nice, aimless evenings. I found that I liked to do the good New Orleans cooking of my childhood and wanted to learn more about the excellent backwoods cooking of my mother's Alabama. I went back to writing short stories in fits of long hours of secret work. But I knew the stories were not very good and so I always put them aside.

Those first few years of marriage included a long trip to Paris, where Arthur worked on a magazine. I wandered around Europe in a jumble of passivity and wild impatience. I believed I was not doing or living the way

I had planned. I had planned nothing, of course. I was bewildered: if I really felt there were a million years ahead of me, why then did I feel so impatient, so restless?

I think we were younger in our twenties than people are now because the times allowed us to be and because we were not very concerned with position or the future or money. (That came to most of us a few years later.) And I was even younger than my friends. I was rash, overdaring, certain only that any adventure was worth having, and increasingly muddled by the Puritan conscience that made me pay for the adventures. I needed a teacher, a cool teacher, who would not be impressed or disturbed by a strange and difficult girl. I was to meet him, but not for another four or five years.

The time came when my idle life didn't suit Arthur and didn't suit me. I wasn't any good at finding jobs or keeping them, and so Arthur found them for me in the theatre. I worked as a press agent for an arty little group who didn't pay me after the second week. I worked as a play reader for Anne Nichols, the author of *Abie's Irish Rose*, who wanted to become a producer. I had a good time for four months in Rochester, New York, working for a stock company and gambling every night for money to spend in Europe that summer. Once, for a few weeks, I went back to the short stories, but I convinced myself that I was not meant to be a writer. I was rather relieved by that discovery — it gave me more time to listen to a gangster who ran Rochester's underworld, more time to win money at bridge from Rochester society, more time to read and drink.

I have no clear memories of those days, those years,

not of myself where and when, not of other people. I know only that I was ignorant pretending to be wise, lazy pretending to work hard, so oversensitive to a breath of reservation that I called it unfriendliness and swept by it with harsh intolerance. It was the fashion then to like the witty insult behind the back, the goose-grease compliment before the face. (That fashion has now returned and we like only those we consider "pleasant.") But I did not want that form of human exchange. I respected only those I thought told the "truth," without fear for themselves, independent of popular opinion. And thus, like so many lady extremists, I began a history of remarkable men, often difficult, sometimes even dangerous.

I did win enough money in those scrubby Rochester days to go to Europe that summer of 1929. I went to Germany, liked Bonn, and decided to study there for a year. I lived in a university boardinghouse waiting for the day of enrollment and went on nice picnics with large healthy blondes. I thought I was listening to a kind of socialism, I liked it, and agreed with it. But one day on an autobus, riding out to the picnic grounds, two of them gave me a cheesy-looking pamphlet about their organization — I cannot remember its name but it was, of course, a youth group publication of Hitler's National Socialism — and asked if I wouldn't like to become a member, no dues for foreigners if they had no Jewish connections. I said I had no other connections that I knew of, although a second cousin in Mobile had married the owner of a whorehouse, non-Jewish. But nobody paid attention to what I said, because Hellman in Germany is often not a Jewish name. I left Bonn the next day and came back to New York.

It has been forgotten that for many people the depression years were the good years. True, my father, like so many of his generation, took a beating from which he did not recover, but Arthur was offered a job as a scenario writer for Paramount Pictures at more money than we had ever seen. We had been living in a beat-up old house on Long Island and I was reluctant to leave it. So Arthur went ahead of me to Hollywood and I fooled and fiddled with excuses until the day when I did go, knowing even then, I think, that I would not stay.

6

WE rented a dark house in Hollywoodland, the hilly section above the already junky Hollywood Boulevard. I do not know why we chose such an ugly house nor why we employed an ex-actress to cook bad dinners. The ex-actress was a sad, lonely woman who gave me my first concern about middle age because she so often cried and spoke about growing bald. Arthur and I felt sorry for her, but my father didn't ever feel sorry for bad cooks, and so, when he and my mother came West for a visit, at the second night's dinner he said to me, "How can you eat salad before the soup and what kind of people eat grapefruit at dinner? What has happened to you?"

He was right. Something had happened to me. Torpor had touched down. I spent most of the day reading in a leather chair and at night I was learning to drink hard. I was out of place and the drinking made uninteresting people matter less and, late at night, matter not at all. I was twenty-five years old that June and I had stepped too early into solitude.

After my father spoke to me, I was worried enough to try again for a job. My husband pulled strings and I was given fifty dollars a week at Metro-Goldwyn-Mayer to read manuscripts and write reports about them. In order to get the job, you had to read two languages — or pretend that you did — and you had to write the kind of idiot-simple report that Louis Mayer's professional lady storyteller could make even more simple when she told it to Mr. Mayer.

Twelve men and two women sat in a large room in a rickety building on stilts, and every small tremor — and California had a number of tremors that year — sent the building atilt. When you finished a manuscript (you were expected to read at least two a day) you went into another large room and waited your turn for one of the half-broken typewriters. It was said that if your reports showed signs of promise you would be promoted to what was called a junior writer position, but after that I don't know what became of you because I was never promoted. The job didn't matter to me after the first few weeks' pleasure of having any job at all, but it did matter to the learned Austrian who sat next to me, and to the former English lady writer who sat by herself in a corner, and most of all it mattered to what had been a most respected editor of a New York publishing house who had left his wife to live with a young girl and ended up here. I used to stare at him a good deal hoping we could become friends, but while he was polite to me, as he was to all others, I was the one person in the room who knew about him and thus most to be avoided. (I knew the girl he had run away with and the fact that she was an ugly girl somehow made the whole story more interesting.) In the third or fourth month of our bowing acquaintance, his girl picked him up one evening and invited me to dinner the following week. I looked forward to the evening, but a few days before the dinner he did not appear in the office, and the head lady of the typewriters told me that his daughter had killed herself and he had returned to New York. I tried to find his girl, but the landlady at the sad little half-house said she had moved without leaving an address. I was never to see or hear from them again, although many years later he did a distinguished piece of scholarly research.

The days and the months went clipclop along, much as they had done in the leather chair in our ugly house, except that now I was reading junk when, alone, I had been with good books. I would leave home at eight-thirty, drive to Culver City carrying a small basket with my lunch and a bottle of wine. I would, by one o'clock, have a vague headache that would disappear as I ate my picnic on the back lot of the studio and got fuzzy on the wine and the surrounding dream of old movie sets piled next to one another, early Rome at right angles to the painted roses of a girlie musical, at the left of a London street, side by side with a giant, empty whaling ship.

It was not a good place to eat lunch, but it was better than going to the studio commissary where I had to pass a large table for famous directors and writers, some of whom knew my husband and thus had to make the kind of half rise-bow, acknowledged in all worlds where classes are sharply marked to mean you are above the ordinary but not enough above it to include you in the circle. Nor was I interested in looking at the almost stars, and occasional real stars, who sat at special tables spooning the chicken soup that was Mr. Mayer's special pride. (I did not know then that the glamour of theatre people was never to mean anything to me, which was forever to make me difficult for those who have the right to think it should.) I remember once seeing Garbo there and thinking she was the most beautiful woman in the world, and I often remember John Gilbert, whose career was about to come to an end because his voice shocked the talking picture audiences, and Norma Shearer, the face unclouded by thought. (Years later, after *The Children's Hour*, Mrs. Patrick Campbell, broke and anxious for a job, borrowed four hundred dollars from me "to go to dinner with Shearer and her husband Irving Thalberg, because he's the head of the studio, duckie, and crazy about her the way Jews are about women who aren't." I didn't understand why that should cost four hundred dollars until a few days after the dinner when Mrs. Campbell showed me a dress she had bought for the occasion. Four hundred dollars was a fortune for a dress in those days, but I thought it a splendid gesture for a proud old lady and asked her if Thalberg had given her the job she wanted. "No, duckie, and I don't think I'll get it. So I'll give you a few of Bernard Shaw's letters as repayment." I said I didn't want Mr. Shaw's letters, but by this time she was giggling and playing with a little dog called Moonbeam. Through the giggles she said, "You see, dearie duckie, I was doing rather splendidly at first. And then, well, it's true, isn't it, and *that's* the important thing, I said to Mr. Thalberg, 'Your wife has the most beautiful little eyes I've ever seen.' ")

69

After my picnic lunch, warm with wine, I would go back to work and try for a nap if the head lady of the typewriters was out of the building. But two and sometimes three and four reports of plays or novels is a lot of work for one day, and by four o'clock there wasn't a face in the room that didn't show the strain. But I would stay late, always with the excuse that I wasn't finished or the typewriter had broken or that I was waiting for somebody to call me.

In truth, I was avoiding the ride home. I do not know why that drive in the dark of six o'clock was so terrible to me. Maybe because the flat, soggy land of the main road was the kind of country I had never seen before, maybe the awful speed and jerkiness of California drivers, maybe the ugly house I was going home to, maybe because I knew this shabby job had solved nothing. Maybe all of that and maybe little of it, I don't know anymore, but the drive had become so bad for me that I would tremble as I got into the car and would often have to stop the car and press my hands together to stop the movements they were making. Sometimes when I stopped I fell asleep for a while; once I leaned from the window and screamed; once I left the car, went to a small hotel and phoned to say I couldn't get home and didn't want anybody to come for me; twice I had minor accidents and once I killed a rabbit and sat by it for a few hours. I did not yet know about "inhuman cities" or roads built with no relief for the eye, or the effects of a hated house upon the spirit. I didn't even understand about my marriage, or my life, and had no knowledge of the new twists I was braiding into the kinks I was already bound round with.

Certainly I did not know that fear, to many, was no disgrace. Like most of the middle class I had been brought up to swim, drive cars, climb around. Irrational fear was no part of your own world and you had contempt for the few times you had seen it in other people. Now here it was, out in the open, and I realized it had been with me before, and would now be with me forever unless I did something, a favorite phrase of my time. I did nothing more than go home because I had no place else to go.

That is the way I saw it then, because that is the way I wrote about it then, but now I know it is not a whole nor a true picture. We often had nice weekends in Tia Juana, where my father found an oyster shucker he had known in New Orleans. The oyster shucker owned a small restaurant and was so happy to see my father that he would go quail shooting at dawn and broil them for us at breakfast, drinking pernod as he told us of the old days when he would open oysters for my father and the other young bloods and their "girlies." Once, when he told about a ball in New Orleans that had lasted three days and punched my father in the ribs with teasing about "seven girlies" in those three days, my mother's pleasant face changed so sharply that I thought she was sick. She went to the ladies' room and I followed her there. She was sitting in a chair, staring at the floor. I don't think we spoke, but I remember thinking that I had never in my life been jealous about a man and had contempt for what I was watching. A few years later, when I had gone to live with Dashiell Hammett, I remember being ashamed of that contempt and always wishing to apologize to my mother for it.

And we had pleasant evenings with our best friends, Laura and Sidney Perelman and Laura's brother, Nathanael West. The five of us, and a few others, stayed close together not only because we liked each other but because we were in what was called "the same salary bracket." Then, and probably now, if you were a writer who earned five hundred dollars a week you didn't see much of those who earned fifteen hundred a week. That was O.K. with me because other, richer and more important groups puzzled me and made me disorderly: the remarkable gadgets in their houses, the then new swimming pools, the earnest talk made me irritable and nasty. It took me years to understand that it had been a comic time, with its overperfect English antiques that were replacing the overcarved Spanish furniture and hanging shawls; the flutey, refined language — one producer spoke often of his daughter's "perberty," and Hammett phoned me one night from Jean Harlow's house to tell me that she had rung the bell for the butler and said, "Open the window, James, and leave in a tiny air" — and the attempt, running side by side with the new life, to stand by the old roots: Jewish mama stories and Jewish mamas proudly imported from the East; French cooks and stuffed derma; and one studio executive who lived in a Colonial house with early American furniture and a mezuzah above the door encased in pickled pine. And there was the wife of a composer who had two ermine coats exactly alike in case one should burn, and the ex-star, our neighbor, who often came calling to show me the knife cuts on her body put there the night before by a very religious movie director, and over our own fireplace in the ugly house there was a portrait of a lion whose eyes lit up if you pressed a button, and we knew a pug dog who would not eat his meat unless his Polish mistress flavored it with what she called a *soupçon d'ail.*

More interesting to me was the foggy edge-world of people who had come to Hollywood for reasons they had long ago forgotten. They lived in the Murphy-bed, modern apartments that were already the slums off Hollywood Boulevard, or in the rickety houses that stuck out like broken tree-geraniums from the Hollywood mud hills. There were still traces of the days when most of them had wanted to act or write or paint, but those days passed into years of drinking and doping or grubbing. I saw this world only after I knew Hammett but, because of my nature and theirs, I saw it only through a crack in the door. It seemed to me a world of independent spirits and I envied the long, free nights and the sleeping days, but they thought my envy was something else, and were suspicious of me. I remember an older woman asking, "Where did you get that suit?" And before I could answer she said, "It takes too damned long to tell that your clothes are good." They saw me, I think, as a tight, tense sightseer, and believed that my unspoken romantic view of them was an outlander's patronage. Hammett saw this world for what it was, and turned to it only during drinking bouts, turning sharply away when they were over. Pep West saw it through his own wonderfully original mind and wrote, in *The Day of the Locust,* the only good book about Hollywood ever written. (Fitzgerald's *The Last Tycoon* was a sentimental view of Irving Thalberg: Scott had written magnificently of the rich and powerful in the East and in Europe, but he got sticky moon-candy about a man who was only a bright young movie producer.)

The people of that world are now, in my memory, rolled into one mass in one room, and I cannot be sure that I do not mix up the men with the women, their dogs with their children or mothers. But I do remember an artist who went barefoot along the streets and picked up a job when he had to as a first-rate captain or engineer on one of the yachts of the rich. His leaning house in the hills was full of china and glass and sheets bearing the names of the many large boats from which they had been taken, and he did funny imitations of movie moguls on the water.

And I remember a small, faded woman called Sis who lived with and exchanged men with her mother. Sis was always too doped to talk much, and as she sat in a chair holding a small dog on her lap, silent, waited upon by her vigorous green-blonde mother, she seemed to me an interesting girl, but the one time I tried talking to her she suddenly slapped my face. She died a few months later when, according to her mother, she was so drunk that she fell to the floor and hit her head on a radiator. Hammett said he didn't believe that because he had never known anybody who doped heavily to drink heavily, and evidently somebody agreed with him because there were a few days of excitement when the mother was arrested and charged with throwing Sis against the radiator during a fight. Nothing ever came of that except a party the mother gave when the police could prove nothing, or didn't want to. And there was a man, an ex-actor, who played the flute and lived with a fat woman everybody said was a man, and there was the American Indian who sold postcards on Hollywood Boulevard and went to every fancy movie opening in top hat and tails. One night Hammett and I were having dinner in the Brown Derby and the Indian came in, pushing his way past the head-waiter, to sit down next to Hammett. He said, "My grand-father was chief of the Sioux, my great-grandfather was killed by . . ."

"How much do you want?" Hammett asked.

"Nothing as a gift from you. You told me once you arrested an Indian for murder . . ."

Hammett put his wallet on the table and said, "Take it any way you want, but don't tell me what you think."

The Indian opened the wallet and took out five twenty-dollar bills. "Be sure I do not take it as a gift. I take it as a loan. You are better than most, but you . . ."

Hammett said wearily, "Arrested an Indian for mur-der. That's right."

The Indian said, "And thus it is impossible for me . . ."

"Sure, sure," Hammett said. "Mail it to me someday." The Indian bowed, kissed my hand, and was gone.

I said, "He's proud, isn't he?"

Hammett said, "No. He's a Negro pretending to be an Indian. He's a no-good stinker."

I said, "Then why did you give him the money?"

"Because no-good stinkers get hungry too."

But all that came after I left the job at Metro. I was there for about a year, and then one night, driving home, I knew I could not make that drive again. It had, of course, become a symbol of much else that had gone wrong. A short time later Arthur and I separated with-out ill feeling and I went back to New York.

I forgot about those rides in the car, don't think I ever thought about them again until seven or eight years later. By that time I had written two plays and two movies, was earning a lot of money, and was able to write a clause in a contract with Samuel Goldwyn that allowed me a choice of scripts and did not require me, except for short periods, to go to Hollywood.

And so I was living on an island off the shore of Connecticut when the Spanish Civil War began in 1936. Never before and never since in my lifetime were liberals, radicals, intellectuals and the educated middle class to come together in single, forceful alliance. (The present feeling against the war in Vietnam is stronger, of course, and more widespread. But it took us four or five years to realize that *we*, our own people, my hairdresser's husband, and the son of my friend's friend, and a former student of my own at Harvard, and a garage mechanic who should never have been trusted with a penknife, had all been drafted to murder for reasons neither they nor we understood.) Therefore when Archibald MacLeish, in 1937, suggested that he, Hemingway, Joris Ivens and I make a documentary movie about Spain, I jumped at the chance to do something. Sitting in New York it was easy enough to write a check, but too hard to write a shooting script, or even an outline, about a war I did not know in a place I had never seen. I decided to join Ivens in Spain, but I came down with pneumonia in Paris, came home, and didn't get to Spain for another eight or nine months. But Hemingway was already in Spain and he was much better qualified than I to make the picture.

In 1938, after I had been to Spain and was back in Hollywood for a short stay, Ernest and Joris brought the final cut of *The Spanish Earth* to California. It was a good picture, with remarkable work by Ivens and a narration by Ernest that I still like — I saw the picture again about a year ago — because he felt deeply enough not to care that he often sounded like a parody of himself. Frederic and Florence March offered us their house for a private showing of the picture. We invited a few well-heeled people and raised thirteen thousand dollars, a great deal of money in those days, to buy ambulances for Spain. (We all felt so good that night that nobody much cared that Errol Flynn, invited because he claimed he had been to Spain during the war — Ernest said that Flynn had crossed the border and crossed right back again — went to the toilet during the money raising and was not seen again.)

When we left the Marches, Dorothy Parker asked a few of us to her house for a nightcap. (She had known Ernest for many years, and while they didn't like each other, the night was pleasant enough to make both of them affectionate.) I had met Scott Fitzgerald years before in Paris, but I had not seen him again until that night and I was shocked by the change in his face and manner. He hadn't seemed to recognize me and so I was surprised and pleased when he asked if I would ride with him to Dottie's. My admiration for Fitzgerald's work was very great, and I looked forward to talking to him alone. But we didn't talk: he was occupied with driving at ten or twelve miles an hour down Sunset Boulevard, a dangerous speed in most places, certainly in Beverly Hills. Fitzgerald crouched over the wheel when cars honked at us, we jerked to the right and then to the left, and passing drivers leaned out to shout at us. I could not bring myself to speak, or even to look at Fitzgerald, but when I saw that his hands were trembling on the wheel, all my rides from Metro came rushing back, and I put my hand over his hand. He brought the car to the side of the road and I told him about my old job at Metro, the awful rides home, my fears of California drivers, until he patted my arm several times and then I knew he hadn't been listening and had different troubles.

He said, "You see, I'm on the wagon. I'll take you to Dottie's but I don't want to go in."

When we finally got to Dottie's, he came around to open the door for me. He said softly, "It's a long story. Ernest and me."

In those days I knew no stories about Hemingway and Fitzgerald, just that they had been friends and weren't anymore, but I remembered that Dottie had once told me that she and Scott had slept together years before I knew her, in a casual one or two night affair.

I said, "But Dottie wants to see you. Everybody in that room wants to meet you."

He shook his head and smiled. "No, I'm riding low now."

"Not for writers, nor will you ever. *The Great Gatsby* is the best . . ."

He smiled and touched my shoulder. "I'm afraid of Ernest, I guess, scared of being sober when . . ."

I said, "Don't be. He could never like a good writer, certainly not a better one. Come. You'll have a nice time."

I put out my hand and, after a second, he smiled and took it. We went into the hall and turned left to the living room. Nobody saw us come in because the four or five people in the room were all turned toward Ernest, who stood with his back to the door, facing the fireplace. I don't know why he did it, or what had gone on before, but as we started into the room, Hemingway threw his highball glass against the stone fireplace. Fitzgerald and I stopped dead at the sound of the smashing glass: he stepped back into the hall and turned to leave, but I held his arm and he followed me through a swinging door as if he didn't know or care where he was going. Dottie and Hammett were in the kitchen talking about Errol Flynn as they watched Alan Campbell, Dottie's husband, grow irritable about ice trays.

I said, "Ernest just threw a glass."

Dottie said, "Certainly," as she kissed Fitzgerald.

I moved toward Dash and said in a whisper, "Please help Mr. Fitzgerald. He's frightened of Ernest and the glass throwing didn't help."

Hammett, when he was drinking heavily, and he was that night, seldom paid any attention to what anybody said but continued with whatever was in his head at the minute.

So now he said, "Ernest has never been able to write a woman. He only puts them in books to admire him."

By the time I asked what the hell that had to do with what I was saying, he was out of the kitchen, and when I went back into the hall he was saying the same thing to somebody else. The rest of the evening was quiet, but I don't remember how long Fitzgerald stayed and I was never to see him again.

But somewhere through the liquor fog of that night, and many others like it, what had been said to him, or what he had seen or sensed himself, stayed in Dash's mind. (Often he would forget a night or a week, could not remember where or with whom he had been, only to discover that many of the details of such periods were recorded almost accurate.)

A year or so later, we were in the Stork Club and the table grew, as it so often did, until it included Ernest and Gustav Regler, a German writer I had known in Spain. (Ernest and Dash had seemed to like each other — they had dined alone a few times when Ernest was in New York — and once I had said, "Ernest is generous about your books, that's nice." Hammett laughed. "Must mean I'm a bad writer.")

The Spanish War was just ended and many Republicans and their supporters had been caught in France, or in northern Spain, and had to be bailed or bought out. We had all given money to make that possible, but Ernest was in a bad humor that Stork Club night and gave small jab lectures about safe people in New York. People began to leave our table until nobody was left but Ernest, Regler, Dash and me, and by that time Dash had had as much to drink as Ernest, and had grown too quiet. Now he put his head in his hands as Ernest spoke again of the friends who must be saved.

Ernest said, "What's the matter with you, Hammett?"

"I don't always like lectures."

I remember an angry silence, and then suddenly Ernest seemed in a good humor and Dash in a bad humor as they talked of saving intellectuals or saving ordinary people, and when Regler or I tried to speak neither of them cared. When I came back from a trip to the ladies' room, Ernest had a tablespoon between the muscles of his upper and lower arm and was pressing it hard. Hammett was staring down at the tablecloth. Just as I settled myself the spoon crumpled and Ernest threw it down with a happy grin.

He turned to Hammett, "All right, kid, let's see you do that."

Kid looked up, stared at Ernest, returned his head to his hands, and I knew there was going to be trouble. I tinkled and giggled and chatted and chittered, but nobody paid any attention. I didn't hear anything for a few minutes until Ernest said, "So you're against saving the intellectuals?"

Hammett spoke through his hands. "I didn't say that. I said there were other people in the world." He turned to me, "Come on. Let's go."

He half rose. Ernest's hand shot out and held him down. Ernest was grinning. "No. Let's see you do the spoon trick first."

Dash stared at Ernest's hand, settled in his chair again, put his head back in his hands. Regler began to talk about something, but I don't remember what he said. Ernest was holding out another tablespoon as he whispered to Dash.

Dash said, "Why don't you go back to bullying Fitzgerald? Too bad he doesn't know how good he is. The best."

The hand on Dash's arm came away and the fingers spread open as the grin disappeared. Ernest said, very sharply, "Let's see you bend the spoon."

Dash got up. He was drunk now and the rise was unsteady. He said, very softly, "I don't think I could bend the spoon. But when I did things like that I did them for Pinkerton money. Why don't you go roll a hoop in the park?"

He left the table and by the time I got up to follow he was nowhere to be found on the street.

7

Two years earlier, in the late summer of 1937, I had been invited to a theatre festival in Moscow. I showed the cable to Dash and suggested he might like to make his first trip to Europe. I pointed to four handsome volumes he had just bought on the art of the Hermitage. "You could see the pictures for yourself."

"The books will do me fine. Why are you going?"

I said I had never been to Russia, that I wanted to see the Russian theatre.

Dash said, "No, you don't."

"Why do you think I don't?"

He shrugged. "I'll write it down for you some day soon."

A few days later I left for Paris en route to Moscow.

I wanted to get out of Hollywood partly because George Gershwin had died a few weeks before, and although I could not yet believe in the terrible death, I was sleepless with the memory of a night when what we all thought was a mildly sick, overanxious man came downstairs for dinner in a dressing gown and, as usual, went immediately to the piano. I was talking to somebody, only half listening to the piano, when I turned my head: his fingers had moved to the wrong notes for a passage of *An American in Paris.* Startled, I went over to the piano, but by the time I reached it, George had stopped playing and was staring at his hands as if he had never seen them before. Then he looked up and saw me, but I don't think he recognized me and the shock of thinking that kept me from speaking. In a minute, George's brother Ira came into the room and we all went in to dinner. George was a bewildered man that night, but the diagnosis had not as yet been made and there was no further sign of the brain tumor that would kill him a week later.

About the third week I was in Paris, in reply to two letters asking him to tell me why he was so certain I didn't want to see the Russian theatre, Hammett wrote: "I think, I don't know, of course, but I think that you would not betray anybody for any reason about anything — and I am not a man who thinks in such terms — unless somebody offered you a free subway ride to Jersey City and then we'd all be in danger. That's one reason you made this trip, and always will. So have a good wasted time but stop telling yourself you want to see the theatre. You don't. You'll see three plays and I'll bet you'll leave all of them by intermission. Then somebody'll give you a party and if the guests include an electrician or a property man, you'll find him and not want to talk to anybody else. I am told that foreigners like to gather cultivated questions for their cultivated guests, so when they get around to asking you your work methods and such, your face will grow very stern because you won't, thank God, know what they're talking about. Or you will be asked about your theatre experiences, and you'll say you never have had any, and you'll believe what you're saying. The truth is you don't like the theatre except the times when you're in a room by yourself putting the play on paper."

Like, not like, were not the words, but there was enough truth in what Hammett wrote to worry me. But now, many years and many plays later, I know as little as I knew then about the conflict that would keep me hard at work in a world that is not my world, although it has been my life. I have had great benefits from the theatre, liked and enjoyed many people in it, count a few of them as my close friends, had pleasure in success and excitement even in failure, but I have wandered through it as if I were a kind of stranger. (Except when I was writing, or the plays were in rehearsal: then all the natural instincts are at work the way some people play a musical instrument without a lesson and others, even as children, understand an engine.) Maybe it happened because I started out wanting to write novels and didn't have much interest in the theatre or movies; maybe my own nature does not fit the rushing strong tones of the theatre, although certainly my own tones are often shrill; maybe because I am not good at collaboration, the essence of the theatre; maybe because I like fame, but don't like, and am no good at, its requirements; or maybe vanity of any kind other than my own seems to me at first funny and at last boring. But most of all, the theatre is not a natural world for those who question whatever is meant by glamour. One must, one should, pay fame the respect it demands, or leave it alone and find someplace else to go. I have not been able to do either and thus have often made myself and other people uncomfortable.

It was in those pre-Moscow Paris weeks that I had first met Ernest Hemingway, although his bride-to-be, Martha Gellhorn — we didn't know then that she was to marry him, and I doubt that she was sure of it, either — had crossed on the boat with Dorothy Parker, her husband Alan Campbell, and me. Martha spent a good deal of her time in the boat's gymnasium, where, Dottie said, all of Ernest's ladies began their basic training for the life partnership.

I liked Ernest. It would have been hard for a woman not to like him if he wanted you to, tried for it. He had just come out of Spain — this was the second year of the Spanish Civil War — and had come up to Paris for a holiday before he and Martha returned to Spain.

And it was that same week that I first met Sara and Gerald Murphy, although I had heard about them for years. I suppose they were in their late forties, remarkable people who seemed to me as original and stylish as they had been described. Years before I met them the Murphys had moved to Europe with their three children to escape their rich, solid background. (Sara's sister, Hoytie Wiborg, was a kind of Henry James heiress in London and Paris society and a rather amusing irritant to the Murphys.) Gerald had become an interesting painter who soon ceased to paint for a high-flown reason that everybody explained to me but that I no longer remember. In Paris and on the French Riviera, which they founded as a summer resort, they were the center of a brilliant world of writers and artists attracted by the originality of their style as people. The rules that the Murphys had overturned seemed to anybody of my generation interesting but not important, but they had attracted and influenced Hemingway, Fitzgerald — the Murphys had introduced the one to the other in a famous first meeting where Ernest told Fitzgerald that Zelda was crazy — Benchley, Dorothy Parker, MacLeish, Picasso, Stravinsky, Léger, and many others. Tales were still told of an apartment in Paris the Murphys kept almost empty so that they could redecorate it every month, or for every party, with junk stuff that nobody else had dreamed could be made to look beautiful; of the small dinners they gave in Antibes, one of which Fitzgerald described in *Tender Is the Night;* of the remarkable guests who came for a night and stayed for a summer.

I liked them both. Gerald was witty and almost self-mocking elegant. Sara was pretty and warm and hidden-shrewd. Not long before we met they had lost their two sons, and certainly that strengthened the bonds with their old friends Hemingway and Parker, who did not like each other but who in those weeks were trying hard to mask it from the Murphys. But it was Gerald's often overcivilized hand that kept Ernest and Dottie, when they were drinking, edge-polite, too polite. I think it was my first knowledge of people who dined and drank together and couldn't wait to talk about each other afterwards. Ernest would confide that Alan Campbell acted toward Dottie as if he were the manager of a movie actress or a prize fighter, and Dottie would whisper that Ernest was a God-damned snob — there were, indeed, a great many social names in his conversation, and once an

American polo player, arrogant with money and little sense, joined us for an evening until Gerald rapped him away. And almost every night, starting with baklava sweetness, Dottie would try to get Ernest to admit that he'd knocked a few years off his age, or to get Gerald to pretend he'd read somebody she'd invented. It was witty, all of it, but I remember feeling awkward: my generation was perhaps all round duller and certainly less talented, but loyalty, or the rhetoric of it, had come back into fashion with the depression, and these four remarkable people — I don't remember that Martha Gellhorn joined us, perhaps she was not in Paris — came from another world and time.

One night after dinner, when we usually parted, the Campbells and I, led by Ernest, moved around Paris from whiskey to scrambled eggs to their old acquaintances at the Deux Magots or Lilas to a place with blaring, bad jazz. By that time I was drunk and headachy and left a note with a waiter saying goodnight.

I had been asleep for two or three hours when there was a loud pounding on the hotel door. Ernest was there with a bottle of Scotch and a package. He was in good humor and we had a large drink of Scotch from his bottle, a talk about my coming to Spain after Moscow, some conversation I didn't understand about the women in his life, and then he threw the package on my bed.

He said, "The proofs of *To Have and Have Not*. Want to read them? Right now?"

It wasn't that I was so young that year, it was that I was younger than I should have been about respected literary men and I had forgotten that I had told him earlier that evening that when I worked at Liveright's I had swiped the first copy of *In Our Time* as it came from the printer, sitting with it at the office through a forgotten dinner date, taking it home with me to read again that night, coming down to the office at eight o'clock the next morning so anxious to talk about the book that I had forgotten other people wouldn't be there at that hour, and had paced up and down the street, and then run up and down the stairs, until Horace and Julian Messner and Tom Smith finally arrived.

So I was pleased to be sitting up in bed, fighting a hangover, flattered that Ernest had brought his new book for my opinion. He sat by the window, drinking, looking through a magazine, mostly watching me as I read the book. I wanted him to go away and leave the book, but when it was good, which wasn't always, I forgot about him. And it was good, and then suddenly very strange, right before I rubbed my eyes and turned off the lamp as daylight came in the window. I went back and reread two or three pages.

"There are missing pages in these proofs."

Ernest said, "Where?"

He came to the bed and I showed him what I thought was a puzzling jump in story and in meaning.

"Nothing is missing. What made you say that?" His voice had changed, not to sharpness, but to a tone one would use with an annoying child or an intrusive stranger, and these many years later I can still hear the change. I tried to say why I thought what I thought, but I got out only half sentences and even those stopped when he kissed me on the forehead, picked up the page proofs and walked out the door. I was puzzled and hurt and, after a minute, angry. I followed him into the hall and stood staring at him as he waited for the elevator.

He came back toward me, pulled me within arm's length, and said, "I wish I could sleep with you, but I can't because there's somebody else. I hope you understand." He smiled at me, patted my head, went down in the elevator, and I was so surprised that I stood in the hall until it was too late to run down the steps and say — Say what? So I went to wake Dottie in the room next to mine. She shook her head at me for a long time.

"You mean I shouldn't have read it or I shouldn't have said anything?"

"Oh, who wouldn't? How were you supposed to know that Max Perkins persuaded him the book was too long and Ernest wouldn't let Max cut it so he made the cuts himself and they're bad, evidently, and you guessed it. And you've only just met Ernest and nobody told you, poor girl, that you're not allowed to think a comma could be in the wrong place, or that the book isn't the greatest written in our time although that's hard to follow, isn't it, because his previous book was always the greatest?"

I said, "What was that about not sleeping with me? Who asked him? Who the hell even thought about him?"

"Revenge, Lilly. Made him feel better. And if that's all he ever says or does you'll be lucky, because he's not a man who forgives people much."

The next day I left for Moscow, changing trains in Berlin. I had been warned that I might have trouble in Berlin — I had a four or five hour wait and a change of railroad stations — and a young Russian consular officer met me at the station. There was no trouble, or I didn't think so, until the second train was nearing Warsaw and then I went to look for my small trunk. It was missing, the Polish conductor claimed, but certainly, he said, I would receive it in Moscow, the Nazis were not barbarians, a mistake had been made, my name was German, and so on. When the trunk did arrive from Berlin two weeks later the insides had been slashed to pieces, every book had been torn apart, every bottle had been emptied.

Although I have long ago lost the diary of that trip, Dash was right: I did not enjoy the Moscow Theatre Festival, except for a production of *Hamlet* with the Prince played as a fat young man in a torpor. I went to one official party and saw no other Russians. (I had sent off a few letters of introduction, but when they weren't answered I put it down to the Slav habit of postponement.) I did not even know I was there in the middle of the ugliest purge period, and I have often asked myself how that could be. I saw a number of diplomats and journalists but they talked such gobbledygook, with the exception of Walter Duranty and Joseph Barnes, that one couldn't pick the true charges from the wild hatred. Most of them, our diplomats, certainly, were frivolous men who might have functioned well in the Vienna of Franz Joseph. Some of what they said in those days most certainly turned out to be the truth, but it is hard to understand fact from invention when it is mixed with blind bitterness about a place and a people.

I went back to Paris after a few weeks in Prague. My first night in Paris I had dinner with Otto Simon. Simon had been born in Prague as Otto Katz, gone to a German university and become a well-known journalist. When Hitler came in, he moved to Paris, compiled and wrote an interesting book, one of the first about Nazism, called *The Brown Book of the Hitler Terror*. He was a Communist who, the year I met him, was a kind of press chief for the Spanish Republican Government. He was a slight, weary-looking, interesting man who had moved in many circles. At dinner that night a famous and beautiful German movie star crossed to our table to kiss him and to speak with him in German. Otto took for granted that my German was good, and so when she left the table he said, "Please forget what you heard. We were in love with each other when she was young and I was not so *triste*."

He was a brave, kind man who stayed in Spain until the very last days of the Franco victory, when, in New York, a few of us found the bail to buy him out and to send him on to Mexico. After the war he returned to Prague, had an important job in the government, and was executed by the regime who thought up the insane charge of Zionism to kill his independent spirit.

But that was a long time later. That dinner night in Paris he persuaded me that I must go to Spain. It didn't take much persuasion: I had strong convictions about the Spanish war, about Fascism-Nazism, strong enough to push just below the surface my fear of the danger of war.

8

FROM a diary, 1937:

Valencia, October 13

It was a long, dusty trip. Valencia seems quiet and so far I have not seen an air raid, although last night Steven and Luigi, from the International Brigades, here on recovery leave, said I should ask the hotel to put me in another room away from the glass skylight. I tried that this morning, but it got me nowhere so I ate a can of quenelles from the box of mostly ridiculous canned goods from Paris that Hemingway told me I must bring with me, but I am sure he thought I'd have sense enough to buy meat or fish. I have been nervous, and last night I dreamed of Amélie's black dress without Amélie in it, floating in and out of the Marais, speaking to Victor Hugo.

[1968 — Amélie Bogeat cleaned and washed for me

in Paris. At this minute, twenty-eight years and two months later, I am looking at a recipe for chocolate mousse that she sent me in early 1939, with a letter saying she believed France was on the edge of war. I had left with Amélie ten letters to be sent my father in New York so that he wouldn't know, and worry, about Spain. But a few weeks later he had to know because I did a radio broadcast from Madrid. In New York, Louis Kronenberger went with him to the broadcast to help with the fears we both were certain my father would have. Louis reported later that my father's only comment was to tell him that he knew a not too expensive tailor who would make Louis the dinner jacket my father thought he needed. It might have been his way of not showing anxiety; it might have been that he had none.]

Steven and Luigi and a Spanish girl whose name I never heard took me to a cafe and we drank a great deal of warm beer. The owner said we could have a supper of fried sardines. They didn't seem to mind, but the oil was so rancid I couldn't manage, so I went back to the hotel for another can of quenelles and everybody thought them splendid. By midnight we were all tipsy and the girl was telling Luigi in eight or ten mispronounced English words that Steven mustn't worry so much because the part could not mend with the head. I thought I was well out of that conversation until Luigi shouted at her to quit and Steven got up and left us. Luigi and the girl walked me to the hotel and Luigi said I wasn't to worry. I wasn't worried: increasingly I find myself most comfortable with conversations I don't understand.

October 14

I get up early and go to the dining room for coffee. Everybody bows and I bow and I can't remember any of their names or what they are doing here. I know some of them are journalists, some of them are working for the government, and most of them are foreigners, but they swim as one except for a tall, pale young Frenchman and a German couple who shake hands with affection as they part each morning in front of the hotel. I have done nothing since I am here and I recognize the signs. I have presented my credentials, as one must, gone once to the Press Office where I was pleasantly welcomed by Constancia de la Mora, had two telephone calls from her suggesting I come back to the office and meet people who might like to meet me, and have not gone. This is nothing new: part the need to make people come to me, part not wanting to seem important. But then why have I come here, what will I see, or do, what good will I be to these people as I eat their food or use their cars or lie on a bed reading Julian Green? I settle it by going for a walk.

A few blocks from the Press Office, where I tell myself I am certainly going this morning, there is a flower market. I stop to buy flowers and some green leaves I have never seen before, and go around a corner and down a strange street and another one. By now I have lost my way and can't get to the Press Office and feel better walking in the hot sunshine watching a cat that is about half a block ahead of me. I didn't hear anything until I saw the cat sit down in the street, its head raised at a queer angle. Then suddenly the cat took off under the grating of a store as a woman with a market push-cart picked up a little girl, threw the girl in the cart, and began to run down an alley. Maybe the child's screams kept me from hearing the sirens, or maybe I had heard them earlier because a long-sensitive tooth made me know that I had clamped my jaws very tight. Two women ran past me and called out something I couldn't understand, and then I began to run toward a square I had never seen before, telling myself that as long as I heard the sirens the planes had not arrived. In the middle of the square I saw a policeman gesturing toward people I couldn't see. I slowed down hoping to figure out what he meant, but I couldn't, and so I ran on toward an open treeless stretch. The policeman was shouting at me now, but I didn't know enough Spanish to understand him. He was angry as I waited for him. I said, *"No sé donde lugar voy."* He pointed under a bench, shoved me, and ran on. As I crawled under the bench, the sirens had stopped. I was lying face down into the heavy smell of my flowers. In the distance I heard a great, swelling sound, as if a storm wave had finished its move into shore. And then another, this time further away, or so I thought. I don't know how many minutes I stayed under the bench, but I knew that being alone there frightened me more than it was worth. I stuck my head out, tried to figure what streets I had crossed, and made a dash across the square. All streets were empty now and I knew that I was acting as I had been warned not to act in an air raid, but I desperately wanted that shabby hotel room because in it were a few dresses, a toothbrush, a raincoat, a few books. It was all that belonged to me in this strange land. It was home.

When I got to the corner of the hotel, I had come to the end of running. I stopped at the convent wall next to the hotel, too troubled with breathing to notice immediately that now the planes were overhead, flying fast. Two Spanish soldiers stood in the door of the convent and one of them was eating from a bunch of grapes. He nodded to me, pointed with his grapes, and said in English, "Italian bastards." As he spoke, one plane dropped down and from it slowly floated what looked like a round gift package. The soldier with the grapes stepped into the street, shook his fist and screamed into the air as the bomb, and another, exploded. Then he turned, called to his friend, and began to smile as he pointed south to four planes coming toward us.

He came toward me. "Ours." He pulled off some grapes, wiped them on his sleeve and handed them to me. "O.K. Now. O.K."

But it wasn't O.K. In the section around the port, about five minutes later, the Italian bombers killed sixty-three people.

October 17

I have been to the Press Office, I have met La Pasionara and paid a visit to Rubio, the Press Chief, who gave me some candy, and I have dined with the charming and witty del Vayo and some other government people. A great many people have told me a great many things — atrocities on one side and the other; nuns and priests torn by the limbs in Republican villages; peasants and intellectuals burned alive on Franco's side; why what government fell when; the fights among the Anarchists and Communists and Socialists; who is on what side today who wasn't yesterday — but this is not the way I learn things and so I have only half listened, although my

97

head will soon come off from the polite up-and-downs it has been making, and the fixed smile might grow into a tic. If I have anything to do here, anything to say or write, I am better off by myself.

Two days ago, I discovered a pleasant square near a building that has a large amount of bomb-scarred statuary in its courtyard. I was staring at the statuary, wondering how I'd find out about the house, when a man and a woman in black came either from it or from around the side of it. The man stopped and looked at me and then they both moved on. A few steps further, he stopped again and turned. Then the woman turned and they both stood watching me. I thought, I've intruded on their house and I'll go say I'm sorry, but as I moved toward them I knew I couldn't say that in Spanish. As I got near them, the woman turned sharply, pulled the man by the sleeve, and they moved off. I went on toward the pleasant square, sat reading for about an hour, walked back to the hotel. As I passed the house with the statuary the man and woman were standing in the courtyard. The man came toward me, the woman moved behind him. When I smiled they stood still, and after a minute the woman said something to the man, who put his hand to his head in a salute, clicked his heels and marched behind a broken statue of a horse and peered from behind its injured head. They're having a nice time about me, I thought, but why?

October 19

Last night Steven and Luigi, the girl and I walked down to the bombarded port area. (The planes had been around all afternoon and the mess was new and looked hot.) The filthy indignity of destruction, I thought, is the real immorality, as I slipped and turned my ankle. Steven said he would take me back to the hotel and wouldn't allow Luigi and the girl to come along.

When I had wrapped my ankle in a torn pair of pants, I sat on a chair and Steven propped my foot up on another chair, and gave me a pain-killer from his pocket. Then he told me what the girl had meant the other night by the mind not healing the part: he had been wounded in the penis, the wound repaired, but the future unknown. He said he didn't have a regular girl, didn't want one now, but would want one when he got back to Kansas City and didn't yet know if he could ever have one again.

I said, "I never thought of anybody being wounded in the penis. How little I know about any of this. Just feeling and jabber."

Steven smiled. He borrowed Julian Green and said goodnight.

October 20

I went up to Benicasim this morning with Gustav Regler. Regler had been a captain in the German army during the First World War, had become a fairly well-known novelist after the war, and had left Germany when Hitler came in. Now a high-ranking officer and a hero of the German section of the International Brigades, he had been badly injured here, in what was called "the little war," when his car was bombed to pieces going up to the front lines. Driving fast toward Benicasim, we talked about writers and writing and I was sorry when we reached Benicasim at dinnertime. This safely based recovery hospital is mostly occupied by the International Brigades wounded and some of their wives have been allowed to join them here.

They obviously respected Regler and when, in a sad little after-dinner meeting, he made me and my visit too important, one man, with a huge scar on his face, rose to say that they were sure that now many other intellectuals would come to Spain and go home and write the truth and Mr. Roosevelt would then send the guns and planes to a people who were fighting for freedom. Before he finished, an older man got up and said didn't my people have sense enough to know that it was here that Fascism would live or die, no charity was needed, just enough to let them kill it here, save American lives later on, and would I please tell that to Roosevelt? When I didn't answer, he repeated the question slowly and carefully, adding that if the United States sent supplies, the Spaniards and the International Brigades would do the job, were willing to do the dying, I must say that immediately. He choked and coughed and waited for an answer. I said that wasn't the way things worked, it didn't matter what people like me said or thought. They were silent for a second and then a woman applauded politely and everybody went off to bed.

I was given a straw bed next to the Prague-born wife of a Yugoslav officer. Lying there, with a small candle between us on the floor, we talked of my recent weeks in Prague. I told her about the famous doctor and his wife with whom I had stayed, their friends, the visits to the opera, and concerts, and my shock when they spoke of Hitler's domination of Czechoslovakia as almost certain, and seemed so resigned and passive in the face of it.

She said, "I have not lived in Prague for many years. Goodnight." She gave me the candle for my side of the bed and turned away from me.

I could not read by the candle, so I smoked until the candle went out. Then the Czech lady said, "Of course, I know Dr. ———. He is a good man, a Jew, impressed with his fool of a wife. Who were the other people you saw?"

I told her about two brothers who owned a newspaper, and a music critic, and an educated divorced lady, friend to the doctor's wife.

She said, "Yes, I could have guessed. The brothers are related to me. Liberal pigs. Pigs. They will kill all the rest of us with their nothing-to-be-done-about-it stuff. They will save themselves when the time comes, the dirty pigs. There isn't a man in this hospital, if he lives, who will ever be all well again. Those dirty pigs. Goodnight."

I didn't sleep much that night thinking about what she said and how this war was like no other. Men had come great distances to fight here and when the war was over, if they came out alive, or with enough arms or legs or eyes to seem alive, there would be no world for them and no reward. They seemed to me noble people. Because I had never used that word before, it came hard to say it to myself even in the dark, and, as if I had had a vision of what I had missed in the world, I began to cry.

The next morning Busch, the American doctor, and Thomas, the political cheerleader, insisted I come on a round of visits to the wounded. The ward was large. Leading off it was a room with beaver board partitions for the very badly wounded and in one of them were two young men. One was a Canadian and the other was a New York boy with the small white face that is so common in poor people who live in cities. The Canadian had lost his left foot but he didn't know it yet. The New York boy was lying on his side, breathing hard, his face moving in pain. I was afraid to look at him, and when Busch went over to examine him I stood by Thomas, a fat little fellow who himself had just recovered from a bad wound in the spine. The New York boy cried out and then screamed.

I closed my eyes and Thomas said, "He was shot up. Kidneys, thigh, neck. Thigh wound won't close right."

"Isn't there any dope for him?"

Thomas nodded. "Sure. Busch will give him something. But the kid's a hypochondriac."

October 21

Last night I went looking for Luigi and Steven, but they are not to be found and I guess maybe they've gone back to their brigades. The hotel clerk says Otto Simon came by and will come again. I didn't know what to do with myself most of today, so I took a notebook to the pretty, small square and wrote about Benicasim.

I looked up from my notebook. The statuary-courtyard man and woman are on a bench opposite me. She is knitting something small and ugly brown. He is intently poking a cane into the bush in front of him. As I see him, he looks up at me. The staring has gone on long enough. I bow, he bows, the woman bows, he bows again, the woman bows again, I go back to my notebook.

In a minute he is standing over me. His voice is a loud boom. *"Madame, faites-vous un croquis?"*

"Non, monsieur."

He peers down at the notebook. "Ah, you are English," he says in a British accent.

"No, I am an American."

"What a miracle."

The woman has put down her knitting. As he sits down beside me, she half rises. But she settles back as he speaks severely to her.

"Lita!" He turns to me. "That is not her name. What is not your name?"

"Pamela Gigglewitz."

"*Madame* Gigglewitz?"

"Once upon a time."

"You are wise."

I thank him and shift on the bench. He pokes around with his cane, frowning, thoughtful. Then he points to the woman.

"She is a nun *fanée*. But still of the blackest faith. She will ask me if you are Catholic."

The non-Lita said in an unexpectedly deep voice, in good English, "Return please to your bench."

He rose to his feet, laughed, and suddenly bellowed so loud that two men a distance from us stopped and stared. "Answer on demand."

I was so startled by the noise that I didn't know whether he was speaking to me or to the woman.

I said, "No, I am not a Catholic. I was born a Jew," at the same minute that she shouted to me, "Are you of the faith?"

The man said, "*Bon*. O.K. Ssh." Then he moved rapidly out toward the street. The woman followed. When they got near the exit of the square they both turned

and stood staring at me. I realized they were the first
people I had ever seen who were of no age that I could
guess because something had happened to their faces.

October 22

Luis and I first met at seven o'clock this morning when
he arrived two hours late, to tell me that he was my official government guide and protector on the trip to Madrid. (He meant he was the chauffeur.) At four in the
afternoon, coming down the long hot stretch of road to
Aranjuez, I was tired of him. I was tired, too, of the sun
and the road and the warm, squashed grapes lying between us on the seat. We had talked too much: of the
war, of automobiles, of my passport, of the long, purplish
plus-fours that he had bought from a hotel clerk in Valencia. I had been polite about the plus-fours but had
not been polite about his driving, which was based on a
personal relationship with the car — sometimes he loved
it and gave it frightening freedom, and sometimes he
punished it with twists and curses, and once he beat the
hood with his foot. He had been polite about my cigarettes, but had not liked my English. He said over and
over again that I was the only American he couldn't
understand. He said I talked like a Swede, which isn't
true, but ever since early morning when he peered over
the first road guard's shoulder to look at my passport, he
had wanted to make a mystery of me. He liked it that
way.

We had talked of Brunete. Luis said he had been there
as the chauffeur of a General. He said the General
thought him brave and he thought the General brave but

the General, like all Spaniards except himself, knew nothing about automobiles and, therefore, could not appreciate good driving. That was very smart of the General, who is fighting around Huesca now but who would not be if Luis were still driving his car.

But by four o'clock we were too tired and hungry to bother with each other anymore. The mountain road was winding down and Luis dozed from time to time. It is not a good idea to sleep on the Madrid-Valencia road, and when we came too close to an army truck, I shoved him angrily with my elbow. He woke up, put his hand on the horn and kept it there. The truck didn't move because there was no place to move to, and our back wheels scraped the mountain fence as we speeded up to pass it. We passed it and Luis twisted the wheel violently, ignored the next curve to shout back at the truck, to explain to me once again that all Spaniards are brave soldiers and bad drivers.

My head had hit the side of the car as we careened.

"For God's sake," I said, "let me drive."

He said, "A woman could not drive this road."

We had been over this several times during the day and my voice was angry now because my head hurt and I told myself I hadn't come to Spain to die in a car with Luis.

I said, "I've been driving a car since I was fourteen years old."

He said, "All right. But the automobile change too much in all that time. The picture in the passport book look older than it says there. You lie in passport book, yes?"

I laughed too long and too loud. I was sick of the remarks about my passport. When I stopped laughing, he looked at me.

"You need to eat."

I said I didn't need to eat. It has been hard to eat. I can't get used to the smell of the rancid olive oil. Most of the time I feel light and pleasant, but I guess the bad part of hunger is setting in because the last four or five days I have felt weak and irritable. Luis said I could do what I wanted, but he was going to find a place to eat. I said there wasn't much to get from these people along the road, they needed the little they had, so why didn't we wait until we got to Madrid?

He looked at me. "If they have nothing, they will say it. If they have something, they will give it. That is Spanish."

We rode on for a long time without passing a house. Then suddenly, as we came out of the shadows of a hill, the inevitable church appeared, high and handsome above the miserable village.

Luis laughed. "Where there is a church that high, there are people that poor. They will give us something."

We wheeled off the road, went bouncing into the ruts of the little square around the church. This village was like all the rest: the fine church in the dusty square, a few heavy-laden mules, a few children in doorways, dogs sleeping in the gutters, one store that maybe before the war had things in it, the sun that gave no light to the dark houses.

Nobody paid much attention to us except the starving dogs. They moved to the car and stood looking at us. Hot and aching, I groaned my way out of the car and sat down suddenly on the running board. Luis was already across the street eyeing the most likely house, and when a group of soldiers came out of a house and spoke to him, he disappeared. I sat on the running board and stared at the ground, hoping the dizziness would go away. A little girl came along, leading a donkey towards a high hill facing me. I watched her, and it was only when she was halfway up the hill that I saw where the bombs had been on another day. Two houses were mostly gone, and the child turned her head away as she passed them. I patted a dog whose bones were out beyond his frame, and a very little boy, unaccountably fat, came close and said, "*Salud.*"

I said, "*Salud, niño,*" but he said *salud* so many times that I stopped answering him. He was funny standing there, singing it, pleased with himself.

I fell off the running board and a man came towards me from a basement near the car. He had a glass of wine in his hand and he pushed it at me and smiled. I was afraid that it would make me even dizzier, but I drank it. It was raw and bitter and hard to manage. When Luis came bouncing back, looking like a fool in the purple plus-fours and army cap, the man poured him a glass of wine.

Luis was pleased with himself. "It is as I tell you. One hundred O.K. Two eggs and she give a potato for you. I escort you."

We went up a flight of whitewashed steps into a room so dark that I had to wait at the door before I could see my way in. There was a stone fireplace, a bed, a chair, a table, a brilliant red vase. Four women stood around the table as if they had been part of a ritual that was momentarily suspended. They bowed to me. Another woman, sitting at the fireplace, holding a pan, rose and shook hands with me. She was a plump, youngish woman with very bleached hair, black for two inches at the roots. She motioned to the chair, indicated the pan.

I said to Luis, "Please tell her that I do not want any food. Say that I thank her very much, but she must not waste it on me because I am not hungry —"

He looked at me with such contempt that I stopped speaking and sat down. But the blonde woman had understood me. Her English was heavy with that almost German accent that Spaniards so often have.

"It is an honor to share with a friend of the Republic of Spain."

Luis had found a *bota* of wine and was drinking it fast through the funnel as he chatted with the ladies. I didn't understand much of what he said, but I knew he was talking about me because the country women looked at me with shy interest from time to time. The bleached lady paid no attention to Luis, except once when she turned her head and told him to lower his voice, obviously because he interfered with her hospitable monologue to me: she was from Madrid, she therefore knew about American ladies; she did not like this country village, but she had brought her children here for safety, which had been a foolish decision because they were bombed almost every day; her aunt was one of the women at the table and was a bastard Fascist because of the bastards priests; she liked American shoes, how much had mine cost, someday she would have such a pair; her husband had left her when she was nineteen, but who cared; did I have information about Chile where she had a cousin with whom she had been in love; it was for him she had first dyed her hair, but no good had come of that except a pregnancy which she had fixed herself, and now all she had for the passion were two postal cards from Chile. She had scooped the potato from the pan, put the egg on top, decorated it with saffron leaves. It was the first thing I had eaten with pleasure in many weeks, and when I told her that she kissed me, and then turned to listen to something Luis was telling the four women.

"So. He says you write. What do you write?"

Luis said, "On the stage, write, write, write." He took a pencil from his pocket and wrote on the table and made faces with his mouth to imitate acting, and then rose to imitate actors taking curtain calls. He did it for so long that I sighed and the blonde lady laughed.

Luis was annoyed. "So. O.K. Laugh. It is written in the passport that she write. Also, she say that she makes writing in the cinema, but yet she do not know the favorites I name to her. But —" He seemed to have a change of mind, because he now began to speak in Spanish and I heard the name of Charles Chaplin.

The blonde lady said to me, "What an honor. You bring here his family greetings."

I said to Luis, "What are you saying about me?"

"I say you say you are cousin to Charlie."

"And I say I did not say I was cousin to Charlie. I've met Mr. Chaplin and that's all."

Luis said, "There is a saying in Andalusia from where I was born. Goes like 'Do not make yourself so small because in doubt you are so big.' "

"There is a saying in Louisiana from where I was born that you are sometimes a foolish man."

The blonde lady was amused. "He did not say you

were cousin to Charlie. He said you were sister to Charlie."

"O.K.," said Luis. "So I gave pleasure to old women here." He saluted. "Come. My orders say Madrid before the night."

The blonde lady was leaning over my head. Now I felt her part my hair at the top and then on the sides. "You do something to your hair?"

"Sometimes I have it bleached."

"What color you born with?"

"I've forgotten. Something like this, I guess."

She patted my hair back in place. "Soon you will need bleach. That was the work I do. That is where I learn the English. Go to the Calle de Isaac, Maria's. She work good on the hair. Tell her —" She stopped and her face grew sad. Then she smiled and said, "Tell her nothing but do good job for my American friend."

We kissed each other and the four ladies of the table followed us downstairs. I had left my shoes for the blonde lady under the chair. She found them as Luis was making a wild swing around the square, and the last I saw of her was from a window as she shouted for me to come back for my shoes and then, as I waved no from the car, she clapped her hands in applause.

[Four or five days later — I tried to find Maria's. But almost every house in the three or four blocks where it should have been had been bombed away.]

Madrid, October 23

It was after eight o'clock last night when Luis and I got to Madrid. He said I was not to take any wooden nickels and certainly we would meet again. There was a note from Hemingway at the hotel desk telling me where he was eating dinner and inviting me to join him. But I was very tired and fell asleep immediately, only slightly conscious of rumbling sounds in the distance, not thinking much about them until the next day, and even then forgetting to ask what they were.

Early this morning, a young man from the Spanish Press Office came to tell me that Columbia Broadcasting had agreed to give them radio time for me that night and the government people were very pleased because they hadn't had much luck getting air time in America. I wanted to see University City, but I got tired before I got there, and when I came back to the hotel Ernest was in the lobby with a bottle of whiskey for me, and an invitation to have dinner that night at the apartment of an English newspaper correspondent. Madrid bullfight people had given Hemingway a piece of beef. He said I'd better come and share it because I wouldn't see beef again.

[1968 — My diary does not have the name of the English correspondent where I went that night for dinner, but he was a large man with that overknowing air that journalists so often have, and most British have, whatever they are.]

When I arrived Ernest was already there, and Martha Gellhorn, looking handsome in her well-tailored pants and good boots. I took along two cans of sardines and two cans of pâté, and Ernest said he was glad I had brought in canned goods from Paris because John Dos Passos hadn't brought in any food but had eaten everybody else's, and he and Dos Passos had had an ugly fight about that.

The beef from the bull was tough, but the wine was good. I began to hear the noise during the English sugary pudding. I dropped my spoon and Ernest told me that I was hearing my first bombardment.

The Englishman, Ernest, and Martha went out to the balcony to watch — every night at almost the same hour the Franco people bombarded the telephone building — and I sat on the couch in the living room with my head bent low and my eyes shut, hoping I could control the panic I felt. Several times Ernest called to me to come out on the balcony, it was a beautiful sight, he said, and once Martha called, and once the Englishman came to the door and stood looking at me and went mumbling back to Ernest. Ernest came to the door, stared at me, opened his mouth as if to speak, changed his mind, and went back to the beauty of the shelling. After a while the phone rang, and the Englishman said the man at the radio station said the station itself was being hit, it would be too dangerous for me to come there, so would I tell the chauffeur who was already on his way to take shelter somewhere?

About ten minutes later the doorbell rang, a servant admitted the chauffeur, and I went down the stairs with him.

When I was a few flights down, Ernest shouted at me, "You can't go into that shelling." He ran down the steps toward me. "Come back here."

I said I wasn't going to come back, it was important for me to do the broadcast, they probably couldn't get the time on another night. Ernest was holding me by the arm. Then he dropped my arm and said softly, "So you have *cojones,* after all. I didn't think so upstairs. But you have *cojones,* after all."

I said, "Go to hell with what you think."

When the broadcast was over and I was back at the hotel, Ernest knocked on my door. We had a few drinks and I kept wanting to tell him that I would have gone into far more dangerous places to get out of that apartment that night, but I didn't tell him.

[Although I saw Hemingway often in Madrid and a number of times in the years after, I don't think he liked me ever again, and I'm not sure what I felt about him, either.]

October 28

Last night I packed a jewelry case — what a ridiculous thing to have brought to Spain — with a few things I thought I would need for my trip to the front lines. I took a bath, washed my hair, and was drying it when Otto Simon came to see me. We took a long walk. Madrid is a sad city, particularly at night. Otto said all great cities look plague-like in a war, much worse than small towns or country villages.

He said, "Why are you going up to the front?"

I said the Press Office had asked me, I thought I should go, I didn't really know.

"Have courage enough not to go. It is a foolish, dangerous waste."

"I don't want to go, but I haven't guts enough to tell them that."

"I'll tell them in the morning. Don't worry. I'll say I ordered you not to go."

I thanked him and felt much better. We were standing now in the terrible rubble of University City. He sat down on a pile of rock.

"You don't look well, Otto. Is something the matter?"

"Ach. I've been sick for years. In my forties I am an old man."

"It must be hard to be a Communist."

"Yes. Particularly here."

"How long have you been?"

"I can't remember, it's so long ago. A young boy, almost a child."

He got up and took my arm and pressed it hard. "Don't misunderstand. I owe it more than it owes me. It has given me what happiness I have had. Whatever happens, I am grateful for that."

[1968 — When I read of his execution in Prague, in 1952, I remembered the passion with which he spoke that night and hoped that it carried him through his time in jail, his day of death.]

November 3

There doesn't seem to be any sense staying here longer. I have done all the dutiful things — spoken to a group of International Brigade people, made three recordings which will be translated, gone to a nursery and two hospitals, made a speech to be broadcast to Paris, had the forever sardine dinners with government people who said that I and all like me must explain, write, plead that the United States and France must send arms immediately. God in Heaven, who do they think I am, any of us?

November 4

I am going back to Valencia tomorrow so I went around to get my coat from the woman who was fixing the lining. I took her a can of beef soup and she gave me a little green bottle in which there must once have been perfume. Walking back to the hotel, I was shocked to see that a whole block was almost entirely destroyed since I had been past it a week before. I stopped in front of what had been a fine nineteenth-century house converted to apartments, and asked a woman who was standing in the broken doorway when it had been destroyed. She said that the night before twenty-seven people had been killed and nine wounded. I asked her if I could go inside. She shrugged and said she had nothing to do with the house, she came from another neighborhood.

I was careful, I thought, about climbing the broken stairs, but as I got to the second floor, a step crashed under me, and I leaped past it for the landing. Directly in front of me a door was open. The floor seemed safe, but the pleasant center room was a tangle of overturned furniture, and the smell of scorched material was fruity and sour. I called out but nobody answered. I had seen many bombed houses from the outside, but I had never before been inside one and I stood there thinking that the thrown-about objects made their own formal design: a woman's hat was lying next to three daguerreotypes in a triple frame; an unbroken blue tile was on the edge of a table; a couch cover was burned and wet; a bowl of limp lettuce was sitting in a chair. On the burned couch were two small china bottles, with roses painted on one side; a book, printed in French, *La Vie de Mireille,* was open

115

on the floor and on top of it was an overturned kitchen colander with a few grains of cooked rice at the bottom; the skirt of a print dress was on a fallen ironing board; next to it were a white table napkin and a large key. All around my feet were pictures of people in the clothes of other times, other places. I picked up the china bottles with the painted roses, and a daguerreotype of a young girl, and started down the stairs, jumping past the bad step onto what I thought was a good step. I went crashing to the bottom. The noise was very loud and a man came into the hall followed by two children. They stared at me as I struggled up from the broken wood. The bottles were not harmed, although the top of one was badly chipped.

I said to the man, "Where are the people who lived in the first apartment?" He shook his head.

I held up the bottles. "I would like to have something to take back to America" — but the man moved away.

I said to the children, "Where are the people who lived in the first apartment?"

The younger boy said, "Two ladies. They die."

"In the bombing?"

"I don't remember."

[1968 — Transcribing these notes from the diary of that day in Spain, I cross to the fireplace mantel and look at the china bottles and the picture of the young girl. I have carried them with me to many houses for many years.]

Valencia, November 6

It was nice to come back to Valencia, maybe because air raids frighten me less than the nightly bombardments in Madrid. The people in the hotel dining room seemed like old friends and I eat now at the same table with the handshaking German couple, a nervous, minor aide from the Press Office, and an English doctor who has come here to supervise the medical supplies sent down by English organizations. I can't understand much of what the English doctor says, but then he doesn't say much. Foreigners here are not as famous or as important as the ones in Madrid and so there is no big talk and one doesn't have to know or listen to everybody's history.

Last night Constancia took me to a political meeting of about fifty people. I don't know why she asked me because I was the only foreigner there. A dour-looking young man was appointed my translator, but he didn't translate much except the occasional sharp gibes and the one impassioned fight. An elderly Spaniard made an elaborate speech of thanks to two Russians sitting in the back row. He said the Russian planes and guns were of excellent quality, splendid products of socialism, but, unfortunately, that could not always be said of the advisers and technicians that came with them. A young man rose to deny that, another rose to shout him down, there was a great deal of easily understood carryings-on about who was entitled to the floor, and it was finally taken by the man with the deepest voice. He said ingratitude made his ears sharp with pain, but what else could one expect from a Spaniard who had spent his early life in the conservative great houses of England and his later life in the cafes of Paris? He apologized to the Russians, which was amusing because they had long before left the room.

Rubio has arranged a place for me on the Thursday
plane to Barcelona. I have twice put off my departure:
each day I tell myself that I will stay until the war is over
and be of some use, but at night, when I don't feel well,
dizzy and weak, I want very much to leave. I am not
hungry anymore, except early in the morning, and this
morning I took out my last Paris cans — flageolets, anchovies, brandied peaches. I began to wolf the beans.
Without knowing that I did it, I had locked the door of
my room, and maybe that was why I felt sick after the
first large spoonful. I put the beans aside, bought a
withered orange from a street stand, and took my notebook to the pretty square. I must have been there a couple of hours when I saw the strange couple — the nun
fanée and the man in black — sitting opposite me, and
I knew I had come to the square because I wanted to see
them again. The woman was knitting on the same ugly
brown affair and the man was playing with an abacus.

As I looked up, the man bowed and held out the abacus. "I count the days of my life. Then I count my
father's money. What do you read?"

"Good morning. Good morning, madame."

He rose. "Madame? Hah! Answer my question without fear."

"Did you ask me a question?"

"Most certainly. Trust me."

I said I would trust him, but I didn't remember the
question. Very patiently, speaking the words by over-
shaping his mouth, he said, "What do you read?"

"I am not reading. I am writing."

"So." He went back to his abacus. After a second he rose and leaped toward my bench.

"Do you approve of Ralph Waldo Emerson?"

I laughed.

He said, "You find him amusing?"

"No. I find your question unexpected."

"Is it your habit never to answer?"

"No," I said. "It is rather my habit to answer too readily. I've never read much of Emerson. Some of what I've read I like, some of it seems to me pompous."

" 'Pom-pousse'? I do not know the word. Perhaps it will come back to me at bedtime when I eat." He suddenly pointed at the woman. "A greed, she is a greed."

The woman said something to him in Spanish, he answered, then he crossed to stand in front of her and shouted down at her. She went back to her knitting and he sat down next to me.

"My father is very rich. Bottles and many other matters. We were sent away here when they departed." He leaned close and whispered to me. "Very rich, very. Do you know where you are? You are in Valencia. Often I do not know where I am, but I prefer to be on the country estate. She mounted upon me first when I was at the age of twelve, the nun *fanée. Elle m'a monté quand j'avais douze ans. Triste, n'est-ce pas?"*

The nun *fanée* got slowly to her feet and moved down the path toward the exit. The man rose immediately and began to run toward her. He ran past her, left the square, and I could see him running very fast down the boulevard.

Tonight I took the peaches, two cans of anchovies, a box of crackers to the dinner table. I asked the hand-

119

shaking German to open them, but he put his hands in his lap and smiled. I passed them to the young man from the Press Office, but he shook his head. I was puzzled and thought I had offended all of them until the English doctor wrote something in his address book and passed it to me. "They are shy about taking other people's food. Open the cans yourself and pass them around." I started to open the anchovies, but the key got stuck. The doctor opened the cans, and gave them back to me. Nobody would have an anchovy, but each passed the can to the next person with great politeness. When the can came back to the Englishman, he kicked me under the table and said, "You are leaving tomorrow. You have brought these down to have a kind of party. You will be unhappy if we don't share your party, yes?"

I liked him very much as he rose and served each person one anchovy and a cracker. Everbody ate very slowly, and there was no talk. I served the peaches and they stared at their plates, almost as if they were frightened to eat. There were still a few anchovies and so I gave one to the German lady, one to her husband, one to the press attaché. There wasn't any for the doctor or for me. The German immediately put his anchovy on my plate and the German lady leaned over to give hers to the doctor.

The doctor said, "No, thank you. In England we eat them as a savory and I don't like them. Miss Hellman told me that she doesn't like them, either."

I said that was true, I was sick of anchovies, and suddenly both the doctor and I were talking at once. It was a long time before they finished their anchovies, and when the oil of the can was passed around, I heard the German lady make a sound of pleasure. I didn't want a peach, but there was such disbelief when I said so that I ate part of one. This small party had taken an hour and had acted on my table companions as if they had drunk a case of champagne. For the first time in the weeks I had known them they chatted and laughed, and the German told an elaborate joke that everybody pretended to understand. As we left the table, we all shook hands. At the door, I turned to speak to somebody and saw that the German lady was wrapping my half peach in a piece of paper. She handed it to her husband. He shook his head and gave it back and she gave it back to him and this time he took it and kissed the hand that gave it to him. The doctor had waited at the door for me and had seen what I had seen.

In the hall he said, "My God. Hunger is awful."

November 11

Rubio telephoned at five this morning to say that for security reasons the plane, scheduled to leave at noon for Barcelona, would take off in an hour. I was still packing in the airport, and writing farewell notes that I will mail from Paris. Barcelona looked lovely and Rubio said he would show me the city before the train left for France, but after we had walked for a while I got so dizzy that we sat down on a bench until an army car passed us and Rubio asked for a ride to the station. As I got on the train, Rubio introduced me to the tall young French journalist I had sometimes seen in the hotel dining room. As the train pulled out, I knew I would probably never see Spain again, and Rubio's sad, owl face, staring up as the car window went past him, seemed to me a symbol of his country's defeat.

The Frenchman and I, in the same compartment, were as concerned as strangers usually are that they will be bored with each other. I read a book, he slept, he read a book, I slept, and when I woke up he was staring out the window with an empty wine bottle on his lap. He told me he was leaving Spain after a year and a half because he had tuberculosis and was going straight into a hospital in Paris. I said that a friend — I was talking of Hammett — had had tuberculosis, was now cured, it wasn't the disease it had once been, and so on, cheery, but he didn't answer and we didn't talk again until the train pulled into Toulouse.

It made me uncomfortable to arrive in Toulouse, so safe, so untouched by war. The young Frenchman and I wandered around the railroad station long after our bags were cleared. We both wanted to leave immediately, but there wasn't anything but a milk train for Paris, so we decided to spend the night in Toulouse and made a booking for the morning train.

He found us a hotel near the station, good enough to have a bath down a long hall. I stayed in the bath so long that I came out staggering, as if I were drunk. The Frenchman was sitting in my room as I half fell through the door. He helped me to the bed and I tried to light a cigarette but I couldn't hold the match steady.

I said, "It's like being drunk."

He said, "Too little food, and other feelings. Rest a bit."

After a while, I said, "What's your name? Rubio told me but I often can't remember names."

"Pascal. Centuries ago, which is where my family lives, such a name was a road between reason and the Church. I know Toulouse very well. My grandparents lived here. There's a fine restaurant. Let's go and have cassoulet and good wine. We will feel better and sleep well."

It was, indeed, a good restaurant, nineteenth-century rich in dark walls and bright chandeliers, the customers so nice and fat. Pascal ordered Marennes oysters and nothing ever tasted better. We toasted each other in wine and his long, sick-sour face began to have color, and sometimes he would smile to himself.

"Each Sunday my grandparents would bring me to this restaurant. My grandfather supplied it with geese and chickens. They are both dead now from tuberculosis. My mother, too, in Paris later. What did your family die of?"

"My mother and aunt from cancer. I don't know about the others. Everybody dies from something."

"No, they don't. I had two friends who died because they wanted to. I am going to be homesick for Spain. There people are dying for a reason. I tried to be a soldier, but they wouldn't take me in the Brigades. So I am a not good journalist. I bore you."

"No. It's that I don't know what to say that is sensible. How old are you?"

The waiter said, "Pascal has twenty years," as he popped the lid off the cassoulet and brought the dish down for us to see and smell.

Pascal laughed. "Twenty-five. And you, Cowboy, have two hundred."

The waiter laughed, "Not until next year."

The first taste of the cassoulet was wonderful, but on the third taste I began to sweat and knew I was near to vomiting.

In the waves of vomit that were coming close to my throat, I heard Pascal's voice say, "I am sorry. I am sick."

When I had choked back the waves and knew I wouldn't be sick at the table, I looked up and saw Pascal on the sidewalk, his shoulders rising and falling as if he were in pain. Cowboy was standing at a distance from him, but when he came close and put his hand on Pascal's arm, Pascal moved away. I sat at the table for a long time, and when I was ready to leave Cowboy said the check had been paid, not to worry, and maybe cassoulet wasn't a proper dish "to reenter civilization." Back at the hotel, I knocked on Pascal's door, but he didn't answer. I went to bed sure that I would see him on the morning train.

But he was not at the station and was not on the train. Two days later, in Paris, I called his office. Three telephone calls later — I didn't know Pascal's last name — a very irritable man told me that he was in a hospital and gave me the address. That afternoon I went around to the hospital, almost opposite the hotel on the Rue Jacob where my husband and I had once lived. My French has always been bad, sparse and timid, the accent still patois New Orleans, and the French enjoy not understanding me. The nun at the desk had a good, long joke with me that day until she finally said that my friend was, indeed, in the hospital, but was too ill to see anybody. I left him a note with my address, asking if I could come and see him soon again, but I did not hear from him. A week later I went back to the hospital and an older nun told me that he was dead. She said that he had refused to see his father, had often, in the final days, thought he was in Spain, had died alone, had refused the last rites.

*W*orld *W*ar *I*, for many intelligent people, ended in a revulsion against the high-toned rhetoric that could not hide a dislocated world and a dangerous future. *W*orld *W*ar *II* was, in the first years, fought in Europe in a bewildered, half-crazed confusion of inefficient defense, and then, too late, in patriotic protection of homeland. The strength of the patriotism came only after the Germans had started their long, terrible and triumphant march toward the north, south and east.

Many people here who were neither callous nor cowards remembered the palaver of *W*oodrow *W*ilson, and while they were revolted by Hitler and Mussolini, they fought the war in good-natured consent only because they had been conscripted, and you fought for your country when your country said it needed you. *W*e forget that it took us a long time to believe in the German death camps for Jews and political dissenters because it took us a long time to stop the dismissive talk about the little Austrian house painter and the Italian clown with the frown.

There wasn't much to say about the Korean War and almost nobody said it. There is much to say about the dirty Vietnam War and some good stuff has been said, but it remains a puzzling time out, and one still wants to turn one's face away from the memory of American kids doing murder, being murdered, and from those of them who remain in our hospitals, crippled forever by the Washington loonies and the boys who tell the loonies how to think.

But among these wars, tucked away, there was a so-called little war in Spain, a minute of history that caught the imagination not only of the generation that is old enough to remember it, but of the present young who, in every college where I have ever taught, know more of the Spanish Civil War and ask more questions than they do about World War II or even Vietnam, about which they are surprisingly ignorant. (Where are history departments now and what do they teach?)

The Spanish Republicans, politically denouncing each other every minute of the way, managed to fight with extraordinary force for nothing more radical than the right to continue free elections. We approved of that, and so did the French, but approval did not mean guns or planes. Only the Russians supplied those and then not enough, and under such accusations from the squabbling political parties of the Left that even that amount driveled down to almost nothing towards the end.

But the Spanish were fighting for their country, as we all would, given an enemy of danger. The International

127

Brigades, however, were made up of strangers to Spain, men from all over Europe and America who came to fight against Fascism: middle-aged Germans; Yugoslavs, including Tito; young Englishmen from Oxford and Cambridge. And us. And us was something of a sight. Young men came from the Middle West who had been auto mechanics and were sudden geniuses with planes and tanks. And boys like Jim Lardner just out of Harvard. (I will remember all my life the night before Lardner left Paris, only a short time before he was killed in Spain, when I tried all during dinner to persuade him not to go. He listened politely and then asked me if I wanted to see a puzzle he had just invented.) And slum kids who had never been out of their own neighborhoods in the giant cities of their birth. They were an extraordinary bunch: strangers in a country with an unattractive history, often wounded and sent to inadequate hospitals, many of them dying without recognition or honors or enough pain-killers to make death anything but weeks of agony.

In the Abraham Lincoln Brigade, the American section of the International Brigades, there were a large number of Jewish kids. Ernest Hemingway said three or four times to me and to other people, "God damn it, these little Jews fight fine." I do not believe he meant anything anti-Semitic. I think he never could understand that lower middle class kids could fight as well as his sporting types raised on fine guns and rods. A basic conviction of Hemingway's life was shaken, but not so shaken as to alter the nature of his war heroes or his personal taste ever.

Any form of the word "ideal" has suspect meanings, but the foreigners in the Brigades were more than ideal-

ists. *You become more, I think, when you lay yourself on the line. That must, has to be, a very pure state of being and I think the cleanness and clarity of it is what the present generation recognizes, envies, or wants for itself.*

And yet and yet. My pieces here about Spain do not say all or even much of what I wanted to say. I knew it when I first wrote them, I knew it when I included them in this book, and I knew it last week when I read them again. I wish I understood why. Somehow they do not include the passion that I felt, my absolute conviction that when the Spanish War was lost, we were all going to be caught in a storm of murder and destruction in another, larger war. It does not console me that almost nothing that has been written about Spain includes what I missed. Certainly not "For Whom the Bell Tolls," nor the brilliant but limited political stuff of Orwell's. Certainly some of Malraux, but not enough, and on and on. Maybe passion, passion on paper, takes more than most of us have.

9

Most people coming out of a war feel lost and resentful. What has been a minute-to-minute confrontation with yourself, your struggle with what courage you have against discomfort, at the least, and death at the other end, ties you to the people you have known in the war and makes, for a time, all others seem alien and frivolous. Friends are glad to see you again, but you know immediately that most of them have put you to one side, and while it is easy enough to say that you should have known that before, most of us don't, and it is painful. You are face to face with what will happen to you after death.

I had, from so short and relatively safe a visit to Spain, little right to such feelings, but I had them, and the few weeks I spent in Paris when I came out were unpleasant. But Paris was never my city, and at the time I told myself that was in part my reason for depression over the pieties of Léon Blum, the fashionable parties being given for Spanish orphans, the sad chatter among intellectuals as they assured one another that the Republic of France would never allow the Republic of Spain to be defeated. I crossed to London.

On my first night in London I went to dinner at the house of an old friend. Louise and I had grown up together, and if she had married for money and nothing else, the money boy never did anything worse than laugh in the wrong places. The people at the table were, I thought, intelligent enough to eat with, which in those days in London didn't have to be very intelligent in exchange for a French chef.

Louise told the table that I had just come out of Spain. A man to her right said the English version of "Really" several times and then, "I've never been able to fathom the issues."

Louise, nervous, said, "Perhaps Lillian will tell you."

The man said, "Which side did you choose to visit, Miss Hellman? Each has an argument, I dare say."

I said, "I chose Franco, of course. He's got more money."

Louise's husband said, "Now, now, no harm intended, I'm sure —" and a lady opposite me, hurrying in, said, "I'd love to go to Spain again, the Prado, Toledo. Is it very interesting there now?"

After a minute a titled gentleman sitting next to me, in an accent as clear as can be managed with a mouth constructed of hot gruel, said, "You didn't answer my wife's question."

It isn't easy to be ruder than upper-class Englishmen, although I told myself that wasn't any reason for not trying, but as I opened my mouth to say, "Who could have guessed you had a wife?", I thought, My life, all I felt in Spain, is going out in drip-drops, in nonsense, and I suddenly was in the kind of rampage anger that I have known all my life, still know, and certainly in those days was not able, perhaps did not wish, to control. I left the table so fast that I turned over my chair, left the house so fast that I forgot my coat and was not cold on a winter night, threw myself down so hard on the hotel bed that I slipped to the floor, had a painful ankle and didn't care.

If I have remembered that unimportant evening in London, it's because I had broken my ankle and was in bed, or a chair, for the next few weeks.

Nothing, of course, begins at the time you think it did, but for many years I have thought of those days in the lonely London hotel room as the root-time of my turn toward the radical movements of the late thirties. (I was late: by that period many intellectuals had made the turn. So many, in fact, that some were even turning another way.) It saddens me now to admit that my political convictions were never very radical, in the true, best, serious sense. Rebels seldom make good revolutionaries, perhaps because organized action, even union with other people, is not possible for them. But I did not know that then and so I sat down to confirm my feelings with the kind of reading I had never seriously done before. In the next few years, I put aside most other books for Marx and Engels, Lenin, Saint-Simon, Hegel, Feuerbach. Certainly I did not study with the dedication of a scholar, but I did read with the attention of a good student, and Marx as a man and Engels and his

Mary became, for a while, more real to me than my friends.

In 1939, soon after *The Little Foxes,* I bought a Westchester estate, so called — large properties were cheaper in those days than small ones — and turned it into a farm. Hammett, who disliked cities even more than I did, came to spend most of his time there, and maybe the best of our life together were the years on the farm. At night, good-tired from writing, or spring planting, or cleaning chicken houses, or autumn hunting, I would test my reading on Dash, who had years before, in his usual thorough fashion, read all the books I was reading, and a great many more. They must have been dull and often irritating questions I threw at him — my father had once said that I lived within a question mark — but Hammett used to say he didn't mind the ragging tone I always fall into when I am trying to learn, because it was the first time in our life together I had been willing to stay awake past ten o'clock.

But this time the ragging, argumentative tone came for a reason I was not to know about for another ten years: a woman who was never to be committed was facing a man who already was. For Hammett, as he was to prove years later, Socialist belief had become a way of life and, although he was highly critical of many Marxist doctrines and their past and present practitioners, he shrugged them off. I was trying, without knowing it, to crack his faith, sensed I couldn't do it, and was, all at one time, respectful, envious, and angry. He was patient, evidently in the hope I would come his way, amused as he always was by my pseudo-rages, cold to any influence. I do not mean there were unpleasant words between us. None, that is, except once, in 1953, after he had been in jail and gone back to teaching at the Jefferson School. I was frightened that his official connection with the school would send him back to jail and was saying that as we walked down 52nd Street. When we were a few steps from Sixth Avenue, he stopped and said, "Lilly, when we reach the corner you are going to have to make up your mind that I must go my way. You've been more than, more than, well, more than something-or-other good to me, but now I'm trouble and a nuisance to you. I won't ever blame you if you say goodbye to me now. But if you don't, then we must never have this conversation again." When we got to the corner, I began to cry and he looked as if he might. I was not able to speak, so he touched my shoulder and turned downtown. I stood on the corner until I couldn't see him anymore and then I began to run. When I caught up with him, he said, "I haven't thought about a drink in years. But I'd like one. Anyway, let's go buy one for you."

A few years after I bought the farm, the United States declared war. It was useless now to say yes, many of us knew it was coming; during the war in Spain, Hitler and Mussolini could have been stopped, the bumblers and the villains led us into this. (I had tried to write some of that in *Watch on the Rhine.*)

When the war came I thrashed around trying to find something useful to do, but all the jobs offered were official, tame, bound to high-sounding titles enclosed by office doors. Then Hammett disappeared for a few days and reappeared having enlisted as a private, although he'd had a tough time convincing the doctor who found the old First World War tubercular scars on the X-rays.

After he left Pleasantville, I felt lonely and useless, jealous of his ability to take a modest road to what he wanted. I spent the next year or so doing what I knew to be idle lady stuff: I wrote a few speeches for people in Washington, I planted a granite field that broke two plows, I made speeches at rallies for this or that bundles for something-or-other, I watched other people go to a war I needed to be part of. And then, suddenly, I was invited to go on a cultural mission to the Soviet Union.

I was invited because a month after we declared war William Wyler, the movie director, and I, both under contract to Samuel Goldwyn, had agreed to make a documentary film of the war in Russia. (Wyler and I had made a number of pictures together by that time and were old friends.) I no longer remember exactly how the plan started because its origins were kept from us, but Harry Hopkins, without involving President Roosevelt, had set it in motion. The Russian news was very bad that winter of 1942, but all of America was moved and bewildered by the courage of a people who had been presented to two generations of Americans as passive slaves.

Both Wyler and I were wild to do the picture and so Goldwyn flew East to consult with us, and the famous cameraman Gregg Toland agreed to come along. Wyler and I went to Washington to see Ambassador Litvinov, whom I already knew and liked. But Litvinov said our plan was impossible, wouldn't work without full co-operation from the Russian government, and that they were too hard pressed to give it. When Litvinov described the horrors of the German sweep through White Russia to Moscow, Leningrad and Stalingrad, we felt like young schoolchildren who had heard of *Oedipus* and thought it excellent to stage in their lunch hour.

But the next afternoon, Litvinov telephoned to ask me to come immediately to the embassy. Molotov had arrived that morning in Washington, Litvinov had mentioned our movie, and to his surprise Molotov thought it a fine idea and said the Russian government would guarantee a bomber, camera crew, and whatever else we needed for however long we needed it.

It was a wonderful day. Wyler went to see Hopkins, I made long-distance telephone calls, Wyler knocked down a drunk who was making anti-Semitic speeches in front of our hotel, we ran around in circles missing each other at the airport, and arrived back in New York that night for a meeting with Mr. Goldwyn in his apartment at the Waldorf Astoria Towers. Something about the Towers, the ill-proportioned apartments, the carefully guarded guests, has always depressed me as I enter the lobby, and so it is possible I was looking for trouble when the conference began. But Goldwyn was as pleased as we were, and we quickly agreed — a rare occurrence in Hollywood circles — that we would leave as soon as possible, that no script or outline could be made until we saw what Wyler could photograph, that we would make a full-length picture that would, of course, have a regular commercial release. Because of the enormous American admiration for the Russians in those days, we were an almost guaranteed success before we started. Goldwyn recognized that, of course, and knew that a large part of the cost of the picture — planes, camera crew, extras — would be supplied by the Russians. The three of us were, for a change, in complete accord on all details. (This had not always been so. Once Mr. Goldwyn had fired Wyler for twenty-four hours because he claimed Wyler made the set of *Dead End*, a picture about New York slums, look dirty, and I had quit in sympathy.) But this was a most pleasant meeting until Wyler said that while he was in Russia he'd like his salary paid in monthly installments for the support of his wife and children. This simple request caused Goldwyn's face to change, and I remember knowing immediately that something was going to happen. (I had, by this time, worked for Goldwyn for seven years.) I had nobody to support, but I thought I'd better do something, so I said I'd like my salary paid half on the day we started photography, half on the day I arrived home, even if I came back in a coffin. My attempt to lighten the air was a failure: we were in for the silent staring that always precedes a Goldwyn shocker.

Finally Sam spoke. "You say you love Russia. You say you are radicals. So you say."

Wyler said, "I don't know what you mean. Who is radical and who says they love Russia? What's that got to do with anything?"

It was as if he had not spoken. Goldwyn's tones were now very soft, an old and ominous sign. "You say you love America, you are patriots you tell everybody —"

"What?"

"Everybody. Everybody, you both go around saying. Now it turns out you want *money* from me, from *me* who am sacrificing a fortune for my government because *I* love my country."

Wyler turned to look at me and I knew he didn't understand the purpose of the conversation. It was, indeed, often hard to understand Sam's shockers, but I had been at it for longer than Willy.

Wyler said, "I don't understand what you're saying, Sam. This picture is being made for commercial release and you intend to profit on it as you profit on any other movie. You're not putting up a nickel for 'your government.' The Russians, as a matter of fact, are giving you most of a free ride."

I said, "We'll be paid as we are paid on any picture, so let's cut out the nonsense and go home to bed."

Sam rose to his feet. *"Nonsense?* You call it *nonsense* to take money away from your government?"

Wyler was walking slowly toward Sam as if he were coming out of a dream. "Are you really suggesting that we take no salary, you take the profits, and that makes you a patriot and us hypocrites?"

The anger was now ready. Sam kept it in a properly blessed tin box, with a touch-spring top. Reason would, from now on, have no further place and words no meaning.

So before the box could be opened, I said, "Sam, you think you are a country with rivers and mountains and cities, inhabited by people who will, of course, risk their lives to protect the riches of the country called Samuel. Two of your citizens, servants called Wyler and Hellman, doubt that you are a country. Therefore we are traitors. So off with our heads and let's take them home to bed."

Wyler laughed and we went home. We would, of course, have won that ridiculous argument — Sam never intended not to pay us, he only hoped we'd reduce our usual fee — but by the time relations had been mended, other things intervened: Wyler enlisted in the air force and I didn't want to make the trip with anybody else.

But Goldwyn and I — and Washington, behind the scene — went on talking about a Russian picture and finally came to what seemed like, and could have been, a sensible solution: we would do a simple, carefully researched, semi-documentary movie to be shot in Hollywood. I have, during the last year, read again my script for *North Star*. It could have been a good picture instead of the big-time, sentimental, badly directed, badly acted mess it turned out to be. Halfway through the shooting, Mr. Goldwyn and I parted company. (The picture, now called *Armored Train* when it is shown on television, has printed titles explaining the Russians were once our allies but haven't turned out so nice. If apologies were needed, and they were needed for the silliness of the movie, then the picture should have been scrapped. But the convictions of Hollywood and television are made of boiled money.)

But I think the picture was one of the reasons why the Russians invited me on a cultural mission in 1944 and why Washington — acting with faceless discretion — wanted me to go. (True, that when I got to Moscow I found they thought *North Star* a great joke, but I guess outside Moscow there were some simple peasant folk glad to find themselves so noble on the screen.)

In September of 1944, I flew to Fairbanks, Alaska, where the Russians were to pick me up for the journey across Siberia. I am glad I was too ignorant to know what Robert Lovett, Assistant Secretary of War and an old friend, told me on my return — that it was so dangerous a journey that he would have forbidden it if he had known I was going that way.

The trip was made in a C–47, a two-engine plane capable of a maximum speed of 240 miles an hour. It carried cargo, a full crew, few instruments, and a nineteen-year-old boy called Kolya, a Russian mechanic stationed in Alaska, who had conned a ride home by convincing the top Russian brass in Fairbanks that he spoke English, and was therefore a fit escort for the lady guest. His English consisted of "and," "so," "O.K." "Hell" — I was known all through the trip as Miss Hell — "lie up," which he used to mean lie down or sit up, "stockings" and "Betty Grable." The Russian commanding officer wished me a happy trip, said I would be in Moscow in three days, and gave me a fine sleeping bag.

The trip took fourteen days because the crew had been instructed to take no chances with their guest. Those two weeks were, physically, the hardest time of my life. Kolya and I sat, or lay, on packing boxes in the rear of the plane, where the heating system ceased to work on the second day. (When it got so cold we couldn't stand it any longer, one of us would go into the pilot's compartment, and the radio operator would move out.) We flew only when the weather was good and that meant that for days at a time we were lodged in log cabins on Siberian airfields. The crew, unfriendly at first because I was the reason for their long, cautious journey, soon came to understand that I didn't like the command delays any more than they did. None of them talked English, but Kolya and I spent four hours a day teaching each other English and Russian, and while I can never really learn any language, by the time we were halfway across Siberia he could understand almost everything I said and translated for me with remarkable intelligence. His bright, round, child's face, his hands shaking from the cold as he held my dictionary, is still with me. I owe a dangerous pneumonia to his overconfidence about the English language.

We had come down in Yakutsk. The first night there was pleasant: a spinster schoolteacher who spoke excellent English had met the plane, the sleeping quarters were less rugged than usual, and the teacher had spent dinner hour through 3 A.M. reading and translating for me the poetry of Yesenin. (She was as in love with him as earlier ladies had been with Byron after his death.) But on the second day I turned my once-broken ankle in the ice ruts and Kolya, convinced that I would be crippled, and anxious to show off Soviet medicine, insisted I go to the clinic. The clinic was a long way in a jeep riding on ice, and when we arrived there the doctor was absent. Two nurses, understandably, were bewildered by Kolya's insistence that I "had been crushed by ice." The twisted ankle was diagnosed as just that, but I made the mistake of asking for a laxative. Kolya was carrying our English-Russian pocket dictionary and he and the nurses turned many a page before they seemed to find the word. One of them shook her head over the word but the other one seemed convinced and Kolya, pounding his chest in some kind of show of military authority, made firm demands. I was presented with a small bag of salts in rough, large chunks. Kolya, with gestures, explained that I must dissolve them in water and all would be "excellence," his now favorite word. I don't know why I believed any of it, but I drank most of the filthy stuff that afternoon.

I was too sick for the next few weeks to make entries in a diary, but, between hours of sleep or passing out, I remember certain scenes, although I am not always sure where they happened, or if I have remembered them in their proper order. I remember crawling through the fifty below zero cold of Yakutsk to an outhouse, the sweat pouring into my eyes; two visits from a doctor who seemed dead drunk; a yellow liquid that Kolya and the pilot poured down my throat; being carried up the icy ramp of the plane, then strapped down with ropes to keep me from falling off the packing crates; Kolya lying on a cot outside my door at each night's lodging; hot milk which made me sick and a sour pickle that I wanted very much as Kolya shook his head and said it was not fit for a lady who had not eaten in five days; no longer wanting to go to the pilot's compartment for warmth and fighting with Kolya and the radio operator who carried me there; endless miles of pine trees seen from the window; and once, coming out of a long sleep into a fit of laughter — I was composing, dreaming, a death prayer — and then into a fit of crying that scared the crew so badly that they turned the plane back to the place where we had stayed the night before; and another doctor; and then a day when Kolya said, "Urals. Look down, Miss Hell"; and another day, soon after, when a woman in uniform came on our plane and Kolya said, "Now, all O.K., Miss Hell," and when I said I didn't know what he meant, he explained that the co-pilot had been bad, very ignorant, would not be allowed to fly again, but this lady was famous and would "bring us good into Moscow." On the fifteenth day, about two in the afternoon, Kolya woke me up because he wanted to open one of my suitcases. He took out a toilet bag, handed it to me with a mirror. I shook my head, either because I didn't understand or didn't care.

He said, "All good now, Moscow soon, maybe one hour."

I said that was nice and tried to go back to sleep. But he propped me up and made disapproving faces and then fiddled in the bag and wiped my face with cream, combed and brushed my hair, smudged lipstick on my face, wiped it clean, tried again, until I laughed and managed it myself. Then he pulled a dress from the suitcase and said, "Take off pants. No good Moscow committee. Fix nice dress. Stockings not O.K. now. I fix." He took from his bag an ugly pair of brown stockings he had bought in Fairbanks and gave them to me. He unlaced my boots, smoothed out the dress, pulled me to my feet.

"I go now there," he said, pointing to the pilot's compartment. "Please fix nice for people."

I said, "Kolya, I wish you had been born to me."

He laughed. "I tell this to my mother."

An hour later we were in Moscow, and there were men and women carrying flowers who ran toward the plane. But I remember only Sergei Eisenstein, who said in perfect English, "We know you have been ill. I have insisted there be no speeches. You must come to the hotel now and rest for a long time."

But I thought I felt fine. I was excited about being in Moscow, and soon after Eisenstein left me an embassy man came around and we went off to dinner and a long talk afterwards. After that, for the next five days, I remember nothing. When I came to, I was in a bedroom at Spasso House, Ambassador Harriman's Moscow residence, because George Kennan had moved me there. The embassy navy doctor told me I had had a bad pneumonia, so bad that he had decided to chance the first shot of penicillin he had ever given. He said the penicillin had worked like magic but that he needed a vacation. Months later, when I told Eisenstein that the sickness had begun in Yakutsk and seemed to be connected with a dose of rough salts, he took my dictionary home with him and came back the next afternoon to say that there was no word for laxative in the Russian language and that the salts had been meant to soak my ankle in. He said, "Lilishka, is there something the matter inside your head from time to time?"

I stayed in the Soviet Union for the next five months. I lived most of the time, through the generous invitation of Averell Harriman, at Spasso House, but I kept my rooms at the National Hotel for work, or for bad nights when the snow made it hard to get back to the Arbat district, or when the rather heavy atmosphere of Spasso made me want to eat alone.

In those five months I kept diaries of greater detail and length than I have ever done before or since, but when I read them last year, and again last week, they did not include what had been most important to me, or what the passing years have made important. I know, for example, on what date I went to Leningrad, and there are many pages about a terrible evening during which Olga Bergholz, the poet, and four other people told me about the siege and famine of their city, but I see and hear more clearly a woman and a boy of about seven or eight walking close behind us on the Nevsky Prospect.

The mother said, "The sausage is better lately. Not so much grain in it."

The child said, "Why doesn't he stand up the way he used to?"

"He can't stand up."

"But why?"

"Because he can't."

"But *why?*"

My Leningrad translator turned to face the woman and the boy. The woman spoke directly to her. "My husband. We had one pair of valenki between us." (Valenki are long, felt boots.) "He went across Ladoga to help bring in the first food after the siege. The valenki froze to his legs and when he tore them off, to save them for me, his skin came off, too. I wear the valenki today."

When my translator had finished telling me all that, the woman and the boy moved on. My translator began to cry as we went past Pushkin's house — closed during the war — and when we stopped to look at the house she raised her hand to make the right-left Orthodox cross. She said, "It was like that with all of us. During the siege my boy ate a little piece of candle every day."

And my notebooks tell what people I saw, what the usually glum dinner conversation at Spasso was about, the bad plays that the Russians were convinced I wanted to see, my impatience with the foreign colony's ill-humored complaints, and then my own increasing ill humor in the gray, terrible Moscow winter of 1944–1945, but nowhere is there a record of how much I came to love, still love Raya, the remarkable young girl who was my translator-guide. Nor how close I felt then and now to a State Department career man whose future, seven or eight years later, went down the drain for no reason except the brutal cowardice of his colleagues under the hammering of Joe McCarthy. And there are many entries about Sergei Eisenstein and our almost daily cup of tea, but I didn't know, couldn't know, that twenty-one years after his death he is more real than many of the people I saw last week. And I know the name, because it is written down, of the three-year-old fat, blond orphan who threw himself at me the first time I ever saw him and who, when I went to see him twice every week, would sit on my lap and feel my face because the lady who ran the orphan school said I looked like a picture of his mother, but I couldn't know then that I would think about him for years afterwards, and dream as recently as last month that I was riding with him on a toboggan.

But the most important few hours are not even recorded in the diaries. I had gone to a hospital for the severely wounded and was making the handshaking, false-smile clown-sounds that healthy people make when they are faced with the permanently injured, when suddenly a man came into the room. I think he was in his late twenties, I think he was blond, I think he was tall and thin. But I know that most of his face had been shot off. He had one eye, the left side of a piece of a nose and no bottom lip. He tried to smile at me. It was in the next few hours that I felt a kind of exaltation I had never known before.

10

F<small>ROM</small> a diary, Moscow, 1944:

The Kremlin is the political heart of the Soviet Union
and the geographical heart of Moscow. The city grew
up around the great thirteenth-century walls that en-
close the buildings of the Kremlin and has continued to
grow away from them into what is called the A Circle
and the outer B Circle. The A Circle includes the Kremlin, the important government buildings, the main shopping district, many of the theatres and the big hotels.
The National Hotel faces St. Basil's Cathedral and the
main gate of the north Kremlin wall. Between the cathedral and the wall is that famous cobblestone passage
which has seen so much of Russian history: in the seventeenth century a czarist massacre of friendly petitioners;
in the nineteenth century it was here that Napoleon
turned loose his cannons on the burning city; in 1917

the Bolsheviks and the White Guards fought until the cobblestones were slippery with frozen blood, the passage blocked by bodies.

I am told that to the pure in art, St. Basil's is one of the architectural freaks of the world: to me it has the daring self-assurance of a great work. It is true that within one lifetime it would not be possible to see all that is of it or all that is on it. It is not a large church, but it has no lonely half inch. Maybe the architect-churchmen omitted the sculptured eye of a toad or a mandrake root, but you cannot be sure that if you looked again they wouldn't turn up. The cathedral rises to violate all rules, and maybe it reflects the nature of the people who move past it today as truly as it reflected the sixteenth-century men who built it for Ivan the Terrible.

The Germans never came closer to Moscow than the airport, which, of course, was close enough, but the city was spared the horrors of Stalingrad and Leningrad. But now, December 1944, the people here look tired, cold, shabby and exhausted-sick in this, the easiest,* winter of the war.

Russians are so accustomed to cold that they seldom speak about it, but when they describe the first winter of the war they speak about it even before they tell you of the evacuation of women, children and Jews, the re-settlement in the Urals when families were lost to each other for months, the strange diets in places forced to feed refugees — a friend of mine, her mother and child ate nothing but caviar and milk for seven weeks — the

---

* This was the word used in 1944. In 1966, three Muscovites told me it had been the hardest winter of the war. I think this conflict of memory came about because in 1944 they knew they were on the way to victory and an end. In 1966 they remember only the deprivation and the misery.

arrival of the Siberian army that is credited with saving Moscow, and the young student army that fought the Germans at and near the airport. The students had been in classes the day before, they had no training, many of them had no guns, there was no air cover, no large artillery. They were volunteers and most of them were killed in the first week. When they tell you about the students somebody, maybe two people, start to cry, and the others are silent. Almost everybody by this year of 1944 has lost a husband, a father, a son, and usually more than one man in a family has been killed. But it is for the students that they cry or start to cough until the crying stops. I think they cry, in part, for their own endurance during these last awful three and a half years, in pride for that endurance.

Russians have always had a deep love of their country, but now they are in love with each other. They do not say they like bread: they say, "All Russian people like bread," as if liking bread was a medal won in a school of high morals. They no longer say, "Pushkin wrote . . ." but "Pushkin, one of the greatest poets who ever lived" — and a few days ago, a woman said to me, "We have no bald men in Russia." It's a kind of national coming-of-war-age pride. They don't boast about the Red Army or the near starving civil population, but they hurry to tell you about the millions of books sold last year, the forty theatres that are filled at every performance, the people who wait in line through the freezing nights to buy tickets for a ballet or a concert. The Russian intellectual has had a hard life. If he is now in his late thirties, forties or fifties he has gone through the revolution and the hunger, privations

149

and upheavals that followed the revolution. The 1930's were the first promise of something better, but the promise was soon followed by the hurricane of the 1937–1938 purges that sent him whirling, looking for the protective walls that were not there. The accusations against his friends or his heroes were only half understood and were, therefore, more frightening. Such men and women tell you that one day they knew a criminal charge of treason or disloyalty could not be true, the next day felt uncertain, and within a short time were half convinced that perhaps their country, their revolution might have been betrayed. Great honor must and will be paid those who did protest the criminal purges. It is hard to judge those who tossed about in silent doubt and despair, but it is even harder to believe that they did not understand what was happening.

Those years of struggle from the dark centuries of ignorance and poverty, then famine, then hope, then nightmare ideological upheavals, and, finally, war on a scale that has never been seen before, have made deep marks on all of them. The least important scar, perhaps, is a chip-on-the-shoulder feeling toward foreigners that often takes the form of looking for the insult. Last week a woman I like came to see me. She is in her forties, a pleasant lady who translates French and English poetry. Her face was tense and twitchy. She began almost in the middle of a sentence, "Last night he said across the table, 'Where is Akhmatova? Gone, gone, with so many others.' What do you think of that," she asked me, *"What do you think of that?"*

I said, "Is it so terrible? You told me only last week about the trouble Akhmatova has had —"

She ran toward me, pulling up her sweater as she came. "There are scars here," she shouted, "although they were not made with a knife. All over me, all over all of us. But I don't show them to strangers, I don't sip cognac at tables and lift my clothes to show the long scar called Akhmatova, my friend Akhmatova, or the scar called Mandelstam — You will not hurt my scars. But *he* wanted to put his fingers in them so they would bleed again."

Russians puzzle us, we puzzle them. Their pride is the pride of poor people, the manners they require from others must be more elegant than ever could have been known at Versailles. And in so many ways their recent social customs have run counter to ours: they are, for example, romantic and dawn-fogged about sex, and I often find the talk about love and fidelity too high-minded for my history or my taste.

But it is easier for me than for most foreigners. Two plays, *The Little Foxes* and *Watch on the Rhine,* are in rehearsal. (Rehearsals have been going on for six months.) Certainly there are other foreigners who have good relations with Russians, but most of the journalists, diplomats, military and trade commissions live on islands of each other, cut off from all Russians except waiters, cooks, translators, and various forms of bribe takers such as whores and telephone operators.

The largest of these islands is the Metropole Hotel, teasing close to the walls of the Kremlin. It was built in the nineteenth century, and while it is often referred to as run-down elegant, it could never have been more than large and ostentatious with the carved gewgaws and marble that the Russian rich liked so much. (It was in the Metropole that the last holdout aristocracy of Moscow barricaded itself during the revolution, but that story has too many versions to believe any of them.) Now the hotel is in a state of disrepair and smells of cabbage, but its vast corridors burst with the kind of international high jinks that should attract a magazine novelist, except that the high jinks are not very high and always have an aimless, frivol-out quality.

Most of the foreign journalists live at the Metropole and they have a long list of understandable grievances: the press censors are suspicious, irrational, arbitrary; they have never been allowed to visit the front lines, seldom been allowed to travel anywhere; they see few important government people and must get information out of Russian newspapers or on the rumor circuit; there is nothing to buy with money they would like to spend; Moscow winter weather is terrible and darkness comes depressingly early in the afternoon and moves into lonely nights.

Journalists cannot, therefore, do a proper job and it is a bad life for them, but with the exception of Alexander Werth, John Hersey and a few others, they are men used to bullying their way around the world and their daily defeats turn dinner into a sour stew of complaints unless one turns off the ears and plays the game of who is that at the next table or across the room?

Who is that, on a recent evening, was a trade commission from Iceland; two unidentified men from Mongolia; a repatriated Russian tenor and his family who had been living in Shanghai; an American who is here to sell farm machinery and who plays the piano very well; part of the English military mission whose chief had been a spy in the First World War and author of a famous book about his experiences as a foreign agent — but who considers it unjust, or pretends to, that the Russians think he is possibly still spying; and four young, and one not so young, whores, accompanied by a very small Russian man. We were joined at dinner that night by a magazine writer who had arrived only a week before and had just been through his first rough days of Russian press censor officials. When he had had enough to drink he talked very loud about all Russians being savages, and when I had had enough to drink I said I didn't think so, and he said he did, and I said what difference did that make, and he said something else, and I said lots of people who had just learned not to sleep in their underwear thought that other people were savages, and it was all high-class talk like that until the American farm machine gentleman got up to drown us with the piano.

I can't seem to stay away from the Metropole: it is a highly colored small station in the somber world of the embassy where I live, and a relief from the painful world of my Russian friends. It's a grubby joint but it's lively and I have taken to dropping over almost every day to listen to the stories about the night before, or the ones that Alex Werth remembers from the first year of the war, or Henry Shapiro remembers from even further back. Then I wander up and down the corridors, looking for people to talk to.

The third floor is the most interesting: two Turkish diplomats who never seem to be at home have the rooms opposite the elevator; across the hall from them are two Japanese military attachés and, in an adjoining cubicle, their Japanese chauffeur. Next to him is a journalist of a neutral country who is very proud that his mistress was once the mistress to a group of Uzbeks. This lady laughs too loud and too much and is the reason why the repatriated Russian tenor, who lives next door with his family, spends his mornings demanding a new suite of rooms. Next to the Russian tenor is a recently arrived middle-aged American who works in our consulate. He is disturbed by the almost nightly arrival of a big Russian girl who pushes into his room, looks around, and screams. The American knows no Russian, the big girl no English, and nobody will tell him that the girl is called Dempsey because she once, when hitting a man, reminded somebody of Jack Dempsey. Now she mourns the former occupant of the room who left Moscow without telling her and she thinks the middle-aged American had something to do with her lover's disappearance.

Across the hall lives a lady called Miss Butter Fingers, radical in the politics of her own country and most sympathetic to the Soviet Union, except on the day, long before my arrival, when she stole an icon on a visit to a German-destroyed monastery near Moscow. Her journalist colleagues were disturbed and forced her to return the loot with the threat of a kangaroo trial in the lobby of the hotel. Since then she does not often appear in the dining room.

Yesterday the Russian tenor spoke to me. Shanghai had taught him a little English, I knew a little French, but I did not know until the end of our half hour that he greeted me so warmly because he thought I was Australian and had been sent by the British Embassy to help him arrange a larger and quieter hotel apartment with what he called *un piano propre*. I have no idea why he thought the British would be willing to tangle with anything like that, but by the time I got around to asking, the tenor had given me up as an impostor. In any case, he loves his homeland with all his hearts, he wishes to sing once again for his peoples but how practice without *un piano propre* and with four children? I tried, occasionally, to speak, to ask why and how he had come back to Moscow, but his handsome wife appeared about that time and he introduced her, adding the information that she was his first wife and his fourth wife and his cousin.

Down the hall from the tenor, in two apartments, live the fur buyers. The fur buyers are three men of no age except vague middle age, interchangeable in color and size. They interested me more than anybody in the hotel and so I tried to do a little research on them. But any research was limited because they have been in the hotel so much longer than anybody else that nobody is sure of anything about them except "the trouble."

The fur buyers are American by citizenship. This was established by the embassy, and so Mr. Harriman invited them, along with all other Americans in Moscow, to a Christmas party. I did my best to speak with them, to bring them food and drink, even to ask one of them if he would dance with me. We did dance for a few minutes, but I got nothing more than nods and what I guess were smiles, and my attempts at conversation produced little except an occasional half-recognizable sound in English, and other sounds in a language I could not identify. (Russians say the fur buyers speak very little Russian, but seem to understand the language.)

Some of their hotel mates claim they are Latvians, others insist they are Bessarabians, but the information at our consulate is that they were employed by United States merchants as experts on the raw fur pelts that were, before the war, sold at giant auctions. Evidently, they used to spend six or eight months a year traveling around the Soviet Union and were caught in Moscow by the outbreak of the war. But none of this explains why they are still here: they are American citizens and they could have gone home long ago. When I asked Alex Werth about this he said, "Where's home for them?" I guess that's the answer, although another man I know feels that they wish to stay here in the belief that the war will end any minute and they will be the first on the scene to bid for the valuable wild minks and chinchillas who, unlike the hunters, must have grown fatter and more beautiful during the war.

"The trouble" involved the transshipment of a Russian prostitute. (Each fur buyer has a girl, but they are men who believe in class distinctions, because the girls never appear at their dining room table and nobody has ever seen them with the girls in the lobby or in the corridors.) I first heard of "the trouble" from a British Third Secretary, but the very mention of it caused him to choke with giggles and I could make little sense of what he was saying. Last week I went to a large official Russian party and spent most of the evening talking to Maxim Litvinov who had recently returned to Moscow. [1968 — I knew Litvinov first when he was Ambassador to Washington and liked and admired him. Mrs. Litvinov had been the very British Ivy Low. I found Ivy — a combination of Bloomsbury and Russian Revolution —

charming, but Hammett didn't. She had come for a weekend visit to the Pleasantville farm. On the second night
Dash didn't appear for dinner. I went upstairs to find him
reading on his bed. He shook his head. I nodded mine. He
shook his and I knew that no amount of arguing would
bring him to dinner. Angrily I said, "Why?" He said,
"Because she's the biggest waste of time since the par-
cheesi board."] Litvinov and I sat at a table watching
the dancers, who were mostly diplomats. Maxim doesn't
think well of diplomats and spoke of them as buyers
and sellers of world herring. One passing dancer was,
he said, "the highest-ranking pederast" in Moscow, and
when another gentleman, too tall and too handsome,
went by Litvinov laughed and said, "It was the custom
in his time to choose for foreign service on the basis of
length of body and bone in nose, as with butlers. You
can imagine their surprise when they first saw small,
fat me." Then he raised his finger, pointed to a young,
very blond man and said sharply, "That one tries too
many tricks. We think he managed the girl in the trunk
for the fur buyer. But why did he do it?" Before I
could ask about the girl in the trunk, Litvinov was called
to the phone and did not appear again that night.

The next day I pinned down the British Third Secretary who had had the giggles. There had been a long box
in the lobby of the Metropole marked, in Russian, COF-
FIN OF A CHILD FOR TRANSSHIPMENT. The box carried
whatever are the proper papers for a coffin and a Stock-
holm receiving address. It got through the Leningrad customs until a train official got curious about some odd-
looking holes in the box. He poked into them with some
kind of poking instrument that went, unexpectedly,

through to another series of holes. Strange sounds began to be heard, and when the coffin was broken open there was a trunk inside the coffin and a Russian girl in whatever form of hysteria you get from being in a trunk that is in a coffin. The investigation turned up the news that the trunk belonged to one of the fur buyers and so did the girl. The girl was released, returned to Moscow, and no further action was taken. That seemed odd because the Russians are very severe about exit visas, but when I asked my British friend why, he shrugged and said, "Maybe they are giving everybody enough rope. They don't like the embassy Swedes, but they can't seem to get anything on them."

"But what about the fur buyer who shipped her?"

He said, "I don't know. He says he didn't ship her. He says she stole his trunk and made her own coffin."

Last month came the good news of our naval victory in the Philippines. But on the third floor of the Metropole the news got mixed up: the Japanese radio announced it as a victory for *their* navy and so the Japanese military attachés decided to celebrate with a refined, small party, where, according to the Russian tenor, tidbits were served, classical music came from the phonograph, and the guests were in their own beds quite early. But the Japanese chauffeur, in his cubicle, only got going about three in the morning with the noise of crashing glass and muffled female sounds. A half hour was not enough to worry his corridor mates of the Metropole, but when the female sounds became screams of fear, a few of the more humane rose from their beds. Sleepy, annoyed figures gathered in the hall. Out came the Turks, out the Mongols, out the ex-mistress of the Uzbeks, out the tenor and his children, out, even, the fur buyers to the edge of the gathering. Although the screams were now steady and agonized, the observers seemed reluctant to move. A reason was found that had not before occurred in the tolerant international life of the hotel: nobody wanted to mix himself into the affairs of a country at war with the United States, particularly since it had now been firmly established that it was our naval victory and not the Japanese. But a solution was finally reached: one of the Turks — a neutral — would not go directly to the chauffeur's room, but agreed to knock at the door of the strangely absent Japanese attachés and bring the screams to their attention. This was done, and the Japanese attachés, evidently awake and prepared for the summons, padded down the hall in Bond Street dressing gowns carrying a long pole used for opening windows and several smaller implements. They broke open the door. On the floor, in a corner, were two crouching women, one of whom had her leg stretched at an odd angle. (It was later found that she had a broken foot. She told the police that she had fallen over her girl friend during a game of tipsy hide and seek.) Several windows were smashed, all mirrors were broken, and an overstuffed chair was slashed to pieces. At this moment, the hotel manager pushed his way through the crowd, entered the room, held up his hand for silence and said in English, "I wish to say that this is simply not nice."

There are, of course, many quiet days at the Metropole. Last week very little happened. A journalist returning from London brought a girl he knew three pairs of nylon stockings. She thought them a mingy, unloving gift, so she wrote a short account of their life together and sent one copy to his newspaper and a carbon to his wife. A code clerk in a minor embassy slapped the oldest child of the Russian tenor and the Russian tenor says that he regrets his return from Shanghai into the company of barbarians. One of the fur buyers received a box of eggs that exploded in the main lobby with such force that the manager had him frisked for a gun.

The night the child got slapped John Hersey and I went to the opera. The streets around the Bolshoi were as crowded as they always are on the night of any performance. The Tchaikovsky-Pushkin *Pique Dame* was being performed. The cold, tired, hungry audience seems to feel at home with the lush nineteenth-century aristocrats on the stage. Maybe they would enjoy the comedy dramas in the Metropole across the street.

11

A FEW weeks after I arrived in Moscow, the Foreign Office invited me around for a visit. I met with two cordial gentlemen who each made the same formal speech of welcome. The Soviet Union was my host and, in their tradition, a guest was to be honored and trusted. (There was a hint here that lesser people did not always act with such courtesy.) Would I, therefore, tell them what I would like to see, where I would like to go. They could promise nothing definite at the moment, but they could promise that I would move with as much freedom as war conditions allowed because I had come to them not only as a "cultural representative of my country" but because my plays were deeply admired by the Russian people. (This was, indeed, odd: *Watch on the Rhine* and *The Little Foxes* were still in rehearsal and were to stay in rehearsal so long that I never saw a public performance.)

High-class official visits have never been up my alley. I am ill at ease, prefer another kind of flattery, and after a short time cease to hear what is being said. That would always have been true, but pneumonia had left me tired and foggy that day in the Foreign Office, and so it took me a long time to understand that thank you so much, but I don't want to go anywhere, I've hardly seen Moscow, was causing the older of the men to sigh, twist in his chair, and finally to rap on his desk.

He said, "Thank you very well. Now we proceed to make list of your desires."

Would I like to go to Leningrad? Would I like to go to Kiev? Perhaps there was a chance, very doubtful to be sure, that I would be allowed to join the army at the front lines. Now. With whom would I like to meet? I said I didn't ever think about meeting people, but maybe later on, I'd come back another day. The older gentleman was once more rapping on his desk.

"Madame Hellman, offers have been made for your pleasure that are not usual. Yet you reply that there is no person in the Soviet Union with whom you wish to meet."

I tried to say that wasn't what I'd meant, was sorry if it sounded that way, but before I finished the younger man rose and said, very sharply, "Comrade Stalin does not give interviews, although of course we will inform his secretary of your request to see him."

That night, and in the next days, I told Mr. Harriman and a few friends about my visit, but they all said not to worry, I wouldn't be allowed to go anywhere, it was all a lot of official palaver. I felt better and forgot about the whole thing until late October when Raya came to the hotel to say that we had been granted permission to go to Leningrad the next day. This didn't seem to me very special, but it caused a good deal of interest in the foreign colony. I no longer remember whether I was the fourth or fourteenth foreigner to be allowed to visit Leningrad after the siege was lifted, but the visit was still rare enough to make me, on my return to Moscow, more interesting than I had been to foreign embassies. Dinner invitations came thick and fast, one enclosed in a leather edition of *The Kreutzer Sonata*, one nestled in a large bouquet of flowers — hard to find in Moscow — and one tied to an electric heater, more desirable that winter than the return of youth. The gentleman who sent the heater was the head of his country's military mission and had, during the Russian Revolution, been an adviser to the White Armies. Shortly after, he coauthored a book about his experiences as a spy. The day after the gift of the heater, the spy grown older — he was now a brigadier general — arrived carrying a bottle of fine prewar vodka and a tin of fresh caviar. I remember that when we had exhausted ourselves on the vodka and caviar, we moved on to the strange color of my hair, the need for bleach, then to praise for a suit I was wearing and straight into how chic were the women of Leningrad when he first knew them. From then on the conversation was extraordinary: the loaded questions would alternate with the innocent as if he were a metronome and I a child at the piano. When the child took to staring out of the window, and no sound came, his teeth clamped together, the mouth pulled back, and then, as if this were an old habit he worried about, he put his hand over his mouth and coughed for a long time. The child said she didn't much like questions, was weary, uncomfortable. He said he understood, none of us got enough sugar, he'd go and fetch me some candy from his rooms. I guess he came back, but I don't know, because I left the room immediately after he did and sat for a long time on a bench in the Gorki Street subway station wondering whether shabby jobs made people insensitive and arrogant, or whether arrogance doesn't usually lead to stupidity. The next day I returned the electric heater and the general never spoke to me again.

On December 20 I was to have the second proof that the gentlemen in the Foreign Office had meant what they said. Raya came to see me, her pleasant, overstrained young face in a happy grin, all weariness gone, with what she called "the greatest possible good news." When she had teased me for a while, and I couldn't guess, she kissed me and said that permission had been given for a trip to the front and we would leave within the next few days at any hour we were notified. It was not good news to me. I saw no point to the trip. I was not a journalist and didn't wish to report on the war, I was uncertain I could take the hardships with any grace, I was frightened, and when I told her I would not go, she shook her head and said I must sleep on it, please not to decide, it was of great importance. I slept that night at the hotel, not anxious to face the occupants of the embassy. By morning I was more than ever certain that I must not fake, or test myself where I knew the test would fail and make a permanent scar because it had failed.

I don't remember why I changed my mind. Probably because everybody was in a state of shock that this amazing, unprecedented offer was being turned down. I don't remember anybody putting pressure on me, but in a few days I was packing and unpacking and repacking a small bag, borrowing a padded army coat from General Deane, mending woolen underwear, knitting myself a new pair of socks, doing the fussy things I have done all my life to avoid facing the turmoil that any decisive travel movement sets up in me.

On December 27, in the early afternoon, a tall, blond major met Raya and me at the railroad station. When he had bowed, paid compliments, saluted too many times, he gave Raya instructions to be translated: I must not ask the route of the train; I must not ask our final destination; I must ask no questions upon arrival "with the army"; I must not ask questions "upon exit"; all arrangements, decisions, "tours," were entirely at his discretion, and Raya would serve only as translator. She said it was cold standing in the station and would he pick up our luggage and give the rest of his orders on the train?

The first car moved out with only Raya, myself, and the major. There were two cars behind us, but the major pulled down our shades so that we couldn't see who boarded the train. This primitive blackout was ignored by the pleasant lady attendant-conductor who, as she set up a samovar at the end of our car, told us that we were headed for Kiev, that the car behind us was "full of Polish people" and the one behind that "full of other strange foreigners." Toward night, when the train stopped at what had once been a station and was now a total ruin, we got out to buy hot sausages from two old ladies who were selling them from baskets. "The foreigners" turned out to be Moscow journalists, many of whom I knew and was happy to see. But I was treated rather coldly and I did not know why until years after the war was over, when John Hersey told me that they were all understandably resentful that having asked to go to the Russian front in letters unending, they were now being sent to the Polish front while I, who didn't want it, was being allowed the journey they had all been begging for. The "car full of Polish people" turned out to be members of the Polish government in exile, going home to declare itself in Lublin because the Germans were still in Warsaw.

It was a long, roundabout journey. I was, of course, sorry that I had come, but there I was, grotesque of costume, unwashed, cold, less frightened than I had been because I was no longer in my own hands. (As others grow more intelligent under stress, I grow heavy, as if I were an animal on a chain.) There were endless cups of tea, nights in the train when I kept Raya awake reading to her from Mann's essays on Wagner and Freud; the boredom and stupidity of the Moscow major; a stop in Kiev, a walk down the destroyed Kreshchatik, which must have been a street of great beauty, and a night there when Raya and I wandered around the city long after the curfew, and then ran back to the hotel through the black, empty streets, stumbling over bricks and wood and beams, being too tired to care where the long running steps would take me.

The train moved up to Lublin. Major Kazakevitch was at the station to meet us. He was a charming young man. (I was told many years later that he wrote a good novel after the war and died in the 1950's of cancer.) I liked him immediately because he turned on the Moscow major

Julia Newhouse (wearing the false front of the period)
before her marriage to Max Hellman

New Orleans: with Sophronia

Key Largo

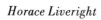

Horace Liveright

*Early 1930's: Robert Coates, Dashiell Hammett, Nathanael West,
Laura and Sidney Perelman*

Pleasantville

(photo by Ham.

New York

(photo by Irving Penn)

Moscow, 1945: with Sergei Eisenstein

Pleasantville

Dashiell Hammett

Dorothy Parker

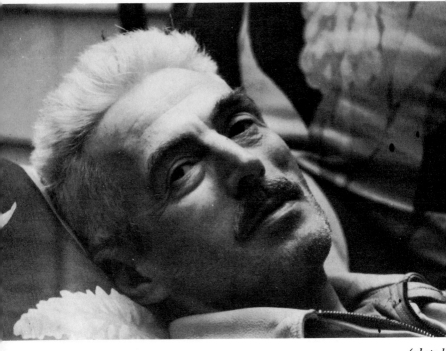

(photo b

and said, "Spare us the punctilio of the Moscow desk officer."

The hotel in which we stayed that night was a strange place: it was empty, it was heavily guarded, the rooms were warm, the windows were barred. (Two weeks later I was told that it was the quarters of Marshal Zhukov, the commander of the First and Second White Russian Armies facing the Germans across the Vistula.) All through that night there were shots in the distance and twice during the night there were the sounds of many men in heavy boots running by the hotel. (There were still pockets of trapped Germans in the city and the suburbs.) At seven o'clock the next morning I opened the steel shutters of our room. The day was brilliant with sun on clean snow. Across the street was a little girl in a fine squirrel coat and hat, and gray suede gloves that matched her boots. She was with a woman in a full English nanny costume and cap. They were a strange pair, moving quietly past the rubble of a destroyed apartment house, and I leaned far out on the balcony to watch them turn into a church two blocks away.

That morning, that afternoon, that what of time, did not have then, does not have now, any measure of hour-space or land-distance as I ever knew it before. We had driven to the concentration camp of Maidanek, taken from the Germans only a short time before. I was down in the blackness of deep water, pushed up to consciousness by monsters I could smell but not see, into a wildness of lions waiting to scrape my skin with their tongues, shoved down again, and up and down, covered with slime, pieces of me floating near my hands. A diary written six months later tells me that an elderly Polish couple were our guides, that the smell of iodoform was sickening, that I was in an enormous rectangular cement chamber filled with bins that held thousands of shoes arranged by size and color, that I touched a pair of red shoes, that as we moved around that endless, wired horror of flat earth, we came to the death ovens, large for men and women, small for children, that smoke was still faintly puffing from a large brick center structure whose purpose was variously translated as "for burning bones," "for waste," "for fire to heat the ovens," so that to this day I do not know what it was, that we moved again and there were trenches with human bones, that, turning now, we faced a building that had a long worm crawling up the wall, that I asked myself how a worm could survive in the terrible cold, that I chewed on a piece of gum to keep from vomiting and then did vomit, but not food, something yellow with red spots, that I repeated so many times, "I don't believe it, I don't believe it," meaning the worm — since there was nothing else that day to believe or not believe — that the Polish old lady was annoyed with me and said to the translator, "Hellman is a German name, isn't it?", that I went to sleep in the car riding back to Lublin and have no other memory until the car, the next day, the day after, whatever day, was approaching a river.

Major Kazakevitch said, "We are almost there."

The Moscow major said, perhaps for the tenth time, "Please do not inquire where you are, please do not ask number of men, guns, planes, present battle action, location of villages, forests —"

I said, "How often can you go on saying the same

thing? How often can I tell you I don't give a damn, and wouldn't know a platoon from an army corps or maybe even a gun from a plane?"

The Moscow major said, "That is difficult to believe," and when Kazakevitch stopped laughing he said, in English, "I am looking forward to his meeting with the General."

The meeting took place a few hours later when we went to join the General and two of his officers for dinner. (The General was, I think, the tallest man I have ever seen, or maybe the handsome high fur hat made him seem that way.) We had not finished shaking hands before the Moscow major said, "I salute you, sir, as a great hero of the Union of Soviet Socialist Republics. Now I report to you my orders from Moscow. This foreign lady has been allowed by our government the enormous distinction of a visit to your front lines. Carrying with such permission goes the order that she must ask no questions of location of men or villages, numbers of soldiers, planes, guns —"

Kazakevitch was grinning with pleasure as he translated for me the General's interruption: "I dare say somebody will bring you a message when and if you are ever needed."

It was a good dinner, the best I had had in Russia. Meat and bread, cucumbers, tomatoes, Georgian wine, fine beer, with a beat-up phonograph playing from a chair. They were healthy men of good spirits, good manners. We made awful jokes which got worse in translation and one of the colonels did a kind of jig, and the General and I waltzed to something that wasn't a waltz, and everybody sang a song of their region, but the beer made me forget most of the words of "Dixie" or maybe I never knew them.

From a diary:

January 3, 1945

I am sitting in a pine forest, propped against a tree. Not a sound can be heard, although there must be three thousand men spread out in the forest and a thousand horses, resting or being fed. It is a scene from another, long ago war, or the background for an opera. I put down my notebook to stroke the face of a horse who is pushing his nose into the snow and I am back in Pleasantville on another winter day, sitting in the snow, hot from the sun, patting the heads of a pony and a poodle. I want to be where I am. I want to stay in this forest.

Later that day

An hour or so later, we arrived at Divisional Headquarters, and as we sat around General Chernov's fine, two-room dugout, he asked me what I would like to see. I said I wanted to go back to the pine forest and live there for a while. He laughed and said that was O.K. with him, they'd build me a pine room and come back for me after the war. We drank tea and spoke of his past: he had been a lieutenant in the czarist army, then had fought with the Red Army for three years in Siberia and had taken Vladivostok. He said, "In this war, I was the man who had to surrender Kovel and retreat to Stalingrad. But God has been good. I lived to take back Kovel and I will live to help with Warsaw. Would you like to see the German encampment?" He carried his binoculars to a small glass opening in his dugout wall, focused the glasses, moved me into his position, putting my hand over the top of the glasses. I suppose the Germans were five hundred feet from us and I was so shocked at their nearness that I dropped my hand. There was an immediate answer of grenades and heavy guns as Chernov pushed me to the floor. Lying there I saw the major pressed against one wall and Chernov against another. The major said, "Stay where you are. You moved your hand from the glasses and they caught the reflection."

"I'm sorry. That was so foolish —"

General Chernov laughed. "They'll stop. What they are doing is useless. But for a minute I thought I might not get to Warsaw."

January 7

I sat up all last night a safe distance from the glass of the windows, watching shells explode into the heavy snow, the river brilliant with signal flares. Once the house shook so hard that I was thrown against the table, and that shell must have caused a fire, because I saw high flames from a building and heard shouts of running men. At four this morning Kazakevitch stuck his head in the door, said not to worry, none of it amounted to much, he'd send over some hot tea. It occurred to me then, and only then, that I had not been frightened. Did I lose the fear on the train or at Maidanek? I take out my diary and decide to write about Maidanek, but I cannot make the second sentence — the first doesn't seem to be in my handwriting — and know that I can't write about it now or maybe ever.

It had been a busier night than I knew. At breakfast we are told there had been heavy firing along the whole Vistula line, Russian patrols had brought in large numbers of prisoners, and nine S.S. men had deserted and were about to be questioned. Did I want to sit in on the session? I didn't understand why the nine desertions seemed so important until somebody told me that S.S. men were the élite troops of the German army and these were the first men ever to desert from it.

General Kusmean said, "There is never a first in a war. All we know is that they are the first ever to desert to us. I would guess the S.S. are now taking slobs and none of this means much." He waved to the two colonels and Kazakevitch and left the room, passing a tall, thin, sick-looking German who jumped to get out of his way.

The German gave his name as Techler, 61st Regiment of the 5th Tank Division, former worker in an aircraft factory until it had been destroyed by American bombers in August of 1944. He had been conscripted immediately and moved to the Vistula front five days ago.

Colonel Zeidner said, "Why did you desert?"

Techler answered in a polite, tired voice, "We tried to desert the first day. We hear your offensive is going to start and we don't want to get hurt."

The other colonel said to the table, "The General was right. Waste of time. They've put men like this in the front danger spots to divert the first blows from the good S.S. troops. Get out."

Techler went out of the room slowly, as if he were

sorry to leave. As he passed the hot stove, he put out his hand to touch it. Watching him, I did not see another man come into the room. Now I heard his voice.

"Max Makosh, 7th Platoon, 70th Regiment, 73rd Infantry Division. I do not believe in the ideals of the Nazi party —"

"Keep your ideals to yourself. Where born and so on?"

"Yes, sir. Born in Ruda, Poland, a mine worker, my wife is going to have a baby. We have no fight with the Russians, but the Germans came and took me —"

The major said to me, "Upper Silesia. Germans who emigrated to Poland and are solidly Nazi. This one understands a little Russian, of course, and it's making him feel good. Too good."

Zeidner said, "How many coal mines in or near Ruda, what quality coal, are Germans in charge of the mines?"

Makosh thought for a long time. "Yes, sir. But I know only about where I worked. Germans run the office so that a man down in the mines, like me, doesn't see them much and doesn't know —"

Zeidner leaned across the table and pushed Makosh's right hand with his left hand. "You are not a miner. Stop lying."

Makosh put his cap over his hands and coughed. "I used to be a miner sometimes."

Zeidner said, "There is a prison camp in Ruda. Describe it."

"I don't know about it, sir."

"When you do know about it, come back. In the meantime —"

"I know, of course, what I was told. The prisoners are mostly Poles, some French and Russians —"

"Are the Russian prisoners treated in the same way as the other prisoners?"

Makosh said, very softly, "I have heard they are treated bad. My mother's uncle works in the place and he said the Russians get only half food rations and sleep in a filthy place. Many die, he said, and have green feet. He told us all that and we said a prayer."

The other colonel had been scratching the table with his penknife. Now he threw the penknife over the head of Makosh into a door, crossed to the door, pulled out his penknife, spoke very angrily in Russian, and left the room.

Zeidner turned to look at me. "Do you wish to write about this, have you anything to ask?"

I said, "Ask him about the Jews in Ruda."

Makosh said, "*Pana,* I knew two nice Jew boys when I was young. But you know how it is with Poles. They do not like Jews, *pana* —"

"Please stop calling me *pana.* I am not a Polish lady."

The soft voice said, "I am a religious man. Therefore, I do not lie. The Jews were taken away to be killed. I did not help the Jews."

He bowed his head. When nobody spoke he moved toward me. "No, I did not help them. I am a small man who does not know what is outside his village. I don't even know how many men in a regiment, or a brigade."

Zeidner leaned forward and pushed him away from the table. Then he looked down at a paper on the table. "You have been a member of the Nazi party since 1931. You told your friend Techler that you killed three Russian prisoners." Zeidner rose now and shouted. "You're wearing Russian boots from the green feet of the men you killed. Get out before we kill you."

We walked over to join the General for dinner. The colonel was already there, slumped in a chair. When a soldier brought in the food, he said the General was busy and would not be joining us. (The Moscow major was, for the first time, at dinner with us.) The talk was listless and gloomy.

Zeidner said to me, "The first Nazi is hard for everybody. Drink some wine."

The colonel said, "It is our sad duty to say goodbye to you, Miss Hellman. We wish you to know that your visit has been valuable. A plane will take you back to Moscow tomorrow morning."

I said, "Oh. Have I done something?"

The Moscow major wagged a finger. "No questions, madame."

The colonel turned to look at him, turned back. "We are going into Warsaw."

There was a gasp and rattle from the Moscow major and the colonel laughed. "The offensive will begin in a few days and we will either take Warsaw on the sixteenth or seventeenth or we will surround it and continue on. General Zhukov says that he has learned many a lesson from your Civil War." He turned his head to the Moscow major. "The Civil War took place in the United States of America. Please report that I have given this secret to Madame Hellman."

After dinner, as a farewell present, I think, it was arranged that Raya and I were to have a steam bath. We were pouring water on each other's hair when a sharp rapping was heard at the door. The modest old man who presided over the stove came out from hiding and shouted that two ladies were bathing and officers would have to wait. But Zeidner's voice could be heard demanding that Raya come to the door immediately. He and Raya talked over each other as she said she couldn't, she was wet and naked, and he said to get unwet and unnaked immediately, he had a most important piece of news.

We made a strange pair going up the steps of the General's house into the small room where we ate each night, shivering from the extremes of high heat and night cold, no guns heard for the first time, our wet heads wrapped in towels, my American army coat looking even worse with nothing under to pad it out, a scarf holding the front together. Raya said, "You look like a poor czarist widow come to collect her husband's pension, wearing his coat to prove her poverty."

The penknife colonel was there and Zeidner and, a few minutes later, Kazekevitch. The colonel said immediately that although the plane was ordered for eight the next morning, the General wanted me to know that I did not need to go back to Moscow, I could move with the army into Warsaw, and stay with it on the march to Berlin, which might, would, take six months or more, but was certain of its destination.

Zeidner said, "Certain?"

"Yes, certain. Maybe five months, maybe seven, but certain. There comes a time when an army cannot be stopped. We know it and so does the German General Staff."

Raya, who seemed smaller than usual, her face bright

with excitement but clouded with something else, said, "But Moscow has ordered us back —"

"Moscow has nothing to do with it. It is the General's decision and Miss Hellman's."

When I did not speak, Kazakevitch said, "Your head is wet, you're cold. Go to bed now and I will come at seven."

I did not want to go to bed. I thought: I will not sleep tonight, whatever I decide, or the next night or the next, until I will feel too sick not to sleep, and after that will come, as it always has, a hatred for the side of me that either falls into action or avoids it without thought, aimless, giving in and over to people or places, or slamming doors in anger or fear, all the same coin. But it was not like that. I fell asleep immediately, woke up at six o'clock, tore a sheet from a notebook, thanked the General, said I would remember the offer all my life but I hadn't the courage for such a journey, not in fear for my life, but in fear of my nature, and hoped that we would both live long enough for me to understand myself and be allowed, if that should happen, to explain it to him.

The major came at seven and I gave him the note to read. He smiled and went off with it and we got ready for the plane. At eight-thirty he reappeared with the Moscow major and a small box. I still have the gift. It is a cigarette lighter made from a gun barrel. Carved on it, in awkward Latin letters, are the words: *From the First White Russian Army as pleasant memory of your visit, January, 1945.*

In the late afternoon of January 17, the Russian who operated the switchboard at Spasso House rang my phone, mumbled, disconnected the phone, rang again, mumbled something else and then announced, "His Honor wishes a line to you."

His Honor was a pleasant voice who said he was secretary to Prime Minister Stalin and that the Foreign Office had informed him of my wish to do an interview. (The Foreign Office, if it had learned nothing of what I wanted, had certainly not forgotten anything that it wanted.) I said no, I'd never said that, certainly not, it would be an imposition, no, indeed —

The voice said, "Because of the important events of today, it is impossible for Comrade Stalin to see you on the date you proposed. However, we are prepared to make an appointment on February second or third, if that is convenient for you."

I said I was sorry, so sorry, but I was leaving Moscow in a few days en route to England to make a war documentary, but how courteous, how gracious, how other-things-or-other I thought the invitation. The voice sounded pleased with the news of my departure and we exchanged elaborate good wishes for the future of his country and mine.

The Russian telephone operator and I had never liked each other. (He listened in on all conversations, even in languages he said he didn't understand, and sometimes he made a point of coughing into the phone to let you know he was there.) I went out in the hall, guessing what he would do. He was already half up the stairs to report my call to Mr. Harriman.

One of his pretenses was deafness, so I shouted at him, "Know what Chekhov said? He said to hell with the great of this world."

As I turned back to my room, the first big gun went

off, then the second and the tenth and the fiftieth in the loudest salute of victory I had ever heard. I ran downstairs to find out what it meant and bumped into General Deane, who called out, "They told you the truth. They took Warsaw today."

I stood in the hall thinking that I could have been there and then told myself to shut up, I couldn't have been there, and must not have such fake regrets again.

But I often thought about the General, and when the Russians took Berlin I wanted to send him a cable but was too lazy to find out how to do it. In any case, he wouldn't have received it. When I returned to Moscow many years later, I tried to find him. He had been killed two days after Warsaw.

12

TWENTY-TWO years later, the same week in October when I had arrived during the war, the plane lowered for the Moscow airport. I put out my cigarette, took off my glasses, closed my book and was shocked to find that I was crying. All women say they do not cry very much, but I don't because I learned long ago that I do it at the wrong time and in front of the wrong people. The two young English commercial travelers opposite me stared and then turned their heads away, but the German in the next seat made no secret of his interest, and a Russian across the aisle shook his head at me. I shut my eyes on all of them. What fragment at the bottom of the pot was the kettle-spoon scraping that it had not reached before?

I told myself that maybe I was worried about seeing my old friend Raya: it is not easy to see an old friend after so many years, and certainly not women because they change more than men. But I knew the tears were not for Raya: they were for the me who had, twenty-two years before, been able to fly across Siberia for fourteen days in an unheated plane, lying in a sleeping bag on top of crates, knowing the plane had few instruments even for those days, starting to be sick in Yakutsk, unable to explain in a language I didn't know, not caring, thinking that whatever happened the trip was worth it, although when the pneumonia did come, I changed my mind about that. The tears had to do with age and the woman who could survive hardships then and knew she couldn't anymore. I was sorry I had come back to Moscow.

The pretty, fat young stewardess said in Russian and then in English, in a singsong voice, "And now we have come to the end of the road and we must take our parting. A god journey to you, ladies and gentlemen."

I laughed, and the tears stopped, or so I thought, until I came down the long ramp toward the visitors' gate and saw Raya before she saw me. I leaned against the wall, knowing that I did not want to greet Raya until the weariness had passed.

The fat young stewardess came past me, stopped, turned and said, "Madame, we have come to the end of the road and now we must take our parting."

I said, "Thank you, but that is a mournful sentence in English and you must find another."

She was annoyed. "My teacher was English from England."

That is, or was, a favorite sentence of Russians, and as I shook my head her face became the big face of a fat girl named Martha Judge who used to hit me when I was six years old in New Orleans, and I said to myself, "To hell with this memory nonsense," and moved down the ramp.

I had no need to worry about seeing Raya again. She was twenty-four or twenty-five when I last saw her, a girl with a sweet, gentle face, a small girl, now a small woman, but very little changed. Her first husband had been killed, before I met her, in the famous student defense of Moscow when raw boys with guns that had to be shared marched out to the airport to hold back the Germans. By the time I met Raya the daughter of that marriage was four years old. (The daughter is twenty-six now and has a baby of her own.) But neither Raya nor I talked about the past for five whole days except in an occasional, shy sentence, but when the memories did come, they came pell-mell strong.

In the immediate postwar years after I left Moscow in 1945, we had written many letters, but after a while I no longer heard from Raya and put some of it down to Slavic putting-off-until-tomorrow, but knew, also, that some other wall had gone up for both of us. Now, in wanting to explain, she was shy, stumbling, finally saying that she did not know how to write about herself or her country in the postwar Stalin years, and so had postponed the letters until it seemed too late to take them up again. I felt my own kind of pain in this mishmash summary of the years that had passed: I was also shy and stumbling when I tried to talk about the McCarthy period which had changed my life, and when Raya asked me about the farm in Pleasantville, I had a hard time telling her that I had sold it in 1952, guessing what the future would be for Hammett and myself. I tried to explain why Hammett had gone to jail and why I, who offered to testify about myself but not about other people, had not gone to jail, but that was tough going with a foreigner, the legal complications, and the personal — Hammett and I had not shared the same convictions — and so I gave up, saying finally that I guessed you could survive if you felt like it, but you only knew that after you had survived.

We were in a restaurant, Raya and I, when we talked of those years. Neither of us said any more than was necessary, both of us soon fell silent. When I got back to my hotel through the cold November rain, I fell asleep, and for the first time in many years dreamed of the farm in Pleasantville: a dream of the walnut trees and the weeping beech, of November pig killing, of spring scilla, and pickerelweed and skunk cabbage when it is purple, and the lovely mush that was spring. I woke before curtain time for the Bolshoi and canceled the tickets because I didn't want to move from the room. The dreams had brought back a time of me and I needed to spend the evening with it, knowing now that the tears from the day on the plane would come back again if I continued to bury this period of my life. I would not have chosen the gloomy National Hotel in Moscow for the digging up of frozen roots, but there I was.

The night was confused. I felt as if I had a fever, and it is possible that I was half drunk during the night because sometime that evening a waitress brought me bread, caviar and a small bottle of vodka, and there was no vodka left the next morning. The sessions of sweet, silent thought were not always silent: that night in the hall, somewhere near my door, a man and a woman were having an argument in French about Intourist food tickets; and downstairs somewhere somebody was playing the piano and singing in German; and my bathroom pipes clunked as the heat faded; and during the night I knocked over a large china figure of a Greek athlete and crawled around the floor trying to find his hand; and after that I washed my hair and fell against the tub and bruised my arm.

The memories mounted with the cigarettes and, I guess, with the vodka. They were not bad memories, most of them, and I was not disturbed by them, or so I thought, but I knew that I had taken a whole period of my life and thrown it somewhere, always intending to call for it again, but now that it came time to call, I couldn't remember where I had left it. Did other people do this, drop the past in a used car lot and leave it for so long that one couldn't even remember the name of the road?

The road had to be to the lake in Pleasantville. But at first, I could only remember the last day I had ever walked it. After the moving vans had left the house, I had gone down to the lake remembering that we had left two turtle traps tied to a tree. I climbed up and around to bring in the traps, and then wondered what to do with them, how to ask the storage people to keep turtle traps safe for the future. Then the memory of the turtle traps brought back the first snapping turtles Hammett and I had caught, the nights spent reading about how to make the traps, how to kill the turtles, how to clean them, how to make the soup; and the soup brought back the sausage making and the ham curing, and the planting of a thousand twelve-inch pines that must now be a small forest; and the discovery of the beaver dam, and the boiled skunk cabbage and pickerelweed for dinner, in imitation of American Indians, that had made everybody sick but me; and working late into the night — I had written four plays at the farm and four or five movies — and then running, always with a dog and sometimes four, in the early summer light to the lake for a swim, pretending I was somebody else in some other land, some other century. And then back again to that last day: I had carried the turtle traps back to the house, forgetting, until I got to the tree nursery along the lake road, that I didn't own the house anymore. I stopped there to look at the hundred French lilac trees in the nursery, the rosebushes waiting for the transplant place they would never get, the two extravagant acres of blanched asparagus, and standing there by the road that May afternoon of 1952, I finally realized that I would never have any of this beautiful, hardscrabble land again. Now, in the Moscow room, I was glad it was gone, but sorry that the days of Joseph McCarthy, the persecution of Hammett, my own appearance before the House Un-American Activities Committee, the Hollywood blacklist, had caused it to be gone. There could never be any place like it again because I could never again be that woman who worked from seven in the morning until two or three the next morning and woke rested and hungry for each new day.

From a diary, 1966:

Tanya came to see me this afternoon after a long journey from the country. What had been a sharp, unhappy young face is now charming-plump, and her laughter is as deep as I remembered it. When Tanya was young she knew a man, liked him, didn't think much about him until she met him again in 1955 when he had just returned from ten years in a Siberian camp. She had divorced a drunken first husband but was full of happy stories about her life with Alex. She wanted me to like him, she said, because she likes him so much. We had dinner together. He is the head of a provincial art institute, a decent scholar, I was told, and I liked him immediately. (It is always pleasant to find an intellectual who looks like a peasant, instead of the often weak-handsome and the more often stunky-meek.) During the next days I found that their Moscow friends referred to Alex as the Saint, a man who gave anything to anybody, a man who, in the words of one of their friends, "did not care to be afraid." Alex and I got along fine although we had an argument last night about the Germans. His defense of Germans seemed to me odd for a Jew who fought with the Russian armies all the way to Berlin, and I might well have gone too far with the argument had Alex not risen to speak to a friend who passed our table in the restaurant. The man sitting next to me explained fast that Alex had been sent to the Siberian camp in "eternal banishment" because he had protested the behavior of Russian troops in Germany. When Alex sat down again, I think he knew that somebody had told me his history. Gently he said that he knew my ancestors had been Germans and maybe that made me less forgiving. I said maybe, I didn't know, but that Harriman, when he was ambassador, had told me that he had called on Stalin to relay a request from Roosevelt that all the Allied armies be instructed to act with care and decorum as they entered Germany. Stalin had laughed and said he would so instruct the Russian armies, but he didn't believe that men who had been fighting for years could be kept from rape and loot. But Stalin is not a good man to quote these days and Tanya and Alex and their friends were silent.

Moscow was always an ugly city except for the Kremlin Red Square and a few rich merchant sections, but now it is much uglier, as if Los Angeles had no sun and no grass. The city sprawls around, is inconvenient and haphazard with brash new buildings pushing against the old, as if bright mail order teeth were fitted next to yellowed fangs. There is a brutality about modern architecture in America, but in Moscow the brutality is mixed with something idiot-minded, as if their architects could loll about, giggling, poking at each other at a tipsy party given in honor of nothing.

There are still some fine nineteenth-century houses in Moscow — it has very few from the eighteenth century — and while they never could have compared to the great houses of London or Paris, now they seem lovely and soft, often in pinks and fading yellows, next to the new shabbiness on the next block. More churches are open, more have been restored since I was last here during the war, and St. Basil's, opposite my window at the hotel, is a wonderful building, as if wild bands of children had painted the brilliant onion domes and put the cheerful blocks into rounded shape. The light comes up late in Moscow in November, but there is never a morning that I don't want to walk across Red Square to look at St. Basil's. But you can't walk across Red Square anymore: I guess it was smart to allow no dangerous foot traffic in the giant spaces of the Square, but it is a tiring nuisance to go down the subway steps through the long corridors, up again and down, pushed and shoved, simply to find yourself across the street. True, it is very nice when you get there: nice to see the crowds all day, every day, waiting to look in religious reverence at Lenin's body, nice that the grounds of the Kremlin are now open to the public, wonderful to be able to go inside the exquisite small churches. Greek Catholicism, Russian form, has a warmth and coziness unlike other architectural church forms, as if God needed only brilliance of color and carving to feel praised.

The Palace of Congresses, the new building inside the walls of the Kremlin, is less bad than most, but it was vanity to put it so close to the wonderful old Kremlin buildings and ask it to compete. The new apartment buildings, spread out in all directions in the flat, ugly land, have no color and no form. The new hotels are imitations, I guess, of Abramovitz, or maybe men of the same time share the same vulgarities. The Danes and the Swedes have done some decent modern design, but the Russians have ignored their close neighbors and seem to be intent on imitating the mess we have made of our cities. But then everybody who has been in the Soviet Union for any length of time has noticed their concern with the United States: we may be the enemy, but we are the admired enemy, and the so-called good life for us is the to-be-good life for them. During the war, the Russian combination of dislike and grudging admiration for us, and ours for them, seemed to me like the innocent rivalry of two men proud of being large, handsome and successful. But I was wrong. They have chosen to imitate and compete with the most vulgar aspects of American life, and we have chosen, as in the revelations of the CIA bribery of intellectuals and scholars, to say, "But the Russians do the same thing," as if honor were a mask that you put on and took off at a costume ball. They condemn Vietnam, we condemn Hungary. But the moral tone of giants with swollen heads, fat fingers pressed over the atom bomb, staring at each other across the forests of the world, is monstrously comic.

Today Frieda Lurie, an official of the Writers Union, and I went to a shabby old building, climbed a lot of steps, came into a room where twenty women were working at desks, and told a scrawny lady that we had come to collect my royalties. (Not for the performances of the plays, although I don't know why, but for the publication of the plays.) The scrawny lady had known for a week that we were coming, and why, but she had a few minutes of pretending she couldn't quite place my name or the title of the book. Then she handed over ten bundles of rubles and I stuffed them into a paper bag that held some toys and a jar of caviar. She angrily pushed at the paper bag and told Frieda that this was most irregular, I must count the rubles before I signed the release papers. I said I wasn't going to count them, I didn't like to count money and didn't do it very well. The lady said that it was a necessary legal requirement. I said not for me and we were about to have trouble when I said, "Tell her I like what money buys, but I don't like handling it, and won't, and that's that." She understood English, because she smiled suddenly, nodded, and handed over the papers that had to be signed. On the walk back, I wondered why

189

I had made such a fuss, if my dislike of counting money could have started at my grandmother's Sunday dinners where they spoke of things in exact dollar amounts — the rug had cost two thousand four hundred three dollars and seventy-four cents, the chauffeur had used up four dollars and thirty-two cents of gas on a drive of two hundred and two miles — or whether it came much later, from the opening night of *Another Part of the Forest,* when my father counted crisp bills throughout the performance, throwing the actors and causing angry mutters in the audience around him. My father, who had little concern with money, had never done anything like that before, although he had been acting odd, speaking odd, for many months before that night. At the party after the performance, I was angry with my father until Gregory Zilboorg, the psychoanalyst, said to me, "Your father has senile dementia. You must face it and do something about it very soon." The shock of that sentence is still with me now, over twenty years later, but I didn't do anything about it for another six months, and then only when the terrible crack-up came that sent my father to a hospital. He blamed me for his being in the hospital and thus I lost my father, as he lost his mind, for two years before his death.

A few days later, at dinner again with Tanya and her friends, one of the women said the scrawny lady, who was her cousin, had been amused that I refused to count my royalty money. She said it was Russian of me, not to care about money. I said I did care about money, cared so much, in fact, that I pretended not to care, and maybe that was the reason I had always been so attracted by

Russians, who are nonsavers, noncomputers, generous about sharing and giving, no middle-class calculations about what you take or give back. My hosts were pleased, but assured me that Russian openhandedness had nothing to do with Socialist theory, they had always been like that, maybe because Russia had skipped the middle-class revolution, maybe because the poverty had been so great, maybe even religion; and so we batted all that around for a while and finally got to Dostoevsky's *The Possessed*, and had an argument about the book because I liked it more than they did. By this time we had all had a lot to drink and, of course, we ended the evening with somebody reciting Pushkin, long, long, long. That's the way I remembered many nights during the war, somebody reciting Pushkin, long, long, long.

In 1945 I had met a young captain who was home from the front, just out of the hospital after a bad leg wound. Captain K was in his middle twenties then, his graduate degree interrupted by the war. He had been doing his thesis on modern American novelists and wanted to use his recovery leave to work on it. We had talked a lot in those days: Hemingway wasn't well published in the Soviet Union, but the captain was hungry for knowledge of him. I tried hard to sell him on Faulkner and Fitzgerald, but although he had heard of both men, he knew nothing of them. Russians are extra dogmatic about what they don't know, and so he was sure they were not as good as Hemingway.

Now, on this trip, I asked about Captain K, but nobody knew what had happened to him. Toward the end of my first week, he telephoned me from the lobby of the hotel. I opened the door to a man I would not have recognized: the face had become too large, and folded around itself; the blond hair was now a darkish red; the manner, once eager and sharp, was now so withdrawn and quiet that he didn't answer my greeting, but moved directly past me to the table and sat down. At the end of ten minutes of forced chitchat from me — I don't like myself when I do that and often end up not liking the person who forces it on me — he said, "I am glad to see you, Lilishka. The rain is not coming now. Shall we make a walk?"

We walked in silence, going past the old building of Moscow University. Then he stopped, turned, went back to the building and stood in the courtyard, staring at it.

He said, "I have not seen it for years. I do not now come to this neighborhood. The last time I came down that staircase, I held my thesis in large bag. I was to go to front lines that night. I think there will be much time to finish my thesis at front in the long nights."

I said, "Is that the thesis on American novelists that you used to talk about?"

"Yes," he said, "but by the time I knew you I had long lost it. I did not want to tell that. I was not wounded that time, by the fence that was mined, but I was thrown a distance and my thesis was gone. In the army they called me Comrade Thesis and then later Captain Thesis. No, I did not resume to work on it again." After a long silence he said, "You were O.K. right. Faulkner is fine writer, best. You have Faulkner books with you?"

I said I didn't, but I would send them to him.

He said, "Tell me about the book *Sanctuary*."

192

I don't know how to tell about books, and I thought he meant just good or bad, but he wanted the characters and the plot. It's a complicated book, *Sanctuary*, and there was something ridiculous about describing Popeye on a cold Moscow day when, for me, Popeye is the South I knew, full of vines and elephant ear leaves, heavy with swamp air and Spanish moss, home and frightening land, so I told him instead about the time in the early 1930's when Hammett and I had first come to New York together. I think we had just met Faulkner, and for the length of Bill's visit in New York the three of us would meet each night, sometimes early in the evening, sometimes very late, usually at Dash's place, arguing about books and drinking through until morning, when I would fall asleep or pass out, and they would eat breakfast or start another bottle. I told the captain that Faulkner was on a kick then about *Sanctuary* — I am told he stayed on the kick throughout his life — claiming that it was a potboiler and he had only written it for money. Hammett used to be irritated by that and would answer that nobody ever deliberately wrote a potboiler, you just did the best you could and woke up to find it good or no good. Usually, by the time of such talk they were both too drunk to listen to each other and each would speak at the same time, or to me, or in space. The captain said he didn't know much about drinking, he had skipped his youth, did I still drink a lot? I said no, not as much, I couldn't, but I'd like a drink now in the cold drizzle that had started. We wandered around looking for a place, and by the time we found it I realized that we were in the Arbat section. The neighborhood has changed a great deal since I lived in Spasso House during the war.

Spasso, which had once belonged to a nineteenth-century sugar millionaire, could never have been a beauty, and during the war it was a seedy kind of embassy, but now it looks spruced up and prosperous-gay. Standing in front of it I remembered all the dinners, sometimes pleasant and homey with Harriman, his daughter, and the few foreign career officers who lived in the house, sometimes just aimless off-tempered, a table of people living in a place they didn't like, waiting to be cheered by anything, even by my discovery of fresh onions in the cellar. And I remembered a small, crazy dog that lived in the room next to mine; and the visits to the house of the great dancer who, wherever she sat, always faced a mirror, her eyes unwavering; and siphoning off gasoline from the embassy car to clean my hair, and falling over and over again in the courtyard as I practiced walking in flat, high felt boots; and Prokofiev urging me to leave a chamber music concert because he didn't like music "played"; and the nice kid from Kansas City who ran the army P.X. and gave lectures about the possible state of my liver, and a hundred other faces and voices from so long ago.

I was looking now for the miserable, state-owned antique store where so often I had tried to find something, anything with color, to cheer me in the cold, gray misery of wartime Moscow. The store is gone now and a brassy department store has taken its place, but I laughed as I remembered the day when John Melby and I had found two nineteenth-century children's picture books and were on our way out to the street. Then he touched my arm and pointed to a high shelf. On the shelf was a large photograph of the real faces of Garbo and the director Rouben Mamoulian, with crudely faked bodies arranged in one of the poses of love. Both Melby and I advanced toward the picture in movements evidently so furtive that the two ladies who attended at the store came toward us. I put out my hand to take the picture but John shook his head and pulled me to the door. When we were on the street, I turned to go back, but he held my arm and said that of course some joker had put it there, but as foreigners we would never be forgiven for buying it. He only got me back to Spasso by promising that he would get one of the Russian employees at the embassy to go around and buy it for me. But two days later, the Russian messenger said the picture was gone. Maybe, maybe not.

Captain K knocked at my door a few mornings later. Again he went immediately to the table, picked up a magazine, read it for a while without speaking to me. (I like people who refuse to speak until they are ready to speak.) I went back to reading Malamud's *The Fixer*.

After an hour or so, I said I had to go out for lunch. He immediately picked up *The Fixer* and asked if he could stay on and read it. When I came back in late afternoon, he had finished the book and was lying on the couch, his right leg propped up on two pillows. I was not meant to see that, because he jumped to his feet and put the pillows into place too fast.

He said, "I came this morning to speak with you about Eisenstein. After he died, we found engraved little box with greeting from him to you. I had the intention to mail it to you. But time went by and then I cannot find it."

"All of you," I said.

"All of us?"

"Slavs," I said. "I would like to have had something from Eisenstein. You must have known that."

Eisenstein had been at the airport to meet me when I landed in 1944, and after that we met three or four times a week during the months I was in Moscow. We would often walk in the afternoon darkness and, in the early days, I would suggest that he come to Spasso for tea, but he would smile and say goodbye. Perhaps because I asked no questions, he finally told me that it was dangerous for him to be seen at our embassy. (He did come, finally, to my farewell party, but that was the only time, and then so many other Russians came that I guess he felt it no great chance to take.) Eisenstein was, during that winter of 1944, cutting the first part of *Ivan the Terrible*; he would talk about the picture, and his other pictures, and his Baltic youth, and his studies of the human eye, and German literature and English poetry, and music. And sometimes we would go off to rehearsals of *The Little Foxes* or *Watch on the Rhine*. He would be amused at my muttered complaints which he made worse when he translated for the actors and directors. One day an actress in *Watch on the Rhine* broke into tears at an objection I made to the heavy ornamentation she was giving the part. Eisenstein said, "What shall I tell her? I've worked with her many times and the tears will go on all night unless you give some foolish praise, or cry with her."

196

I said, "I don't want to cry with her so tell her she's wonderful and let's get out of here."

He translated that into "Miss Hellman says to tell you that you are wonderful in the hope that we can get out of here immediately."

Eisenstein was one of the most forceful and brilliant men I have ever met, and one of the best to be with. Neither of us ever talked about ourselves, although once he asked me if I was married to Hammett and then he spoke vaguely about a wife. (I had heard from other people that she was not and never had been a wife, but a devoted friend and housekeeper, and some of his friends denied even that.) It is considered a political and social sin in Russia to print news about anybody's personal life. I don't know the origins of this taboo, but it operated as well for the life of Stalin — one remembers that until Svetlana Alliluyeva emerged under Western eyes one did not know how many times he had been married, or what child came from what lady, or what happened to the ladies — as it does for the life of the men now in the Kremlin or the poet or the scientist. It is puzzling, however, because Russians gossip among themselves as people do everywhere, except they know more about each other than my neighbors on the tight little island of Martha's Vineyard. Eisenstein was, at the time I knew him, both in and out of government favor: in enough to be making a large, expensive movie, out enough to be worried about whom he saw, where he went, what was going to happen to his work. Among intellectuals, however, even those a generation younger, he was still a great figure — he has become an even greater figure because of his new published collected work — but nowhere did I hear any gossip about his life, although I was always conscious that caution set in when people talked about him.

One day, a few weeks before I left Moscow in 1945, Eisenstein phoned to say that he had finished a rough cut of *Ivan* and had borrowed the apartment of a friend to show the picture to a few people. The next night Averell, Kathy Harriman and I went to the only luxury apartment I had seen in Moscow. It was flutey and crowded with nineteenth-century bibelots, shawls, and carved furniture. The large piano was draped with six or seven young men, nibbling on sandwiches, who looked as if they were posing for a winter picnic. Surrounding the young men were three or four older men who offered candies and lit cigarettes with the attention of elderly valets to young royalty. *Ivan* was a turgid, dull movie — I think Eisenstein already knew it was — and it was not a pleasant evening.

I said to the captain, "It made me sad, that evening. That great man, the bad movie, the pretty boys —" forgetting that he didn't know what evening I was talking about. "I wrote to Eisenstein when I got home. I wrote several times, but I had no answer. Then I got a cable that said, 'I am ill. Please airmail thirteen mystery stories to bring me luck.' I knew it was a joke but I sent the thirteen mysteries, anyway. Long before they could have reached Sergei I read in the newspaper that he was dead. It was a strange joke for a sick man, wasn't it?"

The captain turned to look at me. "It was not a joke. It was most serious."

"You can't mean that. How could it be serious?"

"Eisenstein was a most superstitious man, of such proportions that he would not speak again in his lifetime to an old friend who once laughed at his misery over salt spilled on a table. Perhaps he hide this from you because you are Western woman. Now tell about writer Norman Mailer."

I was about to say that this telling about books and people was no good for me, but the captain's face suddenly twitched and he leaned down to rub his right leg and then to move it in a quick up-and-down exercise, turning his head away from me. So I said that I had known Mailer for many years, thought *The Naked and the Dead* very good, had never much liked the other novels, but now I admired *Cannibals and Christians*. It was not possible, not the time, to explain the affection and angry teasing that have made the seesaw on which Norman and I have sat out our relationship, but I tried to say, discovering it as I said it, that *Cannibals and Christians* had made me understand the growth of Norman as a man. If I had not given full credit before it was not all my fault: Mailer's growth has been mixed with so much foolishness, his real powers so sprinkled with aimless errands, his true sweetness so buttoned under the meanest-kid-on-the-toughest-street in Slumsville, Harvard, Class of 1943. But that was all too hard to say.

I said, instead, "Mailer is a wonderful writer, a natural, the best kind, who wasted time being famous, but maybe he won't waste it anymore. I don't know. You can't know actors and Norman is an actor."

The captain said, "I like very much Mailer, a brave man, I think. Did you hear ever of historian Smirnoff?"

I shook my head.

"Did you hear ever of the siege of Brest?"

I nodded.

"The Russian garrison fought against the Germans until most were dead. Those who live were taken prisoners, all sick with wounds. Then, years in German concentration camp, bad. So there are not many who live when war is finished. They go home. But no one of them arrive home. *No one.* Smirnoff, the historian Smirnoff, wishes to write of Brest, so he begins investigation for his work. Where are the men who make the fight at Brest? Nobody knows. So Smirnoff sets the task to find out. He find out: they have gone in straight-line train from German prison camp over Urals to Russian prison camp. This man, this Smirnoff is hero, hero, not like in war when there is no other thing to be. This man, this Smirnoff, began to make fight by himself. All the time he go to the Kremlin, knock on one door, knock on other door, day and day, month and month, no fear for himself, day and night — He won. I come back. Me and others." He laughed. "Now poor Smirnoff is famous, like great judge or priest of old days, and nobody gives him rest. From all over people write him about cows are not good, my science teacher is vodka drinker and such, please speak with Kremlin."

I said, "What was the reason, the official reason?"

"The old crazy man Stalin believe that if Germans had you prisoner, perhaps you wished to be prisoner, or perhaps you talk secrets to them. Do you not think Smirnoff is good story of a man?"

I said, "Do you still write?"

"No, I am now pharmacist's assistant. I learn it in the prison camp."

"Are you married?"

"For six years. Then my wife go away with man from hotel desk in Yalta. Last year she send me picture of the house of Chekhov and said I should come look at it."

I said, "You will marry again."

He shook his head. "No. I have not the faith. I make mistake so large I could make mistake more large." He rose. He was limping badly now. "I have brought a list of poets. I would be glad if you could send their books to me. Not thirteen, like Eisenstein. Four."

The list was Wallace Stevens, Auden, William Carlos Williams, and a man called James Senate. Weeks later, in London, I was on my way to buy the books when I realized I had no address for the captain and no way to find it.

*S*ometime during the 1940's, Westchester County, where Hammett and I owned a large farm, banned deer hunting by gun. But they said they would allow, certainly with tongue in teasing cheek, deer to be taken with bow and arrow.

Hammett, who was an excellent shot and had always supplied us with fine game, agreed with the ban on guns, decided he would teach himself to shoot with bow and arrow. This is a difficult sport, but within about two months he was good at it, practicing long hours, far from the house, using the usual supplied target or dead bushes and branches, and finally bringing in two fat squirrels, not easy stuff. I wanted to try, too, and that brought groans and finally, "You can't shoot straight at anything. Haven't you realized through the years that's why I always made you walk in front of me when you carried a gun?"

I was, indeed, a bad shot, but I was peeved this time into a spectacular first feat with a light bow and arrow. On my first lesson, I hit a sitting black duck. I was not to hit anything again, but once, trying for a large buck running almost directly in front of me, I hit a dogwood tree that was over my right shoulder. That night Hammett wrapped my bow and arrow carefully in oiled paper and put them in the attic, where I never discovered them until the day we were forced to leave the farm forever.

I don't know why the history of my bow and arrow career has, on several occasions, reminded me of the charges made against me for "pro-Stalinism." I could have answered some of those charges a long time ago, but it was a complex story and didn't seem worth the try. And, like most people, I don't like explaining myself when I am under attack.

The truth is that I never thought about Stalin at all. I have never had any interest in the one-man-makes-history theory, he and he alone did what and when. One of the reasons I find "War and Peace" such a wonderful book is that it blows the monumental-man-molding-history into comic bits. I do not mean that there are not remarkable or great men, I mean that they come only when history makes it possible and then the times make them if they have the sense and temper to grasp the times. That does not reduce them in interest, but it changes the face of how you see history.

I have written that in 1945 I was offered an interview with Stalin, although I have never been sure it would have come through if I had accepted. But I did not accept and advanced my leaving Moscow by one week to avoid it. I saw nothing in the interview that could interest

*me and, therefore, nothing that could interest him. I
knew I would go in with the jitters and come out with
nothing else.*

*But the term "pro-Stalin" has long ago, in the fash-
ion of hop and skip history (and to malign) come to
mean you are a bad kid, who believes in cruelty and
violence. I did have an interest in the Russian Revolution. Or, to be more exact, all through my childhood and
youth I had an interest in all sharp turns of history. Once
upon a time, I read a great deal about the French Revolution and the men who preceded it and predicted it, and
if I found the English social changes more to my taste it
was only because I am frightened of violence. I was
completely at home, however, in the American Revolution, and, forgetting or not wanting to know all the
economic reasons for it, I grew up in deep admiration
for all men who said, "Enough is enough. We will stand
no more."*

*Russian literature, even the works of Dostoevski, are
almost all an indictment of the cruel flouting of peasant
misery and ignorance, the daily acts that had no bounds
in inflicting pain and cruelty. I was a child when the
Russian Revolution was made, but in my early twenties
I read Lenin. (There was, later on, very little to read of
Stalin, and the little I read seemed empty stuff.) I began
reading Lenin because I had just met Mayakovski on
what I think was his only visit to New York. I had dinner
with him, alone and with others, three or four times, and
whatever caused his unhappy end, on that visit he was
full of fine tales about what the revolution had done for
his people. It is certainly possible that he was sent here
to say just that, but I don't believe good poets lie in that*

fashion — he was not a man to carry a propaganda bag.

I was, indeed, late to believe the political-intellectual persecutions under Stalin. When I first visited Russia in 1937 I knew nothing about the purges until I got home and read about them in the newspapers. But I met and saw almost every day many people in the American embassy and did not always believe in their reports or their dinner talk. They were limited men: although a great deal of what they saw and reported was based on fact, much was embroidered with personal dislike and understandable, unaccustomed diplomatic discomfort. Later, when I knew about the purges, I bought a history of the Moscow trials and Hammett and I read aloud from it, saying things like "lawyers are lawyers wherever their training," and about Vishinsky, the prosecuting attorney, "what a tricky old bastard," "the disgusting cheap-jack," "so socialism picked up all the bad junk, after all."

I was not to see the Soviet Union again until the autumn of 1944. It was wartime, of course, and Russia was an ally. Then, along with President Roosevelt, for one, and most of America, I was impressed with what my Russian friends told me of Stalin as military leader. True, that I could not understand the treatment of Akhmatova and other intellectuals, but a woman writer who was a close friend of Akhmatova told me she wasn't quite sure what the beloved poet had done, if anything, to deserve her punishment, but something strange, perhaps personal, must have taken place.

I have always sent money to the early dissidents, who have sometimes used it to eat with or, more often, shared it with others who needed it even more. A number of people took it in for me, some bewildered, some knowing the risks. When the attacks on "Scoundrel Time" came I had a letter from one man who transmitted money for me many times. He offered to write a public letter and say that. It was brave of him, because he is a journalist and it would have cost his job.

We each, I guess, make political statements in our own way. In 1948 I was severely criticized by radicals here and in Moscow because I flew to Belgrade to do a series of interviews with Tito after the Russian-Yugoslav break. I had seen the Russian bullyboy side and I sympathized with the Yugoslavs, although on a level important only to me, I was amused by the medal-covered chest of the man I faced each morning, and I did not much like the man, although I was impressed with him. Those interviews were printed here and are a matter of record.

I returned to Moscow in 1966, for the first time after the war. My oldest and best friends were now among the leading dissidents. They would guarantee my sympathy and, even more important, my practical help for their colleagues. In 1967, at an invitation whose motive still remains unclear, I returned as a guest of the Writers Union. The union's officials and I were on immediate bad terms and so I was shocked when, without asking me, and because somebody else had canceled out, I was suddenly announced as a delegate to the Writers Congress. I fought that designation until I received assurances that I could make any speech I wanted to make.

I sat waiting all afternoon in the great hall, speech in hand, refusing to allow anybody to read it. Then it became clear that I was not going to make the speech at all unless somebody — and to this day I do not know who — saw it before I would be allowed on the platform. I handed over the speech, my turn was skipped, an hour passed, I left the hall, went back to the hotel, telephoned the New York Times, gave them the speech, packed my bags and took a morning plane to Paris. My speech was published here and in Europe.

None of this disproves my critics or confirms them, either. In truth, I was nobody's girl. That is a position that for many reasons did not, does not, please or satisfy me, but I did my best within the limits of myself.

13

F<small>ROM</small> a diary, 1967:

Paris, April 23

For two days now I have asked myself why the French frighten me. I came here the first time when I was very young, lived here for four months, and have come back many times since. True, I am ashamed of the patois French that New Orleans taught me and won't take part in conversations with educated people, but waiters and taxi drivers think I talk just fine. I have felt more at home in Copenhagen in three days and more comfortable in a frozen outskirt of Irkutsk. I can't remember being frightened of the French when I was young and poor, so why should I be now when I am not poor? I stay at the best hotels, go to the best restaurants, can buy in good shops, can afford meals for those old friends who didn't share in the French boom. (Most intellectuals didn't.) And yet, in the last years, I am timid as I walk along the lovely streets. It's as if all of France had become a too thin lady. Very thin ladies, any age, with hand sewing on them, have always frightened me, beginning with a rich great-aunt and her underwear embroidered by nuns. The more bones that show on women the more inferior I feel.

I know my way around Paris and yet each day I get lost and it's no longer possible, as it was even three years ago, to say to hell with all that, today I go once more to see Ste. Chapelle or to the Marais or to wander around the Rue de la Université, trying to sort out all those houses that Stendhal is supposed to have lived in, and then take myself alone to a small place to eat and rest. I have, this week, bought a dress and a bag, no better and no cheaper than New York, have kept myself from the angry question of why a dress should need four fittings, and have had dinner or lunch with old friends. (I have written to Aragon and Elsa but, for the first time, they have not answered me, and yet I know they are in Paris. It is understandable: they are growing old, they work hard, and who, after a certain age, wishes to see anybody at intervals of two or three years?) The dinners and lunches were not as good as they used to be, but the talk is still good, or, at least, high class. It may be the only country in the world where the rich are sometimes brilliant.

April 24

We are at the Château Choiseul Amboise. It has been a good day: I feel at my best when somebody else drives the car, gives the orders, knows me well enough to see through the manner that, as an irritated theatre director once pointed out, was thought up early to hide the indecision, the vagueness. The hotel and gardens are charming, the dining room high and white, the dinner of Loire salmon is excellent, and I feel very close to the man opposite me. The years we have known each other have made a pleasant summer fog of the strange, crippled relationship, often ripped, always mended, merging, finally, into comfort. I am comfortable now. I feel young again on this journey that was his idea. We have a local marc in the garden, we have been talking as old friends should talk, about nothing, about everything.

R says, "I must say something to you. I should get married again. My feeling for you has kept me from marrying."

I have heard this many times before. I mumble that to myself.

"What did you say?"

"Nothing. Are you marrying a theory or a woman?"

"I met a girl in Berlin. We've been living together. I have been in a panic since she went home."

I push my chair back. I know now why this trip was arranged. It is not the first time he has done this. I go to my room, drink too much brandy, and the anger turns in against myself. The next morning we cancel the rest of the trip and drive back to Paris. I have a stinking hangover and don't speak on the ride back, don't even think much except to tell myself how much jabber there is in the name of love. The next day R sends me flowers just as the porter is carrying down my luggage for the plane to Budapest.

Budapest, April 30

Is it age, or was it always my nature, to take a bad time, block out the good times, until any success became an accident and failure seemed the only truth? I can't sleep, I have had a headache for three days, I lie on the bed telling myself that nothing has ever gone right, doubting even Hammett and myself, remembering how hard the early years sometimes were for us when he didn't care what he did or spoiled, and I didn't think I wanted to stay long with anybody, asking myself why, after the first failure, I had been so frightened of marriage, who the hell did I think I was alone in a world where women don't have much safety, and, finally, on the third night, falling asleep with a lighted cigarette and waking to a burn on my chest. Staring at the burn, I thought: That's what you deserve for wasting time on stuff proper for the head of a young girl.

Edmund Wilson's friends are nice people. Mrs. S is a bluestocking but handsome and with good manners. Her husband, much older than she, is an art expert. Bluestockings are the same the world over, but the European variety has learned a few graces: Mrs. S, of course, chose the table in the restaurant and ordered the dinner, but she pretended that her husband did and he was pleased. When I got back to the hotel I felt cheerful, for the first time in a week. I sat on the balcony outside my room and looked at the old church across the square. In the park the hotel night clerk was drinking something from a glass. I thought about Mrs. S and her husband, their age difference must be what mine was to Hammett.

But Dash was not grateful, or ungrateful, either, for a much younger woman, and I didn't choose tables or food or anything very often. He used his age to make the rules.

One day, a few months after we met, he said, "Can you stop juggling oranges?"

I said I didn't know what he meant.

He said, "Yes, you do. So stop it or I won't be around to watch."

A week later, I said, "You mean I haven't made up my mind about you and have been juggling you and other people. I'm sorry. Maybe it will take time for me to cure myself, but I'll try."

He said, "Maybe it will take time for *you*. But for me it will take no longer than tomorrow morning."

And so I did stop for long periods, although several times through the years he said, "Don't start that juggling again."

Many years later, unhappy about his drinking, his ladies, my life with him, I remember an angry speech I made one night: it had to do with injustice, his carelessness, his insistence that he get his way, his sharpness with me but not with himself. I was drunk, but he was drunker, and when my strides around the room carried me close to the chair where he was sitting, I stared in disbelief at what I saw. He was grinding a burning cigarette into his cheek.

I said, "What are you doing?"

"Keeping myself from doing it to you," he said.

The mark on his cheek was ugly for a few weeks, but in time it faded into the scar that remained for the rest of his life. We never again spoke of that night because, I think, he was ashamed of the angry gesture that made him once again the winner in the game that men and women play against each other, and I was ashamed that I caused myself to lose so often.

And so I told myself that it was unjust to hold in contempt R, who is another juggler. Unjust. How many times I've used that word, scolded myself with it. All I mean by it now is that I don't have the final courage to say that I refuse to preside over violations against myself, and to hell with justice.

I have sent two cables to the Writers Union in Moscow, saying that I would arrive on Sunday night. A few hours ago, a call comes from Moscow, a man's voice makes sounds that I can't hear. I make sounds that he can't hear, I hang up, he calls again, and then Tomas comes on the phone to ask if I would like a picnic, free, no charge, with his children. I say yes, the man in Moscow goes on shouting through Tomas, an operator shouts at him in Russian, and he hangs up.

Tomas is a taxi driver whose cab I took my first day here. He speaks good English, is wry and funny, makes fancy hints about his fallen station in the world. Every morning he calls to see if I want to hire him for the day, and sometimes I do.

Yesterday, when I left him, I said, "Thank you for calling every day. It is kind of you to be so nice to a stranger."

He stared at me. "That is not it, you do not count very well. You have been giving me large amounts of forints."

"I have? How much?"

"That is for you to decide. For me, I would not like to ruin the golden goose."

Now the golden goose is lying on her back in the hills above Budapest. Tomas's two little girls are playing with Tomas's shoes.

Tomas says, "They had different mamas. Both ladies departed from me. But me, their papa was the same, or so is my hope, who cares."

I close my eyes. A few hours later the sun is down, and I wake up shivering. One of the little girls is running down the hill and the other is crying. Tomas brings me the one who is crying and I rise and walk with her as he lopes down the hill to catch the older girl. That is what she wants, because she turns, laughing, and waits for him. He carries her back up the hill, looking very tired, shaking his head at me as he speaks of his age and weight.

On the way back to Budapest he says, "The older one gives trouble. She is like her mother, the one who departed from me, although the second departed from me also. You know why she departs? I tell her that my rich uncle in San Francisco will send washing machine because when I am sixteen the rich uncle writes and says he will send washing machine when I marry. You know what he sends when I write and say now I marry? He sends ten-dollar American bill. For three years I try to send back ten-dollar American bill. It is forbidden here, of course, to send foreign money outside. Communism!" He turns his head and speaks in Hungarian. The older girl fishes out from her dress a last-century largish locket, opens it, shows me a folded ten-dollar bill. The child is grinning, but when I smile back, her face goes cold and she slumps in her seat.

Later that evening, Mr. B, a literary politician in any country, arranges to have a young poet come to escort me to a reception for the president of PEN, an Englishman. I always find this kind of gathering difficult, but was made to feel rude when I said that I would like to skip it. Even when I was young, when we didn't know the good word square, we knew PEN was square, and for writers with three names. But it is explained to me now that the organization has become important because it arranges an exchange of visits between Communist writers and Western Europeans — only the Soviet Union has refused to participate — that might otherwise never take place.

The reception is unexpectedly pleasant and I speak for a long time with a tall, sad-faced man without knowing that he is Geza Ottlik, a novelist about whom I have heard. (On the way back to the hotel, my poet escort says that Ottlik is considered a "master" by the younger generation, but that he doesn't write novels any longer.) In a small group at the party — I have a bad ear for foreign sounds and thus for anybody's name — we sit talking of *Encounter*, and the CIA scandal, and the possibility, mentioned in the press, that the CIA paid for certain delegates to the last PEN meeting. A fat man says the CIA has ruined itself forever, it will not again appear on the cultural scene, don't I agree? I say no, I do not agree: what he calls a scandal is only a minor discomfort to be forgotten in a few weeks. The fat man bristles and says his American friends have told him otherwise. I do not like such arguments, seldom trust people who make them, and so I shrug and shut up. But the fat man is annoyed with me and demands that I explain what I mean. It is not easy to explain to a foreigner, maybe to anybody, that what you had thought was a small, primitive concept

215

of dignity, the early voice that says nobody can buy me, became in our time so corrupted by anti-Communism that bribes were not thought of as bribes, particularly if they came in the form of trips to foreign lands, or grants for research, and were offered by Ivy League gentlemen to a generation of intellectuals who were jealous of the easy postwar money earned by everybody around them. Intellectuals can tell themselves anything, sell themselves any bill of goods, which is why they were so often patsies for the ruling classes in nineteenth-century France and England, or twentieth-century Russia and America. I try to say that and end up by saying, "Ach, I don't know." The fat man begins to talk about the English nineteenth century and after a while a young man says to me, "He talks of everything like an encyclopedia, on and on." Somebody laughs and people rise and move off. A lady takes my arm and moves me to the punch bowl.

"He is a spy, as you so quickly guessed."

"The fat man? No, I did not guess. A spy for what?"

She giggles and says, "The government," and pokes me in the ribs.

May 6

It has been ten days since I have slept more than a few hours or eaten more than one meal a day. I have lost eight pounds. That would usually please me, but I look tired, sad, and that does not please me. You can do and you can take almost as much as when you were young, but you cannot recover fast. I tell myself that I must forbid myself these upheavals because I can no longer afford them. But how often I have said all that before, what good does it do, how little my nature allows me to carry out the resolute wisdom of night. For a minute I wish age would strike with the bad health I have never had, then immediately frightened, superstitious, I jump from the bed, put on a coat, cross the park, and look for the first restaurant that might have coffee. On the way, I argue, I lecture, I determine. I am suddenly so sick of myself that I spit in the street. I stand staring at the spit, laughing.

I remember: Hammett and I are having breakfast with friends in the country, served on one of those ugly bar arrangements with high stools. Hammett is teasing me. He tells about a hunting trip when, in an attempt to aim at a high-flying duck, I had hit a wild lilac bush. He is saying that I have no sense of direction about anything.

I say, "Don't count on it. I could spit in your eye if I wanted to. How much says I can't do it?"

"The Jap prints," he says, meaning a rare set of Japanese art books he has just bought and loves, "fifty dollars, and anything you want to say to me for a whole not."

I spit directly into his eye and the daughter of the family screams. Hammett had a quiet laugh that began slowly and then creased his face for a long time. It begins now and is increased by the perplexed, unhappy looks of the others at the table. He says, proudly, "That's my girl. Some of the time the kid kicks through."

I turn into a restaurant, happy now at the memory of Dash's long, thin, handsome face at that spitting breakfast more than fifteen years ago. The place is crowded, the people at tables near the entrance stare at my fur-lined coat on this warm day. I move to the back and sit down at a table with two young women. I have coffee and try to order a boiled egg.

One of the young girls says in English, in an excellent accent, "The eggs are at the front bar. May I get them for you?"

She gets up and the other girl asks me in less good English if I am Australian. When her friend comes back we ask and answer questions. They are graduate students, one in English, one in French. Magda is the daughter of a history professor, Charlotte the daughter of a factory foreman. They are pleased that they know two of my plays, they ask if they can show me any part of Budapest or the countryside. I tell them I don't like gypsy music, am sick of hearing it, is there any place to hear jazz?

Magda claps her hands. "Indeed, indeed. My younger brother, if you can tolerate him, plays with a group every Saturday night. Will you come?"

It is past midnight. The apartment must once have been part of a solid private house. I am sitting in a broken chair, my back hurts. Around me are Magda and Charlotte, and Charlotte's beau Sandor, a tall young man of about twenty-four. I count the others, including the band, as eleven, and all eleven are younger, in their teens. The jazz band is not good, very imitative of us. They have been playing since nine o'clock, with few rests, but now they are tired and hungry, I guess, because two girls appear with coffee, pastry, and wine that is too sweet for me. The room having been blown with noise is now silent except for somebody who is whistling. Everybody eats or drinks and a few of them stare at me. Something is expected of me, but I don't know what, and I feel awkward. Finally, one of the younger boys says something and Sandor answers him. Then somebody else speaks and Sandor answers sharply.

He says to me, "They say 'Launch.' "

"Launch?"

"That is the translation. They mean you must have come to this country with a purpose. So launch the purpose here, now. Hungary is bad and poor, America is good and rich, et cetera, et cetera."

"Why would I do that?"

Magda laughs. "My brother says maybe you think they should enlist in Vietnam war against Communist aggressors."

I remember a Harvard seminar when two students wished to bait me. I decide on the answer I made then.

I say, "Tell your brother to go to hell."

Magda translates, and they laugh. She says, "They are young. We are not young, although there is only five or six years between us. We were the believers, they are not."

"Believers in what?"

"Socialism. We grew up believing. Now we are bitter."

Sandor, Charlotte's beau, says to Magda, "Speak for yourself, less for others. I am still a Communist. My own kind of Communist."

Charlotte puts out a hand and touches him. Timeless gesture, and timeless response when he pushes her hand away. She turns to me. "He stays with the workers. He is finding a new Communism."

He says, "Do not explain me. Not that way."

She says something to him in Hungarian. Magda whispers to me, "She is too *triste, éthérée.*"

Charlotte, as if conscious of me again, says, "My brother was to be an engineer, but now he doesn't want to be anything, except not to starve or ask favors of the government. Sandor tells him without work man is nothing."

I say to Sandor, "What do you work at?"

"I do not work." He moves about in front of me. "Something new must come, Marxism must advance. Now we leave it to the protectors of the state. It is too good for them. Something new must come."

Charlotte's brother laughs. "Lady foreigner, turn your ears away. Nothing new will come. There is nothing in this world but now for now."

Then he crosses the room, raises his arm, and the music starts again, for the first time in a kind of folk melody. The guitar player sings, and when the first verse is finished several others sing with him.

Magda brings me some wine. "The song says, 'Shut your heart against the past and the future. Now is for now.'"

After the rather sweet melody is over, the band goes back to jazz. It is two o'clock and I rise to leave. Sandor, Charlotte and Magda walk me back to my hotel, a long distance across the river. Sandor tells me that the new socialism must come from the worker, I say that was the old way, he says that's what people thought but things got off the track, and for a few minutes it seems to me I am young again and Sandor is William and Charlotte is

Gertrude and the conversation is being held on the porch of a house in the Berkshires. I ask Sandor too many questions in order to hide my weariness with what he is saying, and thank them for the evening too many times. We agree that we will meet again before I leave Budapest, but the next day it is raining and I decide to fly to Moscow that afternoon.

Moscow, May 8

I should never have criticized the National Hotel. My hosts, the Writers Union, have put me up at the Pekin Hotel, built in the fifties, and already shabby. It may have been comfortable then for Chinese visitors, but it must always have been strange for other foreigners. (Since I am already known as a difficult lady, I think it best not to complain.) My translator is a gentle, friendly young woman called Maya, doing her doctoral work in English literature. Raya and Lev, dear, good friends, are hurrying back from Tiflis, but Elena and her husband were at the airport to greet me. Elena, who is about my age, looks very like my father's mother — a fine, craggy face filled with life that was and life that is. It is very hot in Moscow and hard to recognize a city that I have known only under snow or cold autumn rains.

Elena arranged for me to hear the Richter concert tonight. As good as he is, the audience is better: old ladies rise after each number, hand their drooping flowers to the nearest young girl, who carries them up to Richter. Richter bows to the young ladies, and the old ladies bow and simper to him. There was a disagreeable crowd at the entrance to the concert hall. The tickets are scarce and there were hundreds around the theatre trying to pick them up at the last minute. Music lovers are a rough bunch, I tell myself, whether they are crowding the Beatles or Richter. A man had pushed so hard around me that my left hand got hurt. I snarl at the man in English, he smiles, Elena scolds him, but she does not like my jokes about the manners of proletarian music lovers.

May 10

There is a large statue of Tolstoi in the courtyard of the Writers Union. They insist this is the house that Tolstoi described for the Rostovs. But during the war I was shown another place that was called the Rostov house and I still believe that is true not only because my guide then was a very old man, a distinguished historian, but because the Writers Union place could never have been big or rich enough for the Rostovs. Mr. Sirkov, the secretary of the union, is away, which is O.K. with me. I have tea with two other officials who tell me how glad they are I chose this time to come to Moscow because, in two weeks, the Writers Congress will begin. This is the first time I have heard that this twice postponed conference will take place at all, and I explain that it will be impossible for me to stay that long because Mike Nichols and I are casting a revival of *The Little Foxes* and I am due home. I am glad that is true because I heard in Paris that the conference will be run by the conservative faction of the Writers Union and that no protests about past or present censorship will be allowed.

May 12

Raya and Lev have returned to Moscow and we had dinner last night and a fine evening. Their pleasure in their new apartment — they have waited so many years to get it — is fun to watch, and the open way in which they live, people wandering in and out to talk, to eat, to borrow books, to sleep for a night or a week, is a way of life I envy, but for which I have no gift.

One of their friends told me that Robert Lowell is expected for the Writers Congress, but I don't believe it. I think Voznesensky has been asked to bring him to Moscow, but I have faith in Cal's instincts of where to go when. Tonight as Raya, Lev and I returned to the hotel, a large group of men and women were moving about on the sidewalk, half of them falling-stage drunk. One woman could not stand up. Three men were holding her as they tried to persuade a taxi driver to take them in the cab. The taxi driver didn't want them. We stand listening to the argument until the woman begins to vomit and the taxi drives away.

As we turn into the lobby, I see Captain K standing at the corner. I start toward him but he shakes his head and puts up his hand. I watch Lev leave the hotel, I wait for a few minutes and then go into the street. One of the drunks moves toward me. He is not smiling and his mumblings sound angry. A friend says something to him, but he shakes his head and follows me to the corner. I don't see the captain until the drunk is against a wall and the captain is pushing the drunk's friend with his other hand. They are the fastest, most efficient moves I've ever seen.

Then the captain takes my arm and we run across Maya-kovski Square.

He says, "I read in paper you come back. I am happy to see you. But you look not so healthy as last time. I am hungry. I do not eat because I wait for you to arrive at hotel."

We go into the subway. On the train, he takes out a small book and reads for the next twenty minutes. Then he rises and we get out. I have no idea where we are. We walk a long block, turn into a dirt road. We are now passing the small wooden houses that I remember so well during the war, with the pretty carved window frames and door ornaments, and the very small, hot rooms. The captain unlocks the door of what looks to be a pink house trimmed in black or dark green, and we go through the front room where a man is sleeping, and then into two small rooms, with a kitchen off one of the small rooms. He smiles, makes a gesture of welcome, moves into the kitchen. The light is dim but I see that books are piled high in corners, under the army bed, under a wooden stool. The room is military clean and there is no decoration except a small bust of Dante and a picture of what seems like a very, very tall man with his face half turned from the camera, holding in his hand a large handker-chief. There are no papers on a desk made from two wooden boxes, but it is piled with books and pamphlets in Russian, English, French and German.

The captain comes out of the kitchen carrying a bottle of vodka, tea, a jar of mushrooms, black bread, a dish of tomatoes. We silently toast each other in vodka. I don't want food, but I eat a piece of bread and have some tea.

I point to the picture. "Your father?"

"My uncle. I lived with him my life."

"He doesn't look like a peasant."

"A peasant?" He laughs. "A peasant? You remember little of what I tell you years ago."

"You didn't tell me much, except about the war and your thesis."

I pick up a worn, leatherbound English edition of Coleridge and suddenly remember the books he had wanted in November.

"I went to buy you the books, then realized I didn't have your address and that you wouldn't have wanted me to write and ask people to find you. I'll send the books immediately I get home."

He nods. "But you. With you something is the matter?"

"Age, maybe."

"Work?"

"I guess so."

"For a long time?"

"I guess so."

"The death of Mr. Dashiell?"

"No, I don't think anymore. Maybe just too much of myself. Or knowledge that has come too late, or wisdom I can't make use of now or don't want to. All kinds of things."

He pours us more tea, picks up a book, puts it down, picks up the magazine *Foreign Literature*. He has forgotten I am in the room.

Finally he mumbles, closes the magazine. "*Merde. Merde.* More polite it is in French, eh? Tell me of yourself. It is safe. I am hermit."

"This 'tell me,' 'tell me,' 'tell me.' How can one talk that way?"

I wonder why I have sounded so irritable and I want to say something friendly to make up for it, but I can't think of anything.

"So you go home from Moscow in 1945. Before you leave you tell me that G. Zilboorg is doing a psychoanalysis. I read *Mind, Medicine and Man* by Zilboorg. Did you return to his treatment?"

I nod.

"I would like to hear of such an experience."

"It was a long, painful business. Then it is over and you can't fit the pieces together or even remember much of what you said or what was said to you. But I no longer have headaches."

"It was good, then?"

"It was better than it was not. That's all, I guess." I have never said that before, never knew I thought it, but having put it into words, it seems mingy and not the whole truth. "I don't drink much anymore. I understand more of what was wrong. I don't know. When life doesn't go well, then it seems to me all that time and money should have done more for me. When things get better, I am grateful for what I learned, glad of the changes in me."

He says, "He is dead, G. Zilboorg. From one foreign quarter I hear that he was much respected." He hesitates. "But from another, I hear strange tales of his last years."

I wonder how, isolated from all others in this distant land, he has heard about Zilboorg in New York. Zilboorg had been a Russian, it is true, but — Then I remember that the captain had started as a medical student and that in the war years he had been reading Freud and Adler and asking questions.

"Yes," I said, "Zilboorg ended odd." But the story is too long, too complicated, too American. "But I respected him and was grateful to him. I went to him in his good years. After he died it took me a long time to believe the ugliness I was hearing. I guess people who mesmerize other people die absolutely on the day they die — the magic is gone."

He nods. "Like Stalin."

"Yes. And then it's hard to know whether the turn against them comes because the magic has gone or because they really were kind of crazy or — I don't think it was all venality with Zilboorg, although it looked like it to many people. He was an old-fashioned Socialist who hated inherited wealth as undeserved, and many of his patients were people like that. But I don't think you can milk the rich anymore."

He writes something in a notebook. "Milk? Milk. American? I like, make note of it."

I rise, move about, and then lie down on the floor. "I have a bad back."

"And something other is bad? Work? The theatre work?"

"I don't like the theatre anymore and yet it is what I do best. I have cut myself away from it, don't go much, don't learn, don't even want to. And I am getting old and I can't understand how that happened to me."

"Did you not marry again?"

"No. And there was a long, long time when I deprived myself of any man."

He smiled. "I did not think that when first I met you."

227

"It wasn't true then. It came with Joe McCarthy." That sounds so wacky that I sit up from the floor laughing. "Do you know about McCarthy?"

"I have read much, but I was in prison camp when he came to your nation."

"Well, I'm religious, I guess, although I don't like to think that. So I told myself then that if they didn't put Hammett back in jail, if he could be sick and die in peace, I would be a good girl, like a nun, and not ask for anything else —"

But now I am laughing so hard that I start to choke and the captain gets me a vodka.

Talking about yourself, when you don't do it much, is heady stuff, so I said, "So the years that are good for many women were not good for me. I didn't know that I wanted anybody, didn't even think about it much, but there, suddenly, was the wrong man, of course, as could be expected, as usual."

"As usual? Mr. Dashiell was not wrong."

"No, that turned out fine, just fine. But it didn't start fine, and maybe only came out fine because I was stubborn. I'm not making any sense. I'm sleepy."

We took the subway back to the Pekin Hotel and it looked more dreary than usual at five o'clock in the morning.

Leningrad, May 16

How good it is to come back here. My room in the Astoria Hotel must be directly below the one I had during the war. I open the old notebook: "It is as if this city had been built by another people who had no connection with Moscow or Kiev. It is a silent, lonely beauty." Now, so many years later, it still seems silent except at rush hours, and people from Moscow don't like what they call its deadness, by which they mean nobody shoves or pushes or has to. The great sweep of squares and parks, the delicacy of the colors — Rossi Street must be one of the most charming streets in the world — the better manners of the men, the better dresses of the women, do not please the vigorous Muscovites.

I walk all day in the spring rain, up and down, up and down Rossi Street as delighted as I was years ago by the imagination that put the pale, delicate southern-yellow buildings in this cheerless, damp northern climate.

Last night we went to the Gorki play. Awful, just awful, decorated and ornamented with direction that can leave nothing unsaid, with actors who can leave nothing undone, including an exit. It was over at one A.M. but I walked the streets for the last half hour, waiting for Raya and Maya. As I left the theatre one usher told another that I was *nyet culturni*. Five hours is, evidently, more cultured than three.

May 18

We went to Pushkin's apartment this morning. It is a charming place, not too much furniture and that very good. It was fun listening to Maya and Raya, rivals in admiration, reciting Pushkin to each other as we wandered along Nevsky Prospect. They are as moved as if the poetry had appeared last month and they had carried tears to his grave yesterday.

Late in the afternoon we went looking for Dostoevsky's apartment. They thought they knew where it was, but they didn't, and it was hard to find anybody who did.

229

But there it was, finally, a middle-class nineteenth-century four-story apartment building, curving around a corner, no plaque to mark it and no way of seeing his apartment because people still live in it. An old woman spoke to us, saying she had lived all her life in the apartment above Dostoevsky's. Wouldn't we use our influence on the "authorities of government" to have the building declared a monument with a proper sign and proper words to mark "the bedding place" of so great a man? It is, indeed, strange that although Dostoevsky has been widely published again not even the most liberated talk about him as a great writer. You can get an argument any time you want about *Crime and Punishment.*

In the afternoon we go to see Olga Bergholz in a hospital. Her friends last night were mysterious about her ailment, and she herself gives it no name, maybe because it is no more, and no less, than too much life behind her, too much, perhaps, ahead. Bergholz is thought to be a good poet and Maya is delighted to come along with me. I am glad to see Olga again, although I was not easy with her when we met during the war, and am not easy now. She was a pretty woman, but the face has turned old-child peevish. The hospital people are affectionate with her as they come and go bringing her a cake, flowers, books. This is her birthday and she has made a small party for us. We have the cake and tea as she speaks of other birthdays spent with her good friend Akhmatova, how generous Akhmatova was to her when she was young. Then she talks of new poems she is writing, asks me what I am writing, but does not wait for an answer as she takes me to the window to look at the lovely hospital garden, and uses the garden, I think, to tell me that the gardener is her great admirer, isn't it wonderful about simple people? I want to go, I want very much to leave the room, although I know she doesn't want us to leave, because she goes with us down the stairs for another talk on the landing.

I feel guilty, so I make Maya find a florist where we buy a great bouquet, take it back to the hospital, and leave it with a nurse. I am conscious that Maya is puzzled about the visit, and so am I, until I realize that Olga has reminded me of Dorothy Parker, who is also sick, and to whom I have not always been a faithful friend these last few years. I go back to the hotel and write Dottie a story that I heard two nights before, knowing it is the kind of thing that will please her.

14

DOROTHY PARKER

I FIRST met Dorothy Parker in 1931, shortly after I moved back to New York with Hammett. She caused a wacky-tipsy fight between us. She had read *The Maltese Falcon* and *Red Harvest*, perhaps a year or two before, and she had written about them, but she had not met Hammett until a cocktail party given by William Rose Benét. I was already uncomfortable at this party of people much older than myself, when a small, worn, prettyish woman was introduced to Hammett and immediately fell to her knees before him and kissed his hand. It was meant to be both funny and serious, but it was neither, and Hammett was embarrassed into a kind of simper.

I had a habit in those days — there are still often hangovers of it on other levels — of making small matters into large symbols and, after enough cocktails, I saw the gesture as what New York life was going to be like for an unknown young woman among the famous. That night I accused Dash of liking ladies who kissed his hand, he said I was crazy, I said I wasn't going to live with a man who allowed women to kneel in admiration, he said he had "allowed" no such thing, didn't like it, but if I wanted to leave right away, he would not detain me. I said I'd go as soon as I had finished my steak, but I guess by that time we were fighting about something else, because a few months later he said if I ever reminded him of the incident again, I would never live to finish another steak.

I was not to meet Dottie again until the winter of 1935 in Hollywood, and then, having glared at her for most of the evening in memory of that silly first meeting, we talked. I liked her and we saw each other the next day and for many, many other good days and years until she died in June of 1967.

It was strange that we did like each other and that never through the years did two such difficult women ever have a quarrel, or even a mild, unpleasant word. Much, certainly, was against our friendship: we were not the same generation, we were not the same kind of writer, we had led and were to continue to lead very different lives, often we didn't like the same people or even the same books, but more important, we never liked the same men. When I met her in 1935 she was married to Alan Campbell, who was a hard man for me to take. He was also difficult for her and she would talk about him in a funny, half-bitter way not only to me but given enough liquor, to a whole dinner party. But she had great affection for Alan and certainly — since she was to marry him twice — great dependence on him. If I didn't like Alan, she didn't like Hammett, although she was always too polite to say so. More important to me, Hammett, who seldom felt strongly about anybody, didn't like Dottie, and in the later years would move away from the house when she came to visit us. He was not conscious that his face would twist, almost as if he had half recovered from a minor stroke, as she embraced and flattered a man or woman, only to turn, when they had left the room, to say in the soft, pleasant, clear voice, "Did you ever meet such a shit?" I think the game of embrace-denounce must have started when she found it amused or shocked people, because in time, when she found it didn't amuse me, she seldom played it. But Hammett found it downright distasteful and I gave up all efforts to convince him that it was the kind of protection sometimes needed by those who are frightened.

I am no longer certain that I was right: fear now seems too simple. The game more probably came from a desire to charm, to be loved, to be admired, and such desires brought self-contempt that could only be consoled by behind-the-back denunciations of almost comic violence.

If she denounced everybody else, I had a right to think that I was included, but now I think I was wrong about that, too: so many people have told me that she never did talk about me, never complained, never would allow gossip about me, that I have come to believe it. But even when I didn't, it didn't matter. I enjoyed her more than I have ever enjoyed any other woman. She was modest — this wasn't all virtue, she liked to think that she was not worth much — her view of people was original and sharp, her elaborate, overdelicate manners made her a pleasure to live with, she liked books and was generous about writers, and the wit, of course, was so wonderful that neither age nor illness ever dried up the spring from which it came fresh each day. No remembrance of her can exclude it.

The joke has been changed and variously attributed to Mischa Elman and Heifetz, but it is hers, because I was there when it happened. We were knitting before the living room fireplace in the country house that she and Alan once owned in Pennsylvania. Upstairs, Alan was having an argument with his visiting mother. The afternoon grew dark, it began to snow, we made the fire very large and sat in silence. Occasionally, the upstairs voices would grow angry loud and then Dottie would sigh. When the voices finally ceased, Alan appeared in the living room.

He said, immediately, angrily, "It's hot as hell in here."

"Not for orphans," Dottie said, and I laughed for so long that Alan went for a walk and Dottie patted my hand occasionally and said, "There, there, dear, you'll choke if you're not careful."

Once she said to me — I quoted it at her funeral and found to my pleasure, as it would have been to hers, that the mourners laughed — "Lilly, promise me that my gravestone will carry only these words: 'If you can read this you've come too close.' "

Long before I knew her she dined in Paris with a group of Lesbians who were seriously talking of the possibility of legal marriage between them. Dottie listened most politely, clucked in agreement. They expected her friendly opinion and asked for it. The large eyes were wide with sympathy. "Of course you must have legal marriages. The children have to be considered."

But for me, the wit was never as attractive as the comment, often startling, always sudden, as if a curtain had opened and you had a brief and brilliant glance into what you would never have found for yourself. Like the wit, it was always delivered in a soft, clear voice; like the wit, it usually came after a silence, and started in the middle. One day she looked up from a book: "The man said he didn't want to see her again. That night she tried to climb into the transom of his hotel room and got stuck at the hips. I've never got stuck at the hips, Lilly, and I want you to remember that."

Dottie was very fond of the Gerald Murphys, but fondness never had anything to do with judgment. The Murphys had been in Europe and she had not seen them for six or eight months. We met to walk to their apartment for dinner. Dottie said, "Make a guess who Gerald will have discovered this time, what writer, I mean."

I said I couldn't guess, I didn't know Gerald as well as she did.

She said, "O.K. Give me three guesses and if I hit one right, will you buy me a drunken lunch tomorrow?"

I agreed and she said immediately, "Madame de Staël, Gerard Manley Hopkins or Philippe de Swarzberger."

"Who is Philippe de Swarzberger?"

"An Alsatian who moved around Tibet. Born 1837, died 1871, or so it's thought. A mystic, most of whose work has been lost, but two volumes remain in Lausanne under lock and key, and Gerald invented him this afternoon."

We had a fine dinner at the Murphys and were drinking our brandy when Gerald produced a small book and asked if he could read a few poems from it. It was, indeed, a volume of Gerard Manley Hopkins.

It was Gerald who told the story that always seemed to me to sum up the contradictions in the Parker nature. Long before I met her, she had an affair of high tragi-comedy with a handsome, rich, wellborn stockbroker, getting extra enjoyment from it because Elinor Wylie had also had her eye on him. Murphy said that one night he called to take Dottie to dinner. She appeared as neat and pretty as usual, but with a black eye, recently caked blood on the mouth, and nasty bruises on the arm. She explained to Gerald that the wellborn had beaten her up the night before, that even worse cuts and bruises were concealed by her dress.

Gerald, horrified, said, "How can you bear that man, Dottie? He's a very dirty cad."

Dottie turned to stare at him, opened the door of the taxi, said softly, "I can't let you talk about him that way, Gerald," and fell from the taxi into the middle of Park Avenue traffic. (The cad, many years and a wife or two later, was to fire a gun into his mouth in the Martha's Vineyard airport.)

Her taste in men was, indeed, bad, even for writer ladies. She had been loved by several remarkable men, but she only loved the ones who did not love her, and they were the shabby ones. Robert Benchley had loved her, I was told by many people, and certainly I was later to see the devotion he had for her and she for him. She had had an affair with Ring Lardner, and both of these men she respected, and never attacked — a rare mark of feeling — but I don't think she was in love with them, because respect somehow canceled out romantic love. (She talked far too much about how men looked — handsome, well-made, and so on.) But then her relations with lovers, and with her husband, were always a mystery to me — perhaps because I had missed the early days of the attempted suicides, the long, famous tape of the broken heart. There is no question she wanted it that way — she wanted the put-down from everybody and anybody, and she always resented it and hit back. The pride was very great, although she never recognized that she so often pleaded for the indignity that offended it.

But she was, more than usual, a tangled fishnet of contradictions: she liked the rich because she liked the way they looked, their clothes, the things in their houses, and she disliked them with an open and baiting contempt; she believed in socialism but seldom, except in the sticky sentimental minutes, could stand the sight of a working radical; she drank far too much, spent far too much time with ladies who did, and made fun of them and herself every inch of the way; she faked interest and sympathy for those who bored her and for whom she had no feeling, and yet I never heard her hit mean except where it was, in some sense, justified; she herself was frightened of being hit, being made fun of, being inconvenienced, yet when she was called by the House Un-American Activities Committee and I went to say that I would come with her, she said, in genuine surprise, "Why, Lilly?" I don't think it occurred to her, or to many of her generation, that the ruling classes were anything but people with more money than you had. She acted before the committee as she acted so often with their more literate, upper-class cousins at dinner: as if to say, "Yes, dear, it's true that I'm here to observe you, but I do not like you and will, of course, say and write exactly that."

But she wrote it too often in sentimental short stories about the little dressmaker or the servant as they are patronized by the people Dottie had dined with the night before. It was her way of paying back the rich and powerful, and if it is understandable in life it is too raw and unshaded for literature. The good short stories, like "Big Blonde," are her imaginative projections of what she knew or feared for herself, and have nothing to do with vengeance on the rich. Her put-them-in-their-place stories are often undigested, the conclusions there on the first page. The other stories, and much of the light verse, I think, are a valuable record of their time and place.

But I am not an intelligent critic of those I like. It is not that I am overgenerous or overloyal, it's that their work, from the very best to the not very good, is too close to what I know about them, or hope to find out, and thus I am so occupied by the revelations of the author in the work that I cannot be cool about the work itself. This has been of value: it has made it possible to be good friends with writers who, in the end, do not require extravagant praise if you make clear that you have little interest in extravagant analysis. A book is good, bad or medium for me, and I usually don't know the reasons why. Years later, I will often think the good was not as good as I once thought, but on the record, my inability to know the why, my rather lumpish, incoherent acceptance or rejection, has often been less mistaken than those who care more or know more of what literature is made.

And so it was with Dottie. I never gave her all the good

words she got from so many others, and I always cut off her praise of my work, never sure that she meant it, never really caring. We were polite, we were reticent, but very little fakery was given or required, although certainly we both lied now and then about each other's work and we both knew it. I once wrote a short story, my first since I was very young, and gave it to her to read. She had warm words for it, but the fact that she picked up a phrase — I no longer remember what phrase — and kept praising its originality and delicacy, worried me. A few months later she asked me what I had done with the story. I said I had decided it was a lady-writer story, not about anything. She protested, she quoted the phrase again, she said how much impressed she had been, and she tripped over a group of poodle puppies that we had brought along on our walk. As she stooped down to console them, I said, "God is not just. He punishes puppies for the lies of pretty ladies to their friends."

She said, "Lilly, I *do* like the story" — but I had walked ahead of her.

In a few minutes she caught up with me and we went in silence to the lake. It was a cold spring, but Hammett and I had decided to set the snapping turtle traps earlier than usual and I was anxious to have a look at them. I hauled up one of the long, wire cages and there was our first turtle of the year. As I put the cage on the ground to look at him, his penis extended in fear.

Dottie said, "It must be pleasant to have sex appeal for turtles. Shall I leave you alone together?" She had paid me back and all was well.

After Dottie married Alan Campbell for the second time — she had phoned me from California immediately after the wedding reception with "Lilly, the room was filled with people who hadn't talked to each other in years, including the bride and bridegroom" — we did not see each other as often as in the years before. But there would be periods when she moved back to New York and would come to stay with me in Martha's Vineyard. It was in those years that Dash would pack and leave the house to return only after Dottie had left. But there was the last painful summer of his life when he couldn't leave any place anymore and I had to lie to Dottie about the reason for putting her up in a guest house down the road. I would sit with Dash as he nibbled on his early dinner and pretend to eat from my tray. Almost immediately he would sleep from the weariness of eating, and Dottie would come soon after to have dinner with me. I never ate a whole dinner that summer, partly because the pretend eating had spoiled my appetite, partly because I was so often silent angry with Hammett for making the situation hard for me, not knowing then that the dying do not, should not, be asked to think about anything but their own minute of running time. Dottie stayed about a month that year without ever seeing Dash, and the measure of her tact was that she never asked a question about a situation she must have understood.

Hammett died that next winter, I sold the Vineyard house, and built myself a new house. The first telephone call in the new house came from Dottie to tell me that Alan was dead from an overdose of sleeping pills. She was very sure that the overdose was not intentional — she believed he had had too much to drink and had forgotten how many pills he had taken. I believed her. Alan was the first person I ever knew to take sleeping pills and I remember a trip to Europe the three of us made on the old *Normandie*.

One day I said to Dottie, "What happens to Alan every afternoon, where is he?"

"Takes a sleeping pill. He hates to toss and turn from four to six."

Less than a year after Alan's death, Dottie moved back to New York. We saw each other, of course, but after the first few times I knew I could not go back to the past. The generation difference between us seemed shorter as I grew older, but I was irritable now with people who drank too much and Dottie's drinking made her dull and repetitive, and she made me sad. I had money again but no longer enough to give it without thought before it was needed, which is the way it used to be between us; but mainly, plainly, I did not want the burdens that Dottie, maybe by never asking for anything, always put upon her friends. I was tired of trouble and wanted to be around people who walked faster than I and might pull me along with them.

And so, for the next five years of her life, I was not the good friend I had been. True, I was there in emergencies, but I was out the door immediately they were over. I found that Dottie's middle age, old age, made rock of much that had been fluid, and eccentricities once charming became too strange for safety or comfort.

Dottie had always, even in the best days, clung to the idea that she was poor. Often she was, because she was generous to others and to herself, but more often it came from an insistence on a world where the artist was the put-upon outsider, the *épaté* rebel who ate caviar from rare china with a Balzac shrug for when you paid. I had long ago given up trying to figure out her true poverty periods from the pretend-poverty periods, and the last sick years seemed no time to argue. She had, many years before, given me a Picasso gouache and a Utrillo landscape, saying as she gave them that she was leaving them to me anyway, so why not have them now? It was her charming way of paying off a debt and I remember being impressed with the grace. A few years after the gift, when I thought she was short of money, I sold the Utrillo and sent her a check. (She never told me that she had received the check, we never spoke of it at all.) Now, in 1965, she needed money and so I decided to sell the Picasso. It was a good, small picture, sold immediately for ten thousand dollars, and I took the check to Dottie the day I got it. Two days later, a woman unknown to me phoned to say that Dottie was in the hospital, sick and without money. I said that couldn't be, she said it was, and would I guarantee the hospital bills? I went to the hospital that day. Dottie and I talked for a long time, and as I rose to go I said, "Dottie, do you need money?"

"She's been calling you," she said, "the damned little meddler. She's called half of New York to make me into a pleading beggar."

"She meant no harm. She thinks you're broke."

"I *am* broke, Lilly. But I don't want people, not even you —"

"You're not broke. I gave you a check two days ago for ten thousand dollars. Where is it?"

She stared at me and then turned her face away. She said, very softly, "I don't know."

And she didn't know, she was telling the truth. She wanted to be without money, she wanted to forget she had it. The check was found in a bureau drawer along with three other checks. It had always been like that, it always would be. After her death, and nobody ever left fewer accumulations, I found four uncashed seven-year-old checks. She never had much, but what she had she didn't care about, and that was very hat-over-the-wind-mill stuff in a sick lady of seventy-four.

What money she had, she left to Martin Luther King, a man she had never met. I was the only executor of the will. I was, I am, moved that she wanted it that way, because the will had been dictated during the years of my neglect. But I had always known and always admired her refusal to chastise or complain about neglect. When, in those last years, I would go for a visit she always had the same entrance speech for me, "Oh, Lilly, come in quick. I want to laugh again." In the same circumstances, I would have said, "Where have you been?"

And in a little while, we would laugh again, not as often, not as loud as in the old days, but enough to give us both a little of the old pleasure. Her wit, of course, was delicate, clear, and sharp. I don't know what mine is, but it isn't that, and I never knew why it amused her. But we were affectionate about each other's jokes, even when they weren't very good, and would endlessly repeat them to other people with the pride of mothers. (She never in her life repeated her own witticisms, perhaps sure that other people would do it for her. I was one of the many who did.)

Among the small amount of papers she left were odds and ends of paid or unpaid laundry bills, a certificate of the aristocratic origins of a beloved poodle, a letter dated ten years before from an admirer of her poems, and the letter from me sent from Russia about six weeks before she died. This is the letter:

Dearest Dottie,

Leningrad is a beauty, Moscow is not, but I think you ought to know that once upon a time not so long ago there was a man called Beria, Stalin's police boy, who liked very young girls. Then there was Madame Comrade Gigglewitz — I was told her name but I can't remember it — whose second husband was a minor GPU official, but not so minor he didn't know Beria's tastes. Madame Gigglewitz waited until her beautiful Natasha, the child of a first marriage, reached the age of fifteen and then, putting Natasha in her baby carriage, she wheeled her over to Beria. You will remember that the sexual act does not necessarily take a long time, particularly when your Mummie is there to help. So clipclop and Natasha is pregnant. Beria likes that and sets Natasha up in an apartment with a curly fur coat, an elderly cleaning woman, a car and chauffeur, and when he isn't too tired from sending people to Siberia he comes around to coo at the baby.

But Stalin, Beria's friend and admirer, ups and dies. For three days Natasha hears nothing from her lover and nothing from the chauffeur who has always taken her on a daily nice drive. On the fourth day she is indignant, as you would be, too. So she calls Beria's secretary and asks when the car can be expected.

The secretary says, "I think never," and hangs up.

Most of us go to our mummies when a secretary is rude, and that's just what she did. Madame Gigglewitz is brighter than Natasha — who wouldn't be? — so in a few hours they are sitting before a judge swearing to a document that accuses Beria of traitorism whispered to Natasha through the years, or bed. Natasha's Ma had guessed right, of course: Beria had been arrested, was tried and condemned, and Natasha's testimony helped to shuffle him off. A year passes — do you remember once asking me what else a year could do? — before Madame Gigglewitz and Natasha thought it wise to petition for the support of Beria's child. They are sentimental here about the sins of the father shall not be visited, so they give the child a nice allowance and Natasha goes to live with Mummie, share and share alike the kid's money.

But Natasha hasn't had enough trouble so she takes to hanging out in an Armenian restaurant. There she meets Mr. X. He's a nice, kindly Jew who has a surprising amount of money and this time it's a real marriage which all goes to show that my people — so, O.K., for the fiftieth time don't tell me you're half Jewish — do not wish to corrupt women the way many of your mother's people so often do. A few years and two children later, over beyond the Urals, strange rumblings are heard in the land. They grow and grow until the storm reveals that Mr. X is one of the bosses of a syndicate, operating, often in caves, with stolen government material to make private light machinery. Scandal, arrest, execution of Mr. X. (Do you remember the story in the *New York Times?*)

Now you can say that Natasha ain't the best luck for a boy, but that kind of talk won't get anybody anything. Anyway, there's always Mummie, and after the two of them have had a good cry, what's there to do but wait, knowing that God has been on their side before.

Now, in time, comes a delegation, half from America,

half from Israel to investigate charges of anti-Semitism in the Soviet Union. Our two cozies hot-foot it over to the delegation to tell the story of Mr. X, a fine fellow, an excellent husband, innocent of all knavery, persecuted only because he was a Jew. This saddens the hearts and confirms the opinions of the visitors, and after several meetings with Natasha, private or public, I couldn't find out, the American delegation begs to be allowed to send a monthly contribution for the support of Mr. X's children. The Israelis cannot afford money, but certainly they are sympathetic.

I have a friend here — I first met him during the war — who is a doctor. Last summer my friend went to the country to visit his brother. Three A.M. and the brother is awakened by a man who says his wife is dying down the road, would the doctor come immediately? The dying lady — she does not die, she is still down the road — is Madame Gigglewitz. During the long hours before a Moscow ambulance arrives she occasionally confuses my friend, the doctor, for a priest, and the tale I've told you is told to him. The house is filled with pictures of the pretty Natasha — she offers one to the doctor — and enormous baskets of fresh and dried fruits. From time to lucid time Madame Gigglewitz raises her voice above a whisper: "Have a piece of fruit, Doctor, it comes regularly from some dirty Jews in Israel."

Around the envelope of my letter was folded a piece of paper that was the beginning, obviously, of a letter Dottie never finished. It said, "Come home soon, Lilly, and bring Natasha on a leash. She'd be such a nice companion for C'est Tout. I —"

C'est Tout, a very small poodle, was with her when she died. I was never to see Dottie again, but even now I don't think of her as dead, and only a few weeks ago, when Peter Feibleman told me a story I had not heard before, I had a nice minute of wanting to reach for the telephone. The story is all of her as age put aside the deceits of youth, as time solidified the courage she didn't want to admit was there.

Feibleman was with her when Alan Campbell's body was taken to the coroner's car. (No charge of suicide was ever made.) Among the friends who stood with Dottie on those California steps was Mrs. Jones, a woman who had liked Alan, had pretended to like Dottie, and who had always loved all forms of meddling in other people's troubles. Mrs. Jones said, "Dottie, tell me, dear, what I can do for you."

Dottie said, "Get me a new husband."

There was a silence, but before those who would have laughed could laugh, Mrs. Jones said, "I think that is the most callous and disgusting remark I ever heard in my life."

Dottie turned to look at her, sighed, and said gently, "So sorry. Then run down to the corner and get me a ham and cheese on rye and tell them to hold the mayo."

15

Helen

In many places I have spent many days on small boats. Beginning with the gutters of New Orleans, I have been excited about what lives in water and lies along its edges. In the last twenty years, the waters have been the bays, ponds and ocean of Martha's Vineyard, and autumn, when most people have left the island, is the best time for beaching the boat on a long day's picnic by myself — other people on a boat often change the day into something strained, a trip with a purpose — when I fish, read, wade in and out, and save the afternoon for digging and mucking about on the edge of the shore. I have seldom found much: I like to look at periwinkles and mussels, driftwood, shells, horseshoe crabs, gull feathers, the small fry of bass and blues, the remarkable skin of a dead sand shark, the shining life in rockweed.

One night about six months ago, when I was teaching at Harvard, it occurred to me that these childish, aimless pleasures — my knowledge of the sea has grown very little with time, and what interested me as a child still does — which have sometimes shamed me and often caused self-mocking, might have something to do with the digging about that occasionally happens when I am asleep. It is then that I awake, feeling that my head is made of sand and that a pole has just been pulled from it with the end of the pole carrying a card on which there is an answer to a long-forgotten problem, clearly solved and set out as if it had been arranged for me on a night table.

On that night I was living in a rickety Cambridge house and went running down the steps at the sound of a crash. A heavy rainstorm had broken the cheap piece of modernity that had been lighting the ceiling and, as I stood looking at the pieces on the floor, I thought: Of course, one has been dead three years this month, one has been dead for over thirty, but they were one person to you, these two black women you loved more than you ever loved any other women, Sophronia from childhood, Helen so many years later, and it was all there for you to know two months ago when, poking about the beach, a long distance from the house Helen and I had lived in, I found a mangled watch, wondered where I had seen it, and knew a few hours later that it was the watch I had bought in the Zurich airport and that had disappeared a short time after I gave it to Helen. The answer now was easy. She never walked much because her legs hurt. Sam had brought it down to the beach and she didn't want to tell me that my dog, who loved her but didn't love me, could have done anything for which he could be blamed.

From the night of that rainstorm in Cambridge, for

weeks later, and even now, once in a while, I have dreamed of Sophronia and Helen, waking up sometimes so pleased that I try to go on with a dream that denies their death, at other times saddened by the dream because it seems a deep time-warning of my own age and death. When that happens, in argument with myself, I feel guilty because I did not know about Sophronia's death for two years after it happened, and had not forced Helen into the hospital that might have saved her. In fact, I had only been angry at her stubborn refusal to go. How often Helen had made me angry, but with Sophronia nothing had ever been bad . . . But the answer there is easy: Sophronia was the anchor for a little girl, the beloved of a young woman, but by the time I had met the other, years had brought acid to a nature that hadn't begun that way — or is that a lie? — and in any case, what excuse did that give for irritation with a woman almost twenty years older than I, swollen in the legs and feet, marrow-weary with the struggle to live, bewildered, resentful, sometimes irrational in a changing world where the old, real-pretend love for white people forced her now into open recognition of the hate and contempt she had brought with her from South Carolina. She had not, could not have, guessed this conflict would ever come to more than the sad talk of black people over collard greens and potlikker, but now here it was on Harlem streets, in newspapers and churches, and how did you handle what you didn't understand except with the same martyr discipline that made you work when you were sick, made you try to forgive what you really never forgave, made you take a harsh nature and force it into words of piety that, in time, became almost true piety.

Why had these two women come together as one for me? Sophronia had not been like that.

I don't know what year Helen came to work for me. We never agreed about the time, although when we felt most affectionate or tired we would argue about it. But it was, certainly, a long time ago. The first months had been veiled and edgy: her severe face, her oppressive silences made me think she was angry, and my nature, alternating from vagueness to rigid demands, made her unhappy, she told me years later. (She did not say it that way: she said, "It takes a searching wind to find the tree you sit in.")

Then one day, at the end of the first uncomfortable months, she said she was grateful, most deeply. I didn't know what she meant, didn't pay much attention, except that I knew she had grown affectionate toward me, even indulgent. Shortly after, she brought me three hundred dollars done up in tissue paper with a weary former Christmas ribbon. I asked her what it was, she said please to count it, I asked her what it was, she said please to count it, I counted it, handed it back, she handed it back to me and said it was the return of the loan for her daughter. I said I didn't know what she was talking about. Her face changed to angry sternness as she said, "I want no charity. I pay my just debts, Miss Hellman. Mr. Hammett must have told you I said that to him."

Hammett hadn't told me she said anything, but it turned out that one night when he had come from the country to have dinner with me, and found he was too tired to return to the country — it was the early period of emphysema — he decided to spend the night in the library. He had been reading at about three in the morning when the phone rang and a frightened voice said there was an emergency, was it possible to call Helen? He had climbed four flights of steps to fetch her, and when she had finished with the phone she said her niece or her daughter or somebody-or-other had had a terrible accident and she would have to go immediately. He asked her if she needed money and, after the long wait she always took when pride was involved, she asked him for taxi money.

Hammett had said, "What about money for the hospital?"

She had said, "Black people don't have it easy in a hospital."

He had said, "I know. So a check won't do you any good. You'd better have cash."

I said to Hammett, "But what's this got to do with me?"

He said, "It's your money she's returning. I took it out of the safe."

He told me how disturbed she had been when he had opened my safe and so he had said, "Don't worry. It's O.K. There's no sense waking Miss Hellman because she can't learn how to open the safe and that makes her angry."

For many years after, whenever I tried to open the safe, she would come as close to mirth as ever I saw her, saying always that I wasn't to get disturbed, she thought my fingers were too thin for such work, and then always reminding me of the night Hammett gave her the money, "before he even knew me, that is a Christian man."

I said to him, "Helen thinks you're a Christian man."

"Sure. She's a convert to my ex-church. We teach 'em to talk like that."

253

"I won't tell her that. She might not like you."

"I won't find that too tough."

"But I'm worried that she might think you don't like her."

"I don't like her."

He didn't like her and he was the only person I ever met who didn't. Sometimes he would say it was because she spoke rudely to me. (He was right: when she didn't feel well, she often did.) Sometimes he would say he couldn't stand Catholic converts, or overbig women, or he would complain that she was the only Negro in America who couldn't carry a tune. Even through the last four and a half years of his life, when he had come to live in the house and when she, a woman older than he by a number of years I never knew, would climb the steps with endless trays or mail or books or just to ask if there was anything he wanted, he never said anything more to her than "Good morning," or "Thank you," or, on special occasions, "It looks like a pleasant day." I think it is possible that the two of them, obsessed with pride and dignity, one of the more acceptable forms of self-love, but self-love nevertheless, had come face to face with a reflection and one of them didn't like what he saw in the mirror.

Other people always came, in time, to like her and admire her, although her first impression on them was not always pleasant. The enormous figure, the stern face, the few, crisp words did not seem welcoming as she opened a door or offered a drink, but the greatest clod among them came to understand the instinctive good taste, the high-bred manners that once they flowered gave off so much true courtesy. And, in this period of nobody grows older or fatter, your mummie looks like your girl, there may be a need in many of us for the large, strong woman who takes us back to what most of us always wanted and few of us ever had.

It is difficult to date anything between people when they have lived together long enough, and so I can't remember when I knew, forgot, knew, doubted, and finally understood that her feelings for white people and black people were too complex to follow, because what had been said on one day would be denied on the next. In the early years, when she told me of the white family in whose house she had been raised in Charleston, her mother having been the cook there, I would dislike the Uncle-Tomism of the memories, and often when the newspapers carried a new indignity from the South we would both cluck about it, but she would turn away from my anger with talk about good and bad among white people, and she had only known the good. During the University of Mississippi mess, I asked her what she meant by good whites, good to her?

She said, "There's too much hate in this world."

I said, "Depends on where you carry the hate, doesn't it, what it's made of, how you use it?"

She shrugged. "I ain't ever hated."

I said, too fast, "Yes, you have. You just don't know it —" and stopped right before I said, You often hate me, I've known it for years and let you have it as a debt I wouldn't pay anybody else but Sophronia.

Oh, Sophronia, it's you I want back always. It's by you I still so often measure, guess, transmute, translate and act. What strange process made a little girl strain so hard to hear the few words that ever came, made the image of you, true or false, last a lifetime? I think my father knew about that very early, because five or six years after I was separated from Sophronia by our move to New York, when I saw her only during our yearly visits to New Orleans, he shouted at me one night, "To hell with Sophronia. I don't want to hear about her anymore."

That night started in Montgomery, Alabama, although why or how we got to Montgomery I no longer remember. My father had, among other eccentricities, an inability to travel from one place to another in a conventional line; if it was possible to change trains or make a detour, he arranged it. And since we traveled a great deal between New York and New Orleans, stopping for business or for friends, we were often to be found in railroad stations waiting for a train that would take us out of our way.

I had been sleeping on a bench that night in Montgomery, Alabama, so I don't know when I first saw the three figures — a young, very thin Negro girl, and two white men. The men were drunk, my father said later, and maybe that accounted for the awkward, shaggy movements, their sudden twists and turns. The girl would move to a bench, sit, rise as the men came toward her, move to a wall, rest, slide along it as the men came near, try for another bench, circle it, and move fast when they moved fast. She was trying to stay within the station lights and, as the train came in, she ran down the platform toward it. But she miscalculated and ran outside the lights. I saw one of the men light matches and move in the darkness. When he caught the girl he put the lighted matches to her arm before he kissed her. The girl dropped her valise and there was the noise of glass breaking. I have no clear memory of the next few minutes until I heard my father say, "Let the girl alone." Then he hit the man and the other man hit my father, but he didn't seem hurt because he picked the girl up and shoved her up the steps of the train, came running back for me, shoved me up the steps of the train, got in himself and suddenly began to yell, "My God, where is your mother?" My mother was on the ground repacking the girl's valise. The two men were running toward her but she smiled and waved at my father and put up her hand in a gesture to quiet him. She had trouble with the lock of the valise but she seemed unhurried about fixing it. My father was halfway down the train steps when she rose, faced the two men and said, "Now you just step aside, boys, and take yourselves on home." I don't know whether it was the snobbery of the word "boys" or the accents of her native Alabama, but they made no motion as she came aboard the train.

The girl was invited to share our basket supper and she and my mother spent the next few hours speaking about the nature of men. I went into the corridor to find my bored father.

Like most other children, I had learned you usually got further by pretending innocence. "What did 'those men want to do with the girl?"

When he didn't answer, I said, "Rape, that's what. You're a hero. Sophronia will be pleased."

His voice was loud and angry. "To hell with Sophronia. I don't want to hear about her anymore."

A few days later, sitting on a bench in Audubon Park,

while the two small boys she now nursed played near us, I told Sophronia the story. When she didn't speak, I said, "Papa was brave, wasn't he?"

"Yep."

"What's the matter?"

"Things not going to get themselves fixed by one white man being nice to one nigger girl."

I thought hard and long about that, as I thought about everything she said, and by the next year's visit to New Orleans I had decided on a course for myself. Sophronia and I had gone to the movies and were returning home on a streetcar. We had always moved back to sit in the Negro section of the car, but this time I sat in the front directly behind the driver and pulled her down next to me. She whispered to me, I whispered back, she half rose, I pulled her down, and she sat still for a minute waiting for me to grow quiet. The conductor had evidently been watching us, because he turned his head.

"Back."

I held so tight to her arm that she couldn't move.

He said, "Get back in the car. You know better than this."

I said, my voice high with fright, "We won't. We won't move. This lady is better than you are —"

And the car came to a sudden jolt in the middle of the street. People rose and an old woman moved toward us. The conductor opened the doors.

Sophronia got to her feet and I screamed, "Come back, Sophronia, don't you dare move. You're better than anybody, anybody —" and the old lady slapped me as the conductor took my arm. I was carrying a book bag and

I threw it at him, turned to push the old lady, turned back to find Sophronia. She had moved between me and the conductor, who looked more surprised than angry. Now she grabbed my arm and pulled me into the street.

I said, "Let's run."

She said, "You run. I'm past the runnin' age."

So we stood together, staring up at the streetcar, waiting for what we did not know. Then the car started up and moved away from us. I was crying as we walked together toward my aunts' house.

After a while she said, "Crybaby."

"I did wrong?"

It was an old question and she had always had a song for it:

> *Right is wrong and wrong is right*
> *And who can tell it all by sight?*

I said, "Sophronia, I want to go away with you for always, right now. I've thought a lot about it all year and I've made up my mind. I want to live with you the rest of my life. I won't live with white people any-more —"

She put her hand over my mouth. When she took it away, I knew she was very angry. She said, "I got something to tell you, missy. There are too many niggers who like white people. Then there are too many white people think they like niggers. You just be careful."

She crossed the street and was gone before I could move. Sleepless that night and miserable the next day, I went on the second day to find her in Audubon Park.

I said, "Aren't you going to see me anymore?"

She said, "I got a no good daughter and a no good son."

I had heard this from my mother, but I didn't know then, and I don't know now, what no good meant to her, and so I waited. We sat without speaking on the park bench watching one little red-haired brother push the other off a tricycle.

She called out, "Stanley. Hugh," and the fight stopped immediately.

After a while, I said, "Aren't you going to see me anymore?"

"You're growing up, a few years away. Time's approachin' to straighten things out."

"You mean I'm no good, either?"

She turned her head and looked at me as if she were puzzled. "I mean you got to straighten things out in your own head. Then maybe you goin' to be some good and pleasure me. But if they keep on pilin' in silly and gushin' out worse, you goin' to be trouble, and you ain't goin' to pleasure me and nobody else."

Many years later, I came to understand that all she meant was that I might blow up my life with impulsiveness or anger or jealousy or all the other things that she thought made a mess, but that day, in my thirteenth year, I shivered at the contempt with which she spoke. (And there I was not wrong. I came to know as she grew older and I did, too, that she did feel a kind of contempt for the world she lived in and for almost everybody, black or white, she had ever met, but that day I thought it was only for me.)

I got up from the bench in maybe the kind of pain you

feel when a lover has told you that not only does the love not exist anymore, but that it possibly never existed at all.

I said, "You mean I am no good and you don't want to see me anymore. Well, I won't hang around and bother you —"

She got slowly to her feet. "You all I got, baby, all I'm goin' to have."

Then she leaned down and kissed me. She hadn't kissed me, I think, since I was three or four years old. Certainly I have had happier minutes since, but not up to then. We shook hands and I went back to the park bench the next day.

There has always been a picture of Sophronia in my house, all of them taken with me as a young child. Some years after Helen came to work for me, I came into the library to find her with one of the pictures in her hand.

I said, "My nurse, my friend. Handsome woman, wasn't she?"

"You look like a nice little girl."

"Maybe I was, but nobody thought so. I was trouble."

"She didn't think so."

I took the picture from Helen and, for the first time in the forty years since it had been taken, saw the affection the woman had for the child she stood behind.

I said, "It takes me too long to know things."

"What?"

"Nothing. I hadn't seen her for two years before she died."

"You didn't go to the funeral?"

"I didn't know she died. Her daughter didn't tell me."

"She was a light-skinned woman?"

I know about that question, I've known about it all my life.

"Yes, very. But she didn't use it, if that's what you mean."

"How old was she?"

"In the picture? I don't know. I — my God. She couldn't have been thirty. I can't believe it, but —"

"Black women get old fast."

"Yes," I said, "watching white women stay young."

"White women never been bad to me."

I was in a sudden bad humor, maybe because she wasn't Sophronia. I said, "Colored women who cook as well as you do never had a bad time. Not even in slavery. You were the darlings of every house. What about the others who weren't?"

She said, "You mean the good house nigger is king boy."

I said, "I mean a house nigger pay no mind to a field hand."

She laughed at the words we had both grown up on. A half hour later I went down to the kitchen for a cup of coffee. She was using an electric beater and so neither of us tried to talk over the noise. Then she turned the beater off and, I think for the first time in her life, raised her voice in a shout.

"You ain't got no right to talk that way. No right at all. Down South, I cook. Nothing else, just cook. For you, I slave. You made a slave of me and you treat me like a slave."

I said, "Helen! Helen!"

"A slave. An old, broken slave."

262

"You're a liar," I said, "just a plain God-damned liar."

"God will punish you for those words."

"He is, right now."

She took a check from her apron pocket — her share of the last royalties from *Toys in the Attic* — tore it up, and held out the pieces to me.

"There. Take it. You think money and presents can buy me, you're wrong."

I said, "I'm going up to Katonah. That will give you a few days to move out."

That night, sitting on a pile of books that had become the only place one could sit in the depressing little cottage filled with furniture broken by the weight of phonograph records and books, ashtrays toppling on the edges of manuscripts, a giant desk loaded with unopened mail that had arrived that day or five years ago, facing a window that had been splintered by the gun of somebody who didn't like his politics, I told Hammett about the afternoon.

He said, "Why do you talk to her about the South?"

"I didn't think she hated me."

"She doesn't. She likes you very much and that scares her, because she hates white people. Every morning some priest or other tells her that's not Christian charity, and she goes home more mixed up than ever."

"I guess so. But I don't care about what she hates or doesn't. I care about what I said to her. I'll wait until she has left and then I'll write and say I'm sorry I screamed liar."

He stared at me and went back to reading. After a

while he said, "You should have screamed at her years ago. But of course you never lose your temper at the right time. Then you feel guilty and are sure to apologize. I've always counted on that, it's never failed."

I said, "All these years, waiting to catch me out."

"Yep. And shall I tell you something else that goes hand in hand, kind of?"

"I am, as you know, grateful for all high-class revelations."

"Well," he said, "when you start out being angry, you're almost always right. But anybody with a small amount of sense learns fast that if they let you go on talking you come around to being wrong. So after you've slammed the door, or taken a plane, or whatever caper you're up to, that fine, upright, liberal little old sense of justice begins to operate and you'll apologize not only for the nonsense part of what you've said but for the true and sensible part as well. It's an easy game — just a matter of patience."

I thanked him and went back to New York. It has long been my habit to enter the house on the bedroom floor, and on that day I did not wish to see the kitchen without Helen, did not wish to face a life without her, so it was four or five hours before I went downstairs. Helen was sitting in a chair, her Bible on the table.

She said, "Good evening. Your hair is wet."

"Yes," I said, "I'm trying to curl it."

We did learn something that day, maybe how much we needed each other, although knowing that often makes relations even more difficult. Our bad times came almost always on the theme of Negroes and whites. The white liberal attitude is, mostly, a well-intentioned fake, and black people should and do think it a sell. But mine was bred, literally, from Sophronia's milk, and thus I thought it exempt from such judgments except when I made the jokes about myself. But our bad times did not spring from such conclusions by Helen — they were too advanced, too unkind for her. They came, I think, because she did not think white people capable of dealing with trouble. I was, thus, an intruder, and in the autumn of 1963 she told me so.

I had gone down to Washington to write a magazine piece about the Washington March. Through Negro friends, through former Harvard students, through a disciple of Malcolm X, I had arranged to meet the delegations from Louisiana and Alabama. Sophronia's grandson, whom I had never seen, was to arrive with the Alabama delegation. Many years before, I had had letters from his older sister, a teacher at Tuskegee. Now, when I wrote to ask if they would like to come to Washington, she had written back that they could not make the trip. Immediately after, I had a letter from Orin saying that he wanted to come if I would send the bus fare, but please not to tell his sister, because she did not approve. I had sent the money and, as far as I knew, he was on his way.

At seven o'clock on the morning of the March, I was sitting on the steps of the Lincoln Memorial waiting for Orin, wondering if he looked like Sophronia, if he had brought me the photographs I had asked for, if his mother had ever told him much about her. At nine o'clock I went to look for the Alabama delegation. They had been in Washington for six hours, but nobody had heard of Orin and they were sure he had never been on the bus, never signed up to come.

It was, of course, a remarkable day. Two hundred thousand people come to ask only what they thought had been promised, still calm, pleasant and gay in the face of the one-hundred-year-old refusal. But as the day wore on, I felt as if a respectable Madison Avenue funeral had gone on too long. When Martin Luther King rose to speak — and there was no question of the pride the audience felt in the man, no question that he represented all that was gentle and kind in this kindest of people — I remembered too many Negro preachers from my childhood and grew impatient with "I have a dream."

I wandered off looking for something to eat. I dropped my pocketbook, spilled the contents, and was helped by a small colored boy who, when I thanked him, said, "O.K., lady, courtesy of the Commonwealth." I laughed and found that his companion, a tall young Negro, was laughing, too.

I said, "What's that mean, courtesy of the Commonwealth?"

"Nothing," said the young man. "Old George tries to learn a new word every day. We were up around Boston last night so today it will be 'Commonwealth.' "

Old George turned out to be fourteen years old, small for his age, and the young man's name was Gene Carondelet.

I said, "That's the name of a street in New Orleans."

He said, "Yep. That's why I took it."

Old George weaved in and out of the crowd, bringing frankfurters and then coffee, while Carondelet told me he had been in jail seven times for trying to register Negroes in Greenwood, Mississippi, and for leading a march in Baton Rouge. He said he had never seen old

George before McComb, Mississippi, where a policeman had hit George over the head and George's mother had hit the policeman. The next day George's mother said, "Take the boy with you. He's in danger here. Take him and teach him."

"He's been with me for eight months. That George can do, learn anything. Makes a mighty fine speech. Make a speech for the lady."

George rose. "You folks better take your black behinds down to vote your way to freedom. The first correlative to freedom —" At the word "correlative" George grinned at me and sat down, saying he didn't feel too well, he had his headache back again. Carondelet explained that in a few days they were coming to New York to see a doctor about the headaches George had been having since he got hit over the head by the policeman.

About a week later, I came in the house to find Carondelet, George, and a gangly popeyed man of about twenty-four sitting in the living room with Helen. Carondelet said they'd been waiting for an hour and now they had to go because George was on his way to the doctor's. As I took them to the elevator, I did not notice that the strange man was still in the living room until George said, "You wanted him, you got him."

"Who?"

"That Orin something."

Carondelet said, "He's silly stuff."

Orin was, indeed, a dull young man, sleepy, overpolite, as anxious as I was to get the visit over with. He had been born long after Sophronia's death, had no memory of his mother's ever having talked about her. What about his uncle, Sophronia's son? Never heard of him. Where was his mother? She'd skipped long ago, maybe dead, maybe still turning a trick. Why hadn't he come to Washington with the Alabama delegation? They weren't his kind. He'd come to New York, been robbed, lost my address, hadn't eaten, where was the men's room? I pointed toward the kitchen, waited a long time, puzzled and sad that this man should be Sophronia's grandson. When he did come back, I said I had to go to work, and rose to shake his hand. He suddenly began to talk in a more animated way, although the words were now slurred. I had become Miss Hellmar or, more often, "man" in puzzling sentences like "Man, this is some town and they can take me to it any time they got enough, man," and "Man, where them two finkies I come here with, and where is here, just where is here at?" After a while I said I'd get him some money for the trip back home if he wanted to make it, and he began to laugh as I went into the hall to find Helen standing by the door.

She said, "He took a shot in the toilet."

"What do you mean?"

"A no good punkie-junkie. Maybe heroin."

The words were so modern, so unlike her, that I stared, amused and puzzled that there was a side of her I didn't know.

"I don't think so. He's just stupid, and uncomfortable with me."

When I came back down the steps, the phonograph was playing very loudly and Orin was moving around the room. I couldn't hear what Helen said, but his voice was very loud.

"Lady man, I'm stayin' right where I fall, see?"

Helen said, "You a sick boy. You going for a cure, or you going to hell."

"Lady man, hell's my place and you my girl, tired and old. Maybe even have to send you on a little errand soon —"

She crossed to him, pulled his arms behind his back, and stepped to one side as he tried to kick her. She held him easily, gracefully, as she pulled him toward a chair.

She said to me, "Go for a walk," and closed and locked the door.

The following morning she said, "You see, things happen to people."

I didn't answer her, and after an hour or so she appeared again — an old habit, conversation without prelude, in space, from hours or days or months before — "I locked the door 'cause I wanted you out of trouble."

"No," I said. "You just didn't think I'd be any good at it."

"Time I told you what I ain't told you. My daughter, same way, same thing."

After a while I said, "That shouldn't have happened to you."

"No good for colored people to come North, no good," she said. "Live like a slummy, die like one. South got its points, no matter what you think. Even if just trees."

I was never to see or hear from Orin again, but when George got out of the hospital he came to stay with us several times, appearing and disappearing without explanation. There was something odd about his relations with Helen, something teasing on his side, cautious on hers.

269

The next summer he came to stay with us for a few days on the Vineyard. He was romping with the poodle on the lawn outside her window, while I read on the porch above their heads.

He said to her, "Hey, Mrs. Jackson, your poodle got fleas."

"Lot of people got fleas," she said.

After a long pause, George called out, "I've been thinking about what you said, and I'm God-damned if I understand it."

"You been sleepin' here, Miss Hellman been sleepin' here. That's all I got to say."

George screamed with laughter. "You mean *we* give the dog the fleas? You some far-out lady, Mrs. Jackson." And a door slammed.

At dinner, a few weeks later, he said to Helen, "Could I have a piece of your cornbread?"

"Where you see cornbread?"

"Why you hide it where you do?"

It had long been her habit to hide any food that was fattening on the pretense that she ate very little and thus had inherited her "fat glands." Now she opened the stove, reached far back into the oven, and slammed down on the table a giant cornbread cake and a pot of greens and fatback.

. "Can I have some," I said, knowing he had made a bad mistake — "nothing in the world like potlikker and corn —"

She said to George, "What you do all day, besides snoopin'? You know more about this island than we ever find out, or want to."

"Sure do," said George, "that my job. Got to find out

before you organize. You, for example. Find out all about you being like crazy with your money. You got so much money, give it to SNCC instead of wasting it on that no good Almira family down in town."

Helen said, softly, "Eat your dinner, son."

George said to me, "Old man Almira leave his family for a fourteen-year-old girl, and Mrs. Jackson here, that makes her sad, so she send money all year round, *all year round*, to the wife and kiddies —"

Helen said, "No good men, that's what you all are."

George said, "And no good kiddies. You some fine picker, Mrs. Jackson. The Almira boy was the one set the fire last week and the girl whores all over the Cape."

"You lie, boy, and you a mighty dirty talker about your own people."

"First," said George, "they ain't my people 'cause they ain't all black, they part Portuguese. Two, bums is bums, forget the color. Three, a revolutionary got no right to defend the baddies even of his own color, kind or faith. Otherwise it comes about —"

I said, "Oh, shut up, George," and Helen hit me on the arm, an old sign of affectionate approval.

George came to visit us the next summer for a few days but I did not see him at all in 1965, until the cold autumn day of Helen's funeral. That night, quite late, he rang the bell, a small suitcase in his hand.

He said, "I wouldn't have come like this, but I'm going back to Atlanta, and I wanted to — Well, I don't know."

We talked for a while about what he'd been doing, where he'd been, and then he said, "You're worried, Miss Hellman."

"Yes," I said, "if that's the word."

"About the funeral. They didn't come to you?"

"I guess that's part of it, but not much. No, they didn't come to me, although they telephoned, the two nieces, and the daughter I'd never heard from before. They asked me what kind of funeral I wanted, but I didn't like to intrude, or maybe — I don't know."

"Stinking funeral."

I said, "It's hard to know what strong people would want. I've been there before. You think they're trying to tell you something, forbid you something, but you don't know —"

"Ah," he said, "the one thing they knew for sure was she didn't want that coffin, all done up for a bishop, with brass. Seventeen hundred dollars."

"My God, I didn't know that. What fools — Well, at least I talked them into burying her in South Carolina. That I know she wanted."

"It's my birthday," George said, so we had two drinks. When he got up to leave he said, "Don't worry about the funeral or the coffin. It's done, done."

"That's not what's worrying me. She got sick on Monday. I wanted her to go to the hospital. She wanted to go home. I was annoyed with her and went for a walk. When I came back she was gone. I phoned the next day and she said she was better, but might not be able to work for a while, and then as if she wanted to tell me something. The next morning she was dead."

"She did want to tell you something. She was getting ready to die."

I said, "You know too much, George, too much you're sure of. I don't believe she knew she was going to die. I won't believe it. And how do you know how much the coffin cost?"

"They told me," he said. "On Tuesday morning, Mrs. Jackson asked me to come round."

"She asked you, she didn't ask me. I'm jealous, George."

"She had things for me to do, errands."

I said, "She always had people doing secret errands. I didn't know you saw each other."

"Oh, sure, whenever I came up North, and then I always wrote to her. My second operation, I stayed in her place till I was better."

"You didn't tell me you had a second operation."

He smiled. "Anyway, there I am on Tuesday. She shows me two Savings Bank things and says they're for her grandchildren. Then she give me orders to pack her clothes and take 'em to the post office, all of them except one dress and shoes."

"Where did she send them?"

"Somebody in Augusta, Georgia. Then I take around the TV radio set and I sell that for her. When I come back, she asked me to make her a lemonade and said she wanted to sleep. I said I'd be back at night, but she said not to come, she wanted rest. Then she gave me one hundred dollars. Eighty-five for me, she said, or wherever I wanted to give it. Fifteen for Orin when I found him."

"*Orin? Orin?*"

"He's still hanging around. She always gave him a little money. But he ain't going to get this fifteen, 'cause I ain't going to find him. She was some far-out lady, Mrs. Jackson. Some far-out Christian lady."

"Sure was," I said.

"I hope you feel better," he said. "Next time I'm here, I'll come see you."

But he never has come to see me again.

16

Dashiell Hammett

For years we made jokes about the day I would write about him. In the early years, I would say, "Tell me more about the girl in San Francisco. The silly one who lived across the hall in Pine Street."

And he would laugh and say, "She lived across the hall in Pine Street and was silly."

"Tell more than that. How much did you like her and how — ?"

He would yawn. "Finish your drink and go to sleep."

But days later, maybe even that night, if I was on the find-out kick, and I was, most of the years, I would say, "O.K., be stubborn about the girls. So tell me about your grandmother and what you looked like as a baby."

"I was a very fat baby. My grandmother went to the movies every afternoon. She was very fond of a movie star called Wallace Reid and I've told you all this before."

I would say I wanted to get everything straight for the days after his death when I would write his biography and he would say that I was not to bother writing his biography because it would turn out to be the history of Lillian Hellman with an occasional reference to a friend called Hammett.

The day of his death came on January 10, 1961. I will never write that biography because I cannot write about my closest, my most beloved friend. And maybe, too, because all those questions through all the thirty-one on and off years, and the sometime answers, got muddled, and life changed for both of us and the questions and answers became one in the end, flowing together from the days when I was young to the days when I was middle-aged. And so this will be no attempt at a biography of Samuel Dashiell Hammett, born in St. Mary's County, Maryland, on May 27, 1894. Nor will it be a critical appraisal of his work. In 1966 I edited and published a collection of his stories. There was a day when I thought all of them very good. But all of them are not good, though most of them, I think, are very good. It is only right to say immediately that by publishing them at all I did what Hammett did not want to do: he turned down all offers to republish the stories, although I never knew the reason and never asked. I did know, from what he said about "Tulip," the unfinished novel that I included in the book, that he meant to start a new literary life and maybe didn't want the old work to get in the way. But sometimes I think he was just too ill to care, too worn out to listen to plans or read contracts. The fact of breathing, just breathing, took up all the days and nights.

In the First World War, in camp, influenza led to tuberculosis and Hammett was to spend years after in army hospitals. He came out of the Second World War with emphysema, but how he ever got into the Second World War at the age of forty-eight still bewilders me. He telephoned me the day the army accepted him to say it was the happiest day of his life, and before I could finish saying it wasn't the happiest day of mine and what about the old scars on his lungs, he laughed and hung up. His death was caused by cancer of the lungs, discovered only two months before he died. It was not operable — I doubt that he would have agreed to an operation even if it had been — and so I decided not to tell him about the cancer. The doctor said that when the pain came, it would come in the right chest and arm, but that the pain might never come. The doctor was wrong: only a few hours after he told me, the pain did come. Hammett had had self-diagnosed rheumatism in the right arm and had always said that was why he had given up hunting. On the day I heard about the cancer, he said his gun shoulder hurt him again, would I rub it for him. I remember sitting behind him, rubbing the shoulder and hoping he would always think it was rheumatism and remember only the autumn hunting days. But the pain never came again, or if it did he never mentioned it, or maybe death was so close that the shoulder pain faded into other pains.

He did not wish to die and I like to think he didn't know he was dying. But I keep from myself even now the possible meaning of a night, very late, a short time before his death. I came into his room, and for the only time in the years I knew him there were tears in his eyes and the book was lying unread. I sat down beside him and

277

waited a long time before I could say, "Do you want to talk about it?"

He said, almost with anger, "No. My only chance is not to talk about it."

And he never did. He had patience, courage, dignity in those last, awful months. It was as if all that makes a man's life had come together to prove itself: suffering was a private matter and there was to be no invasion of it. He would seldom even ask for anything he needed, and so the most we did — my secretary and Helen, who were devoted to him, as most women always had been — was to carry up the meals he barely touched, the books he now could hardly read, the afternoon coffee, and the martini that I insisted upon before the dinner that wasn't eaten.

One night of that last year, a bad night, I said, "Have another martini. It will make you feel better."

"No," he said, "I don't want it."

I said, "O.K., but I bet you never thought I'd urge you to have another drink."

He laughed for the first time that day. "Nope. And I never thought I'd turn it down."

Because on the night we had first met he was getting over a five-day drunk and he was to drink very heavily for the next eighteen years, and then one day, warned by a doctor, he said he would never have another drink and he kept his word except for the last year of the one martini, and that was my idea.

We met when I was twenty-four years old and he was thirty-six in a restaurant in Hollywood. The five-day drunk had left the wonderful face looking rumpled, and the very tall thin figure was tired and sagged. We talked of T. S. Eliot, although I no longer remember what we said, and then went and sat in his car and talked at each other and over each other until it was daylight. We were to meet again a few weeks later and, after that, on and sometimes off again for the rest of his life and thirty years of mine.

Thirty years is a long time, I guess, and yet as I come now to write about them the memories skip about and make no pattern and I know only certain of them are to be trusted. I know about that first meeting and the next, and there are many other pictures and sounds, but they are out of order and out of time, and I don't seem to want to put them into place. (I could have done a research job, I have on other people, but I didn't want to do one on Hammett, or to be a bookkeeper of my own life.) I don't want modesty for either of us, but I ask myself now if it can mean much to anybody but me that my second sharpest memory is of a day when we were living on a small island off the coast of Connecticut. It was six years after we had first met: six full, happy, unhappy years during which I had, with help from Hammett, written *The Children's Hour*, which was a success, and *Days to Come*, which was not. I was returning from the mainland in a catboat filled with marketing and Hammett had come down to the dock to tie me up. He had been sick that summer — the first of the sicknesses — and he was even thinner than usual. The white hair, the white pants, the white shirt made a straight, flat surface in the late sun. I thought: Maybe that's the handsomest sight I ever saw, that line of a man, the knife for a nose, and the sheet went out of my hand and the wind went out of the sail. Hammett laughed as I struggled to get back the sail. I don't know why, but I yelled angrily, "So you're a Dostoevsky sinner-saint. So you are." The laughter stopped, and when I finally came in to the dock we didn't speak as we carried up the packages and didn't speak through dinner.

Later that night, he said, "What did you say that for? What does it mean?"

I said I didn't know why I had said it and I didn't know what it meant.

Years later, when his life had changed, I did know what I had meant that day: I had seen the sinner — whatever is a sinner — and sensed the change before it came. When I told him that, Hammett said he didn't know what I was talking about, it was all too religious for him. But he did know what I was talking about and he was pleased.

But the fat, loose, wild years were over by the time we talked that way. When I first met Dash he had written four of the five novels and was the hottest thing in Hollywood and New York. It is not remarkable to be the hottest thing in either city — the hottest kid changes for each winter season — but in his case it was of extra interest to those who collect people that the ex-detective who had bad cuts on his legs and an indentation in his head from being scrappy with criminals was gentle in manner, well educated, elegant to look at, born of early settlers, was eccentric, witty, and spent so much money on women that they would have liked him even if he had been none of the good things. But as the years passed from 1930 to 1948, he wrote only one novel and a few short stories. By 1945, the drinking was no longer gay, the drinking bouts were longer and the moods darker. I was there off and on for most of those years, but in 1948 I didn't want to see the drinking anymore. I hadn't seen or spoken to Hammett for two months until the day when his devoted cleaning lady called to say she thought I had better come down to his apartment. I said I wouldn't, and then I did. She and I dressed a man who could barely lift an arm or a leg and brought him to my house, and that night I watched delirium tremens, although I didn't know what I was watching until the doctor told me the next day at the hospital. The doctor was an old friend. He said, "I'm going to tell Hammett that if he goes on drinking he'll be dead in a few months. It's my duty to say it, but it won't do any good." In a few minutes he came out of Dash's room and said, "I told him. Dash said O.K., he'd go on the wagon forever, but he can't and he won't."

But he could and he did. Five or six years later, I told Hammett that the doctor had said he wouldn't stay on the wagon.

Dash looked puzzled. "But I gave my word that day."

"I said, "Have you always kept your word?"

"Most of the time," he said, "maybe because I've so seldom given it."

He had made up honor early in his life and stuck with his rules, fierce in the protection of them. In 1951 he went to jail because he and two other trustees of the bail bond fund of the Civil Rights Congress refused to reveal the names of the contributors to the fund. The truth was that Hammett had never been in the office of the Congress, did not know the name of a single contributor.

The night before he was to appear in court, I said, "Why don't you say that you don't know the names?"

"No," he said, "I can't say that."

"Why?"

"I don't know why. I guess it has something to do with keeping my word, but I don't want to talk about that. Nothing much will happen, although I think we'll go to jail for a while, but you're not to worry because" — and then suddenly I couldn't understand him because the voice had dropped and the words were coming in a most untypical nervous rush. I said I couldn't hear him, and he raised his voice and dropped his head. "I hate this damn kind of talk, but maybe I better tell you that if it were more than jail, if it were my life, I would give it for what I think democracy is, and I don't let cops or judges tell me what I think democracy is." Then he went home to bed, and the next day he went to jail.

July 14, 1965

It is a lovely summer day. Fourteen years ago on another lovely summer day the lawyer Hammett said he didn't need, didn't want, but finally agreed to talk to because it might make me feel better, came back from West Street jail with a message from Hammett that the lawyer had written on the back of an old envelope. "Tell Lilly to go away. Tell her I don't need proof she loves me and don't want it." And so I went to Europe, and wrote a letter almost every day, not knowing that about one letter in ten was given to him, and never getting a letter from him because he wasn't allowed to write to anybody who wasn't related to him. (Hammett had, by this time, been moved to a federal penitentiary in West Virginia.) I had only one message that summer: that his prison job was cleaning bathrooms, and he was cleaning them better than I had ever done.

I came back to New York to meet Hammett the night he came out of jail. Jail had made a thin man thinner, a sick man sicker. The invalid figure was trying to walk proud, but coming down the ramp from the plane he was holding tight to the railing, and before he saw me he stumbled and stopped to rest. I guess that was the first time I knew he would now always be sick. I felt too bad to say hello, and so I ran back into the airport and we lost each other for a few minutes. But in a week, when he had slept and was able to eat small amounts of food, an irritating farce began and was to last for the rest of his life: jail wasn't bad at all. True, the food was awful and sometimes even rotted, but you could always have milk; the moonshiners and car thieves were dopes but their conversation was no sillier than a New York cocktail party; nobody liked cleaning toilets, but in time you came to take a certain pride in the work and an interest in the different cleaning materials; jail homosexuals were nasty-tempered, but no worse than the ones in any bar, and so on. Hammett's form of boasting was always to make fun of trouble or pain. We had once met Howard Fast on the street and he told us about his to-be-served jail sentence. As we moved away, Hammett said, "It will be easier for you, Howard, and you won't catch cold, if you first take off the crown of thorns." So I should have guessed that Hammett would talk about his own time in jail the way many of us talk about college.

I do not wish to avoid the subject of Hammett's political beliefs, but the truth is that I do not know if he was a

member of the Communist party and I never asked him.
If that seems an odd evasion between two people we did
not mean it as an evasion: it was, probably, the product
of the time we lived through and a certain unspoken
agreement about privacy. Now, in looking back, I think
we had rather odd rules about privacy, unlike other
peoples' rules. We never, for example, asked each other
about money, how much something cost or how much
something earned, although each of us gave to the other
as, through the years, each of us needed it. It does not
matter much to me that I don't know if Hammett was a
Communist party member: most certainly he was a Marxist. But he was a very critical Marxist, often contemptuous of the Soviet Union in the same hick sense that many
Americans are contemptuous of foreigners. He was often
witty and biting sharp about the American Communist
party, but he was, in the end, loyal to them. Once, in an
argument with me, he said that of course a great deal
about Communism worried him and always had and that
when he found something better he intended to change his
opinions. And then he said, "Now please don't let's ever
argue about it again because we're doing each other
harm." And so we did not argue again, and I suppose
that itself does a kind of harm or leaves a moat too large
for crossing, but it was better than the arguments we had
been having — they had started in the 1940's — when he
knew that I could not go his way. I think that must have
pained him, but he never said so. It pained me, too, but
I knew that, unlike many radicals, whatever he believed
in, whatever he had arrived at, came from reading and
thinking. He took time to find out what he thought, and
he had an open mind and a tolerant nature.

Hammett came from a generation of talented writers. The ones I knew were romantic about being writers: it was a good thing to be, a writer, maybe the best, and you made sacrifices for it. I guess they wanted money and praise as much as writers do today, but I don't think the diseased need was as great, nor the poison as strong. You wanted to have money, of course, but you weren't in competition with merchants or bankers, and if you threw your talents around you didn't throw them to the Establishment for catching. When I first met Dash he was throwing himself away on Hollywood parties and New York bars: the throwing away was probably no less damaging but a little more forgivable because those who were there to catch could have stepped from *The Day of the Locust.* But he knew what was happening to him, and after 1948 it was not to happen again. It would be good to say that as his life changed the productivity increased, but it didn't. Perhaps the vigor and the force had been dissipated. But good as it is, productivity is not the only proof of a serious life, and now, more than ever, he sat down to read. He read everything and anything. He didn't like writers very much, he didn't like or dislike most people, but he was without envy of good writers and was tender about all writers, probably because he remembered his own early struggles.

I don't know when Hammett first decided to write, but I know that he started writing after he left army hospitals in the 1920's, settling with his wife and daughter — there was to be another daughter — in San Francisco. (He went back to work for Pinkerton for a while, although I am not sure if it was this period or later.) Once, when I asked him why he never wanted to go to

Europe, why he never wanted to see another country, he said he had wanted to go to Australia, maybe to stay, but on the day he decided to leave Pinkerton forever he decided to give up the idea of Australia forever. An Australian boat, out of Sydney for San Francisco, carrying two hundred thousand dollars in gold, notified its San Francisco insurance broker that the gold was missing. The insurance company was a client of Pinkerton's, and so Hammett and another operative met the boat as it docked, examined all sailors and officers, searched the boat, but couldn't find the gold. They knew the gold had to be on the boat, and so the agency decided that when the boat sailed home Hammett should sail with it. A happy man, going free where he had always dreamed of going, packed his bags. A few hours before sailing time, the head of the agency suggested they give a last, hopeless search. Hammett climbed a smokestack he had examined several times before, looked down and shouted, "They moved it. It's here." He said that as the words came out of his mouth, he said to himself, "You haven't sense enough even to be a detective. Why couldn't you have discovered the gold one day out to sea?" He fished out the gold, took it back to the Pinkerton office, and resigned that afternoon.

With the resignation came a series of jobs, but I don't remember what he said they were. In a year or so, the tuberculosis started to cut up again and hemorrhages began. He was determined not to go back to army hospitals, and since he thought he had a limited amount of time to live, he decided to spend it on something he wanted to do. He moved away from his wife and children, lived on soup, and began to write. One day the hemorrhages stopped, never to reappear, and sometime in this period he began to earn a small living from pulp magazines and squibs and even poems sold to Mencken's *Smart Set*. I am not clear about this time of Hammett's life, but it always sounded rather nice and free and 1920's Bohemian, and the girl on Pine Street and the other on Grant Street, and good San Francisco food in cheap restaurants, and dago red wine, and fame in the pulp magazine field, then and maybe now a world of its own.

July 18, 1965

This memory of Hammett is being written in the summer. Maybe that's why most of what I remember about him has to do with summer, although like all people who live in the country, we were more closely thrown together in winter. Winter was the time of work for me and I worked better if Hammett was in the room. There he was, is, as I close my eyes and see another house, reading *The Autumn Garden*. I was, of course, nervous as I watched him. He had always been critical, I was used to that and wanted it, but now I sensed something new and was worried. He finished the play, came across the room, put the manuscript in my lap, went back to his chair and began to talk. It was not the usual criticism: it was sharp and angry, snarling. He spoke as if I had betrayed him. I was so shocked, so pained that I would not now remember the scene if it weren't for a diary that I've kept for each play. He said that day, "You started as a serious writer. That's what I liked, that's what I worked for. I don't know what's happened, but tear this up and throw it away. It's worse than bad — it's half

287

good." He sat glaring at me and I ran from the room and went down to New York and didn't come back for a week. When I did come back I had torn up the play, put the scraps in a briefcase, put the briefcase outside his door. We never mentioned the play again until seven months later when I had rewritten it. I was no longer nervous as he read it: I was too tired to care and I went to sleep on the couch. I woke up because Hammett was sitting beside me, patting my hair, grinning at me and nodding.

After he had nodded for a long time, I said, "What's the matter with you?"

"Nice things. Because it's the best play anybody's written in a long time. Maybe longer. It's a good day. A good day."

I was so shocked with the kind of praise I had never heard before that I started out of the door to take a walk.

He said, "Nix. Come on back. There's a speech in the last act went sour. Do it again."

I said I wasn't going to do it again. He said O.K., he'd do it, and he did, working all through the night.

When *The Autumn Garden* was in rehearsal Dash came almost every day, even more disturbed than I was that something was happening to the play, life was going out of it, which can and does happen on the stage and once started can seldom be changed.

Yesterday I read three letters he wrote to a friend about his hopes for the play, the rehearsals and the opening. His concern for me and the play was very great, but in time I came to learn that he was good to all writers who needed help, and that the generosity had less to do with the writer than with writing and the pains of writing. I knew, of course, about the generosity long before, but generosity and profligacy often intertwine and it took me a long time to tell them apart.

A few years after I met Dash the large Hollywood money was gone, given away, spent on me who didn't want it and on others who did. I think Hammett was the only person I ever met who really didn't care about money, made no complaints and had no regrets when it was gone. Maybe money is unreal for most of us, easier to give away than things we want. (But I didn't know that then, maybe confused it with showing off.) Once, years later, Hammett bought himself an expensive crossbow at a time when it meant giving up other things to have it. It had just arrived that day and he was testing it, fiddling with it, liking it very much, when friends arrived with their ten-year-old boy. Dash and the boy spent the afternoon with the crossbow and the child's face was awful when he had to leave it. Hammett opened the back door of the car, put in the crossbow, went hurriedly into the house, refusing all cries of "No, no" and such.

When our friends had gone, I said, "Was that necessary? You wanted it so much."

Hammett said, "The kid wanted it more. Things belong to people who want them most."

And thus it was, certainly, with money, and thus the troubles came, and suddenly there were days of no dinners, rent unpaid and so on; there they were, the lean times, no worse than many other people have had, but the contrast of no dinner on Monday and a wine feast on Tuesday made me a kind of irritable he never understood.

When we were very broke, those first years in New

York, Hammett got a modest advance from Knopf and began to write *The Thin Man*. He moved to what was jokingly called the Diplomat's Suite in a hotel run by our friend Nathanael West. It was a new hotel, but Pep West and the depression had managed to run it down immediately. Certainly Hammett's suite had never seen a diplomat, because even the smallest Oriental could not have functioned well in the space. But the rent was cheap, the awful food could be charged, and some part of my idle time could be spent with Pep snooping around the lives of the other rather strange guests. I had known Dash when he was writing short stories, but I had never been around for a long piece of work. Life changed: the drinking stopped, the parties were over. The locking-in time had come and nothing was allowed to disturb it until the book was finished. I had never seen anybody work that way: the care for every word, the pride in the neatness of the typed page itself, the refusal for ten days or two weeks to go out even for a walk for fear something would be lost. It was a good year for me and I learned from it and was, perhaps, frightened by a man who now did not need me. So it was a happy day when I was given half the manuscript to read and was told that I was Nora. It was nice to be Nora, married to Nick Charles, maybe one of the few marriages in modern literature where the man and woman like each other and have a fine time together. But I was soon put back in place — Hammett said I was also the silly girl in the book and the villainess. I don't know now if he was joking, but in those days it worried me: I was very anxious that he think well of me. Most people wanted that from him. Years later, Richard Wilbur said that as you came toward Hammett to shake his hand in the first meeting, you wanted him to approve of you. There are such people and Hammett was one of them. I don't know what makes this quality in certain men — something floating around them that hasn't much to do with who they are or what they've done — but maybe it has to do with reserves so deep that we know we cannot touch them with charm or jokes or favors. It comes out as something more than dignity and shows on the face. In jail the guards called Hammett "sir" and out of jail other people came close to it. One night in the last years of his life, we walked into a restaurant, passing a group of young writers that I knew but he didn't. We stopped and I introduced him: these hip young men suddenly turned into deferential schoolboys and their faces became what they must have been at ten years old. It took me years of teasing to force out of Hammett that he knew what effect he had on many people. Then he told me that when he was fourteen years old and had his first job working for the Baltimore and Ohio Railroad, he had come late to work each day for a week. His employer told him he was fired. Hammett said he nodded, walked to the door, and was called back by a puzzled man who said, "If you give me your word it won't happen again, you can keep the job." Hammett said, "Thank you, but I can't do that." After a silence the man said, "O.K., keep the job anyway." Dash said that he didn't know what was right about what he had done, but he did know that it would always be useful.

When *The Thin Man* was sold to a magazine — most of the big slick magazines had turned it down for being too daring, although what they meant by daring was hard to understand — we got out of New York fast. We got drunk for a few weeks in Miami, then moved on to a primitive fishing camp in the Keys where we stayed through the spring and summer, fishing every day, reading every night. It was a fine year: we found out that we got along best without people, in the country. Hammett, like many Southerners, had a deep feeling for isolated places where there were animals, birds, bugs and sounds. He was easy in the woods, an excellent shot, and later when I bought the farm, he would spend the autumn days in the woods, coming back with birds or rabbits, and then, when the shooting season was over, would spend many winter days sitting on a stool in the woods watching squirrels or beavers or deer, or ice fishing in the lake. (He was, as are most sportsmen, obsessively neat with instruments, and obsessively messy with rooms.) The interests of the day would carry into the nights when he would read *Bees: Their Vision and Language* or *German Gunmakers of the Eighteenth Century* or something on how to tie knots, or inland birds, and then leave such a book for another book on whatever he had decided to learn. It would be impossible now for me to remember all that he wanted to learn, but I remember a long year of study on the retina of the eye; how to play chess in your head; the Icelandic sagas; the history of the snapping turtle; Hegel; would a hearing aid — he bought a very good one — help in detecting bird sounds; then from Hegel, of course, to Marx and Engels straight through; the shore life of the Atlantic; and finally, and for the rest of his life, mathematics. He was more interested in mathematics than in any other subject except baseball. Listening to television or the radio, he would mutter about the plays and the players to me who didn't know the difference between a ball and a bat. Often I would ask him to stop it, and then he would shake his head and say, "All I ever wanted was a docile woman and look what I got," and we would talk about docility, how little for a man to want, and he would claim that only vain or neurotic men needed to have "types" in women — all other men took what they could get.

The hit and miss reading, the picking up of any book, made for a remarkable mind, neat, accurate, respectful of fact. He took a strong and lasting dislike to a man who insisted mackerel were related to herring, and once he left my living room when a famous writer talked without much knowledge of existentialism, refusing to come down to dinner with the writer because, he said, "He's a waste of time. Liars are bores." A neighbor once rang up to ask him how to stop a leak in a swimming pool, and he knew; my farmer's son asked him how to make a pair of snowshoes, and he knew; born a Maryland Catholic (but having long ago left the Church), he knew more about Judaism than I did, and more about New Orleans music, food and architecture than my father, who had grown up there. Once I wanted to know about early glassmaking for windows and was headed for the encyclopedia, but Hammett told me before I got there; he knew a great deal about birds and insects, and for a month he studied the cross-pollination of corn, and for many, many months tried plasma physics. It was more than reading: it was a man at work. Any book would do, or almost any — he was narrowly impatient when I read letters or criticism and would refer to them as my "carrying" books, good only for balancing yourself as you climbed the stairs to bed. It was always strange to me that he liked books so much and had so little interest in the men who wrote them. (There were, of course, exceptions: he liked Faulkner and we had fine drinking nights together during Faulkner's New York visits in the '30's.) Perhaps it is more accurate to say that he had a good time with writers when they talked about books, but would usually leave them when they talked about anything else. He was deeply moved by painting — he himself tried to paint until the last summer of his life when he could no longer stand at an easel, and the last walk we ever took was down the block to the Metropolitan Museum — and by music. But I never remember his liking a painter or a musician, although I do remember his saying that he thought most of them peacocks. He was never uncharitable toward simple people, he was often too impatient with famous people.

There are, of course, many men who are happy in an army, but up to the Second World War I had never known any and didn't want to. I was, therefore, shocked to find that Hammett was one of them. I do not know why an eccentric man who lived more than most Americans by his own standards found the restrictions, the disciplines, and the hard work of an army enlisted man so pleasant and amusing. Maybe a life ruled over by other people solved some of the problems, allowed a place for a man who by himself could not seek out people, maybe gave him a sense of pride that a man of forty-eight could stand up with those half his age; maybe all that, and maybe simply that he liked his country and felt that this was a just war and had to be fought. Whatever Hammett's reasons, the miseries of the Aleutian Islands were not miseries to him. I have many letters describing their beauty and for years he talked of going back to see them again. He conducted a training program there for a while and edited a good army newspaper: the copy was clean, the news was accurate, the jokes were funny. He became a kind of legend in the Alaska-Aleutian army. I have talked to many men who served with him, and have a letter from one of them: "I was a kid then. We all were. The place was awful but there was Hammett, by the time I got there called Pop by some and Grandpop by others, editor of the paper, with far more influence on us, scaring us more in a way than the colonel, although I think he also scared the colonel. . . . I remember best that we'd come into the hut screaming or complaining and he'd be lying on his bunk reading. He'd look up and smile and we'd all shut up. Nobody would go near the bed or disturb him. When money was needed or help he'd hear about it and there he was. He paid for the leave and marriage of one kid. When another of us ran up a scarey bar bill in Nome, he gave the guy who cleaned the Nome toilets money to pay it and say it was his bill if anybody in the army asked him. . . . A lot of kids did more than complain — they went half to nuts. And why not? We had the worst weather in the most desolate hole, no fighting, constant williwaws when you had to crawl to the latrines because if you stood up the wind would take you to Siberia, and an entertainment program which got mixed up between Olivia de Haviland and recordings of W. H. Auden. But the main worry was women. When you'd been there a year all kinds of rumors went around about what happened to you without them. I remember nightly bull sessions in our hut about the dangers of celibacy. Hammett would listen for a while, smile, go back to reading or when the talk got too loud he'd sigh and go to sleep. (Because of the newspaper his work hours started around two A.M.) One night when the session was extra loud crazy and one kid was yelling, Hammett got off his bunk to go to work. The kid yelled, 'What do you think, Pop? *Say something.*' Hammett said, 'O.K. A woman would be nice, but not getting any doesn't cause your teeth or hair to fall out and if you go nuts you'd have gone anyway and if you kiddies don't stop this stuff I'm going to move into another hut and under my bed is a bottle of Scotch so drink it and go to sleep.' Then he walked out to go to work. We got so scared about losing him that we never said another word like that in front of him."

But, as I have said, the years after the war, from 1945 to 1948, were not good years; the drinking grew wilder and there was a lost, thoughtless quality I had never seen before. I knew then that I had to go my own way. I do not mean that we were separated, I mean only that we saw less of each other, were less close to each other. But even in those years there still were wonderful days on the farm of autumn hunting and squirrel pies and sausage making and all the books he read as I tried to write a play. I can see him now, getting up to put a log on the fire and coming over to shake me. He swore that I would always say, "I haven't been sleeping. I've been thinking." He would laugh and say, "Sure. You've been asleep for an hour, but lots of people think best when they're asleep and you're one of them."

In 1952 I had to sell the farm. I moved to New York and Dash rented a small house in Katonah. I went once a week to see him, he came once a week to New York, and we talked on the phone every day. But he wanted to be alone — or so I thought then, but am now not so sure because I have learned that proud men who can ask for nothing may be fine characters, but they are difficult to live with or to understand. In any case, as the years went on he became a hermit, and the ugly little country cottage grew uglier with books piled on every chair and no place to sit, the desk a foot high with unanswered mail. The signs of sickness were all around: now the phonograph was unplayed, the typewriter untouched, the beloved, foolish gadgets unopened in their packages. When I went for my weekly visits we didn't talk much and when he came for his weekly visits to me he was worn out from the short journey.

Perhaps it took me too long to realize that he couldn't live alone anymore, and even after I realized it I didn't know how to say it. One day, immediately after he had made me promise to stop reading "L'il Abner," and I was laughing at his vehemence about it, he suddenly looked embarrassed — he always looked embarrassed when he had something emotional to say — and he said, "I can't live alone anymore. I've been falling. I'm going to a Veterans Hospital. It will be O.K., we'll see each other all the time, and I don't want any tears from you." But there were tears from me, two days of tears, and finally he consented to come and live in my apartment. (Even now, as I write this, I am still angry and amused that he always had to have things on his own terms: a few minutes ago I got up from the typewriter and railed against him for it, as if he could still hear me. I know as little about the nature of romantic love as I knew when I was eighteen, but I do know about the deep pleasure of continuing interest, the excitement of wanting to know what somebody else thinks, will do, will not do, the tricks played and unplayed, the short cord that the years make into rope and, in my case, is there, hanging loose, long after death. I am not sure what Hammett would feel about the rest of these notes about him, but I am sure that he would be pleased that I am angry with him to-day.) And so he lived with me for the last four years of his life. Not all of that time was easy, indeed some of it was very bad, but it was an unspoken pleasure that having come together so many years before, ruined so much, and repaired a little, we had endured. Sometimes I would resent the understated or seldom stated side of us and, guessing death wasn't too far away, I would try for something to have afterwards. One day I said, "We've done fine, haven't we?"

He said, "Fine's too big a word for me. Why don't we just say we've done better than most people?"

On New Year's Eve, 1960, I left Hammett in the care of a pleasant practical nurse and went to spend a few hours with friends. I left their house at twelve-thirty, not knowing that the nurse began telephoning for me a few minutes later. As I came into Hammett's room, he was sitting at his desk, his face as eager and excited as it had been in the drinking days. In his lap was the heavy book of Japanese prints that he had bought and liked many years before. He was pointing to a print and saying to the nurse, "Look at it, darling, it's wonderful." As I came toward him, the nurse moved away, but he caught her hand and kissed it, in the same charming, flirtatious way of the early days, looking up to wink at me. The book was lying upside down and so the nurse didn't need to mumble the word "irrational." From then on — we took him to the hospital the next morning — I never knew and will now not ever know what irrational means. Hammett refused all medication, all aid from nurses and doctors in some kind of mysterious wariness. Before the night of the upside-down book our plan had been to move to Cambridge because I was to teach a seminar at Harvard. An upside-down book should have told me the end had come, but I didn't want to think that way, and so I flew to Cambridge, found a nursing home for Dash, and flew back that night to tell him about it. He said, "But how are we going to get to Boston?" I said we'd take an ambulance and I guess for the first time in his life he said, "That will cost too much." I said, "If it does, then we'll take a covered wagon." He smiled and said, "Maybe that's the way we should have gone places anyway."

And so I felt better that night, sure of a postponement. I was wrong. Before six o'clock the next morning the hospital called me. Hammett had gone into a coma. As I ran across the room toward his bed there was a last sign of life: his eyes opened in shocked surprise and he tried to raise his head. He was never to think again and he died two days later.

But I do not wish to end this book on an elegiac note. It is true that I miss Hammett, and that is as it should be. He was the most interesting man I've ever met. I laugh at what he did say, amuse myself with what he might say, and even this many years later speak to him, often angry that he still interferes with me, still dictates the rules.

But I am not yet old enough to like the past better than the present, although there are nights when I have a passing sadness for the unnecessary pains, the self-made foolishness that was, is, and will be. I do regret that I have spent too much of my life trying to find what I called "truth," trying to find what I called "sense." I never knew what I meant by truth, never made the sense I hoped for. All I mean is that I left too much of me unfinished because I wasted too much time. However.

*T*his piece about Dashiell Hammett was written in 1966 as an introduction to his collection of short stories, "The Big Knockover," and reprinted here for this book. It was the second time I had written about Hammett and was no more difficult than the day I spoke at his funeral. On that cold January day, having arranged the funeral I knew he would not have wanted, I told myself that he would forgive the funeral, if only I spoke about him.

I did not, I do not, ever wish to write about Hammett again, but these many years later, perhaps I should say some things about myself that perhaps I knew and suppressed or maybe never knew at all.

I have liked a fair number of people, half liked many more, and loved very few. Perhaps it was my time and place, as I have written before, to distrust the word "love," and to refuse its use. If too much distrust had penalties, I still prefer the penalties to the wild use of the word "love" in its present fashion.

I did not learn the suspicion of such talk from Hammett. It was there long before I met him: he contributed to it, but not in a way that suited my more romantic nature.

He expected nothing from anybody and I don't think he ever had. I expected too much, and thus was scared to ask anybody for anything for fear of what refusal would do to me. This has only become clear to me because, in the last two years, I now have a physical disability and find my refusal to believe in help sometimes dangerous, sometimes comic, and often without truth. But Dash's disbelief, based on one set of doubts, certainly played into mine, based in a different direction. I understand now that however different were our roots of disbelief, they both sprang from an almost obsessional pride. And this from vanity, that is often a part of pride.

But his distrust of human nature was less primitive, less sentimental than mine. He made no complaints about people: they were what they were, and that was that. When he came out of jail and the Bureau of Internal Revenue took away all that he earned until the day of his death, I made a list of those who owed him money. It was only a partial list, I didn't know many of their names, but my list was long and most of the sums were big. I wrote pleasant letters, explaining the circumstances and asking for repayment. I never finished reading him the letters: he shook his head, "Forget it."

The argument of whether the letters should be sent went on for many weeks — I was driven by something more important than the collection of money — until one day Hammett said, "Please stop that injustice stuff. There is a very good reason for not sending the letters. Nobody will answer them. They are all shits."

"If they are shits," I asked, "then why did you lend them money?"

"Oh, Lilly, because they needed it, or pretended to, which is worse, and because they are shits doesn't mean I have to be."

One night, some years later, I said, "Did you read Kant when you were young?"

"When I could stand him. Why?"

"Is that where you got a lie is 'an annihilation of dignity'?"

He laughed. "I don't think so. I just think lies are boring."

"That won't wash," I said. "You are, under all the past drinking and wild ladies, and foolish spending, and messy junk Bohemia, you are a conventional man with rigid ideas of what is right and wrong."

"Big news," he said, "that I am conventional, but it is you who have the rigid ideas of right and wrong."

And by that time it was I. Most of us in late childhood or early youth are casting into a boiling storm-sea for values, a set of rules, anything to show us a road ahead. Unfortunately, for many of us, no sooner do we come to even a tattered, blown-about conclusion than somebody destroys it with a forceful statement. I clearly remember listening to an argument in college about the moral implications of stealing from Woolworth's. Almost everybody there had done it and was pleased. But one young lady, a religious girl, I think, and one of sweet-faced force, talked for a long time about one kind of stealing being equal to another, all stealing, even from Woolworth's, being the moral invasion of other people's rights, and could even lead to murder for gain. I can't say how many others in that college room were disturbed, *but I never again took anything more than a washrag from a hotel, and to this day it must always be from a hotel in a foreign land.*

Young people are no smarter now than they were in my day, but I have taught so many of them in so many universities that I know they are more grown-up, more formed. I cannot imagine a young woman of twenty-five, which is what I was when I first met Hammett, as uncertain, as noodle-headed as I was. And I would not forgive her if I met her now. If Pascal found God before he sought him, an experience that must be, at the very least, a miracle of time-saving — and I repeated Pascal's words many times in my twenties — then I had sought in good books and trash books and talk and found nothing to believe in. This is tough for a nature given, without knowing it, to absolutes.

The words "right" and "wrong" are so simple-minded as to be silly. But I know no substitutes for the words "right" or "wrong," short of a profound appraisal by a remarkable mind. When I met Hammett, who believed in neither word but had formed a set of principles (and was to go on forming and revising them) by which he stood in eccentric isolation, I had come across what I needed. His rules were not my rules, but sometimes mine met his and we agreed, although that mattered less to me than Hammett's refusal to deviate from his, whatever the dangers or the temptations. I had found somebody who stood by himself, who was himself. For many people that would not be much to find: for me, even when I disagreed, it came at a time when I was going under.

There are people who think I have made too much of Hammett's virtues, but none of them are people who ever met him, although that, of course, does not make them wrong. I think I see him straight although, as the years pass, my judgments become sharper. Oddly enough, as they become sharper, my affection and admiration grow larger. I always guessed, and certainly I now clearly know, that somewhere along the line I could and maybe should have chosen another way, a safer way. On winter Sundays I am sorry that I didn't. The rest of the week, life worked as it did, and I was lucky.

PENTIMENTO

For Peter Feibleman

OLD paint on canvas, as it ages, sometimes becomes transparent. When that happens it is possible, in some pictures, to see the original lines: a tree will show through a woman's dress, a child makes way for a dog, a large boat is no longer on an open sea. That is called pentimento because the painter "repented," changed his mind. Perhaps it would be as well to say that the old conception, replaced by a later choice, is a way of seeing and then seeing again.

That is all I mean about the people in this book. The paint has aged now and I wanted to see what was there for me once, what is there for me now.

BETHE

THE letter said, says now, in Gothic script, "Bethe will be sailing between November 3rd and November 6th, the Captain of the ship cannot be certain. Be assured, dear Bernard, that we have full trust in intentions you have been kind enough to give to us. Her mother has put aside the pain in knowledge that nothing is here with us for her but a poor life. We have two letters from the Bowmans, Ernest and Carl Senior, assuring us that the arrangement will not be 'forced upon, etc.' and we know that yourself will make the final approval only if the young people should wish joinment. Bethe is well favored, as the sister you remember, some say even more. How strange the name New Orleans sounds to us, in the Southern States of America. As if our daughter is to travel to the lands of the Indies, we think it no less far. But nightly we say prayer that we will live to cross the sea, all our families to meet again."

The letter is blurred and the pages are torn in the folds, but the name Bowman appears several times and it is still possible to make out a sentence in which the writer tells of having sold something to make the voyage possible.

Bethe for a short time lived in the modest house on Prytania Street, sleeping on a cot in the dining room, rising at five o'clock to carry it to the back porch, to be the first to heat the water, to make the coffee, to roll and bake the German breakfast rolls that nobody liked. Then, to save the carfare, she walked the long distance to the end of Canal Street, where she carried shoe box stacks back and forth all day for the German merchant who ran a mean store for sailors off the wharves.

Two or three months after she arrived — there had been, through those months, a few short visits to whichever lesser Bowman was not too busy or too bored — she was taken to one of the great Bowman houses and there, finally, was introduced to Styrie Bowman, the husband planned for her in the long-distance arrangement. Many years later, when people had given Styrie up for dead, I was told that a journalist wrote a book about the period. Bethe entered the book for a reason she did not know on the day she met Styrie. I do not know the book or the journalist's name, but there is a cutting from the book pasted in a family album. "This same Bethe Bruno Koshland married Styrie Bowman, who was cousin to the powerful New Orleans cotton merchants. Styrie came and went so often and so far that it is impossible to trace his years between the time he was twenty and forty. He was described by many as having powerful force with women and yet all reports say that he was about five feet six, one side of his face an earth brown, and of almost fiend-like distortion. But like many ugly men he had success with women. The last traces of him occur in the home of Mrs. Finch of Denver, who supported him in style."

I do not know who Mrs. Finch was. In fact, I never knew much about Styrie, except the bare accounts, told to me so many years later, of the marriage that was arranged between him and Bethe. The Bowmans had been looking for someone who could clean up Styrie, keep him out of the hands of gamblers — there were too many forged checks that bore their names — and nothing better could be found than sensible, handsome, hardworking Bethe, who was also a third cousin and therefore to be trusted.

Two thousand dollars was raised by the Bowmans, a decent sum in those days for young people to begin a life, and a job was found for Styrie in a Bowman warehouse in Monroe, Louisiana. I never heard anybody say what Bethe felt about Styrie or the marriage, but certainly Styrie's feelings were clear, because six months after the marriage he disappeared, and Bethe returned to New Orleans. I remember breakfast talk about all that, and somewhere in those years I knew that Bethe was acting as governess — or whatever word the Bowmans had learned from their fellow Northern industrialists to call those who cared for their children — to one of the less important — less important meant less money — Bowman families.

I know all that I have written here, or I know it the way I remember it, which, of course, may not be the whole truth, because my grandfather was the Bernard of the letter sent from Germany and it was with his family that Bethe slept in the dining room and rose early to make the coffee. I am, therefore, a distant cousin to the Bowmans, but the only time they have ever acknowledged me was once, in a London hotel, when the Queen Mother Bowman complained to the manager that I played a phonograph in the apartment above her head.

Bethe arrived in New Orleans long before I was born, long before my father was married, but my grandfather and my father were great letter writers, competitive in what was then called a "beautiful hand." My father had little style — perhaps because he was so busy with the formation of the alphabet into shaded curls — but my grandfather, who had a few undergraduate years at Heidelberg, made charming, original observations in his letters and in the children's copybooks he used to make bookkeeping-household entries on one side of the page, and comments and memories and family jokes on the facing page. What isn't blurred, or isn't in code, is good to read: his memories of the Civil War — he became a quartermaster general of the Confederate Army in Florida, a job that pleased him because of its safety — oddly phrased comments on New Orleans, his children, his friends, his self-mocking comic attempts to become as rich as his cousins, the Bowmans. Many of these copy-books and letters — he evidently made a copy of every letter he wrote — were lost before I was born, but a surprising number of them remained by the time I first saw them, when I was sixteen, and I remember my pleasure in them, particularly the ingenious mathe-matical puzzles that he invented for himself and his friends.

That year, the year I was sixteen, Jenny, my fa-ther's sister, sold the boardinghouse she had owned for so many years and she and her sister Hannah moved to a small half-house that could not accommo-date the massive furniture, the old family portraits, the music and the books of their long dead father, much of which had come so many years before from Germany. For a few days I made myself useful to my aunts, but then the debris of other lives, the broken stickpins and cameos and ostrich feathers and care-fully wrapped pieces of exquisite embroidery, pleased me so much that I was allowed to carry them to the back porch and sit with them for days on end. This puzzled my aunts, who like all sensitive older people were convinced that youth had no interest in what it sprang from and so were careful not to bore the young with their own fancies or regrets. (I am now at the

315

same age myself and the interest of students in my past has bewildered me and taken me too long to understand.)

My father's family, more than most, I think, did not speak of the past, although, if pressed, they had loving and funny stories of their mother and father. But I never knew, for example, until that time of their moving from one house to another that they had lost a brother in a yellow fever epidemic twenty years before I was born. I think the three of them, my father and my two aunts, had a true distaste for unhappiness, and that was one of the reasons I found them so attractive. In any case, it was on that porch, that sixteenth year of my life, that I discovered my grandfather's letters and notebooks and asked if I could have them for my own. Jenny and Hannah seemed pleased about that and for weeks after interrupted each other with amused, affectionate stories of my grandfather's "culture," his "eccentricities." When I returned to my mother and father in New York, I carried with me a valise with the letters and notebooks.

I suppose all women living together take on what we think of as male and female roles, but my aunts had made a rather puzzling mix-about. Jenny, who was the prettier, the softer in face and manner, had assumed a confidence she didn't have, and had taken on, demanded, I think, the practical, less pleasant duties. Hannah, who had once upon a time been more intelligent than Jenny, had somewhere given over, and although she held the official job, a very good one in those days of underpaid ladies, of secretary to the president of a large corporation, it was Jenny who called the tunes for their life together. I don't think this change-about of roles ever fooled my father, or that he paid much attention to it, but then he had grown up with them and knew about whatever it was that happened to their lives.

And so it was Jenny who wrote before my visit of the following year, asking me to bring back the letters and the notebooks of my grandfather. That seemed to me odd, but I put it down to some kind of legality that grown people fussed with, and carried them back. Perhaps I told them, perhaps I didn't, I don't remember, that during the year I had them, I had copied out some of them for what I called my "writer's book," a collection of mishmash, the youthful beginnings of a girl who hoped to write, who knew that observation was necessary, but who didn't know what observation was. All I really remember was the return of the valise and my conviction that it would come back to me when my aunts died.

Jenny died twenty years later. Hannah, lonely, bewildered, uncomplaining, lived on for another seven years, and one of the pleasant memories of my life is a visit that Dashiell Hammett made with me to see her. She was waiting for me at the New Orleans airport. She had never met Hammett and I had not told her he was coming with me. I was nervous because I knew she had never, could never approve a relationship outside marriage. As I came toward her, old now, the powerful body sagging, the strong face finally come into its own, outside the judgments of youth, the open, great smile faded as she realized that the tall figure behind me was Hammett and that she would finally have to face what she had heard about for many years.

The first day was a strain, but since Hammett was not a man to acknowledge such strains, the week's visit turned into a series of fine, gay dinners that worried Hannah at first by their extravagance, but came to please her when she realized that Hammett didn't even understand her protests. More important, all my father's family liked jokes, good or bad, and when Hammett, on the second day, told Hannah that all he had ever wanted in the world was a docile woman but, instead, had come out with me, the cost of the dinner at Galatoire's ceased to worry her, and she said that she, too, liked docile women in theory, but never liked them when she met them, and didn't he think they were often ninnies with oatmeal in the head. He said yes, he thought just that, but ninnies were easier women to be unfaithful to. She laughed at that and told me on our walk the next day that she thought Hammett was an intelligent man.

A year later I had a telephone call from a doctor I didn't know to say that Hannah was in the hospital. I went to New Orleans immediately to find a quiet, frightened old woman who had never been really sick in her life, and certainly never in a hospital. At the end of the week she seemed better and I made arrangements to go home, sure that she would recover.

(I have gone through my life sure that the people I love will recover, and if, in three cases, I have been wrong, at least I did them no harm and maybe curtained from them the front face of death.) I had, during that week, gone several times to her house to bring underwear or other things that Hannah needed in the hospital and I had seen the valise I had brought back so many years before. It was tied with the same cord I had put on it then, with the same red mark I had scratched on its side. It was standing in a closet next to a portrait of my grandfather and some old photographs, and I remembered that I had seen Jenny put it just there the day that I returned it.

But Hannah did not recover. She died a few days after I left New Orleans and I went back to give away the sad, proud, ugly things of her house. (She had left a will, giving me everything she had, more savings than I could have guessed from the deprived life she and Jenny had led.) Daisy, a Negro woman, who had come once a week for many years to clean the house for my aunts, brought her son and nephew, and as they hauled away the furniture to sell or keep or give away, we spoke about my aunts and what they would have liked me to keep for them. I decided to take a chocolate pot that had once belonged to my mother, my grandfather's portrait, family photographs, all the broken pieces of antique jewelry that had been piled in a tin box, a box of letters I had never seen before and, of course, the valise. But the valise was not to be found.

But I had seen it ten or twelve days before and

Daisy said she had seen it after that. A few hours later we found Hannah's door keys hidden in a flowerpot on the porch. Daisy said that was a habit of my aunts and it meant that somebody had been given the keys and told where to leave them when they were finished. Finished with what, Daisy asked me, but we both knew immediately that Hannah had given instructions to somebody to remove the valise. What friend, most of them too old or infirm to do such an errand? And why? Perhaps, I told myself, the last act of a private life. Or was it suspicion of me, a different breed, a writer, and therefore a stranger? But I had already seen the contents of the valise many years before and so that made no sense. On the plane going back to New York, thinking about it as the only alien, unfriendly act of Hannah's life, I remembered I had never read all that was there and when asked to return the valise I had told my aunts that and protested its return on that ground.

I don't know when in the next few years I came to believe that Bethe and Styrie and Mr. Arneggio had to do with the disappearance of the valise. When I thought about that, forcing myself into sleepless nights, knowing my memory is always best when I am tired, I pictured again old newspaper clippings and at least one long letter from Bethe in a German I couldn't read.

I am all out of order here — as most memories are — and even when I read my own childhood diaries, the notes about Bethe make no pattern, or they make a pattern in terms of years and seasons. But I cannot separate now what I heard described from what I saw or heard for myself.

I first remember Bethe, a tall, handsome woman in her late thirties, come to call on my aunts, always on a Sunday afternoon, carrying a large box of bad candy. Yes, her health was good, her small job was good, no, her coat was not too thin for the sharp damp of New Orleans winters, she had seen a good movie last Sunday and had a good Italian meal in a good Italian place for little money. I suppose it was the constant use of the word good, without a smile, that caused my mother, who was not to be predicted, to say to Bethe on one of the visits, "What a bitter life," and then leave the room with her hand over her eyes.

Bethe never stayed long on those occasional visits and would leave immediately when she was asked to eat supper with us, shaking everybody's hand and mumbling words that I often couldn't understand. Her accent was not German, but some strange, invented mixture as if she had taught herself English without ever hearing anybody speak it.

My aunts felt guilty about her, remembering their father's commitment, but my father would grow bored with their guilt and say that Bethe was a good-looking clod — he once said that she looked like him — and that he didn't believe Styrie's desertion had caused her anything more than a guttural sound in the throat. Jenny didn't like such talk, answering always that women were injured by the loss of husbands, no matter what stinkers, which is why she had never wanted one, and Mr. Crespie, one of my aunt's boarders, a former great lover of the town, would say that he had never thought much of Styrie, God knows, but that any man could be forgiven for leaving a German donkey like Bethe. I liked that kind of talk: I was coming to the age when I wanted to know what attracted men and what didn't; I would have liked to ask Bethe why men thought she was an unattractive clod, a donkey, when I thought her so handsome.

We were in New York when Bethe disappeared from her job with the Bowmans, because I remember Jenny telephoned my father to report it, and to ask him what she should do. He said that if everybody was lucky maybe Bethe had found a job in a nice whorehouse, and I heard Jenny's cackling laugh at the other end of the phone. But we were in New Orleans when Styrie reappeared, came to inquire for Bethe at my aunt's boardinghouse — I was miserable that I had been out at the time — and two days later was found beaten up somewhere along Bayou Sara. The good side of his face, I was told by Carl Bowman, Junior, older than I by a few years, wasn't good anymore, and the word Mafia came into Carl's talk, but I had never heard it before and it therefore meant nothing to me. I know Styrie stayed around New Orleans for a few months after that because Mr. Crespie said he saw him with some people in fancy clothes at a bar on Lake Pontchartrain. And then, suddenly, he was in the hospital.

Something must have worried the Bowmans — they were well known for shrugging off people who did not succeed — because Styrie had a private room and a night watchman was moved from one of the family warehouses to stand guard outside the room. But on the second night the room was shot up by two men in doctors' coats. When it was all over, Styrie was found clinging to a fire escape with his right hand because his left hand was lying on the ground.

I was allowed to stay home that day from school, and toward night I heard that the Bowmans had found Bethe in "a strange neighborhood," but that she had refused to visit her husband, using more sounds than words, finally writing in German that a visit from her might bring him further harm.

Perhaps nobody understood or perhaps the Bowmans were so sure of Styrie's imminent death that they felt anything was worth a respectable farewell. The two elderly Bowman uncles who escorted Bethe to the hospital told my father that Bethe seemed to "change" as she stepped into Styrie's room, because she "demanded" to be left alone with him. They said she came out mumbling in her "low-class syllables," shook hands with them, and disappeared before the two old fellows could find out where she was to be found for the funeral.

But there wasn't to be any funeral because that night the fevered, amputated Styrie disappeared from the hospital — the night watchman from the Bowman warehouse had a doped glass of Coca-Cola in his hand when they brought him around — and appears only once again, ten or twelve years later, in a letter from Mrs. Finch of Denver, reporting his death to Ernest, president of all the Bowmans, and asking for a memento or a photograph to remember him by. I know that caused a good deal of laughter in our house but Carl Bowman, Junior, my friend, said it caused anger in his.

It was a few years after Styrie's disappearance from the hospital — I was about thirteen, I think — that I was sent to Enrico's in the Wop section near Esplanade to buy oyster loaves for my aunts and me because on Sunday nights no dinner was served in the boardinghouse. I always looked forward to these suppers with my aunts, doors closed, jokes flying, Jenny singing after supper in a pleasant voice, regretting the opera that didn't come to town anymore, imitating her old music teachers.

I had chosen to go early for my walk on that pleasant spring night and have a good look at all the foreigners of the section around Enrico's. It was a conviction of my girlhood that only foreigners were interesting, had the only secrets, the only answers. A movie theatre — even now I can see the poster of Theda Bara, although I have no memory of the picture — was breaking between shows as I paused to examine Miss Bara's face, deciding to come back the next day for the movie. Then I saw Bethe. I started to call her name, never finished the sound, because she was with two men, a large, heavy man, and a young boy of about fifteen. When I did call her name, they were crossing the street and could not have heard me. I began to run toward them, but three oyster loaves, or the running time, or some warning, slowed me down and I came to follow so far behind that when they were a block ahead of me I lost them as they disappeared into a corner store. I took a streetcar home.

I don't know why I didn't tell my aunts that I had seen Bethe, but the next day I decided to skip school. I did this so often that my teachers, puzzled, in any case, by a girl who was shuttled between a school in New York for half the year and a New Orleans school for the other half, had ceased to care whether I showed up. I went immediately to the corner store. I walked around it for a long time until I saw two children go in. I followed them, having stopped to examine the window, full of sausages and cheese, canned goods and cheap candy boxes, and came into an empty store that had only two sausages hanging from the ceiling and one sparse shelf of canned stuff. And the children were not in the store. I waited for a long time and then tried a few soft hellos. When nobody came, I went out the door, rang a bell on the outside, and went back in to face the young boy I had seen in front of the movie.

I said, "I'd like a can of sardines, please."

When there was no answer, I said, "I like Italian sardines best. My father doesn't, he only likes the French ones. How much are they, please?"

The boy said, without accent, "We don't speak English here."

I said, knowing that many people in New Orleans liked only to speak the patois, *"Excusez-moi. Les sardines. Combien pour la boîte de sardines?"*

The boy said, "We have no cans of sardines."

"Yes, you have, I see them. Do you know my cousin Bethe?"

There was a sudden sound behind the door, and voices. The boy said, "Go, please, go out."

"That's not a nice way to talk. I wanted only to say hello to my cousin Bethe — " and stopped because I heard a man's voice; and then Bethe appeared in the door, turned to look at somebody I couldn't see, put up her hand, and shook her head at the young boy.

I said, "Good morning, Bethe, I'm — "

She said, very loudly, "How you find me here, *Liebchen?*"

"I saw you at the movies yesterday and I just wanted to say hello."

"Your family send you to this place?"

"No, no. I didn't tell them I saw you. I'm skipping school today, and I'd catch hell if they knew. What's the matter, Bethe, have I done wrong, are you mad with me?"

She smiled, shook her head, and turned to whoever was behind the door. She said something in a language I didn't know about and was answered. She listened carefully to the man's voice and said to me,

"No longer am I German. No longer the Bowmans. Now I am woman and woman does not need help."

She was smiling and I realized I'd never seen her smile before, never before heard her use so many words. But, more important to me, something was happening that I didn't understand. Years later I knew I had felt jealous that moment of that day, and whenever I have been jealous something goes wrong with my face. I guess it was going wrong then, because she said, "Do not sadden, *Liebchen*," and took my hand. She called out something cheerful to the man behind the door and we went for a walk.

We walked a long way, down toward the river, into streets and alleys I had never seen before. I don't remember her asking questions, but I told her about the books I was reading, Dickens and Balzac, about my beloved friend Julia in New York, and a joke about my mother's Uncle Jake and his money, and how bad it was to live without my old nurse Sophronia. As we waited for the streetcar that would take me home, I said, "Please, Bethe. I will never tell my family. I promise. I didn't come to see you for any reason at all except just coming."

But the words fell away and I knew that wasn't the truth. I was on my religious truth kick, having sworn on the steps of St. Louis Cathedral, and then in front of Temple Beth Israel, that I would never again in all my life tell a lie under threat of guillotine or torture. (God help all children as they move into a time of life they do not understand and must struggle

through with precepts they have picked from the gar-
bage cans of older people, clinging with the passion of
the lost to odds and ends that will mess them up for all
time, or hating the trash so much they will waste their
future on the hatred.) And so sitting on that bench
with Bethe waiting for a streetcar, I went into an incoherent out-loud communication with myself, a habit
people complain about to this day, trying to tell her
what was the truth in what I had just said and what
wasn't. When I grew tired, she sighed and said that
she had not had much schooling in Germany, found
it hard to speak and understand English, but was doing better in Italian. I said I would give her English
lessons if she would teach me German or Italian and
Bethe said she would inquire if that would be allowed.

I have no memory of when we saw each other again
because the next meeting is merged with the others
that followed, that year and the three or four years
before she disappeared once more. I think in those
years I saw her eight or nine times, but nothing now
is clear to me except a few sharp pictures and sounds:
I know that I told her about the Druids and that I gave
her my copy of *Bleak House* and that she returned it,
shaking her head; she brought me a photograph of her
father and mother, and I know that only because I
still have it; once we went to the movies and a man behind us touched her shoulder and she pressed his
hand; I brought along my English grammar and tried,
one day in Audubon Park, to explain the pluperfect

as she stared at me, solemn, struggling, and I touched the beautiful, heavy auburn hair to console her and to apologize. I know that led to sad, sympathetic talk about my hair, blonde and shameless straight in a time when it was fashionable to have curls. And one Sunday, when I went to the corner store, she rolled my hair in wet toilet paper rolls and put a scarf around my head, saying that would do it, and after we had gone to sit in a Catholic church where the priest near the poor box seemed to know her, and we had not spoken for a long time, she unwrapped my curlers, and as the hair came from the curlers as loose and dank as always, she kissed me. It was not a good thing to do. I disliked Bethe for thinking I was "unattractive," a word of my generation that meant you wouldn't ever marry. My friend Julia, in our New York school group of four strangely assorted girls, was too rich to think about marriage and I envied her. I was impractical: I wanted to marry a poet. One of us did marry a young poet but he killed himself a few months after the marriage over the body of his male lover.

On another Sunday morning I went to the store to tell Bethe that we would be leaving for New York in a few days. The young boy who always answered the bell said Bethe was in church and so I went looking for her. She was sitting with a tall, bald-headed man so dark of skin I thought he was a Negro. Something kept me from them and I turned to leave. But Bethe saw me. She said something to the man, he answered, rose, and quickly moved ahead of her. She took my hand and we stood outside in the sun, waiting, I think, for the man to disappear.

She was trying to say something. Whenever she was ready to talk, she moved her lips as if rehearsing the words, and now I saw that what she was going to say she didn't want to say.

"Do not again come to church here, *Liebchen.*"

"I'm sorry."

"You are not Catholic. Some do not like it so, your coming."

"But you are not Catholic, either."

"I am. I become. I believe now God, Father, Holy Ghost."

I was accustomed to my mother's religiosity, a woman seeking and believing that salvation lay in the God of any church. My mother, therefore, had no church, calling in at many; but now, with Bethe, I recognized the assertive tone of the uncommitted because I had so long heard the tone of the committed.

In those days I said whatever came into my head, in any manner that my head formed the idea and the words. (It is, indeed, strange to write of your own past. "In those days" I have written, and will leave here, but I am not at all sure that those days have been changed by time. All my life I believed in the changes I could, and sometimes did, make in a nature I so often didn't like, but now it seems to me that time made alterations and mutations rather than true reforms; and so I am left with so much of the past that I have no right to think it very different from the present.)

I said to Bethe before I began to cry, "You lie because a man tells you to."

She stared at me, walked ahead of me, motioned to me to follow. We went back to the corner store and she disappeared into the back room and reappeared immediately to ask me if I would like to have a good Italian lunch in a good Italian restaurant.

I could now, I did a few years ago, walk to that restaurant; I could make a map of the tables and the faces that were there that Sunday, so long ago. Freud said that people could not remember smells, they could only be reminded of them, but I still believe I remember the odor of boiling salt water, the close smell of old wine stains. I had never been in such a place. Somewhere I knew I was on the edge of acquisition, a state of nervousness which often caused me to move my hands and wrists as if I were entering into a fit.

Bethe asked me what I wanted to eat, I shook my head, she ordered in Italian from a thin old lady who seemed to know her. We had a heavy sauce poured over something I could not identify and did not like. (The food in our house was good: at one end of the serving table there was always the New Orleans cooking of my father's childhood and, at the other, the Negro backwoods stuff of my mother's Alabama black-earth land. Food in other places seemed inferior.) This Italian food was a mess.

I don't know how long it took me to search each face in the restaurant with the eagerness the young have for strangers in strange places, nor how long it took me to recognize the man who had been in church with Bethe. He was sitting alone at a table, staring at a wall, as if to keep his face from us. I asked Bethe for a glass of water and found her staring at the man, her lips compressed as if to hold the mouth from doing something else, her shoulders rigid against the chair. The man turned from the wall, the eyes dropped to the table, and then the head went up suddenly and stared at Bethe until the lips took on the look of her lips and the shoulders went back against the chair with the same sharp intake of muscles. Before any gesture was made, I knew I was seeing what I had never seen before and, since like most only children, all that I saw related to me, I felt a sharp pain as if I were alone in the world and always would be. As she raised her hand to her mouth and then turned the palm toward him, I pushed the heavy paste stuff in front of me so far across the table that it turned and was on the tablecloth. She did not see what I had done because she was waiting for him as he rose from his chair. She went to meet him. When they reached each other, his hand went down her arm and she closed her eyes. As I ran out of the restaurant, I saw her go back to our table.

Hannah wrote to us in New York a few weeks later saying that Bethe had telephoned twice to ask for me, and wasn't that odd? My father wanted to know why

I thought Bethe had asked for *me*, but I had learned to smile at such questions and my father had learned that what had been childish bucking was, if pushed, turning into sharp, unpleasant stubbornness. We had had an uncomfortable winter; I was getting bad marks in school when, all my life, I had been given good ones; I was locking the door of my room and sometimes refusing to come out for meals; I was disappearing at odd hours, and questions about that were not answered. I had run away from home for a day and a night and was, as spring came, refusing to go back to the girls' camp where I had spent so many summers. And late one night I had tried to climb up ten fire escapes into my room to avoid my parents' questions on why I had cuts on my face. I didn't climb more than three fire escapes before the apartment house was in an uproar.

I did send Bethe a Christmas card, but I didn't see her on our next winter visit to New Orleans. It was to be the last regular visit we ever made. It was finally obvious to my parents that I couldn't be dragged back and forth from a bad school in New Orleans to a good school in New York: I was getting too old for such adjustments. I had, on that last visit, gone immediately to the corner store, but I did not ring the bell, telling myself I would come the next day. But I did not go back again.

I have very little memory of that winter in New Orleans or the summer in Biloxi, Mississippi. I know that I watched every movement that Carl Bowman, Junior, made as he dove off the pier, or pitched in the baseball game, or walked down our block, and one night I was wracked with gagging, the emotion was so great, as he put his arm around me. I must have thought about Bethe, because in my "writer's book" for that period I practiced a code based on her name, but now, looking at the book, I can't understand the code.

The last week of our visit — we had returned to New Orleans from Biloxi — we were sitting around Jenny's dining room table, her boarders having gone their after-dinner way, in the family hour that I always liked. My father was reading the paper, and when he made a sound in his throat I saw Jenny nudge Hannah. Hannah nodded, Jenny put down her sewing, Hannah closed her book, and they watched my father.

He said, "Well the boys are shooting it up again. Have you seen her?"

Jenny said, "No."

"Who?" asked my mother.

"Stay away from her," my father said to Jenny, "do you hear me?"

"Stay away from whom?" said my mother. "What are you talking about?"

My father turned his chair toward Hannah. "Stay away from her, I tell you. These boys are nothing to fool around with."

My mother's voice, soft, rose now to high. "It's always been like this."

Hannah, who liked my mother, whispered, "Now, Julia, he will tell you — "

But I was trying hard to listen to my father and Jenny, knowing from long experience that they would have the interesting things to say, the opinions by which the other two would abide. Jenny had said something I missed, was saying now, "Not for two years, maybe more, although one day I saw her in a car, a *car*, an automobile, I mean, and I hurried over — "

"Don't do that again," said my father. "Don't hurry over. If she comes here, say you're sorry, or whatever you can say that will curb your curiosity."

"Mind your business," Jenny laughed.

"I don't care who she sleeps with," said my father, "nor how many. I care that this one is a danger and you're not to go near her with any excuses to me later on."

"It is my belief," said Jenny, "that Hannah and I earn our own living — "

"Oh, shut up that stuff," said my father, "and be serious. These boys are killers."

"Killers," said my mother. "It's always been like this. You never answer me, I'm never told the secrets."

"O.K.," said my father, "you have relatives who are killers."

"Whatever you think of them," said my mother, "my family are *not* killers and even you have never said that in all the years."

"Oh, Julia," said Hannah, "you always let him tease you. You always do."

"What a sucker," said Jenny.

"Don't interfere between man and wife," my father said. "What is it you want to know, Julia?"

"My relatives are not killers and you ought not to say so in front of our child."

My father turned to me. "Your mother's family are not killers of white people. Remember that and be proud. They never do more than beat up niggers who can't pay fifty percent interest on the cotton crop and that's how they got rich."

"The child has no respect now," said my mother, "for my family."

"I didn't say *your* family were killers. I said you were now *related* to killers."

"Oh, God," said Jenny to my mother, "he means us, *our* cousin, Bethe."

"In a proper marriage," said my father, "the blood of one house merges with the blood of the other, or have I misunderstood the marriage vows?"

"You've misunderstood them when you wanted to," said Jenny, and Hannah rose nervously and puttered about. Then my father said something to Jenny in German and I couldn't understand much of it, although I could have managed more if my mother hadn't kept on saying, "Please translate for me," and "That isn't nice. You know I can't understand," and, "Very well, ignore me," until my father said to her, "Bethe's common-law husband, if that's the word," and Jenny said, *"Schweigen vor dem Kind,"* and everybody was silent.

I said, "I will go to bed now so you won't have to

Schweigen vor dem Kind and I've known what that's meant since I was three years old."

"You're smart," Jenny said, "but if you were smarter you wouldn't have told us that."

An hour later, when all the lights were out, I came down to the dining room and found the newspaper. There was a long story about the beating up of some men with Italian names because they were running bootleg liquor, and the headline included the name Arneggio and said he and his brother were being sought by the police in a suspected gang warfare.

At breakfast the next morning I said to my father, "Arneggio is the man in the corner store. You ought to help Bethe."

My father waited a long time, twice put up his hand to silence Jenny. "What corner store? What are you talking about?"

I had made a mistake and I was angry with myself. "I don't know. But you ought to help Bethe. She loves him."

"Come out on the porch," said my father.

"I'm late for church."

"Church? What church?"

"To understand is to forgive," I said, "and love she does, and so does he, and to her aid you must go."

"My God," said Jenny, "help us."

"It's *you* who have taught our child to go to any church and talk that way," my father said to my mother as he took me by the arm. "Come outside and let's have a talk."

"You will bully me," I yelled to my father, who never had, "or you will trick me. And both are immoral and I will not say one more word to a Philistine."

I was at my high-class moral theory stage, from which I have never completely emerged, and I had even had time to learn that it often worked.

"Immoral," I shouted as I ran from the room.

"That's not nice, baby," said my mother, looking in another direction.

"Immoral," I shouted, and sulked under the fig tree, refusing lunch, until late in the day when I asked permission to visit Grace Alberts, the daughter of my father's best friend, crippled at birth from the syphilis of her father. When Jenny said that was very strange because I had often said I didn't like cripples, my mother told Jenny that perhaps I was growing more charitable and she thought the visit to poor Grace was a good idea.

I knew where I was going — the house dictionary having failed me — so I stopped by Christy Houghton's on my way. Christy was the daughter of divorced parents, necked openly with the boys, and was two years older than I. I wanted to ask her what a common-law wife was. She explained it was a fancy name for just a plain old whore in this wide, wide world. The third time she said whore I twisted her arm and held it firm as I forced her to repeat after me, "Does love need a minister, a rabbi, a priest? Is divine love between man and woman based on permission of a decadent society?" and would not now believe those words except I liked them so much that they are written three times in my "writer's book."

When I left Christy Houghton she screamed after me that everybody knew about Bethe Bowman from the newspapers and I came from a family of gangster-whores. (One of the few clear memories I have of the opening night of *The Children's Hour*, almost fifteen years later, is Christy Houghton kissing me and saying, "I married a New Yorker. You're drunk, aren't you?")

But that day I went down to the corner store. It was boarded up and nobody answered the bell. I paced around the block and tried again, worried that I had lost Bethe forever. I took a page from my notebook, wrote a message, and slipped it under the door. As I walked back to the streetcar, a man behind me called, "Hey, young lady," and I began to run. He caught me easily after a block and made sure by a very firm hold on my arm that I couldn't move.

"What's your name?"

I was too frightened to answer. After a minute he took my small purse and went through it to find almost nothing except cigarette butts and my "writer's book."

"What are you doing at Arneggio's place?"

"Nothing."

"Nothing? You don't know the people?"

"I'm on my way home."

"I'll come along with you."

I said, "Please," didn't like myself for it, and heard the fear turn into anger. "Please take your hand off my arm. I don't like to be held down."

He laughed and with that laugh caused a lifelong, often out-of-control hatred of cops, in all circumstances, in all countries. Then the grip lessened and he said, "Nobody's out to hurt you. What's this mean?"

He held out the paper I had put under the door. I had written, "Stendhal said love made people brave, dear Bethe."

"Stendhal was a writer," I started, "who — "

"What do you know about the dame?"

"The *dame?* The *dame?*"

"Look, kid, what were you doing there?"

"Nothing. I told you. I just rang the bell — "

"What's your name and where do you live? Hurry up."

"I am on my way to church — "

I moved away from him. He let me go, or so I thought, until I got off the streetcar on St. Charles Avenue and saw him behind me. He smiled and waved at me and I turned around and got on the Jackson crosstown car. I had a soda in Kramer's Drug Store, felt better for it, and walked home.

Jenny and Hannah were waiting for me on the porch. Jenny motioned me back to the chicken coops, away from the house. She said, "The police were here. Fortunately, we all went to school with Emile. Why don't you mind your God-damned business?"

"No sense getting angry," Hannah said, "no sense."

"Why not? Why not get angry? Miss Busybody here — "

"Tell us," said Hannah.

"Does Papa know the police were here?"

"No. Not yet. But he gets to Memphis tonight."

"Then telephone him," I said, "and don't threaten me. I wasn't doing anything. I was looking for Bethe."

"Bethe? What for?"

Somewhere I knew why, but I didn't want to talk about it, and when they knew I wasn't going to answer, Jenny sailed back to the house and Hannah followed her. When I came in the door the phone was ringing, and as Jenny answered it she put up her hand to stop me from climbing the stairs. When she finished listening she said, "Very well," hung up, went across the room, and whispered to Hannah. I had never seen her face twitch before and was not to see it happen again until a day, many years later, when she first saw my father after he had been confined for senile dementia. It is not good to see people who have been pretending strength all their lives lose it even for a minute.

Hannah said, softly, "Well, don't let's make a fuss. Let's just go."

Jenny said to me, "Go wash your face. Put on a hat. Tell your mother we're taking a cake to Old Lady Simmons. And hurry."

When I came downstairs a taxi was waiting in front of the door. I had never seen my aunts take a taxi before. I think I knew where we were going, because when we drove up in front of police headquarters I wasn't surprised, although I must have taken such a sharp breath that Hannah took my hand.

Jenny, as always, went through the door first, and up to a man at the desk. "I'm Jenny Hellman. Tell Mr. Emile we're here."

"He's pretty busy," said the man, "pretty busy. Is that the girl?"

"Don't speak in that tone," said Jenny. "What is it you want with this child?"

"Is she a child?" said the man, and I thought of the Infant Phenomenon and laughed out of nervousness.

"Sit down, ladies," and the man rang a bell. Hannah gave me her handkerchief as we sat waiting on the bench and I said to her, "I love you."

"Oh, certainly, love is just what we need," said Jenny. "Give Hannah back that handkerchief. It was our mother's."

A man came out of an office, motioned us toward the door.

This time it was Hannah who said, "We'd like to see Mr. Emile. We went to school with him and he's been to our house all his life."

"He told me," said the man. "He isn't here. He's very busy." He turned to me. "How well did you know Al Arneggio?"

I was so surprised that I didn't answer until he repeated the question.

"I didn't know him. I never saw him — I saw him in a restaurant once."

"Who do you think we are," Jenny said, "knowing people like that?"

"I think you're nice ladies whose cousin lives with a man like that, that's what I think," said the man.

"Schweigen vor dem Kind," Hannah said. "I mean that isn't a nice way to talk in front of a young, very young girl."

The man said to me, "What were you doing at that place? At the store? Don't you know it isn't a store?"

"It's a kind of funny store. But it's got some things in it and — "

"How many times have you been there?"

I was growing very frightened, perhaps more of the look on Jenny's face than of the man or the place.

"I don't know how many. I only went to see Bethe."

"Why did you go today? Did you have a message?"

"A message? No, sir. Bethe never wanted my parents or my aunts to know."

"To know what?"

"Where she lived, I guess."

"Or the gangster she lived with?" he said to my aunts.

"We've known," said Hannah. "A man in my office told me. I hope her poor papa is dead long since. In Mannheim, Germany, I mean, he must be."

The man said, "I want to know why the girl went there today."

"I do, too," said Jenny, "although she meant no harm, she never does mean any harm, she is just too nosy and moves about — "

He stood in front of me now. "Why did you go there today?"

I had already come near a truth I couldn't name, so close to it, so convinced that something was being pushed up from the bottom of me, that I began to tremble with an anxiety I had never felt before. It had nothing to do with my fear of the policeman or of my family.

"Answer me, young lady. Why did you go there today?"

My voice was high and came, I thought, from somebody else.

"I don't know. I read about Mr. Arneggio last night. Love, I think, but I'm not sure."

A long time later somebody, I don't remember who, repeated the word love, and I heard Jenny's voice and the man's voice, but I was so busy gripping my knees that I couldn't, didn't, want to look up, or to hear, and didn't care what they said. Somewhere, during that time, I found out that pieces of Arneggio had been discovered a few hours before in the backyard of the store, and I heard the man say to my aunts, "O.K. I'll tell Mr. Emile. But if you should hear anything about Bethe Bowman it is your duty, the Mafia and all, dangerous, and keep the kid away from there."

Hannah it was who poked me to my feet and said to the man, "Thank you. You are most courteous."

I don't think we spoke on the streetcar going home but I don't know because I think of it now as the closest I have ever come to a conscious semiconsciousness, as if I were coming through an anesthetic, not back into a world of reality, but into a new body and time, moving toward something, running back at the moment I could have reached it. I am sure my aunts believed that I was frightened of police consequences or my father's anger. I was glad they thought that and nothing more. Later that night Jenny said that since Emile had not phoned she saw no sense in ever telling my father or mother if I would promise to stay away from Bethe.

The next day and for days after that there were discussions of the murder of Arneggio. Bethe's name was mentioned in every press story but she was never called Bowman. In the boardinghouse so many questions were asked, opinions exchanged, that Jenny grew very sharp and took to defending Bethe, perhaps out of family pride, perhaps from the tangles of her own nature, so sure, so dismissive of "the ninnies of this world," and so sympathetic to them.

From the time I was fourteen until I was twenty-five, I had no news of Bethe, although I often thought of her. I thought of her as I got dressed for my wedding, deliberately putting aside the pretty dress that was intended and choosing an old ugly gray chiffon. As it went over my head, I heard myself say her name, and I saw again the man, Arneggio, in the restaurant. Then I don't believe I ever thought of her again through a pleasant marriage that was not to last, until the first afternoon I slept with Dashiell Hammett.

As I moved toward the bed I said, "I'd like to tell you about my cousin, a woman called Bethe."

Hammett said, "You can tell me if you have to, but I can't say I would have chosen this time."

Later that same year I went to New York from Hollywood to tell my parents about my divorce, and then, on my way back to California, I went to New Orleans to tell my aunts. It was an unpleasant errand: my parents and my aunts liked my husband, knew that I liked him, and had every right to be puzzled and disturbed about me.

I suppose, in an effort not to talk about the present time, my aunts and I talked a good deal about past times, and it was on that visit, as I opened a closet door to get a bath towel, that I saw once again the canvas valise that had been given me and then taken back. As my aunts moved about the kitchen I stood staring at it, wondering about me and them. I wrapped a towel around me and went to stand in the kitchen door.

I said, "Is the letter still there from Bethe? The one that says she now has good Italian friend and that maybe if they marry you will come again to see her?"

Hannah turned her back to me. Jenny said, "What does all that old stuff mean now?"

"It means that long before the day at the police station you knew about Bethe and Arneggio. But you didn't tell me you knew."

"That's right," said Jenny. "Why don't you put on a bathrobe?"

But I wanted to have a fight, or to pay them back, because that night I said, "I know that you will not approve of my living with a man I am not married to, but that's the way it's going to be."

"How do you know that," said Jenny, "how do you know the difference between fear and approve?"

"Because you deserted, sorry, you gave Bethe up, when she loved a way you didn't like. When she was in trouble, neither of you, or Papa, went to help her."

An hour later, reading on my bed, I heard through the walls of the small shoddy house an argument between my aunts. There was nothing remarkable about that — Jenny's temper was as bad as my father's and mine — but something was different, and as I opened my door I realized that it was Hannah who was angry. Neither I nor anybody else, I think, had ever heard Hannah angry, and so I walked into the dining room to find out about it.

Jenny said to me, "Your generation, camp and college and all those fine places, goes about naked all the time?"

"Yes," I said, "all the time. And we sleep with everybody and drink and dope all night and don't have your fine feelings. Maybe that's the reason we don't always spit on people because they live with low-down Wops and get in trouble. Each generation has its standards."

Jenny laughed, but Hannah rose, turned over her chair and said, "Sit down."

Jenny said to her, "We don't have to prove ourselves."

"Why don't you go out in the garden?" Hannah asked Jenny, and as I whistled in surprise at the tone, she turned into her bedroom. I could see she was unlocking a box. Something large had happened between them. I went to get dressed and stalled to give them time.

When I came out, Jenny said to Hannah, "O.K. Go ahead."

Hannah handed me an open savings bank deposit book and said, "Look at the date on that page."

The date was ten years before, in the first days of September. There was a thousand-dollar withdrawal from a total of thirty-three hundred.

I said I didn't understand. Jenny said, "Hannah doesn't want you to think mean of her ever because she loves you more than sense. I, myself, don't give much of a damn what you think. But so be it. That thousand dollars was withdrawn about a week after the police station visit and was used to get Bethe out of trouble. Your father didn't know, nobody knew, and you're to shut up about it."

"You are fine ladies," I said after a while, "the best."

Jenny was angry. "Sure, sure, now put all that sweet-time patter in the shit can."

"My!" said Hannah.

Jenny said, "Bethe paid it back. A long time ago, after she sold the jewelry and other stuff he gave her and when the police finally left her alone, so don't start any stuff about you giving us the money because we are poor virgin ladies."

"I haven't got any money," I said, "but maybe someday."

"Then someday send us a steak."

"I will," I said. (The morning after *The Children's Hour* opened, four years later, I gave a porter on the Southern Pacific ten dollars to carry a package of twelve steaks to my aunts and got back a telegram saying, "Do we have to eat the porter as well?")

The next morning Hannah, who usually left for work at seven-thirty, was still in the dining room at eight-thirty, and as I ate the wonderful breakfast that brought back my childhood — tripe, biscuits, cold crabs, crawfish, bitter coffee — she said that she was entitled to a day's holiday when I came to visit. An hour later, Jenny appeared and said, "Come along, it's a long trolley ride."

I think I guessed where we were going, but I know so little about directions, and the city was so changed and grown, that I didn't bother to ask what direction we traveled in. When we reached the end of the trolley line, we began a long, long walk through flat, ugly, treeless land. Occasionally we would pass a small house, and once an old man came from a dilapidated outhouse to look at us. My aunts were tall, heavy women who never walked more than a few blocks, and now I heard Jenny's heavy breathing and became nervous when I saw Hannah take her hand. Near the end of the road, sitting alone on the plain, was a mean cottage, square against the sun. The half-finished porch had four tilted steps and a broken chair as if to show that somebody had once intended to use it but had grown weary of the effort. Bethe was standing on the steps, her body slanted with their angle, and I stopped at the handsome sight of her. She came down the steps to support Jenny with one arm, Hannah with the other. I followed them into the house.

I don't think many words were spoken that afternoon, and certainly I said none of them. We drank a bitter, black iced tea, we stayed about an hour, we made the long trek home with sighs from Jenny as Hannah hummed something or other off key. That night I telephoned Dash to say I would stay in New Orleans a few days longer, would return to Los Angeles on the weekend.

The next morning I went back to Bethe's, losing my way on the turn of the dirt road, then finding it again. As I came toward her house, I turned and ran from it, around another dirt path and then off into another, coming suddenly into a green place, swampy, with heavy stump trees and large elephant ears. I heard things jump in the swamp and I remember thinking I must be sick without feeling sick, feverish without fever. I don't know how long I ran, but a path brought me in sight of a roof and as I ran toward it, thinking that I must leave the sun and ask for water, I saw Bethe hanging clothes from a line that stretched from a pole to an outhouse. She was naked and I stopped to admire the proportions of the figure: the large hips, the great breasts, the tumbled auburn hair that came from the beautiful side of my father's family and, so I thought that day, had been lost in America. She must have heard the sound of the wet, ugly soil beneath me, because she turned, put her hands over her breasts, then moved them down to cover her vagina, then took them away to move the hair from her face.

I said, "It was you who did it. I would not have found it without you. Now what good is it, tell me that?"

She took a towel from the line, came toward me, and wiped my face. Then she took my hand, we went into the house, she pushed me gently into a chair. After a while she came back into the room, covered now by a cheap sack of a dress, carrying coffee. I must have fallen asleep in the chair because I came awake saying something, losing it, then trying to remember what I had wanted to say. I took a sip of the coffee, finished the cup and, for the first time in my grown life, I vomited. Then I must have gone back to sleep because when I looked down the floor was clean and Bethe was in the kitchen. I went to stand near her as she dropped heavy-looking dough balls into a boiling broth.

She asked me, half in German, half in English, how I was feeling. I tried to say I had never felt sick and, trying too hard, said, "I wasn't sick. Just the opposite. It was that day in the restaurant, you and Arneggio — " and never finished, because as I spoke the man's name she put her hand over my mouth. When she took it away she said, "Now I go in bed maybe seven or eight P.M., in the night. He is plumber and like dinner when come home soon at four-thirty in afternoon. Come for visit again."

I waited for a dumpling to be finished, ate it, didn't like it, shook hands with Bethe, and walked down the road. Not far from the larger dirt road that would join the road of the streetcar back to New Orleans, I passed a very thin middle-aged man, carrying a lunch pail. Maybe he wasn't the plumber, but I think he was.

I was never to find out. Two years later my aunts wrote that Bethe died of pneumonia and they had only known about it because they had a note from a T. R. Carter. They said things like poor Bethe and they wished they had been able to help her, but they were getting old and the streetcar ride was hard for them, although they had always sent a present at Christmas and what they thought was her birthday. My aunts said they had written to Germany, had no reply, didn't know if any of Bethe's family were still alive, but maybe the next time I went to Germany I would try to find out and bring the news.

I never went back to Germany because now it was the time of Hitler, and I don't even remember talking again about Bethe with my aunts, although one drunken night I did try to tell Hammett about Bethe, and got angry when he said he didn't understand what

I meant when I kept repeating that Bethe had had a lot to do with him and me. I got so angry that I left the apartment, drove to Montauk on a snowy day, and came back two days later with the grippe.

WILLY

H E was married to my ridiculous great-aunt. But I was sixteen or seventeen by the time I knew she was ridiculous, having before then thought her most elegant. Her jewelry, the dresses from Mr. Worth in Paris, her hand-sewn underwear with the Alençon lace, her Dubonnet with a few drops of spirits of ammonia, were all fine stuff to me. But most of all, I was impressed with her silences and the fineness of her bones.

My first memory of Aunt Lily — I was named for her; born Pansy, she had changed it early because, she told me, "Pansy was a tacky old darky name" — is of watching one of the many fine lavallières swing between the small bumps of her breasts. How, I asked myself in those early years of worship, did my mother's family ever turn out anything so "French," so *raffinée?* It was true that her family were all thin people, and all good-looking, but Lily was a wispy, romantic specimen unlike her brothers and sisters, who were high-spirited and laughed too much over their own vigor and fancy money deals.

That is what I thought about Aunt Lily until I made the turn and the turn was as sharp as only the young can make when they realize their values have been shoddy. It was only then that I understood about the Dubonnet and recognized that the lavallières were too elaborate for the ugly dryness of the breasts, and thought the silences coma-like and stupid. But that, at least, was not the truth.

Lily was so much younger than her brothers and sisters, one of whom was my grandmother, that I don't think she was more than ten years older than my mother. It was whispered that her mother had given birth to her at sixty, and in my bewitched period that made her Biblical and in my turn-against period made her malformed.

I do not know her age or mine when I first met her, because she and her husband, Willy, their son and daughter, had been living in Mobile, and had only then, at the time of my meeting them, moved back to New Orleans. I think I was about nine or ten and I know they lived in a large house on St. Charles Avenue filled with things I thought beautiful and foreign, only to realize, in my turn-against period, that they were ornate copies of French and Italian miseries, cluttering all the tables and running along the staircase walls and newel posts on up to the attic quarters of Caroline Ducky.

Whenever we visited Aunt Lily I was sent off to Caroline Ducky with a gift of chocolate-covered cherries or a jar of pickles, because Caroline Ducky was part of my mother's childhood. Anyway, I liked her. She was an old, very black lady who had been born into slavery in my mother's family and, to my angry eyes, didn't seem to want to leave it. She occupied only part of the large attic and did what was called "the fine sewing," which meant that she embroidered initials on handkerchiefs and towels and Uncle Willy's shirts and was the only servant in the house allowed to put an iron to Aunt Lily's clothes. Caroline Ducky never came downstairs: her meals were brought to her by her daughter, Flo Ducky. Whatever I learned about that house, in the end, came mostly from Caroline Ducky, who trusted me, I think, because my nurse Sophronia was her niece and Sophronia had vouched for me at an early age. But then her own daughter, Flo Ducky, was retarded and was only allowed to deal with the heavy kitchen pans. There were many other servants in that house, ten, perhaps, but I remember only Caroline Ducky and a wheat-colored chauffeur called Peters. Peters was a fine figure in gray uniform, very unlike my grandmother's chauffeur, who was a mean-spirited slob of a German mechanic without any uniform. My grandmother and the other sister, Hattie, would often discuss Peters in a way that was clear to me only many years later, but even my innocent mother would often stop talking when Peters came into the room with Aunt Lily's Dubonnet or to suggest a cooling drive to Lake Pontchartrain.

Aunt Lily's daughter died so early after they returned to New Orleans that I do not even remember what she looked like. It was said officially that she died of consumption, supposedly caused by her insistence on sleeping on the lawn, but when anybody in my mother's family died there was always the rumor of syphilis. In any case, after her daughter's death, Aunt Lily never again appeared in a "color" — all her clothes, for the rest of her life, were white, black, gray and purple and, I believed in the early days, another testament to her world of sensibility and the heart.

The son was called Honey and to this day I do not know any other name for him. (He died about fifteen years ago in a loony bin in Mobile and there's nobody left to ask his real name.) Honey looked like his mother, thin-boned, yellowish, and always sat at dinner between Lily and his father, Uncle Willy, to "interpret" for them.

I suppose I first remember Willy at the dinner table, perhaps a year after they had moved to New Orleans, although because he was a legend I had heard about him all my life. For years I thought he was a legend only to my family, but as I grew up I realized that he was a famous character to the rest of the city, to the state, and in certain foreign parts. Depending, of course, on their own lives and natures, people admired him, envied him, or were frightened of him: in my mother's family his position in a giant corporation, his demotions, his reinstatements, his borrowings, his gamblings, were, as Jake, my grandmother's brother, said, "a sign of a nation more interested in charm than in stability, the road to the end." By which my grandmother's brother meant that Willy had gone beyond their middle-class gains made by cheating Negroes on cotton crops. But, in fairness to her family, I was later to discover that Willy had from time to time borrowed a large part of Lily's fortune, made money with it, lost it, returned it, borrowed it again, paid interest on it, and finally, by the time I met him, been refused it altogether.

I do not think that is the only reason Aunt Lily and her husband no longer spoke to one another, but that's what Honey's "interpretations" seemed to be about. Uncle Willy, his pug, good-looking, jolly face, drawn by nature to contrast with my aunt's sour delicacy, would say to Honey such things as, "Ask your mother if I may borrow the car, deprive her of Peters for a few hours, to go to the station. I will be away for two weeks, at the Boston office." Honey would repeat the message word for word to his mother on the other side of him and, always after a long silence, Aunt Lily would shrug and say, "Tell your father he does not need to ask for his car. *His* money bought it. I would have been happier with something more modest."

There were many "interpretations" about trips or

cars, but the day of that particular one, Willy looked down at his plate for a long time and then, looking up, laughed at my mother's face. "Julia, Julia," he said. "You are the charming flower under the feet of the family bulls." Then, puzzling to a child, his laughter changed to anger and he rose, threw his napkin in Honey's face and said, "Tell your mother to buy herself another more modest car. Tell her to buy it with a little piece of the high interest she charged me for the loan she made." We stayed for a longer time than usual that day, although Lily didn't speak again, but on the way home my mother stopped in the nearest church, an old habit when she was disturbed, any church of any belief, and I waited outside, impatient, more than that, the way I always was.

Aunt Jenny, my father's sister, who ran a boarding-house, would take me each Saturday to the French market for the weekly food supplies. It was our custom to have lunch in the Quarter at Tujague's, and my watered wine and her unwatered wine always made for a nice time. And so the next day after Willy had told my mother she was a charming flower, I said to Jenny, "Everybody likes Mama, don't they?"

"Almost," she said, "but not you. You're jealous of your mama and you ought to get over that before it's too late."

"Mama nags," I said. "Papa understands."

"*Ach.* You and your papa. Yes, she does nag. But she doesn't know it and is a nice lady. I said you must know your mother before it is too late."

360

She was right. By the time I knew how much I loved my mother and understood that her eccentricities were nothing more than that and could no more be controlled than the blinking of an eye in a high wind, it was, indeed, too late. But I didn't like lectures even from Jenny.

"Uncle Willy likes Mama," I said. "I think that's hard for Aunt Lily."

Jenny stared at me. "Hard for *Lily?* Hard for your Aunt Lily?"

"You don't like her because she's thin," I said to Jenny, who was six feet tall, and heavy, and had long been telling me that my rib bones showed. "I think she's the most interesting, the only interesting, part of our family."

"Thank you," said Jenny. "Your *mother's* family. Not mine."

"I didn't mean you or Hannah," I said, "really, I . . ."

"Don't worry," Jenny said as she rose, "about me, worry about yourself and why you like very thin people who have money."

I asked her what she meant, and she said that someday she would tell me if I didn't find out for myself. (I did find out, and when I told her she laughed and said I was thirty years old, but better late than never.)

It was that year, the year of my mother being a flower, and now, in my memory, the year before my sharp turn, that I saw most of Aunt Lily. I went to the house two or three times a week and whatever she was doing, and she was never doing much, she would put aside to give me hot chocolate, sending Honey to another room as if she and I were ready to exchange the pains of women. I usually went in the late afternoons, after school, but sometimes I was invited to Saturday lunch. The visits were hung in a limbo of fog over water, but I put that down to the way people who had greater culture and sensibility than the rest of us lived their special lives. I don't know what I meant by culture: in Aunt Lily's house there were no books other than a set of Prescott, and once when Jenny and I went to our second-balcony seats for a concert of Verdi's *Requiem* Aunt Lily sent for us to join her in her box. After a while, Jenny said to me, "Would you ask your Cultivated Majesty Aunt please not to hum the Wedding March? It doesn't go well with the 'Libera me' and there are other reasons she should forget it." But I put that down to Jenny's customary sharpness and went on with my interest in Aunt Lily.

Ever since her daughter's death Aunt Lily made soft sounds from time to time and talked even less than before, although unconnected phrases like "lost life," "the hopes of youth," "inevitable waste," would come at intervals. I was never sure whether she was talking of her daughter or of herself, but I did know that, for a woman who had never before used her hands, she now often touched my hair, patted my arm, or held Honey firmly by the hand.

362

And I thought it was the need to deny the death of her child that made possible the scene I once saw when I arrived for a visit while Lily was out shopping. The car came into the driveway to the side door and from the window I saw Peters reach in for Lily's hand. As she stepped from the car, she twisted and slipped. Peters caught her and carried her to the door. On the way there, her head moved down to kiss his hair.

I did not know how to cross the room away from the window, how to face what I had seen, so I ran up to the third floor to call upon Caroline Ducky. Past the second landing I heard Honey's voice behind me. He said, "He does it to her."

"Does what?"

"You're older than me," he said, and ran up ahead of me. He was larger, taller than I, and his face was now sweaty and vacant.

I said, "What's the matter?"

"Ssh and I'll show it to you."

I went by him and was caught by the arm. "Want to see it?"

"See what?"

"My thingy."

I hadn't seen a thingy since I was four years old and maybe my no came too slow, because my shoulders were held with his one hand, my dress lifted with the other, and I felt something knocking against my stomach.

"Open up," he shouted into his future. "Open up."

I sneezed so hard that he fell back against the staircase wall. I was subject to sneezing fits and now I stood in the full force of one violent rack after another. When the sneezing was over, Honey had disappeared and Caroline Ducky was standing a few steps above me. I don't know how long she had been there but I followed her to the attic, was told to press my upper lip and given a Coca-Cola spiced heavily with spirits of ammonia, an old and perhaps dangerous New Orleans remedy for anything you didn't understand.

Caroline Ducky looked up from her sewing. "You be careful of that Honey." (She was to be right: at twenty he raped a girl at a picnic, at twenty-two or -three he was sued by a Latvian girl for assault, and his later years in the Mobile loony bin were in some way connected with an attack on a woman who was fishing in the Dog River.)

Caroline Ducky said, "I knew what he was going to be the day it took him three days to get himself out."

"Out of what?"

"Out of the stomach of his mother."

"What did you know?"

"I knew what I knew."

I laughed with an old irritation. Such answers were, perhaps still are, a Southern Negro form of put-down to the questions of white people.

"His mama didn't want him, his papa didn't want him, and a child nobody wants got nothing ahead but seeping sand."

"Then what did they have him for? They don't like each other."

"She trapped him," said Caroline Ducky. "Mr. Willy, he was drunk."

"Things can't start from birth, that early," I said from the liberalism I was learning.

"That ain't early, the day you push out, that's late."

"What did you mean Aunt Lily trapped him? How can a man be trapped?"

"You too young for the question, I too old for the answer." She was pleased with herself and laughed.

"Then what did you start it for? You all do that. It's rotten mean."

Grown people were always on the edge of telling you something valuable and then withdrawing it, a form of bully-teasing. (Little of what they withdrew had any value, but the pain of learning that can be unpleasant.) And I was a particular victim of this empty mystery game because, early and late, an attempt was made to hide from me the contempt of my mother's family for my father's lack of success, and thus there was a kind of patronizing pity for me and my future. I think I sensed that mystery when I was very young and to protect what little I had to protect I constructed the damaging combination that was not to leave me until I myself made money: I rebelled against my mother's family, and thus all people who were rich, but I was frightened and impressed by them; and the more frightened and impressed I grew the more aimless became my anger, which sometimes expressed itself in talk about the rights of Negroes and on two Sundays took the form of deliberately breaking plates at my grandmother's table. By fourteen my heart was with the poor except on the days when it was with those who ground them under. I remember that period as a hell of self-dislike, but I do not now mean to make fun of it: not too many years later, although old shriveled leaves remain on the stump to this day, I understood that I lived under an economic system of increasing impurity and injustice for which I, and all those like me, pay with ridiculous wounds to the spirit.

"What's rotten mean," asked Caroline Ducky, "you snip-talking girl?"

"Rotten mean, all of you."

"I like your Uncle Willy," she said, "but he ain't no man of God."

She closed her eyes and crossed herself and that meant my visit was finished. She was the only Baptist I ever knew who crossed herself and I doubt if she knew that she used the Greek cross. I left the house and went far out of my way to back-of-town, the Negro section, to put a dime in the poor box of the Baptist Church. I did this whenever I had an extra dime and years before, when my nurse Sophronia had proudly told my father about it, he said to me, "Why don't you give it to the Synagogue? Maybe we never told you that's where you belong." I said I couldn't do that because there was no synagogue for Negroes and my father said that was perfectly true, he'd never thought about that before.

For years I told myself that it was from that day, the day Caroline Ducky said he was no man of God,

366

that I knew about Uncle Willy, but now I am not sure
— diaries carry dates and pieces of conversation, but
no record of family gossip — when I knew that he had
been a poor boy in Mobile, Alabama, working young
on the docks, then as a freight boss for a giant company doing business in Central America, and had married Lily when he was twenty-four and she was thirty.
It was said that he had married her for money and
respectability, but after six or seven years he couldn't
have needed either because by that time he was vice-
president of the company, living with the first fast
cars, a hundred-foot yacht, the St. Charles Avenue
great house, an apartment at the old Waldorf in New
York, a hunting place on Jekyll Island, an open and
generous hand with everybody, including, I think, my
father in his bad years.

Sometimes in those years, years of transition for
me, the dinner table of the St. Charles Avenue house
included other guests — the "interpretations" of
Honey between his mother and father still went on
but were circumspect when these people were present
— fine-looking, heavy men, with blood in their faces
and sound to their voices, and then I heard talk of
what they did and how they did it. I don't know when
I understood it, or if anybody explained it to me, but
there were high tales of adventure, with words like
"good natives," "troublemakers," and the National
City Bank, ships and shipments that had been sabo-
taged, teaching lessons to peons, and long, highly rel-
ished stories of a man called Christmas, a soldier of

fortune who worked for my uncle's company as a
mercenary and had a great deal to do with keeping
the peons quiet. At one dinner the talk was of "out-
breaks," arranged by "native troublemakers" — two
men who worked for my uncle's company had been
murdered — and the need for firm action, revenge.
The firm action was taken by Mr. Christmas, who
strung up twenty-two men of a Guatemalan village,
cut out their tongues, and burned down the village,
driving the others into the jungle. Uncle Willy did not
join in the pleasure of that tale, but he said nothing
to stop it, nor to interfere with a plan to send a boat-
load of guns to Christmas to "insure the future."

The terrors and exploitations of this company were
to become a world scandal, the first use of the U.S.
Marines as private mercenaries to protect American
capital. But even in my uncle's time, the scandal was
of such proportions that the guns and the killings
tapered off enough to convince me that the company
had grown "liberal" as it established schools, decent
houses and hospitals for the natives. When, in 1969,
I told that to a graduate student from Costa Rica, he
laughed and said he thought I should come and see
for myself.

In any case, my reaction to those dinner tales at
Aunt Lily's was an unpleasant mixture: my distaste
for what I heard did not stop my laughter, when they
laughed, at the shrewdness and heroics of "our boys"
as they triumphed over the natives. I believed in
Willy's personal affection and generosity toward the

poor people he exploited. But the values of grown people had long pounded at my head, torn me apart with their contradictions.

But I could not now, in truth, get straight the tangled mess of that conflict which went so many years past my childhood: I know only that there were changes and that one day I felt that Aunt Lily was silly and that I had been a fool for ever thinking anything else. But I went on being sympathetic and admiring of Uncle Willy, interested in the days of his youth when he had ridden mules through Central and South American jungles, speaking always with an almost brotherly admiration of the natives from whom he "bought" the land. I am sure that his adventures made him interesting, the money he earned from them was different to me than money earned from a bank or a store, that his fall from high position seemed to me a protest, which it wasn't. And I had other feelings for him, although I didn't know about them for years after the time of which I speak.

But I already thought Aunt Lily foolish stuff the day of the outbreak. We had arrived in New Orleans only a few hours before she telephoned to ask my mother to come immediately. My mother said she was tired from the long journey, but that evidently didn't suit Aunt Lily because my mother told Jenny she guessed she'd have to go immediately, something bad must have happened. Jenny sniffed and said the something bad that had happened was probably the lateness of the Paris mails that failed to bring Aunt Lily's newest necklace. My mother said it was her duty to go and I said I would go along with her. Since I didn't often volunteer to go anywhere with my mother, she was pleased, and we set off at my mother's slow pace. Lily was pacing around her upstairs sitting room, her eyes blank and unfocused, and, annoyed with seeing me, she said immediately that it was too bad my hair was so straight and muddy-blonde, now that I was fourteen. But she sent for my hot chocolate and her watered Dubonnet, and my mother nervously chatted about our New York relatives until I went to a corner with a copy of *Snappy Stories.*

I guess Lily forgot about me because she said to my mother, "You've heard about Willy."

My mother said no, she hadn't heard about Willy, what was the matter, and Aunt Lily said, "I don't believe you. Jenny Hellman must have told you."

I don't think anybody in her life had ever before told my mother they didn't believe her, and I was amazed at the firmness with which she said that Jenny had told her nothing, Jenny didn't move in large circles, worked too hard, and she, my mother, always tried not to lie before God.

"God," said Aunt Lily. "*God?* He hasn't kept everybody else in town from lying at me. Me and Honey and my brothers and sisters who warned me early against Willy. It isn't the first time, but now it's in the open, now that he says he's paid me back when, of course, he still owes me sixty thousand," and she began to cry.

I saw my mother's face, the pity, the getting ready, and knew that she was going to walk into, be a part of, one of those messes the innocent so often walk into, make worse, and are victimized by. I left the room.

I met Peters in the hall. When he spoke to me, I realized he had never spoken to me before. "Miss Lily with your mama? Miss Lily upsetting herself?"

"I guess so," and started up the stairs toward Caroline Ducky.

"Miss Caroline Ducky don't feel good," he said. "I wouldn't bother her today." I went past him.

When Caroline Ducky answered my knock and we had kissed, I said, "Sorry you don't feel good. Your rheumatism?"

"One thing, five things. They mix around when you getting old. Sit you down and tell me what you reading."

This was an old habit between us. She liked stories and I would sum up for her a book I had read, making the plot more simple, cutting down the number of people, and always, as the story went on, she forgot it came from a book, thought it came from life, and would approve or disapprove. But I didn't want to fool around that day.

"What's Aunt Lily so upset about? She made Mama come right away. Something about Uncle Willy and the whole town knowing."

Caroline Ducky said, "The whole town don't know and don't care. Has to do with that Cajun girl, up Bayou Teche."

I was half crazy with pleasure, as I always was with this kind of stuff, but I had ruined it so many times before by going fast with questions that now I shut up. Caroline Ducky, after a while, handed me her embroidery hoop to work on and went to stand by her small window, leaning out to look at the street. In the last few years she had done this a good deal and I figured it had to do with age and never going into the street except for a funeral, and never liking a city where she had been made to live.

She said, over her shoulder, "I'm making a plan to die in high grass. All this Frenchy stuff in this town. Last night, I ask for greens and pot likker. That shit nigger at the stove send me up gumbo, Frenchy stuff. Tell your ma to cook me up some greens and bring 'em here. Your ma used to be a beauty on a wild horse. A wild Alabama horse."

I suppose there was something wrong with my face because she said, "Your ma's changed. City no good for country folk, your ma and me."

"What's that mean?"

"Your ma's a beauty inside out."

I didn't know why she was talking about my mother and I didn't want to talk about her that day, but I think Caroline Ducky meant that my mother was a country girl and the only comfortable period of her life had been with the Alabama Negroes of her childhood. New Orleans and New York, a worldly husband, a difficult child, unloving sisters and a mother of formidable coldness had made deep marks on my mother by the time I was old enough to understand her eccentric nature.

I said, "Uncle Willy going to marry a Cajun girl?"

"What? *What?* There ain't a white child born to woman ain't crazy," said Caroline Ducky. "Niggers sit around wasting time talk about white folk being pig-shit mean. Not me. All I ever say, they crazy. Lock up all white folk, give 'em to eat, but lock 'em up. Then all the trouble be over. What you talking about, *marry* Cajun girl?"

"All I meant was it must be kind of hard for Aunt Lily. Uncle Willy's being in love. I guess nobody wants to share their husband. My father isn't faithful to my mother."

"How you know that?"

"I found out years ago at a circus when . . ."

"Shut up," said Caroline Ducky, "this house pushing me to my grave."

There were sudden sounds from downstairs, as if somebody was calling. I opened Caroline Ducky's door but nobody seemed to be calling me, so I closed it again and went back to the embroidery hoop hoping to please Caroline Ducky into more talk, but the sounds downstairs grew louder and Caroline Ducky was too busy listening to pay any attention to anything I might ask.

She laughed. "Well, well. Time now for Miss Lily's morphine shot."

This was the richest hour I had ever spent and I was willing to try anything.

"Look, Caroline Ducky, I'll take you back to Demopolis. I'll get the money from Papa or I can sell my squirrel coat and books. I'll take you back, I swear."

"Shut the shit," said Caroline Ducky, good and mad. "Take me home! What I going to do when I get there? Nobody there for me except the rest of your shit catfish family. Home. What home I got?"

The door opened and Uncle Willy came in. "What's going on?" he said to Caroline Ducky.

"She's calling in the securities," said Caroline Ducky, in a new kind of English, almost without an accent. "Taking 'em from the bank."

"Christ," said Uncle Willy. "When?"

"Today's Sunday, tomorrow's Monday."

"God in Heaven," said Uncle Willy. "What a bastard she is, without telling me. That gives me sixteen hours to borrow three hundred thousand dollars. Maybe Peters just told you that to scare me."

Caroline Ducky smiled. "You too smart for what you're saying."

I had never heard anything so wonderful in my life and, although I didn't know what they were talking about, I knew I would, it was just around the corner. I suppose I was straining with the movements of body and face that have worried so many people in the years after that, because Uncle Willy realized I was in the room.

He smiled at me. "Hello, Lillian. Would you lend me three hundred thousand dollars for a month?"

I said, "You bet. If I had it, I'd . . ."

He bowed. "Thank you. Then maybe somebody else will. If they do, I'll take you fishing."

Several years before, Willy had taken my father and me and one of the big-faced men called Hatchey on his large boat and we had had a fine two days fishing in the Gulf. My pleasure in the boat had pleased Willy and there had always been talk of another trip after that. Now he left the room, patting my head as he passed me, and Caroline Ducky fell asleep by the window. I went downstairs. I heard my mother say to somebody that things would be better now that the doctor had arrived.

Walking back to my Aunt Jenny's boardinghouse, I said, "So she is having her morphine. Gets it often, I guess."

My mother stared at me. "What makes you think anything like that?"

"Caroline Ducky. Plenty makes me think plenty. Like what about all that money she's making Uncle Willy pay back because of his Cajun girl?"

"My goodness," my mother whispered. "Please don't speak that way. Please."

And I knew I had gold if I could get the coins together. But it was no use because my mother was moving her lips in prayer and that meant she had left the world for a while.

For the next few days I tried games on Jenny, hinting at the morphine, deliberately mispronouncing it, giving her pieces of the conversation between Uncle Willy and Caroline Ducky, saying that I had read in books that men often had outside women like the Cajun girl and what did she think, but I got nowhere. Jenny said we should mind our own business because rich people like my ma's family often got into muddles not meant for the rest of us.

It was a difficult time for me. I wandered about the house at night and Mrs. Caronne, Aunt Jenny's oldest boarder, complained; I wrote two poems about the pleasures of autumn love; I skipped school and spent the days sitting in front of St. Louis Cathedral and one night I wandered back-of-town and got chased home by a cop. I was, of course, at an age of half understanding the people of my world, but I was sure, as are most young people, that there were simple answers and the world, or my own limitations, were depriving me of a mathematical solution. I began, for the first time in my life, to sulk and remain silent, no longer having any faith in what I would say if I did talk, and no faith in what I would hear from anybody else. The notebooks of those days are filled with question marks: the large, funny, sad questions of the very young.

The troubles of Aunt Lily were not spoken about and my mother, as far as I know, did not return to the house. But I did, every few days, circling it, standing down the street, seeing nothing, not even Honey. But after two weeks that was unbearable and so I decided to take some pickles to Caroline Ducky. As I turned in the back entrance, Uncle Willy came out the side entrance to load his car with fishing rods and a shotgun. He looked fine and easy in old tweed clothes and good boots.

When he saw me he said, "I'm going fishing and maybe a bird or two."

"Oh," I said, "I wish I were going. I do. I do."

"I'd like to have you," he said.

It's been too many years for me to remember how long we drove on the river road, but it was a long way and I was happier — exalted was the word I used when I thought about it afterward — than I had ever been before. It was as if I had changed my life and was proud of myself for the courage of the change. The wilder the country grew, the more we bumped along on the oyster shell roads, the wilder grew my fantasies: I was a rebel leader going to Africa to arouse my defeated tribe; I was a nun on my way to a leper colony; and when a copperhead crossed the road I was one of those crazy lady dancers who wound snakes around their bodies and seduced all men. Willy and I did not speak for a very long time, not one sentence, and then he said, "Oh, Lord, what about your mama, a toothbrush, all that stuff?"

There are many ways of falling in love and one seldom is more interesting or valid than another unless, of course, one of them lasts so long that it becomes something else, like your arm or leg about which you neither judge nor protest. I was not ever to fall in love very often, but certainly this was the first time and I would like to think that I learned from it. But the mixture of ecstasy as it clashed with criticism of myself and the man was to be repeated all my life, and the only thing that made the feeling for Uncle Willy different was the pain of that first recognition: not of love, but of the struggles caused by love; the blindness of a young girl trying to make simple sexual desire into something more complex, more poetic, more unreachable.

Somewhere, after that silent time, we stopped at a small store where Uncle Willy seemed to know the old lady who was sitting on the porch. He telephoned my mother from a back room and came out to say that all was O.K. He bought me a toothbrush and a comb, a pair of boots, heavy socks, a heavy woolen shirt, and twenty-four handkerchiefs. Maybe it was the extravagance of twenty-four that made me cry.

The bayou country has changed now, and if I hadn't seen it again a few months ago I would have forgotten what it looked like, which is the measure of the strangeness of that day because I remember best what things look like and forget what it has been like to be with them. But even now I could walk the route that Willy took that day so long ago as we left the car and began to move north, sometimes on a rough path, more often through undergrowth of strange and tangled roots. Swamp oak, cypress, sent out roots above ground and small plants and fern pushed against the wild high dark green leaves of a plant I had never seen before. There was constant movement along the ground and I was sweating with fear of snakes. Once

Uncle Willy, ahead of me, called out and waved me away. I saw that the swamp had come in suddenly and that he was deep in the mush, pulling himself up and out by throwing his arms around a black gum tree. He was telling me to move to my left but I didn't understand what he meant until I sank into the mud, my feet, my ankles going in as if underground giants were pulling at them. I liked it, it was soft and comfortable, and I leaned down to watch the things moving around me: crawfish, flat small things the shape of salamanders, then the brownness of something the size of my hand with a tail twice as long. I don't know how long I stood there, but I know Willy had called to me several times before I saw him. Above me now he had tied a branch to his pants belt and was throwing it a foot from me. It could not have been easy for him to pull me out as he stood on uncertain ground with my dead weight at the other end. I watched the power of the shoulders and the arms with the sleepy admiration of a woman in love. I think he was puzzled by my slowness, my lack of excitement or fear, because he kept asking me if something had happened and said he had been a fool to try a shortcut to the house.

I don't know where I thought we were going, or if I thought about it at all, but the house was the meanest I had ever seen and, over the next two days, more crowded with people. There was a room with three beds, and two others of Spanish moss on the floor, a kitchen of ells and wandering corners, dirty with

379

coal smoke, filled with half-broken chairs and odd
forgotten things against the walls. Willy was as gay
as my father had always said he was, embracing people who came and went, throwing a small child in the
air, and cooing at a baby who lay in an old box. He
was at home here, this man who was accustomed to the
most immaculate of houses, the imitated eighteenth-
century elegance of Aunt Lily's house. The dirt and
mess pleased him and so did the people. I could not
sort them out, the old from the young, the relations of
the men to the women, what child belonged to whom,
but they were all noisy with pleasure at Willy's arrival, and bowls of hot water were brought from the
stove and an old woman and a young woman cleaned
his boots and washed his feet. A young girl of about
my age took my shoes to dry on the stove and gave me
a bowl and a dirty rag to wash with. I must have
drawn back from the rag — obsessive cleanliness
now seems to me less embarrassing than it seemed
that day, New Orleans being a dirty city when I was
young, with open sewers and epidemics — because
Willy said something in Cajun French and the rag
was taken out of my hand.

It was a good night, the best I had ever had up to
then. The dinner was wonderful: jambalaya, raccoon
stew, and wild duck with bitter pickles, all hot with
red pepper that made the barrel-wine necessary after
each bite. The talk was loud and everybody spoke
together except when Willy spoke, but we were deep
in Cajun country and my school French needed ad-

justment to the omitted sounds and dropped syllables. My pleasure in food and wine was, of course, my pleasure in Willy as he chased wine with whiskey, wolfed the food, and boomed and laughed and was amused, and pleased with me. I remember that a very tall man came into the room, a man in city clothes, and that my uncle left with him to sit on the porch, and everybody else disappeared. But after that I don't remember much because I was drunk and woke up in the bedroom that smelled of other people and saw two women on beds and one on the floor. I have never known whether I heard that night or the next night three quarrelsome voices outside the house, and my uncle's voice saying, "If it goes wrong, and the last one did, I'll get the blame. Nobody else. And that will be curtains." A man kept saying, "You got no choice." I had heard that voice before but I was too sleepy to think about it. Certainly by the time Willy shook me awake at dawn he was in a fine humor, laughing down in my face, saying I must never tell my mother he had got me drunk and to get ready now for the ducks.

I have been duck shooting many times since that early morning, but I have never liked it again because it never again had to do with the pleasure of crouching near Willy in the duck blind. I was then, was always to be, a bad shot and once Willy was angry with me because I ruined the flight overhead, but later he did so well and the dogs made such fine recoveries that we came back with fourteen ducks by nine o'clock. The

house was empty and Willy made us giant sandwiches
of many meats and peppers and said we were going to
the store. We walked around to where we had left the
car and drove down the bayou road to a settlement
of twenty or thirty houses and a store that seemed to
have everything — barrels of coffee, boots, bolts of
cloth, guns, sausages, cheeses and ropes of red peppers, fur hats, oars, fish traps and dried fish.

I was standing on the porch when I heard Willy say
to somebody inside, "Wait a minute, please. I'm on
the phone. Certainly you can see that." Then a young
man passed me carrying to our car a case of liquor,
three or four giant bolts of cloth, a box of ladies'
shoes with fancy buckles, a carton of coffee beans
and a sewing machine. Inside, Willy said, "Hatchey,
Hatchey? Ask them to hold off. No, it's not too late.
Send a cable to the boat." (I don't know if I knew
then the name Hatchey belonged to the man I had met
on Willy's boat, and who had been outside on the
porch the night before, or if I recognized it a long
time later when my father told my mother about the
troubles.) Then Willy came out and got in the car.
The owner of the store called out about a check for
last month's stuff and now all this, but Willy waved
him away and said his office would send it. The owner
said that would be fine, he just hoped Mr. Willy
understood he needed the money, and the car drove
off without me. A few minutes later it made a circle
in the road and came back to the store. Willy opened

the door for me and said, "Forgive me, kid. It's not a good day."

When we reached the house, Willy got out of the car and strode off. I didn't see him again until supper and then, as people thanked him for the gifts, he was bad-tempered and drank a lot. There had been plans for treeing raccoons that night, but Willy wouldn't go and wouldn't let me go. He and I sat on the porch for a long time while he drank whiskey and one of the old ladies brought pitchers of water for him. I think he had forgotten I was there because suddenly he began to whistle, a short call, then a long call. A young woman came down a side path as if she had been waiting there. She sat on the porch steps, at his feet. The second time he touched her hair I made a sound I had never heard myself make before, but neither of them noticed. A long time later, he threw an empty whiskey bottle into space, got up from his chair, toppled it as the girl rose to help him. She moved in back of him, put both arms under his, and they moved down the road. I followed them, not caring that I could almost certainly be heard as the oyster shell path crunched under me. They didn't go very far. There was another house, hidden by the trees, and then I knew I had seen the girl several times before; a big, handsome, heavy girl with fine dark hair.

I went back to the porch and sat there all night in a state that I could not describe with any truth because

I believe that what I felt that night was what I was to feel about myself and other people years later: the humiliation of vanity, the irrational feeling of rejection from a man who, of course, paid me no mind, and had no reason to do so. It is possible to feel many conflicts and not know they are conflicts when you are young: I was at one minute less than nothing and, at another, powerful enough to revenge myself with the murder of Willy. My head and body seemed not to belong together, unable to carry the burden of me. Then, as later, I revenged myself on myself: when the sun came up I left the porch, no longer fearing the swamps. On the way down the road I, who many years later was to get sick at the sight of one in a zoo, stumbled on a snake and didn't care. A few hours after that, a truck gave me a ride into New Orleans. I had been walking in the wrong direction. I did not see Willy again for five years, and if he worried about my disappearance that night, I was never to hear about it.

One July day, three or four years later, on a beach, my father said to my mother, "What's the verdict on Willy?" He was asking what my mother's family was saying.

She said, "I'm sorry for him."

"Yes," said my father, "I am sure you are, but that's not what I'm asking."

"What can they do," she said, as she always did when my father attacked her family. "It isn't their fault that he lost everything."

"Have they forbidden you to see him?"

"Now, now," said my mother.

"So they have forbidden you."

"I'll see him as my conscience dictates," said my mother, "forbid or not, but I don't want fights."

I was old enough, grown by now, to say, "What happened?"

My father said, "He sent down a shipload of guns with Hatchey Moore intended for Christmas to use. They stopped the ship. There was a scandal."

"Guns to put down the natives?"

"Yes."

"You forgive that?" I asked.

"It's always been a disgrace," said my father who, to the end of his life, was a kind of left liberal who had admiration for the capitalist victors. "But it wasn't all Willy himself. He was just acting for the company. He happened to get caught. So they fired him. That old shooting-up stuff isn't liked by the new boys. Too raw. So Willy took the rap."

"And you feel sorry for him?"

"Yes, I do," said my father, "he's stone dead broke. He was good to me."

I said, "He's a murderer."

"Oh, my! Oh, my!" said my mother. "We're all weak vessels."

During those years, because I had started to go to college, we went less often to New Orleans, three or four times, perhaps, for a month. On each visit, my mother went to see Aunt Lily, but I never again went in the front door of the house. I would go to the kitchen entrance to call on Caroline Ducky, the last time a few months before she died. She looked fine, that hot June day, more vigorous than ever. We spoke of Uncle Willy. She took for granted that I knew what everybody else knew: he had been thrown out of "the big company," had started his own fruit import company and was, according to New Orleans gossip, having a hard time. Somehow, somewhere, my aunt's money was again involved, but that made no sense to me because I couldn't see why she gave it or why he once again took it from her. But then I was a young eighteen and so little of what older people did made any sense to me that I had stopped worrying about it, finding it easier and more rewarding to understand people in books.

On one of the visits to Caroline Ducky, she said, "You ever see your Uncle Willy?"

"No."

"Me neither, much. He come around this house maybe once a month, pick up something, sleep in his office."

"Or with the Cajun girl."

"What Cajun girl? The part nigger Cajun girl?"

"I don't know," I said. "It doesn't make any difference to me if she's part nigger."

"Well," said Caroline Ducky's loud voice, "it makes a difference to me, you little white Yankee know-nothing."

I had already come half distance up the slippery

mountain dangers of liberalism. "I think maybe it's the only solution in the end. Whites and blacks . . ."

Caroline Ducky's large sewing basket went by my head. The old lady had remarkable strength, because when she saw the basket had missed me she rose and pulled me from the chair. "Get you down and pick up the mess you made."

As I was crawling around for needles and spools, fitting thimbles back into the pretty old box, she said, "That a nice box. Your mama gave it to me. I leave it to you when I go to die."

"I don't want it. I don't like people to throw things at me."

"You got a hard road to go," she said. "Part what you born from is good, part a mess of shit. Like your Aunt Lily. She made the shit and now she sit in it and poke around."

I was old enough to know what passed for wisdom among ladies: "I guess she's not had an easy time, Aunt Lily. Uncle Willy wanting her money, and his girls and all. That's what many people say."

"Many people is full a shit." With the years Caroline Ducky said shit more often than anybody I ever met except the head carpenter at the old Lyceum Theatre in Rochester, New York.

"Willy's got his side," said the old lady. "Where and why you think the morphine come here?"

I was so excited that I dropped the thread I was rewinding and tried not to shout. "The morphine the doctor gives Aunt Lily for her headaches?"

"He don't give her no morphine 'cause she don't have no headaches. Getting bad now, she won't last long." And Caroline Ducky giggled. (She was wrong. Aunt Lily lived another twenty-three years.) I guess Caroline Ducky was savoring Aunt Lily's death because she kept giggling for a while. Then she said, "That Peters ain't all nigger. His grandpa had a Wop store on Rampart Street. Wops know about stuff like that."

"Stuff like what?"

"Morphine," she screamed. "You wearing me out. And Wops make good fancy men. Peters been with your Aunt Lily long time now, but Mona Simpson down the road had him before that."

Over thirty years later, when *Toys in the Attic* had been produced and published, I had a letter from Honey. I guess he was out of the Mobile loony bin, at least for a while, because the letter had a San Diego postmark. He wanted to know if I ever came San Diego way, were my aunts still living and did I ever visit New Orleans; he himself never went there anymore although he still owned the St. Charles Avenue house, and, by the way, had I meant Mrs. Prine in my play to be his mother and her fancy man to be Peters? If I had, he didn't mind a bit, he'd just like to know. I had not realized until Honey's letter that the seeds of Mrs. Prine had, indeed, flown from Aunt Lily's famous gardenias to another kind of garden, but I thought it wise to deny even that to anybody as nutty as Honey. I showed my denial to Hammett, who talked me out of mailing it, saying that the less I had to do with Honey the better.

And that was because years before the letter, and years after that last time I ever saw Caroline Ducky, Aunt Lily and Honey, on her yearly New York buying sprees for jewelry and clothes and furniture, came twice to visit us on the farm in Pleasantville. I don't know why I invited them, some old hangover of curiosity, I guess, wanting to fill in missing parts of myself.

The first visit was O.K., although Honey seemed even more odd than I remembered and there was some mention of his nervous troubles. After they left, the cook reported that she had seen him kick our largest poodle and put a half-eaten piece of chocolate cake in his pocket.

A few years later Aunt Lily and Honey drove out with my father on a Sunday morning. Honey and I went swimming and I showed him the stables, where he teased a bad-tempered pony who kicked him. At lunch the conversation was disjointed. My aunt, as usual, ate almost nothing, but Honey went four times to the buffet table.

My father said, "You have a good capacity, Honey. The fish is pretty good, but how can you eat that other junk?"

"That other junk," I said, "is sauerbraten. I cooked it for the first time, to please you. It's German and I thought you'd like it."

"It can't be German," said my father, "it's Jewish.

I don't know where you learned to make bad Jewish food."

When Dash laughed I was about to say something about loyalty, but was interrupted by Aunt Lily, who said to Honey, "Go vomit, dear."

Honey said, "I don't want to."

Aunt Lily sighed. Then she turned to my father. "You still see my husband, so called?"

"I'd like to see Willy, but I don't get home much anymore, and Willy doesn't come to New York."

"Oh, yes, he does," said Aunt Lily, "he comes all the time. He just doesn't want to see you anymore. He has no loyalty to anybody."

My father's face was angry. "He doesn't come North and you know it, because he doesn't have any money. None."

"That's right," said Honey through a mouthful of something. "Mama took it all. It's for me, she says, but she gives a lot to Peters."

Aunt Lily seemed to be dozing, so Honey said it again. When he got no answer he said it the third time and added, "That's because of fucking."

My father laughed. "Remember, Honey, my daughter is in the room." Then he said to Dash, "Some nuts." And he got up from the table to get himself a piece of sauerbraten.

Dash said to me, "Your father who hates the stuff has now eaten four pieces of it."

"You have to try everything to know you don't like it," said my father.

Aunt Lily turned to Honey. "I don't like your talk. Shut your face."

My father said to Aunt Lily, "Never punish a child for telling the truth. Haven't I lived by that, Lillian?"

"And by much else," I said.

My father turned to Dash. "Lillian's got the disposition of her mother's family. My family were good-natured. Look what's happening to Honey."

Honey had gone out into the hallway and was standing on his head. Aunt Lily said, "It's his way of adjusting his stomach. The doctor told me Willy has syphilis."

"Oh, Christ," my father said to me, "any time your mother's family get stuck with anything, crazy children, bad stocks and bonds, other people gave them syphilis."

I said to Aunt Lily, "I don't believe you. Uncle Willy is a fine man. I admire him very much."

Dash said, "Watch it, you're not going to like what you're saying."

Soon after lunch, Aunt Lily said she wanted "a lie-down," was there a room to rest in. I took her upstairs, Dash went to his room, my father and I sat reading, and once in a while I watched from the window to see that Honey was doing nothing more than dozing on the lawn. Toward four o'clock their car arrived and I went to tell Aunt Lily. There was no answer to my knocks, but when I opened the door Aunt Lily was not asleep: she was sitting in a chair,

staring out the window at the top of a tree. I spoke to
her several times, moved in front of her, leaned over
her. There was no sign of recognition, no answer. I
went to get Honey. He was sitting in the car. Before
I spoke he said, "She gets like that."

"What's the matter with her?"

"Peters takes care of it, not me. I'll send him back
tomorrow."

"Where are you going?"

"To New York. I got a date."

I said to the chauffeur, "Wait here, please. This
gentleman can't pay for the car without his mother,"
and went off to find Hammett. He put down his book
and went with me to the room where Aunt Lily was
sitting. He pulled a chair up next to her.

"You're a very handsome man," she said. "Handsome people have an easier time in this vale of tears."

"Your car is waiting," he said.

"I hope you are good to my niece. Are you good
to . . ." and faltered over my name.

"Better than she deserves," said Dash. "Please get
up. I will help you to the car."

"In our South," she said, "it is a mark of woman's
trust when she allows the use of her first name. Call
me Lily."

"No," he said, "one is enough," and reaching down
for her arms he brought her to her feet. But he had
not correctly gauged her humor, because she pulled
sharply away from him, moved to the bureau, and
held tight to its sides.

392

I think she saw me for the first time. She said, "What are you doing here? You like Willy. You're no good."

"We'll talk about that another day," Dash said and moved quickly to take away the alligator pocketbook that had been her reason for the move to the bureau.

"Give me my bag immediately," she said, "there's a great deal of jewelry in that bag."

Dash laughed. "More than jewelry. Come along."

I followed them down the stairs and stood on the porch as Dash moved her down the driveway to the car. Once she stumbled and, as he caught her, she threw off his arm and moved away with the overdignified motions of a drunk. As Dash shut the door of the car, I heard Honey laugh and he waved to me as they drove past the porch.

"Well," said Dash, "that will be enough of them, I hope."

"What was that about her pocketbook?"

"She wanted a fix. I don't know what kind and don't want to. A bad pair. Why don't you leave them alone?"

"What did you mean when I said Uncle Willy was a fine man and you said I wasn't going to like what I was saying?"

"You told me that even as a child you hated what his company was doing, the murders, and what it meant to you."

"I never told you Willy did the murders. He's a

good man. He just went where life took him, I guess."

"Oh, sure. Now let's leave that talk for another day or forever."

"Why should we leave it? You always say that when . . ."

"Because I want to leave it," he said, "maybe in the hope you'll find out for yourself."

I thought about that for a few days, sulked with it, then left it and forgot about it.

A year later Dash and I moved to Hollywood for four or five months, each of us to write a movie. Soon after we got there, we had one of our many partings: Hammett was drinking heavily, dangerously. I was sick of him and myself and so one weekend I took off to see my aunts in New Orleans. I would not have liked to live with them for very long, but for a few days I always liked their modest, disciplined life in the shabby little house that was all they could afford since each had stopped working. It was nice, after the plush of Hollywood, to sleep on a cot in the ugly living room, crowded with stuff that poor people can't bring themselves to throw away, nice to talk about what we would have for the good dinner to which one of many old ladies would be invited to show off my aunts' quiet pride in me. Nicest of all was to take a small piece of all the Hollywood money and buy them new winter coats and dresses at Maison Blanche, to be delivered after I left for fear that they'd make me return them if I were there, and then to go along to Solari's, the fine grocers, and load a taxi with delicacies they liked and would never buy, hear Jenny protest over the calves'-foot jelly she liked so much and watch Hannah's lovely, greedy eyes deny the words she made over the cans of giant Belgian asparagus.

The taxi driver and I were piling in the Solari cartons when I saw Willy staring at me from across the street. He was much older: the large body hung now with loose flesh, the hair was tumbled, the heavy face lined and colored sick. I crossed the street and kissed him. He put an arm around me and pressed my head to his shoulder.

He said very softly, "So you turned into a writer? Come and have lunch with me."

He paid the taxi driver to take the stuff to my aunts' house and we walked a few blocks to Decatur Street and turned into an old building facing the river that had a large sign saying, "Guacosta Fruit Import Company." As we went up the steps he said, "This is my company, I am rich again. Do you need anything money can buy?"

Directly opposite the stair landing was an enormous room entirely filled by a dining room table. Along the table, at intervals of ten or twelve chairs, were printed signs, "French," "Mexican," "German," "Creole," "Plain steaks, chops," and seated at the table, sometimes in groups of four or five, occasionally alone, were perhaps twenty men who looked like, and maybe were, the men I had seen at Willy's house on the Sundays so many years before.

Willy put his arm around me, "What kind of food,

kid? There's a different good chef for each kind."
When I chose Creole, he whispered to the two men
who were sitting in that section and they rose and
moved down the table. We must have had a lot of
wine because our lunch lasted long after everybody
left and I didn't get back to my aunts until six that
evening, and then I was so rocky that I had a hard
time convincing them not to send for a doctor and
during the night, through the thin walls, I heard them
talking, and twice Hannah came to turn on the light
and look down at me.

I was in the shower the next morning when there
was a knock on the bathroom door and Willy said,
"Come along. We're going to the country."

Going down the steps, I saw my aunts in the garden.
I called out and Hannah waved, but Jenny turned her
back, and Hannah dropped her hand.

Toward midday we went through the town of Hammond and Willy said, "In a few minutes." The long
driveway, lined with moss oak, ended at a galleried
plantation house. "We're home," he said. It was a
beautiful, half empty house of oval rooms and delicate colors. Beyond the great lawns were strawberry
fields and, in the distance, ten or twelve horses moved
slowly in a field.

I said, "I like my farm in Pleasantville. But there's
nothing like the look of Southern land, or there's no
way for me to get over thinking so. It's home for me
still."

"I'll give you this place," he said. "I'd like you to
have it."

Late in the afternoon, after a long walk in the strawberry acres, I said my aunts would be hurt if I didn't have dinner with them. We had an argument about that, and then we started back to New Orleans. Willy's driving was erratic and I realized that he had had a great deal to drink during the day. When we took a swerve I saw that he had been dozing at the wheel. He stopped the car, said he thought I should drive, and he slept all the way to the outskirts of New Orleans.

I hadn't expected the voice, nor the soberness with which he said, "Pull over for a minute."

We stopped in the flat land that was beginning then to be as ugly as it is now.

"When are you going to Los Angeles?"

"Tomorrow morning."

"Do you have to?"

"No. I don't have to do anything," believing, as I had done all my life that was true, or believing it for the minute I said it.

"I've been faking. I'm broke, more than I've ever been. Stone broke. That lovely house will have to go this week, I guess, and I haven't got the stuff to pay a month's rent on the office. I owe everybody from here to Memphis to Costa Rica."

"I have some money now," I said.

"Don't do that," he said sharply, "don't say it again." He got out of the car, walked around it and came to my window. His face was gay and he was grinning now. "I am going to Central America on Friday. I'll move the way I first went as a boy, on mules. I'm the best banana buyer in the world. I'll get all the credit I want when I get there, San José, Cartago. Three or four months. I can't tell you how I want to go the way I did when I was young. It's rough country and wonderful. Come with me. You'll see with me what you could never see without me. A mule hurts, at first, but if I were your age . . ." He touched my hand. "Anyway it's time you and I finished what we have already started. Come on."

That night, at dinner, I told my aunts I would not be leaving them until Friday. Hannah was pleased but Jenny said nothing. The next morning when I went into the dining room, Jenny pointed to a large florist box and watched me unwrap a dozen orchid sprays. She said Willy had phoned and left the name of a man who made fine riding boots, he had ordered me two pairs and I was to go down immediately, fit them, and come to his office for lunch. I was uneasy at the expression on Jenny's face and went to get dressed. When I came back she was sitting in the hall opposite my door, Hannah standing next to her. She raised her hand and Hannah disappeared.

"You're going riding on a horse?"

"Yes," I said.

"As I remember your riding, you don't need made-to-order boots."

"I'm going to Central America for a few months."

Jenny had rheumatism and always moved with difficulty. Now she got out of the chair, holding to a table. When I moved to help her she pulled her arm away from me.

398

"In that case," she said, "you can't stay here. You have been our child, maybe more, but you can't stay here."

I said, "Jenny! Jenny!" But she pushed passed me and slammed the door of the kitchen.

I lay on the bed for a long time but after a while I packed my bags and went to find a taxicab. It was raining a little and they were scarce that day and by the time I reached St. Charles Avenue there was a sudden, frightening curtain of rain, so common in New Orleans. I went into a restaurant and had a drink.

I phoned the Beverly Hills house from the restaurant. I said to Hammett, "I'm in New Orleans. I'm not coming back to Hollywood for a while and I didn't want you to worry."

"How are you?" he said.

"O.K. and you?"

"I'm O.K. I miss you."

"I miss you, too. Is there a lady in my bedroom?"

He laughed. "I don't think so, but they come and go. Except you. You just go."

"I had good reason," I said.

"Yes," he said, "you did."

"Anyway," I said, "I'll be back in a few months. Take care of yourself and I'll call you when I come back. Maybe then we won't have to talk about reasons and can just have a nice dinner."

"No," he said, "I don't think so. I'm not crazy about women who sleep with murderers."

"I haven't slept with him. And he's never killed anybody."

"No," he said, "he just hired people to do it for him. I was in that racket for a lot of years and I don't like it." He sighed. "Do what you want. Have a nice time but don't call me."

I flew to Los Angeles that night. I didn't telephone Dash but somebody must have told him I was there because after about ten days he called me, said he was on the wagon, and we had a nice dinner together. I never saw Willy again and never had an answer to the letter I had mailed from New Orleans.

On my birthday that year my aunts sent a hand-knitted sweater and the usual box of pralines with a note saying all the usual affectionate things and adding, as a postscript, that Willy had gone into bankruptcy and barely avoided jail for reasons they couldn't figure out. And not many months after that I had a telephone call from a man I knew who worked on a New Orleans newspaper. He said that Willy, driving up the road to Hammond and the strawberry plantation, with two men, had had an automobile accident that killed everybody in the car, and did I want to comment for the obit.

Years later, Caroline Ducky's grandchild, who had worked for Willy as a cleaning woman, said it hadn't been any mystery, that accident, because he had started out dead drunk from a one-room, cockroach apartment he had rented on Bourbon Street.

JULIA

I HAVE here changed most of the names. I don't know that it matters anymore, but I believe the heavy girl on the train still lives in Cologne and I am not sure that even now the Germans like their premature anti-Nazis. More important, Julia's mother is still living and so, perhaps, is Julia's daughter. Almost certainly, the daughter's father lives in San Francisco.

In 1937, after I had written *The Children's Hour* and *Days to Come*, I had an invitation to attend a theatre festival in Moscow. Whenever in the past I wrote about that journey, I omitted the story of my trip through Berlin because I did not feel able to write about Julia.

401

Dorothy Parker and her husband, Alan Campbell, were going to Europe that same August, and so we crossed together on the old *Normandie,* a pleasant trip even though Campbell, and his pretend-good-natured feminine jibes, had always made me uneasy.

When we reached Paris I was still undecided about going on to Moscow. I stayed around, happy to meet Gerald and Sara Murphy for the first time, Hemingway, who came up from Spain, and James Lardner, Ring Lardner's son, who was soon to enlist in the International Brigade and to lose his life in Spain a few months later.

I liked the Murphys. I was always to like and be interested in them, but they were not for me what they had been to an older generation. They were, possibly, all that Calvin Tomkins says in his biography: they had style, Gerald had wit, Sara grace and shrewdness, and that summer, soon after they had lost both their sons, they had a sweet dignity. But through the many years I was to see them after that I came to believe they were not as bonny as others thought them, or without troubles with each other, and long before the end — the end of my knowing them, I mean, a few years before Gerald died, when they saw very few of their old friends — I came to think that too much of their lives had been based on style. Style is mighty pleasant for those who benefit from it, but maybe not always rewarding for those who make and live by its necessarily strict rules.

There were many other people that summer in

Paris, famous and rich, who invited Dottie for dinners and country lunches and the tennis she didn't play and the pools she didn't swim in. It gave me pleasure then, and forever after, that people courted her. I was amused at her excessive good manners, a kind of put-on, often there to hide contempt and dislike for those who flattered her at the very minute she begged for the flattery. When she had enough to drink the good manners got so good they got silly, but then the words came funny and sharp to show herself, and me, I think, that nobody could buy her. She was wrong: they could and did buy her for years. But they only bought a limited ticket to her life and in the end she died on her own road.

It was a new world for me. I had been courted around New York and Hollywood, as is everybody who has been a success in the theatre and young enough not to have been too much on display. But my invitations were second-class stuff compared to Dottie's admirers that month in Paris. I had a fine time, one of the best of my life. But one day, after a heavy night's drinking, I didn't anymore. I was a child of the Depression, a kind of Puritan Socialist, I guess — although to give it a name is to give it a sharper outline than it had — and I was full of the strong feelings the early Roosevelt period brought to many people. Dottie had the same strong feelings about something we all thought of as society and the future, but the difference between us was more than generational — she was long accustomed to much I didn't want. It was true that she always turned against the famous and the rich who attracted her, but I never liked them well enough to bother that much.

I had several times that month spoken on the phone with my beloved childhood friend Julia, who was studying medicine in Vienna, and so the morning after the heavy drinking I called Julia to say I would come to Vienna the next day en route to Moscow. But that same night, very late, she called back.

She said, "I have something important for you to do. Maybe you'll do it, maybe you can't. But please stay in Paris for a few days and a friend will come to see you. If things work as I hope, you'll decide to go straight to Moscow by way of Berlin and I'll meet you on your way back."

When I said I didn't understand, who was the friend, why Berlin, she said, "I can't answer questions. Get a German visa tomorrow. You'll make your own choice, but don't talk about it now."

It would not have occurred to me to ignore what Julia told me to do because that's the way it had always been between us. So I went around the next morning to the German consulate for a visa. The consul said they'd give me a traveling permit, but would not allow me to stay in Berlin overnight, and the Russian consul said that wasn't unusual for people en route to Moscow.

I waited for two days and was about to call Julia again on the day of the morning I went down for an early breakfast in the dining room of the Hotel Meurice. (I had been avoiding Dottie and Alan, all invitations, and was troubled and annoyed by two snippy, suspicious notes from Alan about what was I up to, why was I locked in my room?) The concierge said the gentleman on the bench was waiting for me. A tall middle-aged man got up from the bench and said, "Madame Hellman? I come to deliver your tickets and to talk with you about your plans. Miss Julia asked me to call with the travel folders."

We went into the dining room, and when I asked him what he would like he said, in German, "Do you think I can have an egg, hot milk, a roll? I cannot pay for them."

When the waiter moved away, the tall man said, "You must not understand German again. I made a mistake."

I said I didn't understand enough German to worry anybody, but he didn't answer me and took to reading the travel folders until the food came. Then he ate very fast, smiling as he did it, as if he were remembering something pleasant from a long ago past. When he finished, he handed me a note. The note said, "This is my friend, Johann. He will tell you. But *I* tell you, don't push yourself. If you can't you can't, no dishonor. Whatever, I will meet you soon. Love, Julia."

Mr. Johann said, "I thank you for fine breakfast. Could we walk now in Tuileries?"

As we entered the gardens he asked me how much I knew about Benjamin Franklin, was I an expert? I said I knew almost nothing. He said he admired Franklin and perhaps someday I could find him a nice photograph of Franklin in America. He sat down suddenly on a bench and mopped his forehead on this cool, damp day.

"Have you procured a German visa?"

"A traveling visa. I cannot stay overnight. I can only change stations in Berlin for Moscow."

"Would you carry for us fifty thousand dollars? We think, we do not guarantee, you will be without trouble. You will be taking the money to enable us to bribe out many already in prison, many who soon will be. We are a small group, valuable workers against Hitler. We are of no common belief or religion. The people who will meet you for the money, if your consent is given, were once small publishers. We are of Catholic, Communist, many beliefs. Julia has said that I must remind you for her that you are afraid of being afraid, and so will do what sometimes you cannot do, and that could be dangerous to you and to us."

I took to fiddling with things in my pocketbook, lit a cigarette, fiddled some more. He sat back as if he were very tired, and stretched.

After a while I said, "Let's go and have a drink."

He said, "I repeat. We think all will go well, but much could go wrong. Julia says I must tell you that, but that if we should not hear from you by the time of Warsaw, Julia will use her family with the American ambassador there through Uncle John."

"I know her family. There was a time she didn't believe in them much."

"She said you would note that. And so to tell you that her Uncle John is now governor. He does not like her but did not refuse her money for his career. And that her mother's last divorce has made her mother dependent on Julia as well."

I laughed at this picture of Julia controlling members of her very rich family. I don't think we had seen each other more than ten or twelve times since we were eighteen years old and so the years had evidently brought changes I didn't know about. Julia had left college, gone to Oxford, moved on to medical school in Vienna, had become a patient-pupil of Freud's. We had once, in the last ten years, spent a Christmas holiday together, and one summer, off Massachusetts, we had sailed for a month on her small boat, but in the many letters we had written in those years neither of us knew much more than the bare terms of each other's life, nothing of the daily stuff that is the real truth, the importance.

I knew, for example, that she had become, maybe always was, a Socialist, and lived by it, in a one-room apartment in a slum district of Vienna, sharing her great fortune with whoever needed it. She allowed herself very little, wanted very little. Oddly, gifts to me did not come into the denial: they were many and extravagant. Through the years, whenever she saw anything I might like, it was sent to me: old Wedgwood pieces, a Toulouse-Lautrec drawing, a fur-lined coat we saw together in Paris, a set of Balzac that she put in a rare Empire desk, and a wonderful set of Georgian jewelry, I think the last thing she could have had time to buy.

I said to the gray man, "Could I think it over for a few hours? That's what Julia meant."

He said, "Do not think hard. It is best not to be too prepared for matters of this kind. I will be at the station tomorrow morning. If you agree to carry the money, you will say hello to me. If you have decided it is not right for you, pass by me. Do not worry whichever is decided by you." He held out his hand, bowed, and moved away from me across the gardens.

I spent the day in and around Sainte-Chapelle, tried to eat lunch and dinner, couldn't, and went back to the hotel to pack only after I was sure Dottie and Alan would have gone to dinner with the Murphys. I left a note for them saying I was leaving early in the morning and would find them again after Moscow. I knew I had spent the whole day in a mess of indecision. Now I lay down, determined that I would not sleep until I had taken stock of myself. But decisions, particularly important ones, have always made me sleepy, perhaps because I know that I will have to make them by instinct, and thinking things out is only what other people tell me I should do. In any case, I slept through the night and rose only in time to hurry for the early morning train.

I was not pleased to find Dottie and Alan in the lobby, waiting to take me to the station. My protests were so firm and so awkward that Alan, who had a remarkable nose for deception, asked if I had a reason for not wanting them to come with me. When he went to get a taxi, I said to Dottie, "Sorry if I sounded rude. Alan makes me nervous."

She smiled, "Dear Lilly, you'd be a psychotic if he didn't."

At the railroad station I urged them to leave me when my baggage was carried on, but something had excited Alan: perhaps my nervousness; certainly not his claim that they had never before known anybody who was en route to Moscow. He was full of bad jokes about what I must not say to Russian actors, how to smuggle out caviar, and all the junk people like Alan say when they want to say something else.

I saw the gray man come down the platform. As he came near us Alan said, "Isn't that the man I saw you with in the Tuileries yesterday?" And as I turned to say something to Alan, God knows what it would have been, the gray man went past me and was moving back into the station.

I ran toward him. "Mr. Johann. Please, Mr. Johann." As he turned, I lost my head and screamed, "Please don't go away. *Please*."

He stood still for what seemed like a long time, frowning. Then he moved slowly back toward me, as if he were coming with caution, hesitation.

Then I remembered: I said, "I only wanted to say hello. Hello to you, Mr. Johann, hello."

"Hello, Madame Hellman."

Alan had come to stand near us. Some warning had to be made. "This is Mr. Campbell and Miss Parker there. Mr. Campbell says he saw us yesterday and now he will ask me who you are and say that he didn't know we knew each other so well that you would come all this way to say goodbye to me."

Mr. Johann said, without hesitation, "I wish I could say that was true. But I have come to search for my nephew who is en route to Poland. He is not in his coach, he is late, as is his habit. His name is W. Franz, car 4, second class, and if I do not find him I would be most grateful if you say to him I came." He lifted his hat. "I am most glad, Madame Hellman, that we had this chance to say hello."

"Oh, yes," I said, "indeed. Hello. Hello."

When he was gone, Alan said, "What funny talk. You're talking like a foreigner."

"Sorry," I said, "sorry not to speak as well as you do in Virginia."

Dottie laughed, I kissed her and jumped for the train. I was nervous and went in the wrong direction. By the time a conductor told me where my compartment was, the train had left the station. On the connecting platform, before I reached my coach, a young man was standing holding a valise and packages. He said, "I am W. Franz, nephew, car 4, second class. This is a birthday present from Miss Julia." He handed me a box of candy and a hatbox marked "Madame Pauline." Then he bowed and moved off.

I carried the boxes to my compartment, where

410

two young women were sitting on the left bench. One girl was small and thin and carried a cane. The other was a big-boned woman of about twenty-eight, in a heavy coat, wrapped tight against this mild day. I smiled at them, they nodded, and I sat down. I put my packages next to me and only then noticed that there was a note pasted on the hatbox. I was frightened of it, thought about taking it to the ladies' room, decided that would look suspicious, and opened it. I had a good memory in those days for poems, for what people said, for the looks of things, but it has long since been blurred by time. But I still remember every word of that note: "At the border, leave the candy box on the seat. Open this box and wear the hat. There is no thanks for what you will do for them. No thanks from me either. But there is the love I have for you. Julia."

I sat for a long time holding the note. I was in a state that I have known since I was old enough to know myself, and that to this day frightens me and makes me unable even to move my hands. I do not mean to be foolishly modest about my intelligence: it is often high, but I have known since childhood that faced with a certain kind of simple problem, I sometimes make it so complex that there is no way out. I simply do not see what another mind grasps immediately. I was there now. Julia had not told me where to open the hatbox. To take it into the corridor or toilet might make the two ladies opposite me suspicious. And so I sat doing nothing for a long time until I realized that I didn't know when we crossed the border — a few minutes or a few hours. A decision had to be made but I could not make it.

Childhood is less clear to me than to many people: when it ended I turned my face away from it for no reason that I know about, certainly without the usual reason of unhappy memories. For many years that worried me, but then I discovered that the tales of former children are seldom to be trusted. Some people supply too many past victories or pleasures with which to comfort themselves, and other people cling to pains, real and imagined, to excuse what they have become.

I think I have always known about my memory: I know when it is to be trusted and when some dream or fantasy entered on the life, and the dream, the need of dream, led to distortion of what happened. And so I knew early that the rampage angers of an only child were distorted nightmares of reality. But I trust absolutely what I remember about Julia.

Now, so many years later, I could climb the steps without a light, move in the night through the crowded rooms of her grandparents' great Fifth Avenue house with the endless chic-shabby rooms, their walls covered with pictures, their tables crowded with objects whose value I didn't know. True, I cannot remember anything said or done in that house except for the first night I was allowed to sleep there. Julia and I were both twelve years old that New Year's Eve night, sitting at a late dinner, with courses of fish and meats, and sherbets in between to change the tastes, "clear the palate" is what her grandmother said, with watered wine for us, and red and white wine and champagne for the two old people. (Were they old? I don't know: they were her grandparents.) I cannot remember any talk at the table, but after dinner we were allowed to go with them to the music room. A servant had already set the phonograph for "So Sheep May Safely Graze," and all four of us listened until Julia rose, kissed the hand of her grandmother, the brow of her grandfather, and left the room, motioning for me to follow. It was an odd ritual, the whole thing, I thought, the life of the very rich, and beyond my understanding.

Each New Year's Eve of my life has brought back the memory of that night. Julia and I lay in twin beds and she recited odds and ends of poetry — every once in a while she would stop and ask me to recite, but I didn't know anything — Dante in Italian, Heine in German, and even though I could not understand either language, the sounds were so lovely that I felt a sweet sadness as if much was ahead in the world, much that was going to be fine and fulfilling if I could ever find my way. I did recite Mother Goose and she did Donne's "Julia," and laughed with pleasure "at his tribute to me." I was ashamed to ask if it was a joke.

Very late she turned her head away for sleep, but I said, "More, Julia, please. Do you know more?" And she turned on the light again and recited from Ovid and Catullus, names to me without countries.

I don't know when I stopped listening to look at the lovely face propped against the pillow — the lamp throwing fine lights on the thick dark hair. I cannot say now that I knew or had ever used the words gentle or delicate or strong, but I did think that night that it was the most beautiful face I had ever seen. In later years I never thought about how she looked, although when we were grown other people often said she was a "strange beauty," she "looked like nobody else," and one show-off said a "Burne-Jones face" when, of course, her face had nothing to do with Burne-Jones or fake spirituality.

There were many years, almost twenty, between that New Year's Eve and the train moving into Germany. In those years, and the years after Julia's death, I have had plenty of time to think about the love I had for her, too strong and too complicated to be defined as only the sexual yearnings of one girl for another. And yet certainly that was there. I don't know, I never cared, and it is now an aimless guessing game. It doesn't prove much that we never kissed each other; even when I leaned down in a London funeral parlor to kiss the battered face that had been so hideously put back together, it was not the awful scars that worried me: because I had never kissed her I thought perhaps she would not want it and so I touched the face instead.

A few years after that childhood New Year's Eve, I was moved to a public school. (My father was having a bad time and couldn't afford to pay for me anymore.) But Julia and I saw each other almost every day and every Saturday night I still slept in her grandparents' house. But, in time, our lives did change: Julia began to travel all summer and in winter holidays, and when she returned all my questions about the beauties of Europe would be shrugged off with badly photographed snapshots of things that interested her: two blind children in Cairo — she explained that the filth carried by flies caused the blindness; people drinking from sewers in Teheran; no St. Mark's but the miserable hovel of a gondolier in Venice; no news of the glories of Vatican art but stories about the poverty of Trastevere.

Once she returned with a framed photograph of a beautiful woman who was her mother and an Englishman who was her mother's husband. I asked her what she felt about seeing her mother — in all the years I had never heard her mention her mother — and she stared at me and said that her mother owned a "very fancy castle" and the new husband poured drinks for all the titles who liked the free stuff, but there was also mention of Evelyn Waugh and H. G. Wells and Nancy Cunard, and when I wanted news of them she said she didn't know anything about them, they'd said hello to her and that she had only wanted to get out of the way and go to her room.

"But I didn't have a *room*," she said. "Everybody

has a suite, and there are fourteen servants somewhere below the earth, and only some of them have a window in the cell my mother calls their room, and there's only one stinking bath for all of them. My mother learns fast, wherever she is. She does not offend the host country."

Once, when we were about sixteen, we went with her grandparents at Easter time to their Adirondacks lodge, as large and shabby as was every place they lived in. Both old people drank a good deal — I think they always had, but I had only begun to notice it — and napped after every meal. But they stayed awake late into the night doing intricate picture puzzles imported from France, on two tables, and gave each other large checks for the one who finished first.

I don't remember that Julia asked their permission for our camping trips — several times we stayed away for weekends — on or near Lake Champlain. It wasn't proper camping, although we carried blankets and clean socks and dry shoes and canned food. We walked a great deal, often I fished for trout, and once, climbing a high hill, Julia threw a net over a rabbit, running with a grace and speed I had never before seen in a girl, and she showed me how to skin the rabbit. We cooked it that night wrapped in bacon and it is still among the best things I ever ate, maybe because *Robinson Crusoe* is one of the best books I ever read. Even now, seeing any island, I am busy with that rabbit and fantasies of how I would make do alone, without shelter or tools.

When we walked or fished we seldom did it side by side: that was her choice and I admired it because I believed she was thinking stuff I couldn't understand and mustn't interfere with, and maybe because I knew even then she didn't want to be side by side with anybody.

At night, wrapped in our blankets, the fire between us, we would talk. More accurately, I would ask questions and she would talk: she was one of the few people I have ever met who could give information without giving a lecture. How young it sounds now that although I had heard the name of Freud, I never knew exactly what he wrote until she told me; that Karl Marx and Engels became men with theories, instead of that one sentence in my school book which mentioned the Manifesto. But we also talked like all young people, of possible beaux and husbands and babies, and heredity versus environment, and can romantic love last, mixing stuff like that in speeches made only for the pleasure of girls on the edge of growing up.

One night, when we had been silent for a long time because she was leaning on an elbow, close to the fire, reading a German grammar, I laughed at the sounds coming from her mouth as she repeated the sentences.

She said, "No, you don't understand. People are either teachers or students. You are a student."

"Am I a good one?"

"When you find what you want, you will be very good."

I reached out and touched her hand. "I love you,

Julia." She stared at me and took my hand to her face.

It was in our nineteenth year that she went away to Oxford. The second year she was there I went to visit her. There are women who reach a perfect time of life, when the face will never again be as good, the body never as graceful or as powerful. It had happened that year to Julia, but she was no more conscious of it than she had been of being a beautiful child. Her clothes were ugly now, loose, tacky, and the shoes looked as if they had been stolen from an old man. Nobody came to her rooms because, as one smitten young Indian gentleman told me, she never asked anybody. She was invited everywhere in Oxford and in London, but the only names I remember her speaking of with respect were J. D. Bernal and J. B. S. Haldane. Once or twice we went up to the theatre in London, but she would sigh halfway through and say she had no feeling for the theatre, only Shakespeare on the page, and sometimes not even then.

The following year she wrote to tell me that she was leaving England for medical school in Vienna, with the probably vain hope that Freud would someday accept her as a student.

I wrote a number of letters that year, but the only time I heard from Julia was a cable on my birthday, followed by the Toulouse-Lautrec drawing that hangs today in my house. I was pleased that she thought I knew the excellence of Toulouse-Lautrec, because I didn't, and had to be told about him by a fellow student who used to buy me hamburgers in order, I think, to tell me about his homosexual experiences. (He was a very decorated hero during the Second World War and was killed a week before it ended.)

A few months later I had a letter from Anne-Marie Travers, a girl whom Julia and I had both known in school, but I knew better because we had gone to the same dreadful summer camp. Anne-Marie was an intelligent girl, flirtatious, good-mannered with that kind of outward early-learned passive quality that in women so often hides anger. Now, it seemed, she was in or near Vienna and her unexpected letter — I don't think we had seen each other for four or five years — said she had bumped into Julia on the street and been "snubbed," had heard from people that Julia was leading a strange life, very political, pretending not to be rich and living in the Floridsdorf district, the Socialist working-class "slums." Julia ranked second in the medical school, she had been told, the first candidate being an American also but of a German inheritance, a very remarkable boy from San Francisco, handsome in the Norwegian way, she, Anne-Marie, didn't like. It took knowing Anne-Marie to realize that German and Norwegian used in the same sentence was a combination of put-down and admiration. Anne-Marie added that her brother Sammy had recently tried to kill himself, and was I still torn between being a writer or an architect? There was something strange about the letter, some reason, some tone I didn't understand, didn't like. Then I forgot it for a month or so until her brother Sammy rang to ask me for dinner, saying that he had been living in Elba and thinking of me. He said it again at dinner, having had four whiskeys with beer chasers, and asked me if I was a virgin. This was not like Sammy, who had no interest in me, and I sensed something was to follow. At about four in the morning when we were sitting in Small's in Harlem, and there had been many more whiskeys and beers, he asked me why I had got a divorce, why hadn't I married his older brother Eliot, whose rich Detroit wife had lost all her money in the Depression, and so Eliot was again open to bids and would be right for me, although he himself thought Eliot a handsome bore. He said he rather liked his sister Anne-Marie, because he had slept with her when she was sixteen and he was eighteen. Then, perhaps because I made a sound, he said who the hell was I to talk, everybody knew about Julia and me.

It is one of the strange American changes in custom that the drunks of my day often hit each other, but never in the kind of bar fight that so often happens now with knives. In those days somebody hit somebody, and when that was finished one of them offered his hand and it would have been unheard of to refuse. (James Thurber had once thrown a glass of whiskey at me in the famous Tony's speakeasy, Hammett had pushed Thurber against a wall, Thurber had picked up a glass from another table and, in an attempt to throw it at Dash, missed and hit the waiter who was Tony's cousin. Tony called the police, saying over and over again that he had had enough of Thurber through the years. Almost everybody agreed with Tony, but when the police came we were shocked and went down to the police station to say nothing had happened except a drunken accident of a broken glass; and while I don't think Thurber liked me afterward, I don't think he had liked me before. In any case, none of us ever mentioned it again.) And so, at that minute at the table at Small's, there seemed to me nothing odd about what I did. I leaned across the table, slapped Sammy in the face, got up, turned over the table, and went home. The next day a girl called me to say that Sammy couldn't remember what he had said but he was sorry, anyway, and a large amount of flowers arrived that evening. The girl called again a few days later: I said there were no hard feelings, but Sammy was a bigger dope at twenty-five than he had been at seventeen. She said she'd tell him that.

I wrote to Anne-Marie saying that whatever Julia thought or did was bound to be interesting, and that I didn't want to hear attacks on her beliefs or her life. My letter was returned, unopened or resealed, and it was to be another year before I knew why.

Not long after, I had a letter from Julia suggesting that I come to Vienna for a visit, that Freud had accepted her, that there were things I ought to learn about "the holocaust that is on its way." I wrote back that I was living with Hammett, didn't want to leave, but would come maybe next year. Subsequent letters from her talked of Hitler, Jews, radicals, Mussolini.

421

We wrote a great deal that year, 1933–1934, and I told her that I was trying to write a play, hadn't much hope about it, but that Hammett was pulling me along. I asked her if she liked *The Children's Hour* as a title and was hurt when she forgot the question in her next letter, which was angry with news of the armed political groups in Austria, the threat of Hitler, "the criminal guilt of the English and French in not recognizing the dangers of Fascism, German style, the other one is a peacock." There was much in her letter I didn't understand, although all of us by that time knew that the Nazis would affect our lives.

I could not write a history of those years as it seemed to us then. Or, more accurately, I could not write my own: I have no records and I do not know when I understood what. I know that Hitler — Mussolini might have escaped our notice as no more than a big-talking man in silly uniforms — had shaken many of us into radicalism, or something we called radicalism, and that our raw, new convictions would, in time, bring schisms and ugly fights. But in the early Thirties I don't believe the people I knew had done much more than sign protests, listen to the shocking stories of the few German émigrés who had come to New York or Hollywood, and given money to one cause or another. We were disturbed by the anti-Semitism that was an old story in Germany and some of us had sense enough to see it as more than that. Many people thought of it as not much more than the ignorant rantings of a house painter and his low-down friends, who would certainly be rejected by the Germans, who were for my generation an "advanced," "cultivated" people.

But by 1935 or 1936 what had been only half understood, unsettling, distant stories turned horror-tragic and new assessments had to be made fast of what one believed and what one was going to do about it. The rebels of the Twenties, the generation before mine, now seemed rebels only in the Scott Fitzgerald sense: they had wasted their blood, blind to the future they could have smelled if the odor of booze hadn't been so strong. Scott knew this about himself, and understandably resented those old friends who had turned into the new radicals. But the 1920's rebels had always seemed strange to me: without charity I thought most of them were no more than a classy lot of brilliant comics, performing at low fees for the society rich. The new radicalism was what I had always been looking for.

In 1934, Hammett and I rented a charming house on Long Island and were throwing around the money from *The Thin Man*. It had been a year of heavy drinking for both of us: I drank almost as much as Hammett and our constant guests, but I was younger than most of them and didn't like myself when I drank. In any case, work on *The Children's Hour* was going bad and Hammett, who had a pleasant nature, had resolved on a new, lighter drinking program: nothing but sherry, port and beer. He was never drunker, never ate less, and was in a teasing, irritable mood. I wanted to get away from all of it. Hammett gave me the money to go to Europe.

Because I planned to stay away for a long time to

finish the play, the money had to last as long as possible. I went directly to Paris, to the small and
inexpensive Hotel Jacob, and decided to see nobody.
Once a day I went for a walk, twice a day I ate in
working-class restaurants, struggling through French
newspapers or magazines. They didn't teach me much
but I did know about the formation of the Popular
Front. There had been, there were to be, Fascist riots
in Paris that year. Like most Americans, now and
then, political troubles in Europe seemed far away
from my life and certainly far away from a play
about a little girl who ruined the lives of two women
in a New England private school.

But after a month of nobody, I was lonely and tired
of work. I telephoned Julia — we had talked several
times my first weeks in Paris — to say I'd like to
come to Vienna for a few days. She said that wasn't
a good idea at the minute, nor a good idea to talk on
a telephone that was tapped, but she'd meet me and
would send a message saying where and when. I
think that was the first time I ever knew a telephone
could be listened in on, a life could and would be
spied on. I was impressed and amused.

I waited but no word came from Julia. Then, two
weeks after my phone call, the newspaper headlines
said that Austrian government troops, aided by local
Nazis, had bombarded the Karl Marx Hof in the
Floridsdorf district of Vienna. Socialist workers, who
owned the district, had defended it, and two hundred
of them had been killed. I read the news in a little

424

restaurant called the Fourth Republic, and in the middle of my dinner ran back to the hotel for my address book. But Julia's address said nothing about the Karl Marx Hof or the Floridsdorf and so I went to bed telling myself not to imagine things. At five o'clock in the morning I had a telephone call from a man who said his name was Von Zimmer, he was calling from Vienna, Julia was in a hospital.

I have no memory of the trip to Vienna, no memory of a city I was never to see again, no memory of the name of the hospital, nor how I got to it or in what language. But I remember everything after that. It was a small hospital in a mean section of town. There were about forty people in the ward. Julia's bed was the first behind the door. The right side of her face was entirely in bandages, carried around the head and on to most of the left side, leaving only the left eye and the mouth exposed. Her right arm was lying outside the bed cover, her right leg was lying on an unseen platform. There were two or three people in uniform in the room, but most of the aides were in street clothes and it was a young boy, twelve or thirteen, who brought me a stool and said to Julia, in German, "Your friend has come," as he turned her head so that she could see me with her left eye. Neither the eye nor the hand moved as she looked at me and neither of us spoke. I have no loss of memory about that first visit: there was nothing to remember. After a while, she raised her right arm toward the center of the room and I saw the boy, who was carrying a pail, speak to a nurse. The nurse came to the bed and moved Julia's head away from me and told me she thought I should come back the next day. As I went past the desk, the young boy met me in the hall and told me to ask for a room at the Hotel Sacher. There was another note at the desk of the hotel, a place so much too expensive for me that I was about to take my bags and find another. The note said that the reservation had been made at the Sacher because I would be safe there, and that was best for Julia. It was signed John Von Zimmer.

I went back to the hospital later that evening and, as I got off the trolley car, I saw what I had not seen in the morning. The district was heavily ringed with police, and men in some other uniform. The hospital said I couldn't go into the ward, the patient was asleep after the operation. When I asked what operation, they asked how was I related to the patient, but my German, and much else, had given out. I tried to find out if the hospital desk knew John Von Zimmer's address, but they said they had never heard of him.

I was refused at the hospital the next day and the next. Three days later a handsome, pregnant lady, in a poor coat too small for her, took me into the ward. The same young boy brought me the same stool, and gently turned Julia's head toward me. Her right leg was no longer on a platform and that made me think everything was better. This time, after a few minutes, she raised her right arm and touched my hand. I stared at her hand: it had always been too large even for this tall girl, too blunt, too heavy, ugly. She took the hand away, as if she knew what I thought, and I reached back for it. We sat for a while that way and then she pointed to her mouth, meaning that she couldn't speak because of the bandages. Then she raised her hand to the window, pointed out, and made a pushing movement with her hand.

I said, "I don't know what you mean," and realized they were the first words I had spoken to her in years. She made the motion again and then shut her eye as if she couldn't go on. After a while I fell asleep on the stool with my head against the wall. Toward afternoon a nurse came and said I had to leave. Julia's bed had been wheeled out and I think the nurse was telling me that she was being "treated."

For the three days and nights I had been in Vienna I had gone nowhere, not even for a walk, only once a day to a cheap restaurant a block from the hospital where the old man who ran it talked in English and said he had once lived in Pittsburgh. I don't believe I understood where I was, or what had happened in this city, or why, and that I was too frightened of what I didn't understand to be anything more than quiet. (Fear has always made me unable to talk or to move much, almost drowsy.) I thought constantly about how to find the man called Von Zimmer, but it seemed to me each day that he would certainly come to me. On the fourth night, about ten o'clock, I had nothing more to read, was too restless and nervous for bed, and so I took the long walk back to the restaurant near the hospital. When I got there it was closed and so I walked again until it was long past midnight, thinking how little I knew about Julia's life, how seldom we had met in the last years, how little I knew of what was happening to her now.

When I got back to the hotel the young boy from the hospital ward was standing across the street. I saw him immediately and stood waiting for him. He handed me a folded slip of paper. Then he bowed and moved away.

In the lobby of the hotel, the note, written in a weak, thin handwriting, said, "Something else is needed. They will take me tomorrow to another place. Go back to Paris *fast* and leave your address at the Sacher. Love, Julia."

I was back in Paris before I remembered that when we were kids, doing our Latin together, we would take turns translating and then correcting. Often one of us would say to the other, "Something else is needed"; we said it so often that it got to be a family joke.

I waited in Paris for a month, but no word ever came. A German friend made a telephone call for me to the hospital in Vienna, but they said they didn't know Julia's name, had no record of her ever having been there. My German friend telephoned the university twice to ask for John Von Zimmer, but once somebody said he no longer was enrolled and once they had no information about his address.

And so I went back to New York, finished *The*

Children's Hour, and three nights after it was a success I telephoned Julia's grandmother. I think the old lady was drunk — she often had been when we were young — because it took a long time to explain who I was, and then she said what difference did it make who I was, she didn't know anything about Julia, neither did the Morgan Bank, who had been transmitting huge sums of money to her all over Europe, and she thought Julia was plain crazy.

About a year later I had a letter from Julia, but it is lost now and while I am sure of what it said, I am not sure how it was said by a woman who wrote what had become almost foreign English and was telling me something she evidently thought I already knew. The letter had to do with Nazism and Germany, the necessity of a Socialist revolution throughout the world, that she had had a baby, and the baby seemed to like being called Lilly, but then she was a baby who liked almost everything. She said she had no address, but I should send letters to Paris, to 16 Rue de l'Université, in care of apartment 3. I wrote immediately to thank her about Lilly, then two more times, and finally had a postcard from her with a Zurich stamp.

I can no longer remember how long after that Anne-Marie telephoned to ask me for dinner. I think I was about to say yes when Anne-Marie told me that a friend of hers had seen Julia, that Julia was doing something called anti-Fascist work, very dangerous, and throwing away her money, did I know about the baby and wasn't that nutty, a poor unwanted illegitimate child? I said I was leaving town and couldn't have dinner. Anne-Marie said that was too bad because they didn't often visit New York, but happened to be here on the opening night of *Days to Come* and had to say, frankly, that *they* hadn't liked my play. I said that wasn't illegal, not many people had liked it, and then there was more talk about Julia, something about her leg that I didn't understand, and Anne-Marie said that she wanted me to meet her husband, who, as I certainly knew, had been a colleague of Julia's in medical school in Vienna and was now a surgeon, very successful, in San Francisco. She said he was brilliant and a real beauty. I have never liked women who talk about how men look — "so attractive" was a constant phrase of my time — and to hide my irritation I said I knew she had married but I didn't know his name. She said his name was John Von Zimmer. I am sure she heard me take a deep breath because she laughed and said the next time they came to New York she would call me, and why didn't I ever see Sammy, her brother, who was always trying to commit suicide. I was never to see Sammy again, but certainly he never committed suicide because I read about him in Suzy's society column a few months ago.

In all the years that followed I only once again saw Anne-Marie, with John Von Zimmer, in 1970, when I was teaching in Berkeley. They were in a San Francisco restaurant with six or seven other stylish-looking people, and Anne-Marie kissed me and bubbled and we exchanged addresses. Von Zimmer was silent as he stared at a wall behind my head. Neither Anne-Marie nor I did the telephoning that we said we would do the next day, but I did want very much to see Von Zimmer: I had an old question to ask, and so a few days after the meeting in the restaurant I walked around to his office. But, standing near the great Victorian house, I changed my mind. I am glad now that I didn't ask the question that almost certainly would never have been answered.

But on that day in 1937, on the train moving toward the German border, I sat looking at the hatbox. The big girl was now reading the *Frankfurter Zeitung,* the thin girl had done nothing with the book that was lying on her lap. I suppose it was the announcement of the first lunch sitting that made me look up from the past, pick up my coat, and then put it down again.

The thin girl said, "Nice coat. Warm? Of what fur?"

"It's sealskin. Yes, it's warm."

She said, pointing to the hatbox, "Your hat is also fur?"

I started to say I didn't know, realized how paralyzed I had been, knew it couldn't continue, and opened the box. I took out a high, fluffy, hat of gray fox as both ladies murmured their admiration. I sat staring at it until the heavy girl said, "Put on. Nice with coat."

I suppose part of my worry, although I hadn't even

got there yet, was what to do with the knitted cap I was wearing. I took it off and rose to fix the fur hat in the long mirror between the windows. The top and sides of the hat were heavy and when I put my hand inside I felt a deep seam in the lining with heavy wads below and around the seam. It was uncomfortable and so I started to take it off when I remembered that the note said I should wear the hat.

Somewhere during my hesitations the heavy girl said she was going to lunch, could she bring me a sandwich? I said I'd rather go to lunch but I didn't know when we crossed the border, and immediately realized I had made a silly and possibly dangerous remark. The thin girl said we wouldn't be crossing until late afternoon — she had unpacked a small box and was eating a piece of meat — and if I was worried about my baggage she was staying in the compartment because she couldn't afford the prices in the dining car. The heavy girl said she couldn't afford them either, but the doctor had said she must have hot meals and a glass of wine with her medicine. So I went off with her to the dining car, leaving my coat thrown over the candy box. We sat at a table with two other people and she told me that she had been studying in Paris, had "contracted" a lung ailment, and was going home to Cologne. She said she didn't know what would happen to her Ph.D. dissertation because the lung ailment had affected her bones. She talked in a disjointed stream of words for the benefit, I thought, of the two men who sat next to us, but even

432

when they left, the chatter went on as her head turned to watch everybody in a nervous tic between sentences. I was glad to be finished with lunch, so worried was I about the candy box, but it was there, untouched, when we got back to our compartment. The thin girl was asleep, but she woke up as we came in and said something in German to the heavy girl about a crowded train, and called her Louisa. It was the first indication I had that they knew each other, and I sat silent for a long time wondering why that made me uneasy. Then I told myself that if everything went on making me nervous, I'd be in a bad fix by the time it came to be nervous.

For the next few hours, the three of us dozed or read until the thin girl tapped me on the knee and said we would be crossing the border in five or ten minutes. I suppose everybody comes to fear in a different way, but I have always grown very hot or very cold, and neither has anything to do with the weather. Now, waiting, I was very hot. As the train pulled to a standstill, I got up to go outside — people were already leaving the train to pass through a check gate, and men were coming on the train to inspect baggage in the cars ahead of us — without my coat or my new hat. I was almost out the compartment door when the thin girl said, "You will need your coat and hat. It is of a windiness."

"Thank you. But I'm not cold."

Her voice changed sharply, "You will have need of your coat. Your hat is nice on your head."

I didn't ask questions because the tone in which she spoke was the answer. I turned back, put the coat around my shoulders, put on the hat that felt even heavier now with the wads of something that filled the lining, and let both girls go past me as I adjusted it in the mirror. Coming out on the platform, they were ahead of me, separated from me by several people who had come from other compartments. The heavy girl moved on. The thin girl dropped her purse and, as she picked it up, stepped to one side and moved directly behind me. We said nothing as we waited in line to reach the two uniformed men at the check gate. As the man in front of me was having his passport examined, the thin girl said, "If you have a temporary travel-through visa, it might take many minutes more than others. But that is nothing. Do not worry."

It didn't take many minutes more than others. I went through as fast as anybody else, turned in a neat line with the other travelers, went back to the train. The thin girl was directly behind me, but as we got to the steps of the train, she said, "Please," and pushed me aside to climb in first. When we reached our compartment, the fat girl was in her seat listening to two customs men in the compartment next to ours as they had some kind of good-natured discussion with a man who was opening his luggage.

The thin girl said, "They are taking great time with the luggage." As she spoke, she leaned over and picked up my candy box. She took off the ribbon and

434

said, "Thank you. I am hungry for a chocolate. Most kind."

I said, "Please, please," and knew I was never meant for this kind of thing. "I am carrying it to a friend for a gift. Please do not open it." As the customs men came into our compartment, the thin girl was chewing on a candy, the box open on her lap. I did not know much about the next few minutes except that all baggage was dragged down from the racks, that my baggage took longer than the baggage of my companions. I remember the heavy girl chatting away, and something being said about my traveling visa, and how I was going to a theatre festival because I was a playwright. (It was two days later before I realized I had never mentioned the Moscow theatre festival or anything about myself.) And the name Hellman came into the conversation I could only half understand. One of the customs men said, "Jew," and the heavy girl said certainly the name was not always of a Jew and gave examples of people and places I couldn't follow. Then the men thanked us, replaced everything neatly, and bowed themselves out the door.

Somewhere in the next hours I stopped being hot or cold and was not to be frightened again that day. The thin girl had neatly retied my candy box, but I don't think any of us spoke again until the train pulled into the station. When the porters came on for the baggage, I told myself that now I should be nervous, that if the money had been discovered at the border gate nothing much could have happened because I was still close to France. Now was the time, therefore, for caution, intelligence, reasonable fears. But it wasn't the time, and I laughed at that side of me that so often panics at a moment of no consequence, so often grows listless and sleepy near danger.

But there was to be no danger that day. The thin girl was right behind me on the long walk toward the station gate, people kissing and shaking hands all along the way. A man and a woman of about fifty came toward me, the woman holding out her arms and saying in English, "Lillian, how good it is to see you. How naughty of you not to stay more than a few hours, but even that will give us time for a nice visit — " as the thin girl, very close to me now, said, "Give her the candy box."

I said, "I am so glad to see you again. I have brought you a small gift, gifts — " but the box was now out of my hands and I was being moved toward the gate. Long before we reached the gate the woman and the thin girl had disappeared.

The man said, "Go through the gate. Ask the man at the gate if there is a restaurant near the station. If he says Albert's go to it. If he gives you another name, go to that one, look at it, and turn back to Albert's, which is directly opposite the door you are facing." As I asked the official at the gate about a restaurant, the man went past me. The official said please to step to one side, he was busy, would take care of me in a minute. I didn't like being in the station so I crossed the street to Albert's. I went through a revolving door and was so shocked at the sight of Julia at a table that I stopped at the door. She half rose, called softly, and I went toward her with tears that I couldn't stop because I saw two crutches lying next to her and now knew what I had never wanted to know before. Half out of her seat, holding to the table, she said, "Fine, fine. I have ordered caviar for us to celebrate, Albert had to send for it, it won't be long."

She held my hand for several minutes, and said, "Fine. Everything has gone fine. Nothing will happen now. Let's eat and drink and see each other. So many years."

I said, "How long have we got? How far is the other station, the one where I get the train to Moscow?"

"You have two hours, but we haven't that long together because you have to be followed to the station and the ones who follow you must have time to find the man who will be with you on the train until Warsaw in the morning."

I said, "You look like nobody else. You are more beautiful now."

She said, "Stop crying about my leg. It was amputated and the false leg is clumsily made so I am coming to New York in the next few months, as soon as I can, and get a good one. Lilly, don't cry for me. *Stop the tears.* We must finish the work now. Take off the hat the way you would if it was too hot for this place. Comb your hair, and put the hat on the seat between us."

Her coat was open, and the minute I put the hat on the bench she pinned it deep inside her coat with a safety pin that was ready for it.

She said, "Now I am going to the toilet. If the waiter tries to help me up, wave him aside and come with me. The toilet locks. If anybody should try to open it, knock on the door and call to me, but I don't think that will happen."

She got up, picked up one of the crutches, and waved me to the other arm. She spoke in German to a man I guess was Albert as we moved down the long room. She pulled the crutch too quickly into the toilet door, it caught at a wrong angle, and she made a gesture with the crutch, tearing at it in irritation.

When she came out of the toilet, she smiled at me. As we walked back to the table, she spoke in a loud voice, saying something in German about the toilet and then, in English, "I forget you don't know German. I was saying that German public toilets are always clean, much cleaner than ours, particularly under the new regime. The bastards, the murderers."

Caviar and wine were on the table when we sat down again and she was cheerful with the waiter. When he had gone away she said, "Ah, Lilly. Fine, fine. Nothing will happen now. But it is your right to know that it is my money you brought in and we can save five hundred, and maybe, if we can bargain right, a thousand people with it. So believe that you have been better than a good friend to me, you have done something important."

"Jews?"

"About half. And political people. Socialists, Communists, plain old Catholic dissenters. Jews aren't the only people who have suffered here." She sighed. "That's enough of that. We can only do today what we can do today and today you did it for us. Do you need something stronger than wine?"

I said I didn't and she said to talk fast now, there wasn't much time, to tell her as much as possible. I told her about my divorce, about the years with Hammett. She said she had read *The Children's Hour,* she was pleased with me, and what was I going to do next?

I said, "I did it. A second play, a failure. Tell me about your baby."

"She's fat and handsome. I've got over minding that she looks like my mother."

"I want very much to see her."

"You will," she said, "I'll bring her when I come home for the new leg and she can live with you, if you like."

I said, meaning no harm, "Couldn't I see her now?"

"Are you crazy? Do you think I would bring her here? Isn't it enough I took chances with your safety? I will pay for that tonight and tomorrow and . . ." Then she smiled. "The baby lives in Mulhouse, with some nice folks. I see her that way whenever I cross the border. Maybe, when I come back for the leg, I'll leave her with you. She shouldn't be in Europe. It ain't for babies now."

"I haven't a house or even an apartment of any permanence," I said, "but I'll get one if you bring the baby."

"Sure. But it wouldn't matter. You'd be good to her." Then she laughed. "Are you as angry a woman as you were a child?"

"I think so," I said. "I try not to be, but there it is."

"Why do you try not to be?"

"If you lived around me, you wouldn't ask."

"I've always liked your anger," she said, "trusted it."

"You're the only one, then, who has."

"Don't let people talk you out of it. It may be uncomfortable for them, but it's valuable to you. It's what made you bring the money in today. Yes, I'll leave the baby with you. Its father won't disturb you, he wants nothing to do with the baby or with me. He's O.K. Just an ordinary climber. I don't know why I did it, Freud told me not to, but I don't care. The baby's good."

She smiled and patted my hand. "Someday I will take you to meet Freud. What am I saying? I will probably never see him again — I have only so much longer to last in Europe. The crutches make me too noticeable. The man who will take care of you has just come into the street. Do you see him outside the window? Get up and go now. Walk across the street, get a taxi, take it to Bahnhof 200. Another man will be waiting there. He will make sure you get safely on the train and will stay with you until Warsaw tomorrow morning. He is in car A, compartment 13. Let me see your ticket."

I gave it to her. "I think that will be in the car to your left." She laughed. "*Left,* Lilly, *left.* Have you ever learned to tell left from right, south from north?"

"No. I don't want to leave you. The train doesn't go for over an hour. I want to stay with you a few more minutes."

"No," she said. "Something could still go wrong and we must have time to get help if that should happen. I'll be coming to New York in a few months. Write from Moscow to American Express in Paris. I have stuff picked up every few weeks." She took my hand and raised it to her lips. "My beloved friend."

Then she pushed me and I was on my feet. When I got to the door I turned and must have taken a step back because she shook her head and moved her face to look at another part of the room.

I did not see the man who followed me to the station. I did not see the other man on the train, although several times a youngish man passed my compartment and the same man took the vacant chair next to me at dinner, but didn't speak to me at all.

When I went back to my compartment from dinner the conductor asked if I wanted my two small valises put in the corridor for examination when we crossed the German-Polish border so that I wouldn't be awakened. I told him I had a wardrobe trunk in the baggage car, handed him the key for the customs people, and went to sleep on the first sleeping pill of my life, which may be why I didn't wake up until just before we pulled into the Warsaw station at seven in the morning. There was bustle in the station as I raised the curtain to look out. Standing below my window was the young man who had sat next to me at dinner. He made a gesture with his hand, but I didn't understand and shook my head. Then he looked around and pointed to his right. I shook my head again, bewildered, and he moved away from the window. In a minute there was a knock on my door and I rose to open it. An English accent said through the crack, "Good morning. Wanted to say goodbye to you, have a happy trip." And then, very, very softly, "Your trunk was removed by the Germans. You are in no danger because you are across the border. Do nothing for a few hours and then ask the Polish conductor about the trunk. Don't return from Moscow through Germany, travel another way." In a loud voice he said, "My best regards to your family," and disappeared.

For two hours I sat in bed, doubtful, frightened of the next move, worried about the loss of clothes in my trunk. When I got dressed, I asked the Polish conductor if the German conductor had left my trunk key with him. He was upset when he told me the German customs people had removed the trunk, that often happened, but he was sure it would be sent on to me in

Moscow after a few days, nothing unusual, the German swine often did it now.

The trunk did arrive in Moscow two weeks later. The lining was in shreds, the drawers were broken, but only a camera was missing and four or five books. I did not know then, and I do not know now, whether the trunk had anything to do with Julia because I was not to see Germany for thirty years and I was never to speak with Julia again.

I wrote to her from Moscow, again from Prague on my way back to Paris, and after I had returned to New York from Spain during the Civil War. Three or four months later I had a card with a Geneva postmark. It said, says, "Good girl to go to Spain. Did it convince you? We'll talk about that when I return to New York in March."

But March and April came and went and there was no word from Julia. I telephoned her grandmother, but I should have known better. The old lady said they hadn't heard from Julia in two years and why did I keep worrying her? I said I had seen Julia in October and she hung up the phone. Somewhere about that time I saw a magazine picture of Julia's mother, who had just married again, an Argentine, but I saw no reason for remembering his name.

On May 23, 1938, I had a cable, dated London two days before and sent to the wrong address. It said, "Julia has been killed stop please advise Moore's funeral home Whitechapel Road London what disposi-

tion stop my sorrow for you for all of us." It was
signed John Watson but had no address.

It is never possible for me to cry at the time when
it could do me some good, so, instead, I got very drunk
for two days and don't remember anything about
them. The third morning I went around to Julia's
grandmother's house and was told by the butler, who
came out on the street as if I were a danger to the
house, that the old people were on a world cruise and
wouldn't be back for eight weeks. I asked the name of
the boat, was asked for my credentials, and by the
time we batted all that around, I was screaming that
their granddaughter was dead and that he and they
could go fuck themselves. I was so sick that night
that Dash, who never wanted me to go anywhere because he never wanted to, said he thought I should go
to London right away.

I have no diary notes of that trip and now only the
memory of standing over a body with a restored face
that didn't hide the knife wound that ran down the left
side. The funeral man explained that he had tried to
cover the face slash but I should see the wounds on
the body if I wanted to see a mess that couldn't be
covered. I left the place and stood on the street for a
while. When I went back in the funeral man handed
me a note over the lunch he was eating. The note said,
"Dear Miss Hellman. We have counted on your coming but perhaps it is not possible for you, so I will
send a carbon of this to your New York address. None
of us knows what disposition her family wishes to

make, where they want what should be a hero's funeral. It is your right to know that the Nazis found her in Frankfurt, in the apartment of a colleague. We got her to London in the hope of saving her. Sorry that I cannot be here to help you. It is better that I take my sorrow for this wonderful woman into action and perhaps revenge. Yours, John Watson, who speaks here for many others. Salud."

I went away that day and toward evening telephoned the funeral man to ask if he had an address for John Watson. He said he had never heard the name John Watson, he had picked up the body at the house of a Dr. Chester Lowe at 30 Downshire Hill. When I got there it was a house that had been made into apartments, but there was no Dr. Lowe on the name plates, and for the first time it occurred to me that my investigations could be bad for people who were themselves in danger.

So I brought the body home with me on the old *De Grasse* and tried this time to reach Julia's mother. The same butler told me that he couldn't give me her mother's address, although he knew the mother had been informed of the death. I had the body cremated and the ashes are still where they were that day so long ago.

I should, of course, have gone to Mulhouse before I came home from London, but I didn't, didn't even think about it in those awful days in London or on the boat. After the cremation, I wrote to Julia's grandmother, told her about the baby and that I knew nothing more than that she lived with a family in Mulhouse, but Mulhouse couldn't be so big that they would have trouble finding an American child. I had no answer. I guess I knew I wouldn't, and so I wrote another letter, this time nasty, and got an answer from a fancy name in a fancy law firm saying that everything would be done "in this strange case" about a child only I believed existed and I would be kept informed of any "doubtful results."

In the next few months, I found I dreamed every night about Julia, who was almost always the age when I first met her. Hammett said I looked awful and if it worried me that much why didn't I find a lawyer or a detective in Mulhouse. William Wyler, the movie director, with whom I had made two pictures, had been born in Mulhouse and his family still owned a department store there. It is too long ago for me to be accurate about when and how he got me the name of a lawyer in Mulhouse, but he did, and after a while the lawyer wrote that the investigation was proving difficult, but he thought, in the end, they would certainly find the baby if she was still there.

Three months later the war broke out and I never heard again from anybody in Western Europe until I arrived in London from Russia in March 1944. My second day there — my reason for being there was to do a documentary film for the British government about people on the docksides during the V–2 bombings — I realized I was somewhere in the neighborhood of the funeral parlor. I found it, but it had been bombed to pieces.

Nothing is left of all this except that sometime in the early 1950's, I was sitting on a stone wall at a Long Island picnic at Ruth and Marshall Field's. A man next to me was talking about a man called Onassis — the first time I had heard his name — and a lawsuit by the U.S. government against Onassis, and when he was finished with that he turned to me and said, "My father was the lawyer to whom you wrote about Julia. I am Julia's third cousin."

After a while I said, "Yes."

He said, "My father died last year."

"Your father never wrote to me again."

He said, "You see, I'm not a lawyer, I'm a banker."

I said, "Whatever happened to her family?"

"The grandparents are dead. Julia senior lives in Argentina — "

"The bastards," I said, "all of them."

He smiled at me. "They are my cousins."

"Did they ever find the baby they didn't want to find? I don't care who you are."

"I never knew anything about a baby," he said.

I said, "I don't believe you," got off the stone fence, left a note for Ruthie saying I didn't feel well, and drove home.

*T*he publication of this history of my friend, Julia, brought strange letters: one from a clumsy blackmailer who made a ridiculous guess about her identity; some with odd and dogmatic misunderstandings that were possibly caused by the fusion of the movie, in many places quite different from what is here on the page.

My refusal to reveal her name had many reasons. Previous threats from her family, a fear without base because I have heard nothing from them. Then, most important, I had wanted to write about Julia for years and had to overcome a conviction she would not want it. And there were the lawyers who read the original manuscript for me and for my publishers: they had quite proper worries of invasion of privacy suits and they had those worries to such an extent that I even changed the street where Julia's grandparents lived.

There was no way to answer all the oddities that came

449

to me: was Julia really as tall as Vanessa Redgrave, was she a Jew, part Jew, crazy? But there are a few things that came about after the publication that might be of interest.

Only one person has guessed her identity and she doesn't know she guessed it correctly. Her reasons for the guess are sound: she is second cousin to Julia, an heir to the same fortune, and somewhere in her younger years she had, evidently, heard a version, her family's, of some part of what happened. It is thus not strange that she made the right guess. What is odd is that she is very like Julia. Her life, with her husband and three children, has no relation to Julia's, but her sense of social responsibility, although it springs from another time and place, and without much thought, is very like Julia's. She, too, cares nothing for money and gives it away very well. I hope someday to tell her that.

I had expected to hear from Anne-Marie. But that has not happened, although last year a friend told me that Anne-Marie says that she never really knew Julia, but that I was in love with her husband when we were all so very, very young. As I have written here, I met her husband once and then over a nod in a restaurant. Sammy, Anne-Marie's brother, sent me a warm note after "Julia" and said he was happily married and living in Japan on his father-in-law's money.

A few months after the English edition of the book appeared I had a letter from a Dr. Smith, as I will name him here. He said he had been born in the house to which the wounded or already dead Julia had been brought, that his father was still living, and why had I wanted to involve his father by claiming that he had is-

sued a false death certificate? I answered immediately, saying I had changed his father's name and changed the address. (I am no longer sure that I did change the address. The diary from which I took the notes for this book was written months after Julia's death and I could have meant to alter the address without doing so. But I am sure I changed the name of Dr. Smith's father because I have verified that.) I had no answer from my reply to Dr. Smith, and heard nothing until two years ago when I was in England and an interview with me was published in a newspaper. That night I had a phone call from Smith saying that he believed we should meet. We made an appointment for tea in the lobby of my hotel and I waited for an hour. He did not appear. A few days later I had another phone call. Dr. Smith said his father had persuaded him not to meet me, no good could come of it, and maybe some harm. I said I didn't understand, but please to tell his father that if I had given his correct address I was sorry for the mistake, but certainly I had not given his name. In any case, had any harm come to his father? There was so long a pause that I thought the phone had gone dead. Then Dr. Smith said his father had forbidden him to come to see me because of the younger Smith's "attitude." His father was sitting next to him as he spoke to me now, could not speak to me himself because he had a partial stroke and could speak and write only with difficulty, but wanted me to know that I had done a "great woman" a "little justice." Then there was something garbled, and Dr. Smith said his father was both speaking and writing, would I wait, and when he came back to the phone he said his father wanted me to know that he, and at least five other people, had al-

ways known where Julia's baby was, boarding with a fine man and woman who were part of the anti-Nazi movement and, of course, were among the first to be wiped out by the Germans on their entrance into Alsace. It was now I who made the phone silent: it had not occurred to me that Dashiell Hammett had been right when over and over again he told me that Julia would, of course, have told trusted friends where the baby was located. It is awful to say I was happy about the news of a baby's certain death, but I was. There had, in the end, been nothing I could have done and guilt was gone now, on this phone call. I tried to tell Dr. Smith that, gave up, asked if I might come and see his father or send him something, and Dr. Smith said certainly not, but goodbye and his father said good luck and thanks.

It took me several days to realize that his tone throughout the conversation had been surly, the way a child speaks when a parent is standing by to monitor an action. I have no answer and no guess about Dr. Smith, his letter, his canceled visit or his phone call. I was probably told at least one lie: I looked him up in the present London phone directory and no such name was listed as a doctor, although I guess he could be a research man in an institute. I wanted to ask friends in London if they knew the father or the son, but somehow that seemed wrong: they did not want to see me and their reasons were their own, and maybe because there is no country in the world that pays honor to early anti-Nazis.

Theatre

I T is strange to me that so many people like to listen to so many other people talk about the theatre. There are those who talk for large fees or give it away at small dinner parties and often their stories are charming and funny, but they are seldom people who have done much solid work. You are there, you are good in the theatre, you have written or directed or acted or designed just because you have and there is little that you can or should be certain about because almost everything in the theatre contradicts something else. People have come together, as much by accident as by design, done the best they can and sometimes the worst, profited or not, gone their way vowing to see each other the next week, mean it, and wave across a room a few years later.

The manuscript, the words on the page, was what

you started with and what you have left. The production is of great importance, has given the play the only life it will know, but it is gone, in the end, and the pages are the only wall against which to throw the future or measure the past.

How the pages got there, in their form, in their order, is more of a mystery than reason would hope for. That is why I have never wanted to write about the theatre and find the teaching of English literature more rewarding than teaching drama. (Drama usually means "the theatre," the stories about it, chatter of failure and success.) You are good in boats not alone from knowledge, but because water is a part of you, you are easy on it, fear it and like it in such equal parts that you work well in a boat without thinking about it and may be even safer because you don't need to think too much. That is what we mean by instinct and there is no way to explain an instinct for the theatre, although those who have it recognize each other and a bond is formed between them. The need of theatre instinct may be why so many good writers have been such inferior playwrights — the light that a natural dramatist can see on a dark road is simply not there.

There are, of course, other reasons why I have not written about the theatre: I have known for many years that part of me struggled too hard within it, and the reasons for that I do not know and they could not, in any case, be of interest to anybody but me. I always knew that I was seldom comfortable with theatre people although I am completely comfortable in a theatre; and I am now at an age when the cutting up of old touches must be carefully watched and any sentence that begins "I remember" lasts too long for my taste, even when I myself say it.

But I have certain pictures, portraits, mementos of my plays. They are what I have left of the long years, the pleasure in the work and the pains.

The Children's Hour was my first play. I don't remember very much about the writing or the casting, but I remember Lee Shubert, who owned the theatre, as he did many other theatres in New York, coming down the aisle to stare at me during a rehearsal day. I was sitting mid-theatre with my feet on the top of the chair in front of me. He came around to stand directly before me and said, "Take your dirty shoes off my chair."

I said, "My shoes aren't touching the chair, Mr. Shubert," but, after a pause, he pushed my right leg to the floor.

I said, "I don't like strange men fooling around with my right leg so don't do it again."

Mr. Shubert called out to Herman Shumlin, who was directing the play from the front row. They met in the aisle and I heard Herman say, "That girl, as you call her, is the author of the play," and went back to directing. About half an hour later, Mr. Shubert, who had been standing in the back watching the play for which he had put up the money, came down and sat behind me.

"This play," he said to the back of my head, "could land us all in jail." He had been watching the confession scene, the recognition of the love of one woman for another.

I said, "I am eating a frankfurter and I don't want to think about jail. Would you like a piece of it?"

"I forbid you to get mustard on my chairs," he said and I was never to see him again until the play had been running for about six months and then I heard him ask the doorman who I was.

I've always told myself that I was so drunk on the opening night of *The Children's Hour* because I had begun to drink two nights before. I had gone to have dinner with my mother and father, who had not read the play, had not seen the rehearsals, had asked no questions, but, obviously, had talked to each other when they were alone. Both of them were proud of me, but in my family you didn't show such things, and both of them, I think, were frightened for me in a world they didn't know.

In any case, my mother, who frequently made sentences that had nothing to do with what went before, said, in space, "Well, all I know is that you were considered the sweetest-smelling baby in New Orleans."

She had, through my life, told me this several times before, describing how two strange ladies had paused in front of our house to stare at me in the baby carriage and then to lean down and sniff me. One of them had said, "That's the sweetest-smelling baby in town." The other had said, "In all New Orleans," and when my mother told our neighbor about her pleasure in this exchange, the neighbor had said of course it was true, famously true, I always smelled fresh as a flower. I didn't know that my mother had never until that night told my father or, if she had, he was less nervous than he was two nights before the opening. Now, when she repeated it, he said, *"Who* was the sweetest-smelling baby in New Orleans?"

"Lillian," said my mother.

"Lillian? Lillian?" said my father. *"I* was the sweetest-smelling baby in New Orleans and you got that information from my mother and sisters and have stolen it."

"Stolen it?" said my shocked mother. "I never stole anything in my life and you know it. Lillian was the sweetest-smelling baby in New Orleans and I can prove it."

"It's disgraceful," said my father, "what you are doing. You have taken what people said about *me, always said about me,* and given it to your own child."

"Your child, too," said my mother.

"That's no reason for lying and stealing," said my father. "I must ask you now to take it back and not to repeat it again."

My mother was a gentle woman and would do almost anything to avoid a fight, but now she was aroused as I had never before seen her.

"I will take nothing back. You are depriving your own child of her rightful honor and I think it disgraceful."

My father rose from the table. "I will telephone Jenny and prove it to you," he said.

He was giving the phone operator the number of his sisters' house in New Orleans when my mother yelled, "Jenny and Hannah will say anything you tell them to. I won't have it. Lillian was the sweetest-smelling baby in New Orleans and that's that." She began to cry.

I said, "I think maybe you're both crazy." I went to the sideboard and poured myself a large straight whiskey. My father, holding the phone, said to me, "Sweet-smelling, are you? You've been drinking too much for years."

"Don't pay him any mind, baby," said my mother, "any man who would deny his own child."

I left before my father spoke to his sisters and only found out months later that although my mother and father came to the opening night together, and both of them kissed me, they didn't speak to each other for several days.

On the afternoon of the opening night of *The Children's Hour* I drowned the hangover with brandy. I think I saw the play from the back of the theatre, holding to the rail, but I am not sure: I do remember the final curtain and an audience yelling, "Author, author." It was not all modesty that kept me from the curtain call — I couldn't have made backstage without falling. I wish I had understood and been happy in all the excited noise that comes only when the author is unknown and will never come again in quite so generous a fashion. I remember Robert Benchley pressing my arm and nodding his head as he passed me on his way out of the theatre. It was a nice thing for a critic to do, but I don't think I knew what he meant. I knew only half-things that happened that night: I went to the Plaza Hotel, but I can't remember who was at the table; I went to Tony's with some people who were at the Plaza; I went to Herman's apartment and he told me that the papers were very good indeed and we would be a big hit and he had a bad headache. For the next few hours I have no account. Then I was in a strange bar, not unusual for me in those days, and I was talking to a man and two women. Or they were talking to me and the conversation had to do with the metallic fringe that was on the bottom of the younger woman's dress. Then I was asleep, sitting up, on my couch in the Elysée Hotel. When I woke up one of the women was watering the plants on the windowsill and the other woman was crying, standing against a wall. I said to the man, "Are these your sisters?" and he laughed.

"What's funny about that?"

"Sez you," he said, "sez you."

"I'm going to marry him," said the one who was standing against the wall, "and it's already shit. Everybody has missed the boat, everywhere, everywhere, everywhere and somehow."

"Ssh," I said, "I owe this hotel a lot of money."

"The boat," she screamed, "everybody, everywhere."

There was some more of that. I went to make coffee and when I came back the pair who were going to get married were sitting on the couch holding hands and the one who had been watering the plants was reading my first-night telegrams at the desk. (I was to meet her again a few years later. She was a handsome, boyish-looking woman at every society-literary cocktail party. Her name was Emily Vanderbilt and she was to marry Raoul Whitfield, a mystery story writer. A few years after the marriage she was murdered on a ranch they bought in New Mexico, and neither the mystery story expert nor the police ever found the murderer.) Nobody spoke until the potential bride suddenly pushed her fiancé off the couch, and the one reading the telegrams screamed, "Moxie! Moxie!"

I said — I think it was the sentence I most often used in those years — "Why don't you all go home?"

The man had picked himself up from the floor, was pouring himself a drink, Moxie and her friend were arguing about something or other, when I went in the bedroom shouting, "Why don't you all go home," and locked the door. It was still dark, maybe six o'clock, when I woke up with an awful headache and cramps in my legs, remembering that I should have telephoned Hammett, who was in Hollywood, to tell him the play was a hit. I wanted a cold beer and went through the living room to get it. I thought the room was empty, but as I was returning to bed with my beer, I saw the man sitting at the desk staring out of the window.

I coughed and he turned to me, raising his empty highball glass. "Want to get me a fresh drinkie?"

"What did you do with your ladies?"

"I certainly would like an eensy drink."

"I don't feel well. I have work to do. I have to make a phone call. I had a play open last night."

"You kept saying that," he said. "I'm a doctor."

"*You're* a doctor?"

"Opening an office next week, Park and 80th, going in with my uncle, the heart specialist. Come and see me."

I said I didn't think I'd do that and put a call through to Hammett in the rented house with the soda fountain in the Pacific Palisades. After a long time a woman answered the phone and said she was Mr. Hammett's secretary, what a strange hour to be calling. I sat on the couch thinking about that and feeling very dizzy from the beer.

The doctor said, "What's your name?"

I went back to the bedroom, closed the door, and knew the question had sobered me up. I had wasted what should have been the nicest night of my life. I disliked then and dislike now those who spoil pleasure or luck when it comes not so much because they refuse it — they are a different breed — but because they cannot see it or abandon it for blind nonsense. I had done just that and wanted now to find out about it.

The doctor opened the door. "Do you want to go out for breakfast or Atlantic City? What's your name?"

I said, "What's yours?"

"Peregrine Perry. From Lord Perry of long ago."

"Do they call you Perry Perry?"

"Oh, Christ," he said, "all you have to do is wait for it."

He closed the door, and when I woke up that afternoon the apartment was empty.

(Ten years later I bought a house on 82nd Street and somewhere in that first year I saw him come out of an office with a sign on it that said "Dr. P. John Perry" and get into a car driven by a chauffeur.)

But long before that, two days after the woman had told me she was Hammett's secretary, I realized that I had called Hammett at three A.M. California time and that he had no secretary. We had spoken on the phone a number of times in those days — he was very happy about *The Children's Hour,* proud that all his trouble with me had paid off — but on the day I understood about the secretary and three o'clock in the morning I took a plane to Los Angeles. By the time I got to the house in the Pacific Palisades it was night and I had had a good deal to drink. I went immediately to the soda fountain — Hammett had rented the house from Harold Lloyd — smashed it to pieces and flew back to New York on a late night plane.

The failure of a second work is, I think, more damaging to a writer than failure ever will be again. It is then that the success of the first work seems an accident and, if the fears you had as you wrote it were dissipated by the praise, now you remember that the praise did not always come from the best minds and even when it did it could have been that they were not telling the truth or that you had played good tricks. And you are probably too young, too young at writing, to have found out that you really only care what a few people think; only they, with the change in names that time brings about, will stand behind your chair for good or bad, forever. But failure in the theatre is more public, more brilliant, more unreal than in any other field. The praise is usually out of bounds: the photographs, interviews, "appearances," party invitations are so swift and dazzling that you go into the second work with confidence you will never have again if you have any sense.

Days to Come was written in Princeton, New Jersey. Hammett, who never wanted much to live in New York, had rented the lovely house of a rich professor who was a Napoleon expert. Its overformal Directoire furniture was filled each night with students who liked Hammett, but liked even better the free alcohol and the odd corners where they could sleep and bring their friends. That makes it sound like now, when students are often interesting, but it wasn't: they were a dull generation, but Dash never much examined the people to whom he was talking if he was drunk enough to talk at all.

Even now the pains I had on the opening night of

Days to Come puzzle me. Good theatre jokes are almost always based on survived disasters, and there
were so many that night that they should, in time,
have passed into comedy: the carefully rehearsed light
cues worked as if they were meant for another play;
the props, not too complicated, showed up where nobody had ever seen them before and broke, or didn't
break, with the malice of animated beings; good actors
knew by the first twenty minutes they had lost the audience and thus became bad actors; the audience, maybe
friendly as it came in, was soon restless and uncomfortable. The air of a theatre is unmistakable: things
go well or they do not. They did not. Standing in the
back of the side aisle, I vomited without knowing it
was going to happen and went home to change my
clothes. I wanted, of course, to go to bed and stay
there, but I was young enough to worry about cowardice and so I got back in time to see William Ran-
dolph Hearst lead his six guests out of the theatre,
in the middle of the second act, talking very loud as
they came up the aisle.

It is hard for me to believe these many years later
in the guilt I felt for the failure of *Days to Come;*
the threads of those threads have lasted to this day.
Guilt is often an excuse for not thinking and maybe
that's what happened to me. In any case, it was to be
two years before I could write another play, *The Little
Foxes*, and when I did get to it I was so scared that
I wrote it nine times.

Up to a year ago I used to think of *Days to Come*

as the play that taught me not to vomit. (I have never vomited again.) Reading it then, for a book that includes all my plays, I liked it: it is crowded and over-wrought, but it is a good report of rich liberals in the 1930's, of a labor leader who saw through them, of a modern lost lady, and has in it a correct prediction of how conservative the American labor movement was to become.

Soon after *The Children's Hour* I had had an offer to write movies for Samuel Goldwyn. I think Mr. Goldwyn was in his early fifties when we first met, but he was so vigorous and springy that I was not conscious of his age for many years. He was, as were many of the bright, rough, tough lot that first saw the potential of the motion picture camera, a man of great power. Often the power would rise to an inexplicable pitch of panic anger when he was crossed or disappointed, and could then decline within minutes to the whispered, pained moral talk of a loony clergyman whimpering that God had betrayed him. What I liked best were not Mr. Goldwyn's changes of English speech, although some of them were mighty nice and often better than the original. Certainly "I took it all with a dose of salts" is just as good as a grain; the more famous "a verbal contract isn't worth the paper it is written on" makes sense; he meant to be courteous the day he called down "Bon voyage to all of you" to those of us on the dock, as he, a passenger, sailed away; and when, soon after the war, he was asked to make a toast to Field Marshal Montgomery, and rose, lifted his glass, and said, "A long life to Marshall Field Montgomery Ward," one knew exactly why. But I liked best his calculated eccentricities. When he needed a favor or had to make a difficult bargain and knew a first move was not the best position from which to deal, he was brilliant. I was in his office when he wanted an actor under contract to Darryl Zanuck and demanded that Zanuck's secretary call him out of a meeting. After a long wait, Mr. Goldwyn said into the phone, "Yes, Darryl? What can I do for you today?" And a few years after the McCarthy period, during which I was banned in Hollywood, my phone rang in Martha's Vineyard. Mr. Goldwyn's secretary and I had a pleasant reunion, she said he had been trying to reach me for two days to ask if I wanted to write *Porgy and Bess.* After a long wait Mr. Goldwyn's voice said, "Hello, Lillian, hello. Nice of you to call me after all these years. How can I help you?"

But I think our early days together worked well because I was a difficult young woman who didn't care as much about money as the people around me and so, by accident, I took a right step within the first months of working for Mr. Goldwyn. I had been hired to rewrite an old silly, hoping I could make it O.K., to be directed by Sidney Franklin, a famous man who had done many of the Norma Shearer pictures. It was then, and often still is, the custom to talk for weeks and months before the writer is allowed to touch the typewriter. Such conferences were called breaking the back of the story and that is, indeed, an accurate description. We, a nice English playwright called Mordaunt Shairp and I, would arrive at Franklin's house each morning at ten, have a refined health lunch a few hours later, and leave at five. The next day whatever we had decided would sometimes be altered and sometimes be scrapped because Franklin had consulted a friend the night before or discussed our decisions with his bridge partners. After six or seven weeks of this, Franklin said it was rude of me to lie all day on his couch with my back turned to him, napping. I left his house saying I was sorry, it was rude, but I couldn't go on that way. I took the night plane to New York, locked myself in with some books, and the first telephone call I answered two days later was from Mr. Goldwyn, who said if I came back immediately I could go to a room by myself, start writing, and he'd give me a raise. I said I'd think about it, didn't, and left for Paris. When he found me there a week later he offered a long-term contract with fine clauses about doing nothing but stories I liked and doing them where and when I liked. I had become valuable to Mr. Goldwyn because I had left him for reasons he didn't understand. For many years that made me an unattainable woman, as desirable as such women are, in another context, for men who like them that way.

They were good years and most of the time I enjoyed Mr. Goldwyn. The extraordinary conflicts in a man who wished to make "fine pictures" and climb into an educated or social world while grappling at the same time with a nature made rough by early poverty and tough by later big money amused me, and made him far more interesting than more "civilized" men like Irving Thalberg. (I never understood Scott Fitzgerald's *The Last Tycoon* version of Thalberg: the romanticism that went into that portrait had, in my mind, little to do with the obvious man who had once offered me a job by telling me how lucky I would be to work with him.) But, as in the theatre, I have few memories of the actual work I did in pictures, although I have sharp recollections of much that happened outside the work. And maybe, in the end, they are the same tale.

I had known George Haight in New York as a bright young man from Yale who had written *Goodbye Again*, a funny play. One of his friends, his ex-college roommate, I think, was a director, Henry C. Potter, and now all three of us were in Hollywood, George working as some kind of executive for Goldwyn. No two men, Haight and Potter, could have been more unalike: George was loose-limbed, sloppy, gay, wonderful at magicians' tricks, full of nice jokes; Potter was prep-school handsome, respectable, grandson of a bishop, an unexpected man for the world of the theatre or Hollywood. I was glad to find George working for Goldwyn: it was nice to wander into his office for an hour's exhibition of his newest card tricks or to have him wander into mine for a long afternoon's sleep.

I no longer remember what year I went to Cuba for

a vacation after the opening of what play and on my way to write what movie script. It was the custom then in some parts of Europe and most of Latin America to sell small boxes of wax matches with pictures of movie stars pasted to the box. I don't know what publicity department sent Henry C. Potter's picture out to what match factory — he did look like the cleanest of juveniles — but I came across two boxes and, to please George Haight, gave the head bellboy at the Hotel Nacional five dollars and the promise of a dollar a box for any more he could find. I arrived in Hollywood with nine Henry C. Potter matchboxes and for days George had them laid out on his desk brooding over them. Then he told me that Potter was giving a cocktail party in a few weeks and he thought he had the answer: we were to stamp twenty-seven condoms with the words "Compliments of Henry C. Potter," roll them three to a box, and he, Haight, would distribute them on tables at the cocktail party. Since George was very skillful with his hands and knew where all gadgets were to be bought, we did not foresee, that day of our pleasure, the awful work that was to come.

George bought the stamps, the delicate knives, a small stove to melt the wax that would be used to make the words and, during the first few days, the condoms in the drugstore opposite the studio. I was not skillful, but to my surprise he wasn't either. The carefully carved stamps broke the condoms because hot wax made holes and cool wax wouldn't take. After a time our drugstore ran out of condoms and one of the lasting minutes my eyes will hold is the picture of the owner as he stared at George on his last request for twelve boxes.

When George was unable to persuade me that it was my turn to find a new place to buy condoms, we had a cool day of not talking to each other. But the following morning he showed up with a dozen more boxes, fresh stamps, a more delicate knife, and a new theory for the process. By the third or fourth day of our second week we had given up all other work. Haight's secretary had, from the first, been posted at the door to keep out visitors, but now I refused two conferences with Mr. Goldwyn on the grounds that I first had to try out my ideas on Haight, who had nothing to do with the picture I was writing. And by that time we were not in a good humor with each other — I thought he was not as skillful as he once was, and he said I was clumsy and that he should have known it. One day, in fact, miserable and tired, we raised our voices to the point where the music department, situated in the building directly behind, came to their windows to watch the waving about of ruined condoms, and I yelled at them to mind their business.

I can no longer remember how we solved the stamping, but we did, and there were twenty-seven perfect condoms laid out on a table, all reading in green "Compliments of Henry C. Potter." We quit work early that day, but after enough celebrating drinks we forgot why we had left the studio and went to gamble in the Clover Club and got back to the studio about five in the morning because George said we only had two more days before the cocktail party and I had wasted enough of Mr. Goldwyn's money. It was good we went back so early because a new and even more trying period was ahead: how to roll the things so that three, even two, could go neatly in the small boxes. We rolled them around toothpicks, we whittled sticks, we shaved down pencils, we straightened paper clips and hairpins, but it was obvious they were too wide for the matchboxes.

They were bad days, growing dangerous: Goldwyn's legal department wanted to see me about something or other and reported to Goldwyn that I said I was home with an abscessed tooth. That didn't fit with Goldwyn's having seen me arrive at the studio on William Wyler's motorcycle, so when he called to ask me why I didn't go immediately to a dentist, I forgot what I had told the legal department and said I didn't understand how a dentist could cure a badly sprained neck. Sam said that was odd, would I come immediately and talk to him, something strange was going on. George said I was a dope of a liar; I said I was not meant to spend my life on condoms and was ready to throw over the whole thing. He said I was a fink, and while we were being nasty to each other my elderly secretary, who knew nothing more through those days than that I was missing from my office, opened George's door to say *his* secretary wasn't feeling well and couldn't come to work, and stared down at the condoms. She was an unfriendly woman, but I heard George say to her,

"We have a problem. Have you ever rolled a condom?" I left his office to hide in the toilet and came back to find that she had solved the problem: we were not to roll the condoms, we were to fold them lengthwise, crosswise, and stack them.

George took them to the cocktail party, but either Potter never knew about the condoms or was smart enough not to give George the pleasure of his complaint. In any case, George and I never spoke about them again.

Ten of the twelve plays I have written are connected to Hammett — he was in the Army in the Aleutian Islands during the Second World War for one of them, and he was dead when I wrote the last — but *The Little Foxes* was the one that was most dependent on him. We were living together in the same house, he was not doing any work of his own, but after his death, when much became clear to me that had not been before, I knew that he was working so hard for me because *Days to Come* had scared me and scared him for my future.

If that is true — there is a chance I have made the dependency greater than it was — then it is the more remarkable because it was a strange time of our years together. I don't know if I was paying him back for his casual ladies of our early years — it takes a jealous nature a long time to understand that there can be casual ladies — but certainly I was serious or semiserious about another man and Hammett knew it. Neither of us ever talked about it until I told Dash that I had decided not to marry the man.

He looked at me in surprise. *"Marry? You* decided? There was never a chance you'd marry him."

"It was about to happen," I said. "We had set the day and the place. I thought you knew that."

"I would never have allowed that. Never."

I laughed and he knew why I laughed because a few days later he said, "It was no good. It would never have been any good. The day it is good for you, I'll allow it."

"Thank you," I said, "but if that happens I won't ask your permission and therefore won't thank you for giving it."

"Without my permission you won't ever do it. And you ought to know that by now."

For years after I would say such things as, "May I have your permission this morning to go to the hairdresser, then to the library and on my way home buy an ice cream cone?" But he was not a vain man and, as time moved on, I knew he had been right.

The Little Foxes was the most difficult play I ever wrote. I was clumsy in the first drafts, putting in and taking out characters, ornamenting, decorating, growing more and more weary as the versions of scenes and then acts and then three whole plays had to be thrown away.

Some of the trouble came because the play has a distant connection to my mother's family and every-

473

thing that I had heard or seen or imagined had formed a giant tangled time-jungle in which I could find no space to walk without tripping over old roots, hearing old voices speak about histories made long before my day.

In the first three versions of the play, because it had been true in life, Horace Giddens had syphilis. When Regina, his wife, who had long refused him her bed, found out about it she put fresh paint on a miserable building that had once been used as slave quarters and kept him there for the rest of his life because, she said, he might infect his children. I had been told that the real Regina would speak with outrage of her betrayal by a man she had never liked and then would burst out laughing at what she said. On the day he died, she dropped the moral complaints forever and went horseback riding during his funeral. All that seemed fine for the play. But it wasn't: life had been too big, too muddled for writing. So the syphilis became heart trouble. I cut out the slave cabin and the long explanations of Regina and Horace's early life together.

I was on the eighth version of the play before Hammett gave a nod of approval and said he thought maybe everything would be O.K. if only I'd cut out the "blackamoor chitchat." Even then I knew that the toughness of his criticism, the coldness of his praise, gave him a certain pleasure. But even then I, who am not a good-tempered woman, admired his refusal with me, or with anybody else, to decorate or apologize or placate. It came from the most carefully guarded honesty I have ever known, as if one lie would muck up his world. If the honesty was mixed with harshness, I didn't much care, it didn't seem to me my business. The desire to take an occasional swipe is there in most of us, but most of us have no reason for it, it is as aimless as the pleasure of a piece of candy. When it is controlled by sense and balance, it is still not pretty, but it is not dangerous and often it is useful. It was useful to me and I knew it.

The casting of the play was difficult: we offered it to Ina Claire and to Judith Anderson. Each had a pleasant reason for refusing: each meant that the part was unsympathetic, a popular fear for actresses before that concept became outmoded. Herman Shumlin asked me what I thought of Tallulah Bankhead, but I had never seen her here or in her famous English days. She had returned to New York by 1939, had done a couple of flops, and was married to a nice, silly-handsome actor called John Emery. She was living in the same hotel I was, but I had fallen asleep by the time Herman rang my bell after six hours spent upstairs with Tallulah on their first meeting. He said he had a headache, was worn out by Miss Bankhead's vitality, but he thought she would do fine for us if he could, in the future, avoid the kind of scene he had just come from: she had been "wild" about the play, wild enough to insist the consultation take place while she was in bed with John Emery and a bottle. Shumlin said he didn't think Emery liked that much, but he was certain that poor Emery was unprepared for Tallulah's saying to Herman as he rose to go, "Wait a minute, darling, just wait a minute. I have something to show you." She threw aside the sheets, pointed down at the naked, miserable Emery and said, "Just tell me, darling, if you've ever seen a prick that big." I don't know what Herman said, but it must have been pleasant because there was no fight that night, nothing to predict what was to come.

I still have a diary entry, written a few days later, asking myself whether talk about the size of the male organ isn't a homosexual preoccupation: if things aren't too bad in other ways I doubt if any woman cares very much. Almost certainly Tallulah didn't care about the size or the function: it was the stylish, *épater* palaver of her day.

It is a mark of many famous people that they cannot part with their brightest hour: what worked once must always work. Tallulah had been the nineteen-twenties' most daring girl, but what had been dashing, even brave, had become by 1939 shrill and tiring. The life of the special darlings in the world of art and society had been made old-fashioned by the economic miseries of those who had never been darlings. Nothing is displaced on a single day and much was left over during the Depression, but the train had made a sharp historical swing and the fashionable folk, their life and customs, had become loud and tacky.

Tallulah, in the first months of the play, gave a fine performance, had a well-deserved triumph. It was sad to watch it all decline into high-jinks on the stage and in life. Long before her death, beginning with my play, I think, she threw the talent around to amuse the campy boys who came each opening night to watch her vindicate their view of women. I didn't clearly understand all that when I first met her, but I knew that while there was probably not more than five years' difference in our ages, and a bond in our Southern background — her family came from an Alabama town close to my mother's — we were a generation apart. I first realized it when we were still in rehearsal, about a week before the play was to open in Baltimore.

Tallulah, Herman and I were having dinner in the old Artists and Writers Club, a hangout for newspapermen. Tallulah took two small bottles from her pocketbook, put them on the table, and seemed to forget about them. As we were about to go back to rehearsal, she picked up one bottle and tipped it to put drops in her eyes. She rose from the table, repacked the bottles, led the way to the door, and let out a shriek that brought the restaurant to its feet. Herman rushed to her, she pushed him aside, other people pushed toward her, she turned for the door, changed her mind, and whispered to nobody, "I have put the wrong drops in my eyes." Herman ran to a phone booth, she shouted after him, he called out that he was getting a doctor, she said he was to mind his business, and suddenly, in the shouting and running, she grabbed my arm, pulled me into the toilet and said, "Get Herman off that phone. I put the cocaine in my eyes and I don't tell that to doctors or to anybody else. Tell him to shut up about it or I won't go back to the theatre." She sat down at a table, grinned at everybody, and ordered herself a shot of whiskey. I squeezed my way into the phone booth, told Herman about the cocaine. He moved slowly toward her and said, "Put down the whiskey and come outside."

On the sidewalk he said, "I don't like what just happened. This play is going to open on time and I want you to cut the nonsense."

Tallulah said, in controlled stage-anger, "I'm a professional. It's none of your damn business what I do. I warn you never to talk to me this way again."

As she hailed a taxi, Herman said, "If you don't come back to rehearsals in half an hour, don't come back at all." She slammed the door of the taxi, he and I walked back to the theatre, and ten minutes later Tallulah appeared on the stage.

Cocaine was not mentioned again until the opening night party she gave in her Baltimore hotel rooms. It was, indeed, quite a night. Her father, the Speaker of the House of Representatives, and her uncle, the Senator, had come down from Washington. Hammett had arrived a few days before, then Dorothy Parker and her husband Alan Campbell, with Sara and Gerald Murphy. We were a mixed bag, the cast and guests, trying to circulate in a room too small for us.

With time and booze things got loud and the Senator took to singing "Dixie," spirituals, and a Civil War song, until the fastidious Gerald Murphy said to him, "Lovely. But now you must rest your fine vocal cords."

Tallulah was sitting in a large group giving the monologue she always thought was conversation. I was tired, waiting to go to my room, and I guess I yawned once too often because she began to tease me, in the kind of nagging fashion she used when she knew somebody wanted to leave her. A young Negro waiter moved back and forth, passing drinks, and as he came near us she asked him if he wanted to sleep with her or me. He stood still, frightened. She pulled him toward her and kissed him.

I said to the waiter, "Better get out of here now. She's probably not up to much, but this is Maryland."

He went rapidly toward the door, Tallulah went after him, offering to hit me along the way, and Hammett moved behind her. When things had settled down, she put her arms around Hammett and promised that she'd forgive him because she was a sucker for a handsome man. He thanked her and said he didn't much like to be around people who took dope, in his Pinkerton days he had been more afraid of them than of murderers. They talked that over for a while but I lost track until I heard her shout at him, "You don't know what you are talking about. I tell you cocaine isn't habit-forming and I know because I've been taking it for years."

When I laughed too long she got upset with me

again and Gerald Murphy said he thought I'd be safer in bed.

Unfortunately my bedroom was next door and I lay sleepless until five in the morning. Then I fell asleep to be awakened by a fight that was going on behind my bed. Tallulah and a woman I had met at the party — an assistant or an ex-secretary — were arguing about an income tax claim and what the woman had done with Tallulah's money. (I think that several years later there was a lawsuit between them.) I yelled through the door that I wanted to sleep. Insults came back and then a demand to join them for a drink. When I said I didn't want a drink and why didn't they go knock each other off the hotel roof, one of them began to pound on my door with what sounded like a bottle and, in time, the pounding became, with giggles, the rhythm of "America the Beautiful." I got dressed and decided to go sit in the park, but before I left the room I broke a desk chair against their door.

Tallulah sent commands the next day for me to appear at rehearsals and apologize, but I was with Dottie, Alan and the Murphys in the hotel dining room from ten in the morning until they closed the place at midnight. It was one of the most pleasant days of my life. I was sleepy and content: the play had gotten fine reviews, we all had a lot to drink, and nobody talked about the play or the theatre. I remember dozing on the table for a while and waking to hear Gerald say, "It's not an easy business, the theatre," and Dottie's saying, "Lilly does things the hard way. Why didn't she have sense enough to get Harpo Marx instead of Tallulah?" and then a long discussion about General Sherman, who was Sara Murphy's grandfather.

There are not many good critics for any art, but there have been almost none for the modern theatre. The intellectuals among them know little about an operating theatre and the middlebrows look at plays as if they were at a race track for the morning line-up. It is a mixed-up picture in many ways. One critic who wrote that *The Little Foxes* was a febrile play later called it an American classic without explaining why he changed his mind.

The *New York Times*, for many years, has been the only newspaper that mattered to the success of a play. That is not the fault of the paper, but it is not a good state for a struggling art form. Now, with Mr. Clive Barnes, even that has changed for the worse: a good review by him no longer makes a hit, but a bad review does damage. The *Times* has had a long list of earnest, honest, undistinguished critics. Walter Kerr is the only one, I think, who learned and thrived. Mr. Barnes is the first fashion-swinger in the list but, like most, he can't quite find where the swing is located for the new season.

I knew many of the virtues and the mistakes of *The Little Foxes* before the play opened. I wanted, I needed an interesting critical mind to tell what I had done beyond the limited amount I could see for myself. But the high praise and the reservations seemed to me stale stuff and I think were one of the reasons the great success of the play sent me into a wasteful, ridiculous depression. I sat drinking for months after the play opened trying to figure out what I had wanted to say and why some of it got lost.

I grew restless, sickish, digging around the random memories that had been the conscious, semiconscious material for the play. I had meant to half-mock my own youthful high-class innocence in Alexandra, the young girl in the play; I had meant people to smile at, and to sympathize with, the sad, weak Birdie, certainly I had not meant them to cry; I had meant the audience to recognize some part of themselves in the money-dominated Hubbards; I had not meant people to think of them as villains to whom they had no connection.

I belonged, on my mother's side, to a banking, storekeeping family from Alabama and Sunday dinners were large, with four sisters and three brothers of my grandmother's generation, their children, and a few cousins of my age. These dinners were long, with high-spirited talk and laughter from the older people of who did what to whom, what good nigger had consented to thirty percent interest on his cotton crop and what bad nigger had made a timid protest, what new white partner had been outwitted, what benefits the year had brought from the Southern business interests they had left behind for the Northern profits they had had sense enough to move toward.

When I was fourteen, in one of my many religious

periods, I yelled across that Sunday's dinner table at a great-aunt, "You have a spatulate face made to dig in the mud for money. May God forgive you."

My aunt rose, came around the table and slapped me with her napkin. I said, "Someday I'll pay you back unless the dear God helps me conquer the evil spirit of revenge," and ran from the room as my gentle mother started to cry. But later that night, she knocked on my locked door and said that if I came out I could have a squab for dinner. My father was out of New York but, evidently informed of the drama by my mother, wrote to me saying that he hoped I had sense enough not to revenge myself until I was as tall and as heavy as my great-aunt.

But a few years after I had stopped being pleased with the word spatulate, a change occurred for which even now I have no explanation: I began to think that greed and the cheating that is its usual companion were comic as well as evil and I began to like the family dinners with the talk of who did what to whom. I particularly looked forward to the biannual dinner when the sisters and brothers assembled to draw lots for "the diamond" that had been left, almost thirty years before, in my great-grandmother's estate. Sometimes they would use the length of a strip of paper to designate the winner, sometimes the flip of a coin, and once I was allowed to choose a number up to eight and the correct guesser was to get the diamond. But nobody, as far as I knew, ever did get it. No sooner was the winner declared than one or the other would sulk and, by prearrangement, another loser would console the sulker, and a third would start the real event of the afternoon: an open charge of cheating. The paper, the coin, my number, all had been fixed or tampered with. That was wild and funny. Funnier because my mother's generation would sit white-faced, sometimes tearful, appalled at what was happening, all of them envying the vigor of their parents, half knowing that they were broken spirits who wished the world was nicer, but who were still so anxious to inherit the money that they made no protest.

I was about eighteen when my great-uncle Jake took the dinner hours to describe how he and a new partner had bought a street of slum houses in downtown New York. He, Jake, during a lunch break in the signing of the partnership, removed all the toilet seats from the buildings and sold them for fifty dollars. But, asked my mother's cousin, what will the poor people who live there do without toilet seats? "Let us," said Jake, "approach your question in a practical manner. I ask you to accompany me now to the bathroom, where I will explode my bowels in the manner of the impoverished and you will see for yourself how it is done." As he reached for her hand to lead her to the exhibition, my constantly ailing cousin began to cry in high, long sounds. Her mother said to her, "Go along immediately with your Uncle Jake. You are being disrespectful to him."

I guess all that was the angry comedy I wanted to mix with the drama.

Angry comedy came another way. I was to get my first taste during *The Little Foxes* of the red-baiting that later turned my life into disorder and financial disaster.

The Spanish Civil War — I had been in Spain during the war — had reached the sad day of Franco's victory and many Republicans were trapped on what was known as the International Bridge. Some of them were my friends, some of them I only knew about. Their lives were at stake. Many of us sent all the money we could give or collect and looked around to find other money fast. Herman Shumlin and I decided to ask the cast of *The Little Foxes* if they would do a benefit for the Spanish refugees. Tallulah and the rest of the cast were courteous but well within their rights when they refused, and nothing more was said about benefits until the week after Russia moved into Finland.

I had been in Helsinki in 1937 for two weeks and had turned my head each day from the giant posters of Hitler pasted to the side wall of my hotel. One night a member of our Olympic team, a man of Finnish descent, had taken me to a large rally of Hitler sympathizers and translated for me their admiring speeches. I needed no translator for the raised arms, the cheers, the Wessel song.

Finland's ambassador to Washington was a handsome and charming man who met Tallulah at a dinner party. The day following Tallulah's meeting with the ambassador she announced that *The Little Foxes* would give a benefit for the Finnish refugees. The day following that Shumlin and I announced that *The Little Foxes* would not give a benefit. I can't remember now whether we explained that we had been refused a benefit for Spain, but I do remember that suddenly what had been no more than a theatre fight turned into a political attack: it was made to seem that we agreed with the invasion of Finland, refused aid to true democrats, were, ourselves, dangerous Communists. It was my first experience of such goings-on and I didn't have sense enough to know that Tallulah's press statements, so much better than ours, or more in tune with the times, were being guided by the expert ambassador. Although her anger — she often had the righteousness that belongs to a certain kind of aging sinner — once aroused needed no guidance and stood up well against all reason. And nobody has ever been able to control me when I feel that I have been treated unjustly. I am, in fact, bewildered by all injustice, at first certain that it cannot be, then shocked into rigidity, then obsessed, and finally as certain as a Grand Inquisitor that God wishes me to move ahead, correct and holy. Through those days Tallulah and I were, indeed, a pair.

And so we never spoke again for almost thirty years. Then I met her at a party and heard myself say, "Maybe it's time we said hello." The face that looked up from years of physical and spiritual beatings was blank. I said, "I'm Lillian Hellman," and Tallulah flew toward me in a scream of good-natured greetings and a holiday of kisses. I was pleased for the first half-hour. But reconciliations can be as noisy as the fights that caused them.

Only two diaries written at the end of 1938 could convince me now that *Watch on the Rhine* came out of Henry James, although, of course, seeds in the wind, the long journey they make, their crosses and mutations, is not a new story for writers and even make you hope that your seeds may scatter for those to come.

I was driving back to the farm trying not to listen to the noise that came from two crates of Pekin ducks when I began to think of James's *The American* and *The Europeans.* In the short time since James, the United States had become the dominant country not alone in money and power, but in imposing on other people a morality which was designed in part to hide its self-interest. Was that a new American game or had we learned it from the English who invented it to hold down their lower classes? We still spoke as nineteenth-century Cromwellians in church, home, and university, but increasingly, the more we recognized disorder and corruption at home the more insistent we grew about national purity.

Many Europeans had moved here with the triumph of Hitler in the 1930's. Few of us asked questions about their past or present convictions because we took for granted that they had left either in fear of persecution or to make a brave protest. They were our kind of folks. It took me a long time to find out that

487

many of them had strange histories and that their hosts, or the people who vouched for them, knew all about their past. Two of the perhaps eight or nine that I met turned out to have unexpected reasons for emigration: both had been Nazi sympathizers; in one case, the grandfather wanted to preserve his remarkable art collection from the threatening sounds the "new barbarians" made about modern painting; in the other, bribe money had not been able to suppress a nineteenth-century conversion from Judaism to Luther. I was vaguely related to that family, and when I asked about the truth of the rumor, the son of the family never spoke to me again. But a few weeks later I had a note from his mother saying that she was surprised to find that certain Jews in America claimed a blood connection to her family, when, in fact, they had "no legal or moral right" to do so. I had no right, from my safe place, to feel bitter about such people, but I did and, of course, by 1938 I had been through the life and death of my friend Julia, and had been to Spain during the Civil War, and had been moved by men willing to die for what they believed in.

I wanted to write a play about nice, liberal Americans whose lives would be shaken up by Europeans, by a world the new Fascists had won because the old values had long been dead. I put the play in a small Ohio town. That didn't work at all. Then one night, coming out of a long dream about the streets of London, I knew that I had stubbornly returned to the people and the place of *Days to Come*. I was obsessed with my dream, stopped writing for a month or so, and only started again when I found the root of the dream; then I moved the play to Washington, placed it in the house of a rich, liberal family who were about to meet their anti-fascist son-in-law, a German, who had fought in Spain. He was, of course, a form of Julia.

The dream had taken me back to an evening in 1936 when, on a visit to London, I had a phone call from the famous Margot Asquith. I had never met Lady Asquith, but I remembered Dorothy Parker writing of her *Autobiography*, "The affair between Margot Asquith and Margot Asquith will live as one of the prettiest love stories in all literature." Lady Asquith told me that the novelist Charles Morgan wanted to meet me, would I come to dinner? It was a strange evening: from the minute the butler opened the Baker Street door and said, "Oh, you're bloody *young*," I felt as if I had gone swimming in strong waters and would have to struggle hard to reach land again.

The dinner party was Lady Asquith, her son Anthony, a movie director, her daughter Elizabeth, Princess Bibesco, and the Romanian Prince Antoine Bibesco, her husband. Princess Bibesco had written a number of books and I would have liked to talk to her, being at that point in my life most respectful of lady-books that carried delicate overtones of sadness. There was no Charles Morgan and Lady Asquith was surprised that I thought there would be, but halfway through the dinner a very tall young man sat down next to me and, although I never heard his name through the marshmallow English syllables, there was some reference to his royal cousins.

Tony Asquith was most pleasant, but his mother frowned at me down the table as if she didn't understand why I was there and, as far as I remember, Prince Bibesco said no word. The butlers were plentiful, the conversation so faltering that one had the impression that everybody was ill, and when Bibesco rose, pushed aside his plate, said he'd meet us upstairs, I thought only that he was a sensible man to refuse the bad food.

When we left the savories — that upper-class English habit of drowning the bad with the worse — we joined the prince in a small room off the drawing room. It was filled by a large poker table, the chips already racked, and Bibesco didn't look up from his game of solitaire. Lady Asquith said she was due at a Parliamentary committee, called me Mrs. Dillman as she said goodbye, and left the rest of us to watch the prince play solitaire. When his third game came out fine, he patted me on the arm and asked if I played poker. I said yes, I liked it; he said he did, too, but didn't play much anymore and was out of practice. The semiroyal gentleman coughed, but I thought that was because a Mr. and Mrs. Something-or-Other came into the room.

In a few minutes we were all in a poker game. Elizabeth Bibesco didn't play but sat reading in a room off our room. In the first half-hour of the game her husband made jokes about how you cut cards, in what direction you started dealing, did a straight come before a full house, and by midnight I had lost almost three hundred pounds and semiroyalty had lost over five hundred pounds. I have no memory of what happened to the two strangers: I think they lost or won very little, although the man sneezed a lot through the evening. By the time I decided that my losses were far more than I could afford, I had learned that Bibesco had been the Romanian ambassador to Washington and a regular at the games of Vice-President Charles Curtis, a famous poker player. And I had heard enough to understand that it was not my literary reputation that had gone ahead of me, but a piece in the *New York Herald Tribune* saying that the boys in the famous New York Thanatopsis poker game had thought of inviting me to join them, but finally decided a woman would set a bad precedent. This was verified by the royal cousin, who drove me to my hotel in a high-powered racing car. He was a charming mixture of glum and glee as he said that he knew he was a bad player, always vowed he'd never go back to that particular high-stake game, and went back whenever he was asked. I thought about that poker game for years afterward and came to feel that the evening, the dinner, Bibesco, and Lady Asquith herself were characters sitting in a second-act drawing room because the stagehands had forgotten to tell them that the scenery had changed to the edge of a volcano.

It was a pleasant experience, *Watch on the Rhine*. There are plays that, whatever their worth, come along at the right time, and the right time is the essence of the theatre and the cinema. From the first day of rehearsal things went well. It was a hardworking cast of nice people, with the exception of Paul Lukas, the best actor among them; but his capers were open and comic. (He told me that he had been a trusted follower of the Hungarian Communist Béla Kun, but that the week before Kun fell he had joined Kun's enemies. He saw nothing contradictory in now playing a self-sacrificing anti-Fascist.) But not everybody thought Paul was funny. John Lodge, then an actor and later to be our ambassador to Spain — when Dorothy Parker heard about his diplomatic appointment she said, "Lilly, let us, as patriots, join hands and walk into the water" — was shocked when Paul cheated him at tennis, and Eric Roberts, who played Paul's twelve-year-old son, disliked him so much that some nights he ate garlic before he climbed into Paul's lap and other nights he rubbed his hair with foul-smelling whale oil. I remember all that with pleasure, although a diary tells me that Herman Shumlin and I were having our usual fights.

The Baltimore opening of *Watch on the Rhine* went just fine and gave me a chance to see the medical historian Dr. Henry Sigerist. Sigerist was one of the heroes of my life: a learned man in medicine who read in many other fields; a political radical who was an

expert cook and on whose judgment professional tea
and wine tasters often depended; a tough man who
was gentle; a sad man who did not complain. And
he was a wise political observer: he had left the University of Leipzig, guessing two years before Hitler
came to power what was to come, and several years
before the full flower of Joe McCarthy, during a time
when the rest of us thought McCarthy a clown, he resigned from Johns Hopkins University and moved
back to his native Switzerland.

The week before he left America he came to visit
us at the Pleasantville farm and cooked a great and
complicated meal with our friend Gregory Zilboorg,
and all of us were happy with food and wine and
affection.

I was to see him only once again after that dinner,
in 1953, when, because he believed that McCarthy
might use him against me — I had the year before
been called before the House Un-American Activities
Committee and that year been subpoenaed by a summons that was never served by the McCarthy committee — if I came to visit him and his wife in Switzerland, we arranged to meet in Milan.

It was fine that day in Milan. Henry had gone to
school there and now had pleasure in showing it to
me. We drove a long way to a monastery that had
remarkable early wall paintings and the abbot and
two old priests were openly admiring of this Marxist
unbeliever; we drove further to a small castle on a
hill where the owner, a young woman, had a Cana-

letto he wanted to see again and they talked together of her grandparents; we had lunch and dinner in small, fine restaurants where the owners knew Sigerist and one of them asked for his opinion of a new wine and neither would allow him to pay a bill; we toured the ugly Milan Cathedral and he told me of the difference in the history of the Northern and Southern Catholic Churches; and when we said goodbye he told me he was ill and that I must come back soon because he would have only a few years more to see his friends.

He died on time, as he did everything else.

It is the lifelong problem of only children that they doubt all affection that is offered, even that which has been proved, and so, as the years passed, I told myself that Sigerist had been polite and kind to me, but that I had not gone back to see him because I was not needed or wanted. I only recognized the vanity behind my lack of vanity when his daughter published a part of his diary in which there is proof of what he felt for me. We all have been spared some nonsense and I have been spared caring very much what most people thought about me. But I cared so much for what this distinguished man thought that I cut the words from the book, put them in a frame, and locked the frame in a safe.

Yesterday, nineteen years later, standing in a pretty Wellfleet cemetery at Edmund Wilson's funeral, I thought of Henry Sigerist and knew why. These two men, so different in temperament, in interests, in belief, one so European, one so American, were alike in the kind of wide-ranging mind rare in a time of specialists, alike in the nineteenth-century conviction that culture was applied curiosity. I remembered once telling Edmund that I had asked Sigerist if it was true that he knew thirteen languages and he had said, "No, no. I know only nine. I can read in three others but I cannot say more than a sentence and that not well." Edmund had smiled at that, but a few minutes later told me that he was studying Hungarian and I knew my story had started a charming competitiveness in him and a counting on his fingers.

Watch on the Rhine is the only play I have ever written that came out in one piece, as if I had seen a landscape and never altered the trees or the seasons of their colors. All other work for me had been fragmented, hunting in an open field with shot from several guns, following the course but unable to see clearly, recovering the shot hands full, then hands empty from stumbling and spilling. But here, for the first and last time, the work I did, the actors, the rehearsals, the success of the play, even the troubles that I have forgotten, make a pleasant oneness and have been lost to the past. The real memories of that time are not for the play but for the people who passed through the time of it. President Roosevelt was one of them.

In those days it was a yearly custom for a play to be chosen to give a kind of command performance before the President for the benefit of the Infantile Pa-

ralysis Fund. When *Watch on the Rhine* was invited
to Washington for a Sunday night early in 1942, it
was the first public appearance of President Roosevelt since war had been declared.

John Lodge was a Naval Reserve officer about to be
called up, and a good deal of the train ride from New
York to Washington was taken up with the question
of what he should wear to the White House for a supper party after the performance. A Navy uniform
seemed premature; others of us argued that plain dinner clothes were not quite right for a man of distinguished family about to serve his country, perhaps to
die. I suggested a sword and red ribbon as being neither too little nor too much, but John, who seemed to
like that idea, said it would be impossible because nobody could find such stuff on a Sunday.

While the cast rehearsed light cues and tried the
acoustics of the theatre, I talked an idle assistant
manager into phoning a friend who worked at a theatre warehouse and offering him fifty bucks if he could
come up with sword and wide ribbon. In a few hours
I was backstage ironing the old crushed ribbon and
clanking around with the sword. I guess people
laughed too much because John, who had seemed most
pleased about the idea, now refused the sword in
peevish, stiff terms. I felt bad about that, it would
have been nice, and only came around to feeling better when Mr. Roosevelt entered the theatre. The bold,
handsome head had so much intelligence and confi-

dence that the wheelchair in which he sat seemed not a handicap but an interesting way to move about.

At supper Roosevelt remembered that I had once visited him at Warm Springs, coming, by accident, on the same day as Huey Long. We talked about Long and my native Louisiana, but he was more interested — he asked me several times — in when I had written *Watch on the Rhine*. When I told him I started it a year and a half before the war, he shook his head and said in that case he didn't understand why Morris Ernst, the lawyer, had told him that I was so opposed to the war that I had paid for the "Communist" war protesters who kept a continuous picket line around the White House before Germany attacked the Soviet Union. I said I didn't know Mr. Ernst's reasons for that nonsense story, but Ernst's family had been in business with my Alabama family long ago and that wasn't a good mark on any man. Mr. Roosevelt laughed and said he'd enjoy passing that message on to Mr. Ernst.

But the story about my connection with the picket line was there to stay, often repeated when the red-baiting days reached hurricane force. But by that time, some of the pleasant memories of *Watch on the Rhine* had also disappeared: Lukas, once so loud in gratitude for the play, put in his frightened, blunted knife for a newspaper interviewer, and Lucille Watson, a remarkable actress, changed her written affection for me when she came to work in *The Autumn Garden* almost ten years later. She rehearsed

497

with us then for three days. On the fourth day she did not return. She told another actor that perhaps she could put up with me because I was "a toilet-trained Jew," but she couldn't put up with Harold Clurman, the director, because he was "just plain Jew." The hardest lesson to learn in the theatre is to take nobody too seriously.

It is possible that because the war so drastically changed the world, the small, less observed things changed without being recognized. Now, looking back, I think that after *Watch on the Rhine* much of the pleasant high-jinks of the theatre were never to be seen again because the theatre, like the rest of the country, became expensive, earnest and conservative. The Tallulahs and the Lukases were not easy to take, but they belonged to a time I liked better. Whatever the reason, the theatre pictures behind my eyes for the period after that are fragmented and it would be useless and untruthful for me to order them up from scrapbooks or other people's memories. About the plays that followed that period, the pictures are there, but not many are much more than a camera angle that was part of a whole, of course, but is now seen only by itself.

Of *The Searching Wind* I have very little now except the memory of a wonderful old actor, Dudley Digges, arriving at seven-thirty each night during the run of the play to meet Montgomery Clift, a gifted, inexperienced young actor in his first large part. Together they would sit on the stage until the second curtain call and go through a scene from Shakespeare or Ibsen or Chekhov, or a series of poems, anything that Digges had chosen to teach Monty. It was mighty nice, the two of them, and I took to going to the theatre several times a week just to stand in the wings and watch the delicate relationship between the dedicated old and the dedicated young. I was never to see much of Clift after the closing of the play, but in the years that followed, mostly unhappy ones for him, I am told, I would often get a long-distance call from him, we would arrange to meet, never manage it, but always we would talk of Dudley Digges, who died a few years after *The Searching Wind*.

I had always planned *The Little Foxes* as a trilogy, knowing that I had jumped into the middle of the life of the Hubbards and would want to go forward in time. But in 1946 it seemed right to go back to their youth, their father and mother, to the period of the Civil War. I believed that I could now make clear that I had meant the first play as a kind of satire. I tried to do that in *Another Part of The Forest*, but what I thought funny or outrageous the critics thought straight stuff; what I thought was bite they thought sad, touching, or plotty and melodramatic. Perhaps, as one critic said, I blow a stage to pieces without knowing it. In any case, I had a good time directing the play, not because I wanted to, but because I was tired of arguments and knew no director I thought was right for me. I did a good job, I think, so good that I fooled myself into thinking I was a director, a mistake that I was to discover a few years later. But then and now it gives me pleasure that I found an unknown girl, Patricia Neal, and watched her develop into a good actress and a remarkable woman.

With *Montserrat,* an adaptation I made from the French play by Emmanuel Roblès, I not only cast the play with a kind of abandoned belief that good actors can play anything, but I directed it in a fumbling, frightened way, intimidated by Emlyn Williams, the British actor and writer, who was playing the leading part. I do not blame Mr. Williams for his disapproval of me, although the way he showed it had a bad effect on the actors and thus on the play. He must have known from the first days of rehearsal that fear infects and corrupts what it touches. It is best in the theatre to act with confidence no matter how little right you have to it. It is a special and valuable gift, directing, but it has come to its present power mostly in comedies or musicals. Few dramas can stand up against another assertive talent, even if it is more distinguished than the original creator. Movies have come close to solving that problem: the director and writer are now often the same person, or two people who seen to function as one. But in the theatre, drama, even plain, dull seriousness, is still a business of unsolved delicacy between the writer, the director and the actors.

*   *   *

Many writers work best in time of trouble: no money, the cold outside and in, even sickness and the end in view. But I have always known that when trouble comes I must face it fast and move with speed, even though the speed is thoughtless and sometimes damaging. For such impatient people, calm is necessary for hard work — long days, months of fiddling is the best way of life.

I wrote *The Autumn Garden* in such a period. I was at a good age; I lived on a farm that was, finally, running fine and I knew I had found the right place to live for the rest of my life. Hammett and I were both making a lot of money, and not caring about where it went was fun. We had been together almost twenty years, some of them bad, a few of them shabby, but now we had both stopped drinking and the early excited years together had settled into a passionate affection so unexpected to both of us that we were as shy and careful with each other as courting children. Without words, we knew that we had survived for the best of all reasons, the pleasure of each other.

I could not wait to hear what he thought about the news in the morning paper, about a book, a departing guest, a day's hunt for birds and rabbits, an hour's walk in the woods. And nobody in my life has ever been as anxious to have me stay in a room, talk late into the night, get up in the morning. I guess it was the best time for me, certainly the best time of our life together. Now, I think, that somewhere we both knew — the signs were already there, Joe McCarthy was over the land — that we had to make it good because it had to end. One year later Hammett was in jail; two years later the place where I intended to live the rest of my life had to be sold; three or four years later neither of us had any money and, more important than any of that, all of which can be borne without too much trouble, we were to face Hammett's death around every corner. If we did smell the future, I am glad we had sense enough never to mention it.

I have many times written about Dash's pleasure in *The Autumn Garden*. Now, this minute, I can hear myself laugh at the fierce, angry manner in which he spoke his praise, as if he hated the words, was embarrassed by them. He was forever after defensive — he had never been about my work or his — if anybody had any reservations about the play. A short time after the play opened, I came home very pleased to tell him that Norman Mailer had told me how good he thought the play. Norman had said it was very good, could have been great, but I had lost my nerve.

Dash said, "Almost everybody loses their nerve. You almost didn't, and that's what counts, and what he should have said."

By 1955 I needed money. I wish I could tell myself that was why I adapted Jean Anouilh's *The Lark*. But my reason was not money: I was feeling mischievous and the reasons for the mischief still exist as they were written on a Ritz Hotel menu in London.

My producer, Kermit Bloomgarden, had bought the

play and wanted me to make a new adaptation. I flew to London to see Christopher Fry's version, didn't like it, cabled Kermit that it wasn't up my alley. Then I had lunch at the Ritz with Dr. Van Loewen, Anouilh's agent. I was pleased to meet a doctor-agent having only once before heard of one, Milton Bender, a former dentist, who perhaps had a better right to the title. So I said, "I am sorry, Doctor, but I do not believe this play is right for me. I . . ."

The doctor said, "We, Mr. Anouilh and I, have the greatest respect for your gifts, Mrs. Hellman, but *L'Alouette* comes from the mind of a poet and must, therefore, be adapted by a poet."

"Poet," I said, "*poet?*"

"We have the greatest respect for your gifts, Mrs. Hellman, but . . ."

"You are right. I am not a poet."

"There," he said. "You are a lady of honesty for whose gifts we have . . ."

"You don't need a poet. You need George Bernard Shaw, but he's dead."

The doctor said, "Shaw was not a poet. I do not think he would have been the right adaptor, either."

After I made that note on my menu and thought about foreigners, I said, "Mr. Shaw wrote a fine play about Joan of Arc, without all of Mr. Anouilh's bubble glory stuff."

"Mr. Anouilh is a poet," said the doctor.

"Perhaps," I said, "but not in French," laughed, and felt ashamed of myself.

I don't remember how long it took Bloomgarden to talk me out of the conversation with the doctor, but by the time I agreed to do the play I was convinced that Joan was history's first modern career girl, wise, unattractive in what she knew about the handling of men, straight out of a woman's magazine. The wonderful story lay, as Shaw had seen it, in the miraculous self-confidence that carried defeated men into battle against all sense and reason, forced a pious girl into a refusal of her church, caused the terrible death that still has to do with the rest of us, forever, wherever her name is heard.

And so for good or bad, I scaled down the play, cut the comparisons to the World War II German invasion of France and the tributes to the French spirit. I had doubts about the French spirit and, if the gossip about Mr. Anouilh has any truth, he had doubts; and I didn't like fake doves flying out over the audience to show the soaring spirit of Joan, the victory of idealism, or just to indicate the end of a play. And the fine, straightforward performance of Julie Harris helped make the play the first success Mr. Anouilh had in America, which is possibly why we never again heard from him or from the doctor, although all profits, quite properly, have been accepted by them.

Some kind of confidence, even fake, is needed for any work, but it is particularly required in the theatre, where ordinary timidity and stumbling seem like disintegration, and are infectious and corruptive to other frightened people. I think now that I began to leave the theatre with the production of *Candide,* an operetta with music by Leonard Bernstein, lyrics by Richard Wilbur. (I was not to leave for another two plays, but I am slow at leaving anything.)

I can account for the deterioration of my script from what I think was good to what I know is not good, but any such account would be confused, full of those miserable, small complaints and blames that mean nothing except to the person making them. I was not used to collaboration, I had become, with time, too anxious to stay out of fights, and because I was working with people who knew more about the musical theatre than I did, I took suggestions and made changes that I didn't believe in, tried making them with speed I cannot manage.

All that, I could and did put aside. The confidence went for another reason: I knew we were in bad trouble the day the cast first read and sang the play. I knew it, I said it, and yet I sat scared, inwardly raging, outwardly petty passive before the great talents of Leonard Bernstein, who knew about music, and Tyrone Guthrie, the director, who knew about the theatre. The lady producer knew nothing about either.

All of it, after the nice, hopeful period of work with Lennie and Richard Wilbur, through rehearsals to the closing night of *Candide* — and again, years later, the 1972 Kennedy Center revival with which I

505

refused any connection — was sad and wasteful and did not need to be.

Several months after the play closed in New York, Tony Guthrie said, "Lennie, Wilbur, Oliver Smith, Irene Sharaff, Miss Hellman and Mr. Guthrie were too much talent for a good brew." That is hard for me to believe. Vanity, which I think is what he meant, can be of great use: it was dangerous during *Candide* because it was on a blind rampage.

I think now that Guthrie was as frightened as I was. I should have recognized that the night of the Boston dress rehearsal when Marc Blitzstein, an old friend of Lennie's and mine, walked me back to the hotel. We were depressed, neither of us talked the long way across the Boston Common. At the door of my room Marc said, "You're cooked, kid, and so is the show. I was sitting near Guthrie. He grinned at me once, his mouth full of sandwich and wine, and said, 'Well, Marc, that's that. Lillian is often right, but Lennie is so charming.' "

Guthrie was an imaginative man, bold in a timid business, uncaring about money in a world that cared about little else. It is true that the imagination led to tinkering: he reinterpreted almost every play he directed, but he did it with brilliance.

I turn my head now, look out at a jetty in front of my house, and see again this giant-tall man sitting on the end rock, telling me of his childhood, his university days, and then, as if he had talked more than he meant, suddenly pitching himself into the water at a dangerous angle. In the years after *Candide*, we sometimes saw each other, more often wrote letters. In one letter, I told him that *Candide* had done bad things to me, I wasn't working. He did not answer that letter, but a few months later he was in New York and we met for lunch. As I came in the restaurant door, a voice on my right side said, "Stop the nonsense. Get on with new work, get on with it today."

It was a valuable accident that a few days after that, or so I thought until a week ago, I spent the evening with Elena and Edmund Wilson. During the evening we talked of a man we both knew and Edmund asked why he didn't write anymore. I mumbled something about writing blocks, I had one myself, all of us, and so on.

Edmund said, "Foolishness. A writer writes. That's all there is to it."

For anybody of my generation, so eager for the neurosis, yours if you could manage it, if desperate somebody else's, the hardheaded sense of that was good stuff. But it did not happen a few days after I saw Guthrie. Last week I came back from Edmund's funeral and sat thinking about him most of the night. The next morning I went through old diaries of the many times I had spent with the Wilsons and found that "A writer writes. That's all there is to it," came almost two years after my lunch with Guthrie. But it is true that the next day after Edmund said it I went to work on *Toys in the Attic*.

Months before that day, Hammett and I had walked
down from the house into the beach grass to look at a
quail nest and see how things were going. I had known
about the emphysema since Dash got out of the Army
in 1945, known it had grown worse when he went to
jail in 1951, knew that we could go less and less to
the beach or any place else. But I don't think I had
ever heard the heavy panting breath until that day as
we climbed the steps back to the house. He stopped
and lowered his head. I held out a hand.

He looked away from my hand and said, "I've been
meaning to tell you. There's this man. Other people,
people who say they love him, want him to make good,
be rich. So he does it for them and finds they don't
like him that way, so he fucks it up, and comes out
worse than before. Think about it."

I wrote an act and a half and gave it to Hammett
to read. When he had finished with it, he said, "Take
the boat and go fishing. Forget the play for today.
Maybe by night I'll . . ."

"No," I said. "This time you don't have to tell me
what's wrong. I can write about men, but I can't write
a play that centers on a man. I've got to tear it up,
make it about the women around him, his sisters, his
bride, her mother and — "

"Well," he said, "then my idea's out the window.
Never mind. I'll use it myself someday."

He never lived to use it. But he lived long enough
to have great pleasure from the play, and the last trip
he ever made was to Boston for the opening. We had
fun together, very like the old, first days of jokes, and

wanting to be together, resenting the times we weren't. I skipped rehearsals for a couple of days and we went once more to see Paul Revere's house, Faneuil Hall, the Old South Meeting House, drove out to the Old Manse in Concord and had an argument about Emerson as if we had never had it before. I realized that in the pleasure of those days I had forgotten how sick he was and was worried that he would pay for the tramping about. But for the first time in years he seemed better for it, and we had late, cheerful dinners in our rooms.

I said, "The Ritz Hotel has the best thermoses. I wish I could just up and take one home."

"For years you've thought you were stealing what hotels mean for you to take, washrags, shoe-shine cloths, soap, and then patting yourself on the back for the nerve of doing it. Take the thermos. You'll feel better."

"I can't. And you've never stolen anything."

"I never wanted anything enough."

"That isn't the reason. You think it isn't dignified."

The next day, coming back from a shopping trip with Maureen Stapleton during which I persuaded her into two expensive dresses and an alligator bag about which to this day, whenever there is too much of what she calls wine, she says I bankrupted her forever, Hammett was waiting for me with his suitcase packed.

I said, "You didn't tell me you were leaving today."

He said, "Did we ever tell each other?"

(This morning, twelve years later, I poured myself a cup of coffee from a Ritz Hotel thermos bottle. Dash had put it on top of his clothes, sent for a bellboy to close the valise, and winked at me when the bellboy showed no sign of seeing the thermos. No, I told myself this morning, we had never told each other, never made a plan, and yet we had moved a number of times from West Coast to East Coast, bought and sold three houses, been well-heeled and broke, parted, come together, and never had plans or even words for the future. In my case, I think, the mixture of commitment with no-commitment came from Bohemia as it bumped into Calvin: in Hammett's it came from never believing in any kind of permanence and a mind that rejected absolutes.)

Toys in the Attic, with a splendid cast, was a success. The money came at the right time, because for a year I had known that death was on Hammett's face and I had worried about how we could manage what I thought would be the long last days.

It had been my habit to set the alarm clock for every two hours of the night: I would stumble down the hall to sit with him for a few minutes because he could sleep so little as he panted to breathe. Now it was possible to have a nurse and I looked forward to a whole night's sleep. But it didn't work that way: I didn't like a stranger in his room, I didn't want the night's sleep.

In 1962 I began an adaptation of Bert Blechman's novel *How Much.* The play was called *My Mother,*

My Father and Me and, by the time I finished, was half Blechman, half me. I thought, I think now, that it is a funny play, but we did not produce it well and it was not well directed. More important, I found that I had made some of the same mistakes I had made with *Candide:* I changed the tone midway from farce to drama and that, for reasons I still do not understand, cannot be done in the theatre.

The play waited in Boston for the New York newspaper strike to end. Once again I sat bewildered in a hotel room, making changes I did not believe in, this time under the pressure of how much money was about to go down the drain.

The playwright is almost always held accountable for failure and that is almost always a just verdict. But this time I told myself that justice doesn't have much to do with writing and that I didn't want to feel that way again. For most people in the theatre whatever happens is worth it for the fun, the excitement, the possible rewards. It was once that way for me and maybe it will be again. But I don't think so.

Arthur W. A. Cowan

THEODORE ROETHKE and I stood in the back of the auditorium until the poet Babette Deutsch finished reading. I am a noisy audience in a theatre, moving my body and feet without knowing it, cracking the knuckles of my hands, coughing. But I had been quiet that night because Ted had been tap-dancing in the back aisle to music only he could hear and several people in the last row had objected.

When Babette finished, somebody whose name I do not remember came onstage and said things I wanted to hear but couldn't because Ted said, very loudly, "I have just made up a poem. It begins 'Isn't it thrilling.' Now you write the next line. Go on, write the next line." I smiled because that's usually safe with drunks, but it didn't work.

"You don't want to write a poem with me. I don't

think you want to write a poem at all. O.K. We'll write a play together, just the two of us. What you say to that?"

He said it again and poked me in the ribs. "Sure, Ted. A play," and hoped he wouldn't poke me again.

"You say sure, anything, sure, because no matter how much work *I* do on our play people will think *you* wrote it and I won't get any credit. So we'll sign an agreement to have one name for both of us. What name would you like?"

I said, "Let's go sit down. My feet hurt."

"Not until we find a name. I know, I know, I've got it. We'll sign it with the salmon. How about Irving K. Salmon? I like that, Irving K. Salmon, a good name."

All through dinner there had been talk of a salmon but I didn't know if he was talking about a particular salmon or all salmon because sometimes he talked about their spawning habits, sometimes he talked of one or two or eight fishing trips he had made, and once he told me about a nun he knew in Seattle who had caught a giant fish and given it to him.

Then another man came onstage, Roethke gave a whoop, pulled me by the hand and dragged me down the aisle. "Now stop talking about our play. That can wait. I want to hear Cal."

We started into aisles that were already filled, backed out, crossed a number of annoyed people in the front row, and by this time had the full attention

514

of our side of the house. Robert Lowell had started to read in a rather low voice by the time we finally sat down and I wondered how he would make out if Ted kept on talking. But he didn't. He sat hunched forward, moving his lips to the poems, smiling, applauding occasionally at the end of a line. After a long silence he said in a new, piping, child's voice that carried through our section, "The kid's good." I am sure the kid was good but I hadn't been listening: I was tired after hours of being moved around New York, the pounding, often incoherent talk, the energy that had made us sprint into the zoo, running from monkey house to bird house, and then amble through lunch only to sprint again to visit a friend of Ted's who turned out to have moved from New York two years before.

When the Lowell reading was over, Ted made for backstage. He was ahead of me, forgetting me I think. But I decided not to follow him and walked slowly home, not expecting to see him again until the next time he came East.

In front of my house were Lowell, Ted, Babette, and three other people. Ted lifted me from the ground and said, "I told 'em you'd be right along after you had finished your secret pint."

To this day I do not know who two of the strangers were, but I came to know the third and he is the reason for my writing now about that night. I came to know his face as well as my own, but I have no memory of it that first time, nor did I then know his name.

I remember only that I found myself yawning into the face of a man sitting near me, yawned in another direction, and a few minutes later became conscious that the man had been staring at me for a long time, not with a flirting look, but as if he were trying to understand something.

He said, "Where do you keep your books?"

"Upstairs. There is a kind of library."

"Thank you," he said, "I am glad to know that." And then I was too tired to care that neither of us said anything else. A little while later everybody went home except Ted, who was weaving back and forth in a kind of shuffle, his lips forming words I couldn't hear.

I said, "Ted, I'm sleepy."

He said, "Ssh. I've got it. I've got it. The best poem written in our time. Now listen carefully: 'Isn't it thrilling there's another Trilling?' Got it? 'Isn't it thrilling there's another Trilling?' Got it? 'Isn't it thrilling there's another Trilling?' "

The second time he poked me in the ribs with his pleasure in creation I said, sure, the poem was fine, but why didn't he go home. He gave me a sad, hurt look, fell on me from his side of the couch and went to sleep immediately. I got from under his dangerous weight without waking him, but the next morning when I came down for breakfast he was gone. There was a note on the table: "I tell you it *is* thrilling, the Trilling. And just you remember about Irving K. Salmon."

I don't know how I came to mix up the salmon with the flowers, but four or five days later, Helen, a black woman who had worked for me for many years, suddenly appeared in the reading room of the Society Library. When something important had happened, or she was disturbed, she made military gestures. Now she hit me on the shoulder, made a sign meaning I should follow her, and while we walked the few blocks to our house she said, "Mary is down with it again. This time she got her good reasons."

Mary and her husband Ed had been the janitors of the house for the many years I owned it. They were Irish, feckless, kind, and often drunk, at which time they scattered into excitable pieces over nothing more than the mail being late or a light bulb wearing out.

"What's the matter this time?"

"I tell you this time she got her good reasons. A child's coffin. A child's coffin has come to the house."

"A child's coffin?"

"In a pine box. Dripping."

Indeed there was a pine box in the hall, it was the size of a small child, it was dripping, and most of the red lettering of the sender had been washed away. One could still read, "Mother Joa — " and numbers that still had two eights in them. Mary and Ed were too upset for me to know or care whether they had been drinking, but when I said, "It smells of fish," Mary shrieked, went out into the street and was followed by Ed, who took her arm and led her off, I guess, toward their favorite Lexington Avenue bar.

Helen went to get the handyman from the apartment house next door and when he pried off the lid there was a large salmon lying on what had been a bed of ice. The fish was turning, not enough to make us sick, but enough to make us carry it out to the street and close it up again.

In time, it turned out that Roethke had sent the salmon, and we exchanged a number of letters about it, although it was never clear about "Mother Joa — " A further mix-up came about because while we were opening the salmon box a large basket of flowers arrived, Helen put them on the floor, and somehow they got thrown out in the salmon excitement. I don't know why I thought Roethke had sent the flowers, but I thanked him, and long after I knew he had not sent them, he wrote that they came as a tribute because I liked his greenhouse poems.

A few weeks later another basket arrived. There were two enclosed cards: one from the lady florist who wanted to know if I had received a basket sent a few weeks before, and a second card on which was printed "Arthur W. A. Cowan, Esquire" and then a designation I have long forgotten that meant he had something to do with the State of Pennsylvania. I did not recognize the name Cowan, had never before known an Esquire, wondered when you were entitled to use it. Later that day I tried to phone the lady florist to find out about Esquire, but the phone was busy and I forgot about the whole thing until a third, even fancier arrangement arrived, with the same card and a scribbled sentence that thanked me for a nice evening.

I don't know when or how I connected the name with the man who had asked me about the books. It may have been because Lowell told me that he h never met Cowan before the night of the poetry rea ing but that he knew his name because Cowan ha been a large financial contributor to *Poetry*. Nor do have any memory of how Cowan and I first came to have dinner together, and then to have another, and then to find ourselves good friends.

It is hard, indeed, to construct any history of Arthur, in part because he traveled so much, but mostly because he talked of his own past and present in so disjointed a fashion, often taking for granted that you knew what you could not have known, certain that you were pretending ignorance only to annoy him. He is the only person I have ever known who had no sense of time: he did not know whether he had met people last week or many years before, and once he told me he had been divorced for three years when, in fact, he had been divorced for fourteen. And so, in the first few months I knew him, I could follow very little of the mishmash of what he said, and knew only that he had gone to Harvard Law School, moved on to the Philippines, been poor and grown rich, now practiced law in Philadelphia, had a large number of brothers and sisters, three houses, and expensive motor cars which he was constantly exchanging to buy others.

His no sense of time was tied up with no sense of

place, yours or his, so that he was bewildered and angered if you didn't know the names of his friends or the kind of work he did, even though nothing had ever been said about them. For example, the third time we had dinner he told me that he had spent much of his childhood in a Philadelphia orphan asylum.

I said, "But you're not an orphan. You just spoke of seeing your mother yesterday."

He was at that minute, as at so many other minutes, complaining about the steak he was eating, joking with the waiter about taking it back.

The good humor turned immediately to anger. "God damn it. That's the silliest stuff I ever heard anybody talk. You don't have to be an orphan to get into an orphan asylum. We were poor. We didn't have enough to eat. So they put two of us in the joint. Then sometimes when my father got a job they'd come and get us for a while and then bring us back again. I've told you all that a hundred times before."

In those early days of knowing him, I still believed in reasonability and so I tried to say he could not have told me a hundred times before, we had only known each other a few months. But before I could say that, he was telling the waiter that the steak was fine, but his dinner companion wasn't. I would have been angry, as I was to be many such times in the future, but that night I put down his sharpness with me to painful memories of the orphanage years.

I said, "I'm sorry. It must have been a bad time for you."

"What the hell are you talking about?" he said for the next four tables. "It was the best God-damned time of my life. It was clean, and there was meat every day. They had books and it was there I learned to read. It was the best part of my life and you're an ass. Even you. All women. Every God-damned woman is an ass."

He shouted for the check, left the waiter an enormous tip, put me in a taxi and marched off. The next day almost the same arrangement of flowers arrived and I threw them out.

A few weeks went by, perhaps a month, and then I had a telephone call. He said, very cheerfully, "What's the weather like?"

"It's a sunny day, but not for you and me. How is it in Philadelphia?"

"I'm in London and I called to say that I don't bear any grudge against you. I'll be back tomorrow and will take you to dinner."

I said I didn't intend to eat dinner the next night and he laughed and hung up.

The following night I was having a tray in bed and listening to the phonograph when Helen came in, turned off the phonograph and said, "Can you hear it now?"

"Hear what?"

"There's something bad going on in the elevator."

The house had a small self-service elevator, but once inside you needed a key to get out or somebody to open the door on our side. It was an old elevator, and although nothing much had ever happened to it, we were always conscious that it might stick or fall, or that, without care, we could admit intruders. I got out of bed, went to the elevator door, and when I asked who was there the rhythmic pounding ceased.

A voice said, "Who wants to know?"

"I want to know."

"Who are you?" a second, high voice said.

Helen said, "Tell them to go out the way they came."

The first voice said, "Who said that? How many thieves are in my house?"

The elevator began to move upward. Helen whispered, "Don't open the door. There's more than one." The elevator went past us and continued up to the floor of my tenant.

The high voice said, "Open up or I'll shoot the place down."

My tenants, above me, had an elderly Japanese cook, and after a minute we could hear him running down the service stairs.

Helen said, "There goes the Jap. You can't blame the poor soul."

Like most people my age, I had a hard time believing in city crime, perhaps in any kind of danger. So I said to Helen, as I would not say today, "Let the Jap in our service door and tell him there's nothing to be afraid of."

Then, very loudly, I shouted into the elevator door, "Please leave the house immediately."

"What'll you do if we don't?"

"Call the police. So go immediately."

"I've got a better idea," said a voice, now undisguised. "Get dressed and I'll buy you a decent steak."

A few hours later, sitting next to him in his newest Aston-Martin, having just had a bad steak in a restaurant somebody had told him about — somebody was always telling him about a restaurant; in the years I knew him I don't think we ever went twice to the same place — I said, "Arthur, you're too young for me."

"Without question. How old are you?"

"Forty-eight. Too old for your high-jinks. How old are you?"

He said he was forty-two, and I didn't know that night why he coughed so much after he said it, nor why he stared at me so hard when we reached my door.

I was to find out a few weeks later. It started when the mail brought an engraved invitation for a dinner party to be given in Philadelphia by Arthur W. A. Cowan, Esquire, in honor of Miss Lillian Hellman. Although the engraving proved that the party must have been planned weeks before, I had had on the Sunday before the arrival of the card a most disturbing time with Arthur.

On that bad Sunday, driving to the country on the first, lovely spring day, as the Saw Mill River Parkway went by the turnoff, I said that the farm I had owned for so many years was just around the bend, over the bridge. This was the first time since I had sold it that I found myself so close to it, and if I was silent for a long time it was because I was trying not to cry. After a while, he stared at me and asked irritably why, if I liked the place so much, I had sold it. He knew why, because I had told him, and so I didn't answer until the question was repeated.

"The House Un-American Activities Committee. The Joe McCarthy period. I went broke. I've told you all that, Arthur."

"Yeah," he said, "but I never understood it."

"O.K."

But he was not a man to leave things alone when the toothache of blind contention was upon him and so, after a while, he said again that he didn't understand what Joe McCarthy had to do with the sale of a farm and he thought I was just blaming my mistake on somebody else. I knew, of course, before that day that his politics were eccentric, going in one direction on some days, in another the next. He was solidly conservative, sympathetic to every piece of legislation that benefited the rich, was the attorney for millionaires like Del Webb, and yet was a close friend of Mark De Wolfe Howe of Harvard and the Philadelphia liberal lawyer Thomas McBride. We had had no previous political arguments, in part because the mishmash he talked was too hard to follow, but mostly because I had already learned that I could not, did not wish to explain, or be wise about, or handle the bitter storm that the McCarthy period caused, causes, in me, and knew even then that the reason for the storm was not due to McCarthy, McCarran, Nixon and all the rest, but was a kind of tribal turn against friends, half-friends, or people I didn't know but had previously respected. Some of them, called before the investigating committees, had sprinted to demean themselves, apologizing for sins they never committed, making vivid and lively for the committees and the press what had never existed; others, almost all American intellectuals, had stood watching that game, giving no aid to the weak or the troubled, resting on their own fancy reasons. Years later, in the 1960's, when another generation didn't like them for it, they claimed they had always been anti-McCarthy when they meant only they were sorry he was not a gentleman, had made a fool of himself, and thus betrayed them. That was, that is, to me the importance of the period — the McCarthys came, will come again, and will be forgotten — and the only time I ever heard all that properly analyzed was by Richard Crossman in London, and although I have never seen Mr. Crossman again, I have often wished that he had written it down. It is eccentric, I suppose, not to care much about the persecutors and to care so much about those who allowed the persecution, but it was as if I had been deprived of a child's belief in tribal safety. I was never again to believe in it and resent to this day that it has been taken from me. I had only one way out, and that I took: to shut up about the whole period.

And so on that day, driving in the country, I had

no words. But by the time we returned to New York I was so shocked at the insensibility that forced Arthur to make fun of what had harmed me and had sent Hammett to jail, that I felt nothing more than weariness and that I must not ever listen to such stuff again.

A few days later, I wrote Arthur a note saying that, found the note incoherent, tore it up, telephoned to say that I couldn't come to my party. The operator said he was in Paris. I telephoned him in Paris, the hotel said he was in London. I got him in London, and before I was able to say much of anything he told me that he had just taken a woman to dinner who had on a red coat, he hated red coats, would never see the woman again, didn't know what I was talking about but was in the middle of a meeting and had just bought me a bracelet. He hung up, and when I called him the next day I heard him tell the operator that Mr. Cowan was not available.

Somewhere in the next few weeks, I had dinner with Mark and Molly Howe in Boston. I told them about Cowan's defense of McCarthy. Mark got up from the table and didn't come back for a while. Molly said of course they had heard the same kind of thing, and when Mark came back in the room he said, "Arthur is unbearable, unbearable." He was so disturbed that we ate our dinner almost in silence, only speaking when the Howe children came in and out of the room. Mark and Molly walked me back to my hotel and, as we stood in front of it, Mark's fine face was obviously getting ready for something difficult. He said "He is

unbearable. He is unbearable. But it is only fair to tell
you that his opinions often have nothing to do with
his actions. I once told him about a Communist who
had no money for legal defense. He paid the total bill
and sent the wife a thousand dollars. I don't know his
friend Tom McBride, but I am told he has another
form of the same story." Molly said she thought
maybe Arthur was just plain crazy, but I think both of
them were saying they would understand if I wrote
him off, but they hoped I wouldn't. I didn't.

*   *   *

Thinking about that night a few weeks ago, I wrote
to Molly Howe, who has moved to Dublin since the
death of Mark Howe. She does not refer to that night,
perhaps she doesn't remember it. But she understood
Arthur:

Dear Lillian: What can I say of Arthur? It's like
roaming through a churchyard and picking out the
names of old friends on the tombstones. Mark, Johnny
Ames, Arthur Cowan, Bunny Lang, my old father-in-
law, Felix Frankfurter, McBride, Joe Wall, all of
them strung together by one name — Arthur's.

Arthur becomes a game of true or false. What did
you or I *really* know about him?

I first met him a few years after the war. We had
dinner, Mark, Johnny Ames and I at the Athens
Olympia. He was then triumphing over the winning of
some case in New Jersey, I think, and I think it was
connected with aspirin, which indeed one was inclined

527

to need after a few hours in his rather fevered company.

And after that . . . flying visits into the law school. Everyone knocked out of their legal torpor. Griswold actually took to hiding. Always with a new sports car, wearing frightfully expensive rather gaudy clothes, driving like a madman; off to the Ritz; bursting into the Poets Theatre. You almost knew by the weather when Arthur was coming. Something threatening about those clouds massing in the north. And you never knew he was coming until he was there. And the letters from Paris, from London, from Rome, from Hawaii, from the desk of Arthur Cowan. It must have been a flying desk.

I've never had such a curious relationship with a man before or since. It was purely friendly, almost fraternal. I really confided in him. I wrote him constantly, and the things he told me as well — true or false? To this day I do not know which. Brought up in an orphanage, number 58. That's why the number of our house 58 Highland Street was so important. He was convinced he would die when he was 58! Father killed himself during the Depression. Worked his way through college by professional boxing. Belonged to a delightful club in New York called the Bucket of Blood. Was married once to some girl in Philadelphia who played too much tennis. It broke up. He had girls everywhere. Two of them in London, and he had great difficulty keeping them apart. A girl in Paris — very special. Never liked actresses. Never liked models.

All lesbians at heart and everywhere else. Once caught them in the very act.

Arthur as a houseguest was not good. Stayed with us four days on the Cape in 1954. Would only eat steak and lettuce three times a day. Insisted on going round three-quarters naked with shaven chest. This last revolted Mark. We had some stuffy neighbors to cocktails and Arthur sat in a stately manner (this was six P.M.) naked except for a slight pair of pants, reading a life of Byron. "Arthur," I hissed in passing, "this man is a brother-in-law of the Rockefellers." When I looked round again he had vanished, went upstairs, came down twenty minutes later in an immaculate white linen suit. Unfortunately the Rockefeller contingent had gone. The next night we all went to dinner in Provincetown with Isabella Gardner and her brother Bob. Sudden outbreak from Arthur, who had been curiously quiet all evening. Shouted at Bob Gardner, "You're stupid! Phony! Numb! Ridiculous!" All heads turned in his direction. Nobody could understand it. Belle G. was furious and would never meet him again. A year or two later during the summer he suddenly shouted at Perry Miller — we were having cocktails on the porch, Perry as I remember was offering some learned information on Cotton Mather — "You're posturing. Why are you always posturing?" I don't believe Arthur knew whether Cotton Mather was a textile or a boll weevil, but suddenly something infuriated him. As he was always in very good trim and looked, with that broken nose, like an aging but powerful boxer, nobody cared to take things up with him.

And his health. He was always having mysterious operations. He went through a period of having some-one come in and give him an enema every day. He took royal jelly. Some great man in New York took care of his teeth. A splendid fellow in Switzerland for the eyes. Somebody in Philadelphia for the gallblad-der and he told Mark he had himself sterilized in Paris. He didn't want any trouble of that kind. Pater-nity suits. Can't be too careful. And the diets. I never knew anyone go through such rigorous and varied diets. Do you remember the time he had to have raw parsley and carrots? Then there was the tablespoon of vinegar and all red meat phase and the exercises.

Every time he arrived there was a new and expen-sive camera. Color Polaroid long before anyone else and the constant taking of photographs was a ritual which had to be gone through on arrival and the camera was usually so new, so expensive, so compli-cated he didn't know how to use it. The cursing and swearing was heartrending.

Johnny Ames, for instance. Why did Arthur like such a New England Henry Jamesian old bachelor with very little money, of no importance in the world, because let's face it Arthur did like the Big Names. Why? And Johnny was fascinated by Arthur. They always had to meet when Arthur was in Cambridge. And they always talked about money. Do you remem-ber Arthur talking about money? He talked about it the way some people talk about poetry. The voice was low and reverent, the face radiated a beautiful joy, and Johnny listened as if Arthur was the oracle, and Arthur advised Johnny on how to invest his little bit of capital. Advised him so well that by the time Johnny died he had almost doubled it. They conversed a great deal in French which was another bond and Johnny made the best martinis in Boston.

Why did he like V. R. Lang? A way-out blonde girl who wrote two good plays and some poetry and died of cancer aged thirty — a year after her very happy marriage. He met Bunny at the Poets Theatre, was fascinated by her play and fascinated by her world of Frank O'Hara, Bob Bly, Ted Gorey. It was through Bunny, in some way, he met you, Lillian, and moved into the Big World of Brains and never was happier. It all culminated for me at that wonderful house party, Birthday Party, weekend in Vineyard Haven that you gave for Arthur. How old was he then? It must have been twelve years ago. McBride was there and the Bernsteins and the Warburgs for dinner. Before Mark and I left that Monday morning, Arthur said to me, in that curious falsetto whisper: "It's not often you spend a weekend with all the people you like best. I have a feeling it only happens once." I have often thought of that since. Was it prescience?

He *was* a good friend. When Mark had a bad go of flu from overwork I told Arthur that Mark simply could not go on with the second volume of the Holmes and carry on a full teaching schedule at the law school. It took Arthur only a few weeks to manage that. Mark was relieved of half the law school load and Arthur paid the half of his salary on a grant basis. In fact, if it hadn't been for Arthur, vol. II would never have been written, and if it hadn't been for vol. II, Mark might have lived longer.

Then there was the episode of Little Hel. Do you remember our youngest daughter was always known by Arthur as Little Hel? One afternoon he and Mark went for a walk round Eagle Pond on the Cape and unknown to them Little Hel took it into her head to follow them through bush and through briar a good mile on her own wobbly legs. She caught up with them eventually and Arthur couldn't get over it. The courage! The guts! The determination! He carried her back the rest of the way on his shoulders. He was almost crying. Of course he was going to mention her in his will. That well-known will of Arthur's that you and so many others were going to benefit by.

Did you ever read his poems? He brought out a book of poems I think in the late Forties. I had a copy once. God knows where it went. They were, of course, very bad.

And then those books inscribed to us by authors who had never heard of us, with Arthur standing over them with a gun. "To my dear friends Mark and Mollie Howe from André Maurois, with the compliments of Arthur Cowan." *You* must have several shelves of them.

He was a James Bond character. You remember

the sudden sinking of the voice to a whisper and the shifty look around and quick glance over the shoulder? What *was* he up to?

Well, he died alone on a dusty road in Spain, our friend, and we don't even know the truth about that.

*   *   *

And so I went to the party. I was taken first to what he called the guesthouse — Cowan owned two houses in Philadelphia — and then hustled around to where he lived in the few weeks of the year when he lived in any one place. It was a handsome old house in Rittenhouse Square, the windows spoiled with ugly draperies, the furniture heavy expensive copies of what the movies think is an English greathouse library. I dislike dark rooms and so, without plan, I went to one of the windows and pushed aside the draperies to see the view. Arthur dashed for the draperies, closed them and shrieked at me: "My books! My books! Don't do that."

"Don't do what?"

"Don't let in any light. It will harm the bindings. Why don't you know such things? I'll tell you why — because you don't have a fine binding in the world."

"I don't like them," I said. "If I had the courage, I'd throw out all my books, buy nothing but paperbacks, replace them — "

"I can't stand what you're saying, I can't stand it. You're not fit to touch a book in this house. I forbid you to *touch my books*."

The first guest came in on the shouting. Arthur immediately put an arm around me, his voice low, immensely loving. "This, I am proud to say, is my friend Lillian Hellman."

It was the usual cocktail stuff before dinner, but I was uneasy at being shown off and uncomfortable under the almost constant stare of a pretty girl across the room. At dinner I sat next to Tom McBride, whom I liked immediately. I knew that he had defended two radicals during the McCarthy period, and when I spoke of it and said there weren't many lawyers, certainly not successful ones, who had such courage, McBride pointed down the table to Cowan.

"That nut made it possible. I couldn't afford to take the cases, with a family and growing children, couldn't have involved my law partners. Cowan gave me all I needed through that time even though he hated what I was doing. He's a nut, but you'll get used to him, if you can stay with the nuttiness without wearing out. God knows what goes on in his head, if anything, but he'll kick through every time, without questions, and without wanting thanks, for the few people he has any respect for, and you're already one of them, the only woman it's ever happened with, and you must remember that."

I did remember it a few years later. Cowan said, "What's the matter with you? You haven't said a word for an hour." I said nothing was the matter, not wishing to hear his lecture about what was. After an hour of nagging, by the repetition of "Spit it out," "Spit it out," I told him about a German who had fought in the International Brigade in the Spanish Civil War, been badly wounded, and was now very ill in Paris without any money and that I had sent some, but not enough.

Arthur screamed, "Since when do you have enough money to send anybody a can to piss in? Hereafter, I handle all your money and you send nobody anything. And a man who fought in Spain has to be an ass Commie and should take his punishment."

I said, "Oh shut up, Arthur."

And he did, but that night as he paid the dinner check, he wrote out another check and handed it to me. It was for a thousand dollars.

I said, "What's this for?"

"Anybody you want."

I handed it back.

He said, "Oh, for Christ sake take it and tell yourself it's for putting up with me."

"Then it's not enough money."

He laughed. "I like you sometimes. Give it to the stinking German and don't say where it comes from because no man wants money from a stranger."

I sent the money to Gustav and a few months later had a letter from his wife asking if I knew anything about an American who had appeared at the hospital, left an envelope for Gustav with five hundred dollars, refused his name, spoke fine French, and had asked the nun at the desk if she fucked around very much.

But that day after the Philadelphia dinner party, the day he shoved in my pocket the largest and most vulgar topaz pin I have ever seen, and was strangely silent and thoughtful, was the day that marked our relationship for the rest of his life. We were driving back to New York — it is strange that almost every memory of Arthur is connected to a restaurant or to a car — and I had not talked to him very much because I sensed that he was on the verge of a temper. (I was to realize in the years to come that sadness often looked like temper, often turned into it, as if he were rejecting despair for something healthier.) As Arthur slowed down from his usual speed of a hundred miles an hour to avoid hitting two other cars, he said, "I'm the only good driver in America. Sons of bitches." Then he sighed. "Well, I might as well tell you, that's that. All my friends last night think you're too old for me."

I laughed. "Too old for what?"

"For me. They think that wouldn't be any good. I'm five or six years younger than you are." This was to be accepted throughout the years I knew him.

"What wouldn't be any good?"

He shifted around. He was uneasy, embarrassed, and that was always one step in front of irrationality. I should have been ready.

"You know what I'm talking about. Stop pretending."

"I don't know what you're talking about, Arthur."

"You know damn well. You're a combination of shyster lawyer and Jesuit. I mean you are too old for me to marry. That's what I mean and you made me say it."

I said, "That's not the way it is or ever could be."

"It's always the way it is. For every Goddamn broad that ever lived. Marriage, marriage, marriage."

"Not for me. Twice in my life, maybe, but not about you. I wouldn't marry you, Arthur, I never even thought about it."

"Like hell you wouldn't, like hell." He stopped the car in the middle of the Pennsylvania Turnpike. "You're lying. You'd marry me in a minute. Maybe not for anything but my money, but I'm not marrying you, see?"

I opened the door of the car and got out, getting home late that night by walking a long way to a place that suggested I call another place for a taxi.

But this time, the next day, in fact, I called him. I had not slept much that night, waking up to read, and to think about Arthur. I was what he wanted to want, did not want, could not ever want, and that must have put an end to an old dream about the kind of life that he would never have because he didn't really want it. We have all done that about somebody, or place, or work, and it's a sad day when you find out that it's not accident or time or fortune but just yourself that kept things from you. Years later, when Arthur was telling me about "a beautiful model who double-crossed me when I'd have given her the money without the double-cross," I told him what I had thought that night when he blamed my age and his friends for not wanting to marry me. He patted my arm and said, "Aah. Aah. Sometimes you're not an ass. Why don't I buy you a pound of caviar?"

But when I say years later and things like that, I

am not sure they are accurate. I did sometimes make notes in a diary, I have a large number of letters from Arthur, I remember more about him than I do about most people, and I know I can put together the order of his words with accuracy, but time, in his case, skips about for me, and I often mix up the places where we met, so that something that might have happened in Paris I have possibly transferred to Martha's Vineyard or Beverly Hills. The passing of time, the failure of memory, did not cause those confusions: they were always there. Perhaps because we never shared ordinary days together, more probably because everything about his life, the present and the past, was in jump-bites: he would tell a story about friends but he would start the story in the middle; he would ask you to regret a building he had just sold when he had not told you he had ever owned it; if he told a joke he would start with the last line and go backward; if he wanted to talk about a woman he was tired of, he started to tell you about another woman he had been tired of twenty years before.

I did piece together a kind of history, but I am not sure how much of it happened before I met him or after I knew him, since there was no way of sorting the past from the present. I knew that he didn't practice law much anymore, but that he himself was always suing somebody or some organization, and since that happened at least four or five times a year, I would get the details and the results mixed up. I knew that he had made a lot of money, before I met him, as counsel for a large drug company in a patent suit and that he took stock instead of a legal fee. (It is indicative that Molly Howe remembers the legal fight as having to do with aspirin and I remember it as benzedrine, and it was probably neither.) I knew that he was a large investor in the stock market and a brilliant one. But I only knew that because sometime in the first two years I knew him, he said, "Where is your money invested?"

"I don't have much anymore. I have the house on 82nd Street, but — "

"What the hell did you do with all you earned?"

I said we were on a sensitive subject, the Joe McCarthy period and no work in Hollywood and the Internal Revenue Department's refusal to let Hammett have a nickel of his royalties, and thought we better not get into an argument.

He said, "Don't tell me the reasons. Just go upstairs and get me all your records. Checkbooks, mortgages, everything. You'll starve in the streets without me, that's where you'll end."

The following day I telephoned to say I needed my checkbook because I forgot I was leaving in a few days for London. Arthur said, "I'll give it to you in the airport." Of course I thought he meant the airport in New York and tried to reach him when he wasn't there. He was waiting for me in the London airport and swore that he had told me that. He had a new Rolls-Royce, his third in about two years, and drove me to the hotel. As I was signing, and the manager came to greet me, Arthur said, "One room, not two, and make it a cheap one. Miss Hellman has wasted more money than anybody since Hubert Delahantey."

It was many references later, and many years, before I asked about Hubert Delahantey. It turned out he never existed in life: he was a rich American drunk who threw away all his money and died in a Paris garret in a novel Arthur had once bought at a French railroad bookstand but whose title he couldn't remember.

The following night, when the *Candide* rehearsals were over, Arthur came around to the theatre to take me to a new restaurant somebody had just told him about. After he had gone through his usual denunciation of the steak, he put my checkbook on the table.

"From now on you can have fifty percent of what you earn. I will invest the rest. You know nothing about money and are a disgrace. You'll end in a charity hospital and die without a pot to piss in or a bone to chew."

I said, "You talk too much about my death. And if that's the way it's going to be then I won't die much different from the rest of the world."

"You're the kind of fool who has forgotten more than you ever learned," he said so loudly that the next table of six upper-class English ladies and gentlemen looked down at their plates.

I said, "The English don't raise their voices, Arthur, although they may have other vulgarities."

"Fuck the British. I think they were in collusion with the Germans all through the war."

At the next table one man spoke to another man and the second man got up and came to our table. Arthur rose, grinning with pleasure.

He said, "My dear, good sir. During my attendance at Harvard, a university situated in Boston, the Athens of America, I was middleweight intercollegiate boxing champion and I am flattered that you recognize me. Let me buy you a drink."

The man, who was a tall, good-looking example of Empire, said he did not wish a drink, but he felt impelled to say that he thought insults to the English in their homeland were totally inappropriate for a foreign guest. Arthur gave a mirthless bad-actor laugh and said he wasn't anybody's guest: his hotel and this restaurant were gyp joints, what the hell did guest mean when you paid your way and the billions we spent with the Marshall Plan?

I got up and said, "I'm going to the toilet. Leave a note what jail you're in or what hospital."

When I came back Arthur had joined the English table and was sitting with his arm around the tall gentleman. After he had introduced me he whispered that Sir Francis was a distinguished barrister, they had many friends in common. After half an hour I said I was tired and wanted to go to bed.

Sir Francis said, "You're not going back to the toilet?"

I didn't much understand that or the giggles that went round the table until Arthur, walking me to the hotel, said, "They didn't like your saying toilet. I don't either and have always meant to tell you. Why can't you say ladies' room like other people? Sir Francis didn't like it for his wife. He said, 'I've heard of Hellman. But even an actress needn't say toilet.' "

"And what did you say, Arthur?"

"I said Miss Hellman is a playwright, most distinguished, and they made me name the plays. Anyway, we're invited to dine in the country with them tomorrow. Don't wear that tweed coat. Wear something quiet, black."

When we got to the hotel I said, "I am now going upstairs to the toilet and so I won't be able to go to the country with you tomorrow. If you don't tell them you are a Jew they'll think you're charming, but you can even tell them that if you also tell them how rich you are and very possibly good business for them."

We did not mention Sir Francis again until many months after we had both returned to New York and after somebody told me that Arthur had appointed him his representative in London.

I said, "Nice about you and Sir Francis. Have you given him enough business to install a toilet?"

"So you've heard about her," he said. "Want to see her picture?"

He took out of his wallet one of the many snapshots he was always taking with the most expensive of cameras he had just broken. A youngish woman was standing against a very large house, her entire body and face shaded by giant trees.

"Admit that she's a beauty," Arthur said.

"I can't see her. You can never see anybody in your pictures."

"I should tell you that I may decide to marry her."

"Who is she?"

"She is the niece of Sir Francis. A great beauty. I call her Lady Sarah."

(He did not lie, I guess. He did call her Lady Sarah but it was only last year that I discovered her name was not Sarah, she had no title, and neither, for that matter, did Sir Francis. Arthur had bestowed the titles upon them as a sign of the esteem he then felt.)

It is a strange side of many women that they are jealous even when they do not want the man, but I was old enough to watch for that and wait it out. I suppose I waited it out without speaking because after a while he said, "Don't worry."

I said I wouldn't and he said he thought I should and I asked him why and he said I was hiding things and he didn't like me when I did that. After we had batted that around for a long time, he said, "Don't you, don't you, well?"

"Don't I what?"

It is hard now to believe that I didn't know what he wanted me to feel and say and certainly the stumbling words, so unlike him, the sadness in the face, should have told me. But even if I had known in time I am not sure I could have said it.

"Don't I what?"

The sadness disappeared. He clipped out the words, "Worry about my money. You don't have to. Marry or not I'll take care of you."

I said I was having more trouble than usual finding out what he was talking about, and when he shouted, "My will. After I die. That's what I'm talking about," I thought it wiser to be off in another direction. So I asked him what had happened to the lady in Philadelphia and the one in Paris, had he told them about Lady Sarah?

"I'm through with them. If you ever listened you'd have known that months ago. Tomorrow morning I am flying to Hollywood for a vasectomy. Between that shit orthodontist and the abortions I spent fifteen thousand six hundred dollars last year."

The complaints about the orthodontist were old stuff but the vasectomy was new. I said, "If you're getting married why do you want a vasectomy?"

"Who wants children in this stinking world? I spent my life wondering why they ever had me. Who wants to throw out five thousand six hundred dollars on abortions?"

"You," I said, "for ladies who pocket four thousand of it."

We were at my front door. I said, "Arthur, you know that Hammett lives here now, is very sick, that means I don't get much sleep and am tired most of the time. Good night."

"So you don't want to talk about my marriage? If it worried you, you were going to miss me, that would be something else. But you're just afraid the marriage will cut you out of my will, no money for you. I've told you, and I'll keep my word, I'll take care of you."

And he pushed me through my door and went down the street. I stood in the kind of anger I hadn't known for many years but which, even as a young child, I knew was uncaring of consequence, without control, murderous. I ran down the street and caught him as he was stepping into a taxi. I grabbed his arm and spun him around and spoke in the tones of quiet reasonability which have always been for me the marks of greatest anger. "Stop trying to buy me. You've been doing it too long. Not you or my mother's family or anybody else and just maybe because I am frightened it could happen. So skip me and have your vasectomy and your teeth fixed and your face operated on again and leave me alone and don't mention money or your Goddamn will again."

I stopped in pain at what I had let slip. For two years I had pretended that I didn't know that this interesting-looking man didn't like his face, had had two operations in Hollywood to correct what he didn't like, and neither had corrected anything except to make him look assembled and had taken away the lively brightness, the amusing crinkles of time, all that had been good.

He said quietly, "You don't think the operations made me look better?" Then he turned and took a long time to pay off the taxi driver and when I saw his face the tears in his eyes had stopped. He took my arm and we walked up and down the same Madison Avenue block for an hour or so, neither of us speaking. Then, from the corner, I saw the light in Hammett's room go on, which meant that the night was over for him. We turned down to the house.

I said, "There would be no meaning to any apology, no sense saying I didn't mean to hurt you because I did. When I get like this it's better to be rid of me." We shook hands and I went upstairs.

One likes to think that words are understood, that what has been painful or forbidden will not happen again. But a few weeks later I had a note from Arthur: "I canceled the vasectomy, although I'll probably have it another time. If then I die on the operating table, you'll be a very rich woman."

I can no longer remember how long after that night we let each other rest in a kind of unplanned moratorium, but long after his death, one of his many stockbrokers told me that during that time the market had fallen sharply and that Arthur had put up a good deal of his own money to carry the margin account he had insisted I have; and sometime during that period a puzzling letter arrived from Barclays Bank in London telling me that Mr. Arthur W. A. Cowan had instructed them to notify me that in the event of his death securities had been placed in their vaults for me, although, of course, they could not reveal the nature or the amount. It was with that letter that I knew he had understood nothing of what we had said on our long walk up and down Madison Avenue and that there would never again be any point in telling him that what was proof of friendship to him wasn't, necessarily, for me. I felt self-righteous about that, as I frequently have about other people's money stuff, until Helen, a few days after Christmas, showed me a hundred-dollar bill Arthur had sent her.

"My," she said.

"If you want to send it back, don't worry about me."

"He means no harm," she said. "You never understood that."

Helen was a fine cook, the best I've ever known, and the nicest times we had together were in the kitchen. It had long been our habit, if we were alone, to make each other a gift dinner: she cooked me something I liked and I made her something she had come to like, my "foreign stuff," which she pretended she could never learn. That night I was making her saffron rice.

"Buy yourself a new coat with the hundred. You need it."

"No, I don't. The hundred dollars came pinned to a new coat. It's too small, of course."

Helen was a very big woman and the picture of Arthur trying to guess her size made me laugh.

"The coat be good for my niece. He means well. Men are different. You ain't ever learned that."

"Better than we are, worse?"

"Different. Where is Mr. Cowan?"

I thought I knew what she meant. She could barely

write the alphabet and could spell very few words.

"You can thank him on the phone."

"I ain't worried about thanks and neither is he. *You* ought to write him, it's a shame. He's doing what we all must do, come soon, come late, getting ready for the summons, and you ought to put out a hand."

That kind of talk was a part of her Catholic convert nature: it had happened before. If I argued with her there was a chance of depriving her of what she needed, but to be silent made hypocrisy between us and she had often played at seeing which she could catch me at. But now, although I only half understood, I was disturbed.

"Getting ready for the summons? What do you mean?"

When she didn't answer me, I said, "You talk too much about death. And he's a Jew. We don't get ready for the summons."

"Jew, not Jew. Nobody's anything. We all lost sheep."

I had heard this many times before and I knew I could annoy her by quoting the Reverend Whittier, a famous Negro backwoods preacher of her childhood and my mother's. "Sheep? The Reverend Whittier didn't like sheep. He said, 'Rise up and make yourself in the image of the lion. Throw off the shackles, grab away the whip, cut the chains of your oppressors as the lion would spring from — ' "

"Oh, sure," she said, "sure enough. If we took away

the whip and cut the chains the white man would atom us out."

I laughed because I knew she wouldn't like it. She said, "I ain't talking about black nor white. I'm talking Bible, the summons to the Lord. The horn's over the hill and Mr. Cowan's been hearing it for years."

"Mr. Cowan's been hearing nothing but the sizzling of steaks, the crackle of money and airplane engines. What are you talking about?"

"Write him," she said. "Tell him my coat's fine and the money too."

All my life, beginning at birth, I have taken orders from black women, wanting them and resenting them, being superstitious the few times I disobeyed. So I did write about the money and the coat and for months received no answer. But in June of that year, a few months after Helen, Hammett and I moved to Martha's Vineyard, I had a note from him saying he'd like to come up for my birthday. I postponed telling Dash that he was coming. He had never met Arthur but he didn't like visitors, didn't like their seeing how sick he was, and would disappear into his part of the house during any visit. In any case, I didn't expect Cowan until the 20th, and so on the 17th of June, returning from market with a good many packages, I was surprised and nervous when I saw a Rolls-Royce parked in the drive.

Dash was sitting in the living room. Before I spoke he put up a warning hand and pointed outside to the terrace. The local chief of police was there watching a figure in the distance running up and down the beach.

"What's happened? Cowan was coming in a few days. I forget to tell you — "

Dash said, "He came in here all done up in a motorcycle helmet, carrying a gun. He pointed the gun at me and said, 'Put 'em up, sir, and hand over the jewelry.' It didn't worry me because I know a toy gun when I see it, but it worries the police because he did the same thing at the gas station, where they don't know a toy gun."

Dash was a good-natured man, but in the last, bad, suffering years almost anything was too much for him.

I said, "Sorry. What should I do?"

"Cowan is down on the beach doing push-ups or something. Go upstairs and bring down the toy gun."

When I came back with it — it had been sitting on top of the collected works of Yeats — Hammett went out to the terrace and from the window I could see him and the police chief looking at the gun and speaking words I couldn't hear. The policeman took the gun, waved at me through the window, and climbed the steps to his car.

Hammett went to his end of the house and I followed him up the stairs, bracing myself against the fall I always thought he would have. He put himself on the bed and stared at me as he always did when the years had done nothing to convince him that he knew much about me.

I said, "I didn't know he was coming today."

He closed his eyes. I said, "Is something the matter? Can I get you something?"

"No. I'm just thinking that for the first time in my life I've met a crazy man who is pretending that he is crazy and wondering why you never see danger. Maybe it's what saves you. Let me know when he leaves."

Arthur stayed for three days. He never asked about Hammett, Hammett never asked about him. On the last day of the visit, we took a picnic lunch to an ocean beach. After he had done his push-ups, taken his mile run, we had a nice day, full of disconnected talk about people and places, an occasional passing reference to Lady Sarah. On the ride home Arthur fished out a folded check from the glove compartment. It was made out to me for ten thousand dollars.

"What's this about?"

"It's not a birthday present. You earned it. Remember the Soloway case, the lawsuit I told you about? You said maybe I should just tell the truth because I'd get anything else mixed up."

He laughed with pleasure at the memory and I tried to remember which of the many lawsuits was called Soloway. "Well, only a first-rate shyster mind like yours could have thought that up. I won the case and that's your part. You'll need it when I die."

"Are you going to die again?"

"You're not to ask questions because they've forbidden me to answer."

"They?"

"Yes, this time, *they*. I have taken an important job with the government and an oath not to reveal what it's about. I am telling you that much because my travels may seem odd to you from now on."

"Odder than usual?"

"Odder than usual. That's why I want you to have the check. If I am killed, of course, there will be more for you, the securities at Barclays Bank."

I waited until that night, always his choice for driving because he could reach higher speeds, and put his check in the glove compartment of his car. As he came up the steps with his bags and got into his car, I said, "I don't like CIA spy stuff anywhere, Arthur, and I am too old to waste time talking about how such people are needed, I guess, in every country. I don't ever want another fight with you, so this will be the last time — "

He said, quietly, "Mark Howe said the same thing a few days ago. He believed that I don't lie. Do you?"

"Yes."

"I don't work for the CIA. I never even heard about them until Mark explained. I don't like people who spy on other people, either. It's not the CIA I am working for and I swear to it. But I owe you and Mark the truth. My new bosses did question me about both of you. I said you were about as radical as rice and Mark was the most distinguished man at Harvard and if I had to listen to one word against either of you, then to hell with the whole thing. They're gentlemen, my new bosses, and they apologized."

I said I was glad they were gentlemen and then,

552

somehow touched, I said I didn't have to know what foolishness he was up to and I didn't want to part with him ever.

He said, "We're never going to part. I always knew that," and the car roared out of the driveway.

I telephoned Mark the next morning and asked him who he thought "they" were. He said he didn't know, couldn't believe the job was of any importance because he was going on the assumption that nobody with any sense would allow Arthur to make decisions, except in the field of law, and he wasn't even sure about that.

About a year later, on the opening night of Simone Signoret's production of *The Little Foxes* in Paris, I made the guess that the job had something to do with the Common Market, although there was never anything to prove that true. Arthur had ordered twenty tickets for the opening night and was sitting next to Jean Monnet, who in the few minutes I spoke to him after the play told me that he found Arthur "a brilliant financier" and so did "other countries." I was too sad about the evening to ask the questions that probably wouldn't have been answered anyway. I wanted only to get out of the Théâtre Sarah Bernhardt.

I had arrived for the last two weeks of rehearsals. Arthur met me at Orly Airport and we had a good evening. His love of Paris was always a pleasant thing to watch, but it was the last good evening I was to have until I left Paris the day after the opening of the play.

Much in the theatre always goes wrong, it's as if

from the beginning it was intended that way, but I had never before seen so much go bad so early: it was an awkward, too literal translation of the play; it was in a theatre meant for a pageant or an ice show; the set, which was intended only to show the middle-class indifference of a woman who had all her life been on her way to another house, was cluttered and decorated with the largest and most demanding objects I had ever seen on a stage; and the Texas sombreros chosen for Alabama bankers became a large and dangerous argument between Simone and me when, of course, they were only a small symbol of our irritation with each other.

Simone Signoret is an intelligent, charming woman, as remarkable in front of a camera as she is bewildered by a stage. Not knowing much makes many people in the theatre turn natural sense and humility into nonsense and pretense. It is understandable, it is sad, but it is also difficult and tiresome. And I am often no good with actors or directors. I do not speak when I should, speak out when I shouldn't; I praise in order to hide complaints and that is recognized; and my manners grow excessively good to hide anger that can't be hidden. I thus offend more than if I had had an open fight.

Every evening, after rehearsals, Arthur came to the theatre to take me to dinner, bewildered, he told me later, at a side of me he had never seen before. I would sit silent, unable to eat the good food, drinking too much of the wine, smiling at the wrong places in his complicated stories, shaking my head when I should have laughed. The night before the official opening his patience was coming to an end: why did I worry about an old play when he had made me enough money to live well for the next few years? Why did I make faces about his newest diet, buttermilk with melted butter and cheese? Did I want to see a picture of Lady Sarah in a sable coat he had bought her? Why was there a copy of Büchner on my bed table when I knew how he hated Germans? Had I read *Candy* in the French edition he had given me? I must say immediately what I thought of *Candy*. There was justice in his impatience, but the questions were provocative. I was tired and so, trying not to answer him, I wrote on the back of the menu, "Arthur is a man of unnecessary things. That's sad, but there's no cure. Did I make that up or have I read it?"

He said, "I've asked you three times. What do you think of *Candy?*"

"A nasty way to make a buck." And waited for the trouble.

I don't think he heard me because he said, "Roscoe Pound saved me. At the end of my first year in Harvard Law School I didn't have enough money to come back for the second. Pound called me in and said he'd find the money for me to get through. That was before I married the tennis player whose family had never read a book. They wouldn't have liked *Candy*, either. The ignorant bastards."

"O.K., Arthur, I see what's coming."

"I only started out to say I have been faithful to you in my fashion, Cynara, you and the Harvard Law School, and not much else."

(As I write these words I would not believe them, but I have a letter, written about a week later, in which they are repeated exactly as they came that night.)

"I get tired of other women."

"What's happened to Lady Sarah and the marriage?"

"So Pound got the law school to make me the loan and when he called me in to tell me I could stay, well, I can't tell you — Anyway, I cried so hard afterward that I hit a guy in the cafeteria who asked me why my eyes were red. When I die, I will take good care of my sister, I hate the rest of my family, but I'll leave her enough so she can support them, and then the rest is for the Harvard Law School and you."

I said, "Why don't you do things while you're alive and then not so many people would look forward to your death, which may be the longest in history?"

"O.K.," he said, "I'll buy you a house."

"I have a house."

"Then you'll have two houses. You're no problem, but what should I do for Harvard Law School?"

I started to say fuck the Harvard Law School, I've got other problems, but I said, without interest, "Maybe a scholarship as a thank you to Pound?"

He got to his feet, pulled me up, embraced me until I lost my breath. "Wonderful. When it comes to the clinches, you're not such an ass. That's just what I'll do. Now stop being so sad about *Foxes*, I promise you I am never going to marry Lady Sarah."

A few months later he told me something about the scholarship and I think he remembered to tell me because we were on our way to dine with Ben Kaplan, a member of the Harvard Law faculty. Arthur was in a gay, charming good humor that night — he liked lawyer academics, respected them — until a man sitting next to him spoke of Goethe. Then one of the storms that came across the ocean of his years broke with tornado force, more out of control than I had ever seen before, without sense or reason, from depths so unknown and frightening that even these strangers turned aside in pity or embarrassment. Arthur was shouting to a silent table that Goethe was an old German ass, like all Germans, past and present. Then a woman, maybe the bravest or the silliest, asked about Bach and Beethoven and I knew immediately that would make things worse because Arthur didn't like women to speak when he was angry, maybe because middle- and upper-class men had convinced him against his will that women shouldn't be shouted at or knocked to the floor. He suddenly grew dangerous quiet as he told her that nobody was sure Bach and Beethoven were Germans, and anyway they were musicians and what did that have to do with thinking? I was, as I had been many times before, torn with shame that he was my friend and a strong desire not to deny or desert him. So I made the wrong, nervous remark: I said it all came back to Arthur's never having forgiven the Germans for producing Karl Marx. The quiet tone was gone again: Arthur told the table that my ancestors were German, that I had, therefore, inherited the national villainies, that my grandmother's name was Marx and therefore I was related to Karl Marx, and was even numbskull enough to like Heine. Still mistakenly intent on diverting him — it sometimes could be done and then he was grateful for the extended hand — I said that I had always liked Heine's remark that when the Germans made a revolution they would first have to ask permission. Arthur shouted at me that even I should know that Heine meant the *Nazi* revolution because Heine was an early Nazi and he wouldn't any longer sit at a table with me or anybody else who had an ounce of German blood.

It was that night, at that table, as I watched him leave the Kaplan house and move down toward the beach, that I knew something had gone wrong with Arthur, now forever: the inside lines that hold most of us together had slackened or broken and bad trouble was ahead. The early deprivations, the lost belief that money solved the problems of his life, the wild traveling about, the women, perhaps even the mysterious new job, maybe all of it or only some, certainly much I didn't know about, had made the life into a line on a fishing reel that tangled and couldn't be untangled, held by a hand that didn't have the sense or the courage to cut the line and tie it together in another place. But I had to cut the line of me where it crossed and tangled with his, and that night I did it, although, I am glad to say, he never knew it happened.

I was not angry that night, I was never to be angry with him again. It was no longer possible to pay him the compliment of anger, and I think he knew it and was worried about it. We saw less of each other, but in that next year and a half I had more affectionate letters than ever before, and once he arrived late at night, directly off a European plane, with a charming gold pin, and once he told me he had used the securities in my name at Barclays Bank but not to worry because he had increased my inheritance in his will, and once he told me that I was his best friend and that he loved me, and a number of times we had pleasant evenings and he became, for the first time, almost a suitor, as if he was looking for the affection he felt he had lost. He had not lost it. The truth was more important to us both: he had become to me a man of unnecessary things and often I felt that he knew what he was, was gallant about the pain it caused him and tried to hide it from himself with new cars, new houses, new friends, new women half forgotten at the minute they were half loved, new faces for himself, teeth set and reset, even new writers, here and in France, subsidized too long for their always shabby talents, new banks, new stocks, a new city or village or ocean that

559

he liked so much one year and disliked so much the next.

The last time I ever saw him was an August week he came to stay with me in Martha's Vineyard. An old friend of mine was there, he liked her, and the three of us had a pleasant time. We raced to many beaches in his newest Rolls-Royce, the old having been bought a year before, we walked, we climbed cliffs where he would be waiting for me at the top to say that even if I was six years older than he I was still in bad shape, and he would prove that further by running down the cliff and for a mile stretch on the beach, the fine powerful body no heavier, he said, than when he had been young. And for once there were no boring lectures about new diets: he ate the delicious stuff that Helen cooked and kissed her after each meal.

I said to her, "Mr. Cowan looks fine, doesn't he?"

She stared at me and fished out of her pocket a piece of paper. It read, "Before I fly tonight to Paris, Air France, Flight 972, I wish to bequeath to Helen Anderson in case of my demise the sum of ten thousand dollars in repayment for her kindness during these years."

I laughed. "He does that often, with all the ladies he likes."

"It's not nice," she said.

A few hours later, Helen and I walked with him as he carried his luggage to the car. I said, "Have a good trip."

Behind me, Helen said, "It's not nice, this piece of paper about the money."

I said, "Oh, what difference does it make?"

He kissed us both, said something about coming to visit his new apartment in Torremolinos about which I had not previously heard, and started the engine. I don't think he heard Helen say, "Drive slow, Mr. Cowan. Pray the summons back."

On November 11, 1964, I came into a hotel in Mexico City to hear myself paged. The voice said that Cowan was dead, killed instantly when the Rolls-Royce was smashed in Seville. But the accident was not in Seville and he had not died instantly and he had not been driving the Rolls-Royce. No will was ever found, but Lady Sarah and the pretty lady from the Philadelphia party of so long ago came up with old letters, almost exactly like Helen's, and collected large sums of money. In time, I asked Helen if she didn't want to present her note for collection, the going was good, and for a while she pretended not to know what I was talking about. Then one day she told me she had torn up the note as we stood saying good-bye to him that last day at the car door. The conflicting details of the accident, why a will disappeared that he certainly wrote and rewrote through the years, the failure even to find out what job he had been doing for what agency, all are to this day unexplained. If his life was puzzling, he entrusted the memory of it to people who have kept it that way. He has disappeared. I do not believe he would have wanted it that way. And he was not six years younger than I, he was two years older, and there was a girl with him when he died. She was unharmed in the accident, she was nineteen years old, and she was German.

*T*hings began to happen after the publication of this piece about Arthur Cowan. I received a series of eleven letters, all mailed from Philadelphia, denouncing me and my picture of Arthur. On receiving the fourth letter I noticed that they all had some similarity of phrase or words. I called Philadelphia telephone information for phone numbers, giving the names and addresses on the envelopes. No such people had phones and in none of the four cases was there any such address on the given street. I don't know now where the letters came from, but I have a hunch that a relative of Cowan's didn't like my picture of him, or was worried about my intimation that he had written a will that was never found.

Then, two ladies wrote to me, real ones, to say they had had love affairs with Cowan: one said she found him kind and generous. The other letter came from a young woman who said she had slept with him, "off the Atlantic *coast one summer," a hell of a big place to sleep with anybody. She "deeply hated him" and his treatment of her. I wrote back and said I was sorry, but maybe it was a bad time for him, and such stuff. She didn't like my letter — I am not sure I would have, either, but then I never would have written hers — and she wrote again to say my generation was accustomed to being badly treated by men, hers was not, but she was still shocked at my lack of sympathy. I didn't answer that letter and everything rested for a bit until I had another letter, this time mailed from Denver, claiming that it was I who had kept her romance with Cowan from ending in marriage and that Cowan had told her that. This had to be an unpleasant invention: Cowan would have had his arm torn out before he explained anything to anybody, and certainly not his feelings toward me, nor would he have used me as an untrue excuse. He knew very little about his emotions, didn't ever choose to analyze them, and was always irritated when other people talked that way. I would not have answered that letter except there was a postscript saying that she was writing a short book about Arthur in which, of course, I would appear. I sent her a note saying that I felt he never had any intention of marrying again and I didn't believe he had ever used me to excuse himself from it or from anything else. I had another immediate letter with quotations, stuff he could never have said, and then, about two years later, an announcement of her wedding. On it was written, "You were right. Thank you." I hope she's fine now, but I'm not sure of it.*

Other, more interesting letters came: one from a man who had been Cowan's classmate at Harvard Law School,

*saying he would send me a copy of the poems Arthur
had written when he went to the Philippines after he
graduated. He never sent the copy, which was just as
well because Cowan had given me one the first week we
met, and the poems were awful. Another letter, post-
marked Paris, and signed Emile, asked if it had occurred
to me that Arthur had been killed, deliberately killed. It
had occurred to me, but since I did not know for what
mysterious government agency Cowan had worked, or
with whom, and neither his sister nor his lawyers seemed
anxious to go into that part of his life, there wasn't much
to be gained by an investigation that had so little chance.
One could make a case that he drove cars at such wild
speed, had so many idle, unnecessary operations on his
face and teeth, that he was long headed for death, and
never understood that. One could also make a case that
he enjoyed his high jinks so much that he wanted desperately to live. It is all like that, yes and no.*

*But I believe one thing is certain: he wanted to be re-
membered, and remembered, I think, by Harvard, for
whom, on one of his thousand airplane rides, he had
taken out a life insurance policy. But he wanted, as he
had proved, to give more than money to a place he
looked back upon with great feeling and gratitude, the
best time of his life. He was rich, very rich. And so when
things were still calm between us, I suggested to his sister and to his lawyers that a scholarship fund be set up
for a Harvard Law student in his name as a permanent
memorial. This suggestion was treated with calm and
cool — no answers at first, and then a telephone call saying that he had left very little money and an explanation
of why: garages or buildings he had owned whose value*

565

had been something or other, but were not good now. I didn't understand much of what was being said, except that there was no chance for my idea. Maybe it was true that he died not rich, maybe what I consider rich is not what others think is real money. In any case, a remarkable, generous, valuable, eccentric man has disappeared as quickly as he did on that road in Spain. There was a car, a man, and then nothing. I am sorry for that. He deserved something better than the sentiments of his family, most of whom he disliked, and something better from me if I could only have found it or said it.

"TURTLE"

I HAD awakened at five and decided to fish for a few hours. I rowed the dinghy out to the boat on that lovely foggy morning and then headed around my side of Martha's Vineyard into the heavy waters of West Chop. Up toward Lake Tashmoo I found the quiet rip where the flounders had been running, put out two lines, and made myself some coffee. I am always child-happy when I am alone in a boat, no other boat to be seen until the light breaks through. In an hour I had caught nine flounders and a couple of tautogs that Helen would like for chowder and decided to swim before going home to work. The boat had drifted out, down toward the heavy chop, but there was nothing new in this, and I was never careless: I tied my two-pound stone to a long rope, carried it down the boat ladder with me, and took it out to where I would swim near it. I don't know how long it took me to know that I wasn't swimming but was moving with incredible swiftness, carried by a tide I had never seen before. The boat had, of course, moved with me, but the high offshore wind was carrying it out of the rip into deep water. There was no decision to make: I could not swim to the boat, I could not force myself against the heavy tide. I have very little knowledge of the next period of time except that I turned on my back and knew that panic was not always as it has been described. For a time I was rigid, my face washed with water; then I wasn't rigid and I tried to see where the tide would take me. But when I turned to raise my head, I went down, and when I came up again I didn't care that I couldn't see the shore, thinking that water had been me, all my life, and this wasn't a bad way to die if only I had sense enough to go quietly and not make myself miserable with struggle. And then — I do not know when — I bumped my head against the pilings of the West Chop pier, threw my arms around a post, and remembered all three of us, and the conversation that took place four days after the turtle died when I said to Hammett, "You understood each other. He was a survivor and so are you. But what about me?"

He hadn't answered and so I repeated the question that night. "I don't know," he said, "maybe you are, maybe not. What good is my opinion?"

Holding to the piling, I was having a conversation

with a man who had been dead five years about a turtle who had been dead for twenty-six.

Even in those days, 1940, it was one of the last large places in that part of Westchester County. I had seen it on a Tuesday, bought it on Thursday with royalties from *The Little Foxes*, knowing and not caring that I didn't have enough money left to buy food for a week. It was called an estate, but the house was so disproportionately modest compared to the great formal nineteenth-century gardens that one was immediately interested in the family who had owned it for a hundred and twenty years but who had, according to the agent, disappeared. (This was not true: eight or nine years later a young man of about sixteen or seventeen came by and asked if he could see the house and picnic at the lake. He said he had been born in the house and he took with him a giant branch of the hawthorn tree he said his mother had planted to celebrate his birth.)

In the first weeks, I closed the two guesthouses, decided to forget about the boxwood and rare plants and bridle paths, and as soon as Hammett sold two short stories we painted the house, made a room for me to work in, and fixed up the barn. I wanted to use the land and would not listen to those who warned me against the caked, rock-filled soil. I hired Fred Herrmann, a young German farmer, because I had an immediate instinct that his nature was close to mine, and together, through the years, we drove ourselves to the

ends of weariness by work that began at six in the
morning and ended at night. Many of our plans failed,
but some of them worked fine: we raised and sold
poodles, very fashionable then, until we had enough
profit to buy chickens; I took the money I got from
the movie script of *The Little Foxes* and bought cattle
and three thousand plants of asparagus we bleached
white and sold at great prices. We crossbred ducks
that nobody liked but me, stocked the lake with bass
and pickerel, raised good pigs and made good
money with them and lost that money on pheasants;
made some of it back with the first giant tomatoes,
the sale of young lambs and rich unpasteurized milk.
But all that was in the good years before the place
had to be sold because Hammett went to jail in the
McCarthy period and I was banned in Hollywood after
I was called before the House Un-American Activities
Committee. The time of doing what I liked was over in
1952.

I have a jungle of memories about those days:
things learned and forgotten, or half remembered,
which is worse than forgetting. It seems to me I once
knew a lot about trees, birds, wildflowers, vegetables
and some animals; about how to make butter and
cheese and sausages; how to get the muddy taste out
of large-mouth bass, how to make people sick with
the weeds I would dig and boil up according to all
those books that say you can. The elegant Gerald and
Sara Murphy grew very ill on skunk cabbage I had
disguised according to an eighteenth-century recipe.

But the day I remember best was in the first spring

I owned the place. The snow had gone on the bridle paths and, having finished with the morning's work at the barns, I took Salud, the large poodle, and four of his puppies on an early morning walk to the lake. As we reached the heavily wooded small hill opposite the lake, Salud stopped, wheeled sharply, ran into the woods, and then slowly backed down to the road. The puppies and I went past him to the lake and I whistled for him, sure that he had been attracted by a woodchuck. But when I looked back he was immobile on the road, as if he had taken a deep breath and had not let it out. I called to him but he did not move. I called again in a command tone that he had never before disobeyed. He made an obedient movement of his head and front legs, stared at me, and turned back. I had never seen a dog stand paralyzed and, as I went back toward him, I remembered old tales of snakes and the spell they cast. I stopped to pick up a heavy stick and a rock, frightened of seeing the snake. As I heard Salud make a strange bark, I threw the rock over his head and into the woods, yelling at him to follow me. As the rock hit the ground, there was a heavy movement straight in front of the dog. Sure now that it was a snake about to strike, I ran toward Salud, grabbed his collar, and stumbled with the weight of him. He pulled away from me and moved slowly toward the sound. As I picked myself up, I saw a large, possibly three-foot round shell move past him and go slowly toward the water. It was a large turtle.

Salud moved with caution behind the turtle and as

I stood, amazed at the picture of the dog and the slowly moving shell, the dog jumped in front of the turtle, threw out a paw, and the jaws of the turtle clamped down on the leg. Salud was silent, then he reared back and a howl of pain came from him that was like nothing I had ever heard before. I don't know how long it took me to act, but I came down hard with my stick on the turtle's tail, and he was gone into the water. Salud's leg was a mess but he was too big for me to carry, so I ran back to the house for Fred and together we carried him to a vet. A week later, he was well enough to limp for the rest of his life.

Hammett was in California for a few weeks and so I went alone almost every day to the lake in an attempt to see the turtle again, remembering that when I was a child in New Orleans I had gone each Saturday with my aunt to the French market to buy supplies for her boarding house. There had been two butchers in the market who had no thumbs, the thumbs having been taken off as they handled snapping turtles.

Hammett came back to the farm upset and angry to find his favorite dog was crippled. He said he had always known there were snappers in the lake, and snakes as well, but now he thought we ought to do something, and so he began his usual thorough research. The next few weeks brought books and government publications on how to trap turtles and strange packages began to arrive: large wire-mesh cages, meant for something else but stared at for days until Hammett decided how to alter them; giant fishhooks;

extra heavy, finely made rope; and a book on tying knots. We both read about the origin of snapping turtles, but it didn't seem to me the accounts said very much: a guess that they were the oldest living species that had remained unchanged, that their jaws were powerful and of great danger to an enemy, that they could do nothing if turned on their backs, and the explanation of why my turtle had come out of the woods — each spring the female laid eggs on land, sat on them each day, and took the chance that the hatched babies would find their way to water.

One day, a month later perhaps — there was never any hurrying Hammett when he had made up his mind to learn about something — we went to the lake carrying the wire cages, the giant fishhooks, fish heads and smelly pieces of meat that he had put in the sun a few days before. I grew bored, as I often did, with the slow precision which was part of Dash's doing anything, and walked along the banks of the lake as he tied the bait inside the traps, baited the hooks, and rowed out with them to find heavy overhanging branches to attach them to.

He had finished with one side of the lake, and had rowed himself beyond my view to the south side, when I decided on a swim. As I swam slowly toward the raft, I saw that one limb of a sassafras tree was swinging wildly over the water, some distance from me. Sitting on the raft, I watched it until I saw that the movement was caused by the guyline that held one of the hooks Hammett had tied to the branch. I shouted at Hammett that he had caught a turtle and he called back that couldn't be true so fast, and I called back that he was to come for me quick because I was frightened and not to argue.

As he came around the bend of the lake, he grinned at me.

"Drunk this early?"

I pointed to the swinging branch. He forgot about me and rowed over very fast. I saw him haul at the line, have trouble lifting it, stand up in the boat, haul again, and then slowly drop the line. He rowed back to the raft.

"It's a turtle all right. Get in. I need help."

I took the oars as he stood up to take the line from the tree. The line was so heavy that as he moved to attach it to the stern of the rowboat he toppled backward. I put an oar into the center of his back.

He stared at me, rubbing his back. "Remind me," he said and tied the line to the stern. Then he took the oars from me.

"Remind you of what?"

"Never to save me. I've been meaning to tell you for a long time."

When we beached the boat, he detached the rope and began to pull the rope on land. A turtle, larger than the one I had seen with Salud, was hauled up and I jumped back as the head came shooting out. Dash leaned down, grabbed the tail, and threw the turtle on its back.

"The hook is in fine. It'll hold. Go back and get the car for me."

I said, "I don't like to leave you alone, you shouldn't be handling that thing — "

"Go on," he said. "A turtle isn't a woman. I'll be safe."

We took the turtle home tied to the back bumper, dragging it through the dirt of the mile to the house. Dash went to the toolhouse for an axe, came back with it and a long heavy stick. He turned the turtle on its stomach, handed me the stick, and said, "Stand far back, hold the stick out, and wait until he snaps at it."

I did that, the turtle did snap, and the axe came down. But Dash missed because the turtle, seeing his arm, quickly withdrew his head. We tried five or six times. It was a hot day and that's why I thought I was sweating and, anyway, I never was comfortable with Hammett when he was doing something that didn't work.

He said, "Try once more."

I put the stick out, the turtle didn't take it, then did, and as he did, I moved my hand down the stick thinking that I could hold it better. The turtle dropped the stick and made the fastest move I had ever seen for my hand. I jumped back and the stick bruised my leg. Hammett put down the axe, took the stick from me, shook his head and said, "Go lie down."

I said I wasn't going to and he said I was to go somewhere and get out of his way. I said I wasn't going to do that either, that he was in a bad temper with me only because he couldn't kill the turtle with the axe.

"I am going to shoot it. But that's not my reason

for bad temper. We've got some talking to do, you and I, it's been a long time."

"Talk now."

"No. I'm busy. I want you out of the way."

He took my arm, moved me to the kitchen steps, pushed me down and went into the house for a rifle. When he came out he put a piece of meat in front of the turtle's head and got behind it. We waited for a long time. Finally, the head did come out to stare at the meat and Hammett's gun went off. The shot was a beauty, just slightly behind the eyes. As I ran toward them the turtle's head convulsed in a forward movement, the feet carried the shell forward in a kind of heavy leap. I leaned down close and Hammett said, "Don't go too near. He isn't dead."

Then he picked up the axe and came down very hard on the neck, severing the head to the skin.

"That's odd" he said. "The shot didn't kill it, and yet it went through the brain. Very odd."

He grabbed the turtle by the tail and carried it up the long flight of steps to the kitchen. We found some newspapers and put the turtle on top of the coal stove that wasn't used much anymore except in the sausage-making season.

I said, "Now we'll have to learn about cutting it for soup."

Dash nodded. "O.K. But it's a long job. Let's wait until tomorrow."

I left a note under Helen's door — it was her day off and she had gone to New York — warning her there was a turtle sitting on the stove and not to be frightened. Then I telephoned my Aunt Jenny in New Orleans to get the recipe for the good soup of my childhood and she said I was to stay away from live turtles and go back to fine embroidery like a nice lady.

The next morning, coming down at six to help Fred milk the cows, I forgot about the turtle until I started down the kitchen steps and saw blood. Then, thinking it was the blood that we had spilled carrying the turtle into the house the evening before, I went on toward the barns. When I came back at eight, Helen asked me what I wanted for breakfast, she had made corn bread, and what had I meant by a turtle on the stove?

Going up to have a bath, I called back, "Just what I said. It's a turtle on the stove and you must know about snappers from your childhood."

After a few minutes she came upstairs to stare at me in the bathtub. "There ain't no turtle. But there's a mess of blood."

"On top of the coal stove," I said. "Just go have a look."

"I had a lot of looks. There ain't no turtle on top a stove in this house."

"Go wake Mr. Hammett," I said, "right away."

"I wouldn't like to do that," she said. "I don't like to wake men."

I went running down to the kitchen, and then fast back upstairs to Hammett's room, and shook him hard.

"Get up right away. The turtle's gone."

577

He turned over to stare at me. "You drink too much in the morning."

I said, *"The turtle's gone."*

He came down to the kitchen in a few minutes, stared at the stove, and turned to Helen. "Did you clean the floor?"

"Yes," she said, "it was all nasty. Look at the steps."

He stared at the steps that led to the cellar and out to the lawn. Then he moved slowly down the steps, following the path of blood spots, and out into the orchard. Near the orchard, planted many years before I owned the house, was a large rock garden, over half an acre of rare trees and plants, rising steep above the house entrance. Hammett turned toward it, following a path around the orchard. He said, "Once, when I worked for Pinkerton, I found a stolen ferris wheel for a traveling country fair. Then I lost the ferris wheel and, as far as I know, nobody ever found it again."

I said, "A turtle is not a ferris wheel. Somebody took the turtle."

"Who?"

"I don't know. Got a theory?"

"The turtle moved himself."

"I don't like what you're saying. He was dead last night. Stone dead."

"Look," he said.

He was pointing into the rock garden. Salud and three poodle puppies were sitting on a large rock, staring at something in a bush. We ran toward the garden. Hammett told the puppies to go away and parted the branches of the bush. The turtle sidling in an effort at movement, was trying to leave the bush, its head dangling from one piece of neck skin.

"My God," we both said at the same time and stood watching the turtle for the very long time it took to move a foot away from us. Then it stopped and its back legs stiffened. Salud, quiet until now, immediately leaped on it and his two puppies, yapping, leaped after him. Salud licked the blood from the head and the turtle moved his front legs. I grabbed Salud's collar and threw him too hard against a rock.

Hammett said, "The turtle can't bite him now. He's dead."

I said, "How do you know?" He picked up the turtle by the tail. "What are you going to do?"

"Take it back to the kitchen."

I said, "Let's take it to the lake. It's earned its life."

"It's dead. It's been dead since yesterday."

"No. Or maybe it was dead and now it isn't."

"The resurrection? You're a hard woman for an ex-Catholic," he said, moving off.

I was behind him as he came into the kitchen, threw the turtle on a marble slab. I heard Helen say, "My goodness, the good Lord help us all."

Hammett took down one of the butcher knives. He moved his lips as if rehearsing what he had read. Then he separated the leg meat from the shell, cutting expertly around the joints. The other leg moved as the knife went in.

Helen went out of the kitchen and I said, "You know very well that I help with the butchering of the animals here and don't like talk about how distasteful killing is by people who are willing to eat what is killed for them. But this is different. This is something else. We shouldn't touch it. It has earned its life."

He put down the knife. "O.K. Whatever you want."

We both went into the living room and he picked up a book. After an hour I said, "Then how does one define life?"

He said, "Lilly, I'm too old for that stuff."

Toward afternoon I telephoned the New York Zoological Society of which I was a member. I had a hard time being transferred to somebody who knew about turtles. When I finished, the young voice said, "Yes, the *Chelydra serpentina*. A ferocious foe. Where did you meet it?"

"Meet it?"

"Encounter it."

"At a literary cocktail party by a lake."

He coughed. "On land or water? Particularly ferocious when encountered on land. Bites with such speed that the naked human eye often cannot follow the movement. The limbs are powerful and a narrow projection from each side connects them to the carapace — "

"Yes," I said. "You are reading from the same

book I read. I want to know how it managed to get down a staircase and up into a garden with its head hanging only by a piece of skin."

"An average snapper weighs between twenty and thirty pounds, but many have weighed twice that amount. The eggs are very interesting, hard of shell, often compared with ping-pong balls — "

"Please tell me what you think of, of, of its *life*."

After a while he said, "I don't understand."

"Is it, was it, alive when we found it in the garden? Is it alive now?"

"I don't know what you mean," he said.

"I'm asking about life. What is *life?*"

"I guess what comes before death. Please put its heart in a small amount of salted water and be kind enough to send us a note reporting how long the heart beats. Our records show ten hours."

"Then it isn't dead."

There was a pause. "In our sense."

"What is our sense?"

There was talk in the background noise and I heard him whisper to somebody. Then he said, "The snapping turtle is a very low, possibly the lowest, form of life."

I said, *"Is it alive or is it dead?* That's all I want to know, please."

There was more whispering. "You asked me for a scientific opinion, Miss Hellernan. I am not qualified to give you a theological one. Thank you for calling."

Ten or twelve years later, at the end of a dinner

party, a large lady crossed the room to sit beside me. She said she was engaged in doing a book on Madame de Staël, and when I had finished with the sounds I have for what I don't know about she said, "My brother used to be a zoologist. You once called him about a snapping turtle." I said to give him my regards and apologies and she said, "Oh, that's not necessary. He practices in Calcutta."

But the day of the phone call I went to tell Hammett about my conversation. He listened, smiled when I came to the theological part, went back to reading an old book called *The Animal Kingdom*. My notation in the front of this book, picked up again on a July afternoon in 1972, is what brought me to this memory of the turtle.

Toward dinnertime, Helen came into the room and said, "That turtle. I can't cook with it sitting around me."

I said to Hammett, "What will we do?"

"Make soup."

"The next time. The next turtle. Let's bury this one."

"*You* bury it."

"You're punishing me," I said. "Why?"

"I'm trying to understand you."

"It's that it moved so far. It's that I've never before thought about *life*, if you know what I mean."

"No, I don't," he said.

"Well, what is life and stuff like that."

"Stuff like that. At your age."

I said, "You are much older than I am."

"That still makes you thirty-four and too old for stuff like that."

"You're making fun of me."

"Cut it out, Lilly. I know all the signs."

"Signs of what?"

He got up and left the room. I carried up a martini an hour later and said, "Just this turtle, the next I'll be O.K."

"Fine with me," he said, "either way."

"No, it isn't fine with you. You're saying something else."

"I'm saying cut it out."

"And *I'm* saying — "

"I don't want any dinner," he said.

I left the room and slammed the door. At dinnertime I sent Helen up to tell him to come down immediately and she came back and said he said he wasn't hungry immediately.

During dinner she said she didn't want the turtle around when she came down for breakfast.

About ten, when Helen had gone to bed, I went upstairs and threw a book against Hammett's door.

"Yes?" he said.

"Please come and help me bury the turtle."

"I don't bury turtles."

"Will you bury me?"

"When the times comes, I'll do my best," he said.

"Open the door."

"No. Get Fred Herrmann to help you bury the turtle. And borrow Helen's prayer book."

But by the time I had had three more drinks, it was too late to wake Fred. I went to look at the turtle and saw that its blood was dripping to the floor. For many years, and for many years to come, I had been frightened of Helen and so, toward midnight, I tied a rope around the turtle's tail, took a flashlight, dragged it down the kitchen steps to the garage, and tied the rope to the bumper of the car. Then I went back to stand under Hammett's window.

I shouted up. "I'm weak. I can't dig a hole big enough. Come help me."

After I had said it twice, he called down, "I wish I could help you, but I'm asleep."

I spent the next hour digging a hole on the high ground above the lake, and by the time I covered the turtle the whiskey in the bottle was gone and I was dizzy and feeling sick. I put a stick over the grave, drove the car back towards the house, and when I was halfway there evidently fell asleep because I woke up at dawn in a heavy rain with the right wheels of the car turned into a tree stump. I walked home to bed and neither Hammett nor I mentioned the turtle for four or five days. That was no accident because we didn't speak to each other for three of those days, eating our meals at separate times.

Then he came back from a late afternoon walk and

said, "I've caught two turtles. What would you like to do with them?"

"Kill them. Make soup."

"You're sure?'

"The first of anything is hard," I said. "You know that."

"I didn't know that until I met you," he said.

"I hurt my back digging the grave and I've a cold, but I had to bury that turtle and I don't want to talk about it again."

"You didn't do it very well. Some animal's been at your grave and eaten the turtle, but God will bless you anyway. I gathered the bones, put them back in the hole, and painted a tombstone sign for you."

For all the years we lived on the place, and maybe even now, there was a small wooden sign, neatly painted: "My first turtle is buried here. Miss Religious L.H."

"*Pentimento*" *was written by what psychoanalysis calls, in now weary semi-accuracy, a kind of "free association." I did not know from one portrait to another what I would do next, with the exception of "Julia" where, without much hope, I wanted to try once more. I had not, for example, consciously thought of Bethe for perhaps thirty years; the man I call Willy has been dead for over twenty-five years and in those years I remember only one conversaton about him, with his son-in-law, a few minutes of nothing. When I finished one portrait, there was always a long wait. All kinds of people and places came back, of course, but I knew I was waiting each time not for what had been most important to me, but what had some root that I had never traced before.*

When I finished the Arthur Cowan piece, there was a longer wait than usual. Peter Feibleman was staying with me in Martha's Vineyard, writing a novel, and he says

*that from his room at the end of the hall he would often
hear me talking to somebody, and he would keep his
door closed against my obviously unwelcome visitor.
There was no visitor: I have long had a habit of dividing
myself in two, sometimes three parts: one part is called
Nursie. When I am most disturbed, she says, "My dear
girl, do take things easier" or "A little patience oils the
wheels of life." What Feibleman heard were my answers,
which are usually no more than "Please go to your room
and stay there." She never does, but she smiles so long
and repeats so often that I stop mumbling and speak
loudly: "You have been saying the same things all my
life. Please leave me alone." It is then that she looks up
from her fine needlework and whispers, "I've done a
little good through the years, dear, very little, but more
than you realize." It is at such times that Madame, the
third part of me, who is not very active but is there when
I grow upset with Nursie, begins to say things like "Oh,
you two. What a shame you can't get used to each other,"
and it is then that I speak too quietly: "Your existence,
and yours, Madame, depend entirely on me. Be careful."*

*Both Nursie and Madame had been very talkative in
the weeks following the piece on Cowan because I didn't
know where to go next and felt bad about the long stretch
of wasted time. One night I told Peter I was stuck, depressed, and thought I would put the book away for
a while.*

*He said, "You once told me about a turtle in Pleasant-
ville" — and before he finished the sentence I knew that
I had deeply buried an event which was of great importance to me.*

I have always regretted that my mother, my father,

587

and Dashiell Hammett died in hospitals, and I was thus closed out from them. In the cases of my mother and father, who had to have operations, I guess I could not have avoided hospitals. But I had not wanted Hammett to go away from home and had argued with the doctor against the hospital, losing my nerve when I was told that the proper equipment could not be brought to the house. But I should not have lost my nerve: I should have said what difference does equipment make any longer, what is the difference between Tuesday or Sunday for dying? I am sad that Hammett died away from me not only because it would have been better for him, I think, to have had me with him. I know it would have been better for me, if I had taken care of him. If you are involved in a death that means so much to you then you are involved in your own. That's the way it used to be, before hospitals, that's the way it always had to be once upon a time. But now all of us give the sick to strangers, in part impressed with what they can do that we cannot do, but also wanting to spare ourselves the pain and the fear, and the reminder of our future. Yes, I helped to kill this turtle, and many others after it, but at least I stuck around.

PENTIMENTO

In 1961, a few weeks after Hammett's death, I moved to Cambridge to teach a writing seminar at Harvard. I had thought Hammett would be coming with me and had arranged with the help of Harry and Elena Levin for a room in a nursing home, a pleasant, sprawling nineteenth century house a few blocks away. Now, living with Helen on the top floor of Leverett Towers, a new student building, I could look down on the nursing home from the window and one night, when I couldn't sleep, I went to stand in front of it. That got to be a habit, and two or three times a week I would walk to the house Hammett had never seen, stand until I was too cold to stand any longer, and go back to bed.

The fifth or sixth time I took my late night walk — Helen was a heavy sleeper and I didn't think there was a chance that I could wake her as I dressed quietly in the next room — there had been a snowstorm during the day that made the few blocks hard going and slippery. But I never reached the nursing home that night, turning back for a reason I didn't as yet know, into Athens Street. Long before I reached our corner I saw Helen, looking very black in her useless summer white raincoat, standing with a tall boy who was holding a motorcycle. I felt the combination of gratitude and resentment I had so often felt for her through the years, but I didn't wish to waste time with it that night.

"Bad night," I said as I went past them.

I heard them behind me as I reached the courtyard of the building, and then I heard a misstep and a sound. As I turned, Helen had slipped, but the boy had caught the great weight and was holding to her, sensibly waiting for her to straighten herself. I knew she would not like me to see this, and so I went on into the building, took one elevator, waited until I heard her take another, heard the boy say something outside our door, and closed my own door against whatever she might say to me.

A few days later I saw her cross the courtyard, the tall boy behind her carrying two large bags of groceries. As she opened our door she took the bags from him and said, "Thank you, son. Come whenever you want your good dinner."

That night I said to her, "You've got a good-looking beau."

She had very little humor, but she liked that kind

of simple stuff. Now she didn't answer me and I realized that for the last few days she had said almost nothing to me. She gave me my dinner in silence. After dinner I read for a while, felt restless, and went to get my coat. She came out of her room.

"Death ain't what you think," she said.

"I don't know what it is, do you?"

"A rest. Not for us to understand."

I was used to this palaver, but that night I was ill-humored and made a restless movement.

"I don't want to talk about death."

As I stood waiting for the elevator, she watched me from the doorway.

"You go stand in front of that place because you think you can bring him back. Maybe he don't want to come back, and maybe you don't — " she shrugged, always a sign that she had caught herself at something she considered unwise or useless to continue with.

It was a long time before I knew what she had been about to say, and it was at least a year later, after I had moved back to New York, before I knew that she had discussed me with the tall boy. I thought that was disloyal of her and struggled for months about telling her that, and then knew it wasn't disloyal, and didn't care any more because I had come to like the boy and to understand she had needed him at a lonely time in her own life, in a strange city, living with a woman who did odd things at night.

Soon after the night we had talked about death I

came into the apartment to change my clothes for a
dinner with friends. The boy was sitting at the table,
Helen opposite him. He got up when I came into the
room. We shook hands and Helen said to him, "Sit
you down and eat your soufflé before it falls." As I
went to my room I heard him say to her, "I never
ate a soufflé before. It's wonderful."

"You can have one every night," she said, "a different kind."

When I came out of the bath I could see the boy
from the hall mopping the kitchen floor. Helen came
into my room.

"He eats nice. Two steaks."

I laughed. *"Two* steaks?"

"He asked what you'd think about that. I told him
you got some strange sides, getting stranger, but you
don't think about things like that."

"Thank you."

"He is taking me for a drive Thursday."

"On that motorcycle?"

"His rich roommate got a car. He says his roommate's on the stuff."

This then new way of saying dope, the only modern phrase I had ever heard Helen use, was no surprise. Years before she had told me her son was on
the stuff and she would have to take him back to
South Carolina to the farm her family still owned.

That Thursday, her day off, she got ready early in
the morning and looked mighty handsome and big in
a suit and a great coat.

"This early?" I said. "Doesn't he go to classes?"

"Jimsie is very, very bright," she said.

"What is Jimsie's last name?"

"I don't know," she said, "he's poor."

Jimsie was not as young as his classmates. He was twenty when we met him in his sophomore year. He told me he had had to wait to save a little money and win a scholarship, and when I asked him what his father did he laughed and said that nobody in his family had earned a living for three generations. He came from Oregon and one night he told funny stories about his mother and father, his five sisters and brothers.

I said, "You like them. That's unusual."

"Like them? I don't know."

"You don't know?"

"I don't know what they mean when they use words like that. I like to be around some people, or my motorcycle, and chemistry. I like one thing more than another. But that's all. Is that bad?"

I said I didn't know, I wasn't that kind of teacher. Then he went back to talking about his family and read me a letter from his father. His father wrote that a doctor in Portland had diagnosed stomach cancer but that he himself had cured it with a mixture of hot beer, cloves, and a sweet onion.

Through that first year I spent at Harvard, Jimsie would drop in at least three or four times a week to see Helen, carry her packages from the market, borrow his roommate's car to take her on small trips.

Often he would stay to eat dinner with her and sometimes with me.

It was the period of the early student movement and there was a time when he disappeared into Mississippi and came back beaten up around the kidneys, a favorite place, then and now, for a police beating since it doesn't show. Helen moved him in with us for a week, saying that a roommate who was on the stuff would be no good as a nurse. Jimsie was puzzled, uneasy about the fuss she made over him. And her lack of response to the state of the Negro in the South made him stubborn and nagging. It took years for him to know that it had to do with her age and time: her anger was so great, hidden so deep for so long, that it frightened her and she couldn't face it. He didn't understand her at all, in fact, and there was a funny, nice night in which his attempt to explain to her the reasons for the insanity of the Bay of Pigs was hilarious to hear. She didn't like talk like that: she liked best the times when he played his harmonica, and once she told me with pride that while she had not seen his "report card" another boy in the building had told her he was the most brilliant man in the class who played a harmonica.

In May of that year, about a week before we were to leave Cambridge, I woke up, knocked over an ashtray, and lay sweating with the mess I had been dreaming. After a while I got up, put on a coat and walked to the nursing home, certain that I would never go again. I stood in front of it for a long time, and when I turned to go back, Jimsie was directly behind me. I knew, of course, that Helen had telephoned him, but now, as we walked together, I had no concern for either of them. We didn't speak until I heard myself say, "Pentimento."

"What's that mean?" he said.

I said, "Don't follow me again, Jimsie, I don't like it."

But I don't wish to write about Jimsie; that isn't the point here and he wouldn't like it. Everybody else in this book is dead. We have become good friends, although now, twelve years after I met him, I don't understand him, or why he has decided on a life so different from the one he planned the year I met him. He was a chemistry student then and stayed on, after graduation, to work with Robert Woodward, the Nobel laureate, and spoke of the beauties and mysteries of chemistry with an emotion he showed for nothing else. Then he suddenly switched to astrophysics, and the night he tried to tell Helen what that meant she said he gave her a headache for a week, and because she came down with a bad cold after the headache and died from pneumonia a month later, I have always thought of astrophysics as having to do with her last days.

Jimsie was at the funeral in the ugly Harlem funeral place and I saw him standing in the rear, talking to her son. But by the time I reached the back of the place, through the mass of incompetent relatives she had been supporting for years, he had disappeared, and it was only last year that I found out it was he, not her son, who had taken the coffin by train to Camden, South Carolina, and waited with it on the station platform for a night and a day until her sister and brothers came a long distance over country roads to take it from him.

Somewhere in the years before or after that, I can no longer remember, Jimsie won a Marshall Scholarship, harder to earn than a Rhodes or a Fulbright, and went off to study in Cambridge, England. A friend of mine, an old Cambridge graduate, sent me a letter: "He has dazzled them here. I took him out for a drink, less because you wrote than because he is so interesting. But something has gone awry: I don't think he wants astrophysics, I think the world puzzles him."

I guess that was true, because he returned to Harvard, although I am no longer clear about when or why, except that he was there when I went back to teach in 1968, the year of the student riots. I remember that one day, at the height of the protests, we walked together in the Harvard Yard. George Wald, who had been a hero, and may be again, was not doing well that day as he stood before students making a conciliatory speech, too sure that his audience was with him, he with them. There were angry boos and the boy in front of us took an apple from his pocket and raised his arm for the pitch. Jimsie caught his arm and said, "Put it down, kiddie, a fine way of saying no to an old man." The boy pulled away angrily until he turned and recognized Jimsie, and then he said, "Oh, it's you," and patted him on the shoulder.

I guess he went back to England, because sometime in 1970 I had a short letter: "Do you think I can write? Of course not. But I'm through with astrophysics. I don't intend to work for the bastards and there is no other place to take it." I wrote back to say I didn't think he should try writing and didn't hear again until I had a card with an Albanian postmark that says, "I like these folks. They're willing to fight everybody and they know the reason why. See you soon."

But it wasn't soon, not until last year during the summer, when I had a letter from Oregon saying he was back there, his father had given him forty acres of ruined land, the way everything his family touched was ruined, things were agreeable, but he was sick of communal life except for Carrie, who was clean and hard-working. A few days before this Christmas he called me, said he was in New York, could he take me to dinner?

It was good to see him again. The too bony face and body had grown now into power and full masculine good looks. We ate in a Greenwich Village fancy joint one of his friends had told him about and he whistled when he saw the prices on the menu.

He said, "I can't buy you dinner. I thought I could, but I can't at these prices."

"I'll buy it for you. It doesn't matter."

"Yes, it does, but never mind. You look tired. Is something wrong?"

"I am tired."

"Come to Oregon. I'll take care of you. Carrie has learned to cook and she scrubs around. I can't stand dirt. My mother is such a slob. A pretty, nice lady, but a slob."

"You like Carrie?"

"She's O.K."

"That's all?"

"Isn't that enough?"

"No," I said, "I don't think so."

"Not for you," he said. "For me."

"Do you farm the land?"

He laughed. "I have a good vegetable garden and I had a hundred chickens, but my father killed the chickens for a neighborhood celebration. I earn a living as a carpenter and now, *now*, I'm getting rich. Some ass in Portland, a woman decorator, sells what she calls rosettes des bois and I carve them for her. Got that? I make *rosettes des bois*."

"Somewhere I know those words," I said, "but I can't remember —"

"They're rosettes of wood and you stick them on headboards of beds or old armoires, mostly new junk you fix to make old. She started out paying me five bucks apiece but now she pays me twenty-five. I'll get more when I get around to telling her I want it. Good?"

When I didn't answer, he put down his fork. "Good?"

"Stop it," I said. "You know what I think. Do you want another steak?"

He laughed. "If you've got the money, yes. Helen told you about the two steaks she used to cook me?"

"Yes."

"That great, big, fine lady, doing her best in this world. Do you know she gave me this coat?" He pointed to a sheepskin coat, expensive but old, lying on the chair next to him. "And when I brought it to her, said it cost too much, couldn't take presents from a working lady, know what she did? She slapped my face."

"You once told me you didn't understand about like or dislike."

He said, "I loved Helen."

"Too bad you never told her so. Too late now."

"I told it to her," he said, "the night I looked up your word, pentimento."

SCOUNDREL TIME

For
Barbara and John
Ruth and Marshall
with gratitude for then and now

I HAVE TRIED TWICE BEFORE to write about what
has come to be known as the McCarthy period but I
didn't much like what I wrote. My reasons for not
being able to write about my part in this sad, comic,
miserable time of our history were simple to me,
although some people thought I had avoided it for
mysterious reasons. There was no mystery. I had
strange hangups and they are always hard to explain.
Now I tell myself that if I face them, maybe I can
manage.

The prevailing eccentricity was and is my inability to feel much against the leading figures of the
period, the men who punished me. Senators McCarthy
and McCarran, Representatives Nixon, Walter and
Wood, all of them, were what they were: men who invented when necessary, maligned even when it wasn't
necessary. I do not think they believed much, if anything, of what they said: the time was ripe for a new
wave in America, and they seized their political
chance to lead it along each day's opportunity, spit-
balling whatever and with whoever came into view.

But the new wave was not so new. It began with
the Russian Revolution of 1917. The victory of the
revolution, and thus its menace, had haunted us
through the years that followed, then twisted the tail
of history when Russia was our ally in the Second

World War and, just because that had been such an unnatural connection, the fears came back in fuller force after the war when it looked to many people as if Russia would overrun Western Europe. Then the revolution in China caused an enormous convulsion in capitalist societies and somewhere along the line gave us the conviction that we could have prevented it if only. If only was never explained with any sense, but the times had very little need of sense.

The fear of Communism did not begin that year, but the new China, allied in those days with Russia, had a more substantial base and there were many honest men and women who were, understandably, frightened that their pleasant way of life could end in a day.

It was not the first time in history that the confusions of honest people were picked up in space by cheap baddies who, hearing a few bars of popular notes, made them into an opera of public disorder, staged and sung, as much of the congressional testimony shows, in the wards of an insane asylum.

A theme is always necessary, a plain, simple, unadorned theme to confuse the ignorant. The anti-Red theme was easily chosen from the grab bag, not alone because we were frightened of socialism, but chiefly, I think, to destroy the remains of Roosevelt and his sometimes advanced work. The McCarthy group — a loose term for all the boys, lobbyists, Congressmen, State Department bureaucrats, CIA operators —

chose the anti-Red scare with perhaps more cynicism
than Hitler picked anti-Semitism. He, history can no
longer deny, deeply believed in the impurity of the
Jew. But it is impossible to remember the drunken
face of McCarthy, merry often with a kind of worldly
malice, as if he were mocking those who took him
seriously, and believe that he himself could take
seriously anything but his boozed-up nightmares. And
if all the rumors were true the nightmares could have
concerned more than the fear of a Red tank on
Pennsylvania Avenue, although it is possible that in
his case a tank could have turned him on. Mr. Nixon's
beliefs, if indeed they ever existed, are best left to
jolly quarter-historians like Theodore White. But one
has a right to believe that if Whittaker Chambers *
was capable of thinking up a pumpkin, and he was,
Mr. Nixon seized upon this strange hiding place with
the eagerness of a man who already felt deep contempt for public intelligence. And he was right.

But none of them, even on the bad morning of
my hearing before the House Un-American Activities
Committee, interested me or disturbed me at a serious

* In August 1948 Whittaker Chambers appeared before the House
Un-American Activities Committee. Chambers, a senior editor of
Time magazine, told the Committee that he had once been a Communist and an underground courier. He named ten men as his former
associates, the best known being Alger Hiss, formerly a high official
of the State Department. Chambers accused Hiss of giving him secret
government material, which Chambers preserved by placing it in a
pumpkin at his farm in Maryland. Hiss was indicted, tried twice, and
sent to jail for almost four years. In 1975 the secret pumpkin papers
were found to contain nothing secret, nothing confidential. They
were, in fact, nonclassified, which is Washington's way of saying anybody who says please can have them.

level. They didn't and they don't. They are what they are, or were, and are no relation to me by blood or background. (My own family held more interesting villains of another, wittier nature.)

I have written before that my shock and my anger came against what I thought had been the people of my world, although in many cases, of course, I did not know the men and women of that world except by name. I had, up to the late 1940's, believed that the educated, the intellectual, lived by what they claimed to believe: freedom of thought and speech, the right of each man to his own convictions, a more than implied promise, therefore, of aid to those who might be persecuted. But only a very few raised a finger when McCarthy and the boys appeared. Almost all, either by what they did or did not do, contributed to McCarthyism, running after a bandwagon which hadn't bothered to stop to pick them up.

Simply, then and now, I feel betrayed by the nonsense I had believed. I had no right to think that American intellectuals were people who would fight for anything if doing so would injure them; they have very little history that would lead to that conclusion. Many of them found in the sins of Stalin Communism — and there were plenty of sins and plenty that for a long time I mistakenly denied — the excuse to join those who should have been their hereditary enemies. Perhaps that, in part, was the penalty of nineteenth-century immigration. The children of timid immigrants are often remarkable people: energetic, intelligent, hardworking; and often they make it so good that they are determined to keep it at any cost. The native grandees, of course, were glad to have them as companions on the conservative ship: they wrote better English, had read more books, talked louder and with greater fluency.

But I don't want to write about my historical conclusions — it isn't my game. I tell myself that this third time out, if I stick to what I know, what happened to me, and a few others, I have a chance to write my own history of the time.

I DO NOT KNOW the year when I, who had always been a kind of aimless rebel — not only in the sense that was true of most of my generation, but because I had watched my mother's family increase their fortune on the borrowings of poor Negroes — found that my rebelliousness was putting down a few young political roots. I think that began with the discovery of National Socialism when I was in Bonn, Germany, intending to enroll at the university. It took me months to understand what I was listening to. Then for the first time in my life I thought about being a Jew. But I was not only listening to anti-Semitism. I

607

was hearing from people my own age the boasts of hopeful conquerors, the sounds of war.

I came home to an economic depression that was to break my father, although it treated Arthur Kober, to whom I was married, very well with a job as a scenario writer in Hollywood. But even his good salary meant less than it should have because the storms in the movie industry were so great that the luck of the day was just that and nothing more.

In any case, Arthur's good job didn't matter much to me because I got a divorce in 1931 and couldn't find a job. True, I didn't need one very much because by that time I was living with the writer Dashiell Hammett, who not only earned a great deal but shared it with me, or with anybody else who came along. But that was no answer, either: if you have worked, living on other people's money isn't a solution. For three or four years there was to be no solution for me, although Roosevelt's election gave many people, me among them, our first feelings that maybe we could have something to do with our own futures, through our own government. (Obviously nobody could have anything to do with the governments of Coolidge or Hoover.)

At the end of 1934 my first play, *The Children's Hour*, was a great success. The days of living on other people were over, and it was in many ways a mighty nice time. But success caused a kind of guilt. I am suspicious of guilt in myself and in other people: it is usually a way of not thinking, or of announcing one's own fine sensibilities the better to be rid of them fast. But about this guilt, the guilt that came from my own good luck, I am still pleased because it led somewhere. I am not even displeased with the troubles it was to cause me.

I have written before, and must write again, about Dashiell Hammett because he was so large a part of my life in the Thirties and Forties. (And for much longer, of course, but that is another story.) The middle and late Thirties were a time when many people were turning toward radical political solutions, and he was one of them, with me trailing behind, worried often about what didn't worry him, inhibited by what he ignored. I am fairly sure that Hammett joined the Communist Party in 1937 or 1938. I do not know because I never asked, and if I had asked would not have been answered, and my not asking, knowing there would be no answer, was typical of our relationship. I did not join the Party, although mild overtures were made by Earl Browder and the Party theorist, V. J. Jerome.

I did go, three or four times, with Hammett to meetings: two in an ugly Spanish house in Hollywood; one or two in New York in an apartment I don't remember, with people I don't remember, maybe because I left after a short time. In the Hollywood meetings there were seven or eight people. I knew three of them slightly, but the others were something I then

609

called "unaesthetic." Certainly the fact that what seemed to be the chairman, or leader, had a habit of tying and untying his shoelaces, making strange cutouts from pieces of yellow pad paper and throwing the cutouts to the floor, took my attention away from what might have been a serious discussion. Another man kept using the phrase "the face of the Party," and since all expert phrases interest me, I wanted very much to find out what that meant. Two ladies, one youngish, one middle-aged, talked a great deal, mostly to each other and always in high irritation. The middle-aged lady, I found out later, owned a fashionable dress shop, and I was impressed with the force of the conviction that had made her join a radical group when any gossip about her affiliations would have cost her a fine business. (I didn't need to worry; when the real Red-baiting days began she moved her shop to Santa Barbara and never again spoke to her brother, who went to jail for his Communist Party affiliations.) Either at the first or second of these Hollywood meetings, the Spanish Civil War was discussed. I was surprised that when I complained the Russians had not sent enough supplies — I had just come home from Spain in the autumn of 1937 — but only enough to keep the Spanish fighting and dying for a cause that was going to be lost, nobody disagreed with me or defended the Soviet Union. Maybe they agreed, maybe they didn't think I was worth arguing with.

In any case, whether I signed a Party card or didn't was of little importance to me. I couldn't have known then what importance would be attached to it a few years later. Fear of consequences had nothing to do with my decision. Whatever is wrong with white Southerners — redneck or better — we were all brought up to believe we had a right to think as we pleased, go our own, possibly strange ways. And since few people in the New Orleans of my day had much money, middle-class considerations didn't have much to do with things. This was not true of my mother's rich middle-class Alabama family, but I had revolted against them early on, and took pattern from my father's family, a group of rather mixed-up eccentrics who as deeply believed in the equality of the Negro, for example, as they did in the theory that all black people had a high odor for something called "glandular" reasons. But however confused they were, there was a generosity of spirit and money, an independence of thought, that was attractive to a rebellious child.

My own liking for black people maybe came a few days after I was born when I was put into the arms of a wet-nurse, Sophronia, an extraordinary woman who stayed on with us for years after. It was she who taught me to have feelings for the black poor, and when she was sure I did, she grew sharp and said it wasn't enough to cry about black people, what about the miseries of poor whites. She was an

611

angry woman and she gave me anger, an uncomfortable, dangerous, and often useful gift.

But the traceries from what you were to what you became are always too raw and too simple. Particularly if you are speaking of rebelliousness, which of course is a mishmash of early influences, books read, what teacher taught you what and when, even what you looked like. Most important, what you don't know or remember about yourself and never will. If I were to try such a history for myself from childhood to the evenings of those meetings, I would come out an earnest student, and I wasn't, although there were periods when I was a kind of literary bluestocking, which is quite different: they seldom are interested in anything but theory, rarely in the world around them unless the theory fits the world.

By the time of the late 1930's and early Forties, if I was sure that I would fit into no political party, I was often an admirer of radicals, domestic and foreign. Perhaps because I was not, they seemed to me particularly dedicated, serious people. The overheated arguments, spoken and printed, about dictatorship and repression puzzled me: I couldn't possibly understand how such a state of affairs would ever be tolerated in the United States, and I thought that in the end Russia, having achieved a state socialism, would stop its infringements on personal liberty. I was wrong. But so were many who were right about

Russia: they made use of their anti-Communism to play ball with the wrong people and many of them are still at it.

I am, of course, making my political history too simple: personal conflicts, work problems, whiskey, too much money after *The Children's Hour*, the time of my time, Hammett, all had to do with whatever I believed.

It was true that Hammett became a committed radical and I didn't, but strangely enough when we first met I think it was I, and not he, who had come to certain unshakable conclusions. I remember sitting on a bed next to him in the first months we met, listening to him tell me about his Pinkerton days when an officer of Anaconda Copper Company had offered him five thousand dollars to kill Frank Little, the labor union organizer. I didn't know Hammett well enough to hear the anger under the calm voice, the bitterness under the laughter, so I said, "He couldn't have made such an offer unless you had been strike-breaking for Pinkerton."

"That's about right," he said.

I walked into his living room thinking I don't want to be here, I don't want to be with this man. I went back to the door of the bedroom to tell him that.

He was leaning on his elbow, facing the door, as if he expected me. He said, "Yes, ma'm. Why do you think I told you?"

He seldom talked about the past unless I asked

questions, but through the years he was to repeat that bribe offer so many times that I came to believe, knowing him now, that it was a kind of key to his life. He had given a man the right to think he would murder, and the fact that Frank Little was lynched with three other men in what was known as the Everett Massacre must have been, for Hammett, an abiding horror. I think I can date Hammett's belief that he was living in a corrupt society from Little's murder. In time, he came to the conclusion that nothing less than a revolution could wipe out the corruption. I do not mean to suggest that his radical conversion was based on one experience, but sometimes in complex minds it is the plainest experience that speeds the wheels that have already begun to move.

It is necessary here to repeat what I have written about before. There were perhaps twenty years between my hearing about Frank Little and Hammett's jail sentence in 1951. During those twenty years we did not always live together, did not always share the same house or the same city, and even when we were together we both had unspoken but strict rules about privacy. And so I have no real knowledge of his affiliations to the Communist Party. He went to jail in 1951 for refusing to give the names of the contributors to the bail bond fund of the Civil Rights Congress, of which he was one of the trustees. I don't remember ever hearing the name of the organization until about a month before he was arrested, and that may be because he had never been in their offices. He was sent to the filthy West Street jail in New York, in an unprecedented judgment that allowed no bail, and then moved to the federal prison in Ashland, Kentucky.

He was sickish when he went to jail, and he came out sicker, but he took all of it in fine spirits, obviously pleased with his ability to take whatever punishment had come to him or might come in the future. But his nature was not mine. He had known that if you differ from society, no matter how many pieties they talk they will punish you for disturbing them. No such thing had ever occurred to me; when I disagreed I was exercising my inherited rights, and certainly there could be no punishment for doing what I had been taught to do by teachers, books, American history. It was not only my right, it was my duty to speak or act against what I thought was wrong or dangerous. It is comically late to admit that I did not even consider the fierce, sweeping, violent nonsense-tragedies that break out in America from time to time, one of which was well on its way after World War II.

Hammett's reaction to jail was odd and often irritating: he talked of his time there the way I remembered young men talking about their survival in a severe prep school or a tough football game. He was always pleased that he could adapt to whatever was necessary; he had gone through almost three years of the miseries of the Aleutian-Alaskan weather during the war and several times seriously proposed to me that we move there for good. They were mysterious reactions to me. Now, so many years later, I know they came from plain, old-fashioned self-discipline as it mixed with plain, old-fashioned pride.

In any case, his feelings about jail when I was faced with jail did me no good. I knew that I could not stand what he could stand. I have temper and it is triggered at odd times by odd matters and is then out of my control: if I am kept waiting when I think it is unnecessary, if I am shoved in a bus or subway, finding myself or anybody else treated with disrespect, being unjustly accused of what I didn't do even if the accusation is about something trivial — a whole set of reactions happen which I am unable, at the minute of temper, to recognize as childish. Hammett knew all about me, stuff like that, and so when I was threatened with jail, less than a year after he came out, he used what he knew to try to keep me from what he didn't believe I could safely take. Maybe he was right, maybe he wouldn't have been. I could not know then or now because we did not share what the French call a neurosis for two. We each had our own little bundle, but they did not mix, or cross or rub off on one another. His fears for me began on February 21, 1952.

I OWNED AND LIVED in a lovely neo-Georgian house on East 82nd Street, with one tenant above me. As in most such houses, visitors rang a downstairs bell and then were asked to announce themselves into an instrument. It had never been possible to hear anything but garble from the instrument, so I had grown tired of it and long before had taken to pressing the bell when anyone rang and waiting for the small elevator to rise to my floor. An over-respectable-looking black man, a Sunday deacon, in a suit that was so correct-incorrect that it could be worn only by somebody who didn't want to be noticed, stood in the elevator, his hat politely removed. He asked me if I was Lillian Hellman. I agreed to that and asked who he was. He handed me an envelope and said he was there to serve a subpoena from the House Un-American Activities Committee. I opened the envelope and read the subpoena. I said, "Smart to choose a black man for this job. You like it?" and slammed the door.

I sat with the subpoena for perhaps an hour, alone in the house, not wishing to talk to anybody. There it was, and for some reason there seemed to me nothing to hurry about. I took to looking at the last few days' mail, some of it already dictated for a secretary who came twice a week, some of it yet to be answered. One of the forms I had filled out a few days before, ready for mailing, was the usual questionnaire from *Who's Who in America*. I suppose I found some amusement in reading it again: I had by that day written *The Children's Hour, Days to Come, The Little Foxes, Watch on the Rhine, The Searching Wind, Another Part of the Forest, The Autumn Garden.* I had collected and introduced a volume of Chekhov letters, written movies and tinkered with others, belonged to organizations, unions — all the stuff I always have to look up from the previous *Who's Who* because I can't remember the dates.

Then I took a nap and woke up in a sweat of bewilderment about myself. I telephoned Hammett and he said he would take the next train from Katonah, so to sit still and do nothing until he got there. But the calm was gone now and I couldn't do that.

I went immediately to Stanley Isaacs, who had been borough president of Manhattan and who had suffered under an attack, led by Robert Moses, because one of his minor assistants was a member of the Communist Party. Stanley had stood up well under the attack, although, of course, the episode hurt his very Republican career. (I had gone to him as an admiring stranger as soon as he returned to his own law practice and had brought along with me, in the following years, quite a few people who liked and admired him.) Isaacs was an admirable man, but I think by the time of my subpoena he was more worried than he wanted to admit, and knew that his way back to politics — he was, in fact, never to have a way back — could be mended only with care. Isaacs and I were fond of each other and his face looked pained as he told me that he didn't believe he should handle the case, he didn't know enough about the field, but together we would find the right man.

Together we didn't. Stanley had a number of suggestions during the next few days, but I didn't like any of them, and while I remember that clearly, it is strange that I don't remember how I came, on my own, to phone Abe Fortas. I had never met Fortas, although I had, of course, heard of him and his law firm of Arnold, Fortas and Porter. Mr. Fortas said he was coming to New York the next day and would come by and see me.

But if I don't remember how I came to phone Fortas, I do remember everything about our meeting: the nasty weather outside the tall windows; the thin, intelligent face opposite me in an Empire chair that seemed wrong for him; most of all, the eyes that were taking my measure, a business that has always made me nervous and was making me more nervous on this nervous day. I told him about the subpoena, he asked a few questions about my past, none of any real importance, he admired the china birds on the fireplace, he tried out a few notes on the piano, frowned at the tone, and turned to say that he had a hunch he'd tell me about, but I was not to take a hunch as legal advice.

His hunch was that the time had come, the perfect time, for somebody to take a moral position before these disgraceful congressional committees and not depend on the legalities of the Fifth Amendment. To Fortas the moral position would be to say, in essence, I will testify about myself, answer all your questions about my own life, but I will not tell you about anybody else, stranger or friend. Fortas thought that I might be in a good position to say just that because, in truth, I didn't know much about anybody's Communist affiliations. The Committee would never, of course, believe that, and so my legal rights would be in danger because I would be giving up the protection of the Fifth Amendment. I wanted to tell him that the moral position for my taste would be to say, "You are a bunch of headline seekers, using other people's lives for your own benefits. You know damn well that the people you've been calling before you never did much of anything, but you've browbeaten and bullied many of them into telling lies about sins they never committed. So go to hell and do what you want with me." I didn't say any of that to Fortas because I knew I would never be able to say it at all.

(But for five or six years after my appearance before the Committee, when other troubles came, and I would be sleepless, I would get up at odd hours of the night and write versions of the statement I never made. I was certain that whatever would have been the injuries of jail they could not have been as bad as I had thought in those first days. Then, of course, when I had climbed back into bed to read a new and fancier version of what I hadn't said, I would think it's fine to do all this after the fears are over, you'd better cut it out and start worrying about how you will act when trouble comes again.)

What I did that afternoon of Mr. Fortas's visit was to say that I agreed with him and thought his idea was right for me. But he wouldn't have it that way; he said that I must take a few days and think it out carefully and then call him. I said I didn't need the few days and he said maybe, but he did need them, he wanted to think over what he had suggested. Before Fortas left he said that neither he nor his firm could take my case because they were representing Owen Lattimore and Lattimore could hurt me or I could hurt Lattimore. But he knew a fine young lawyer and we'd talk about him the next time we met.

Mine is often an irritable nature. If the groceries haven't arrived on time, or the corn grows stunted, or the phone rings too much, even with good news, I am, as I have said, sometimes out of control. But when there is real trouble, the nervousness gets pushed down so far that calm takes its place, and although I pay high for disaster when it is long past, I am not sure that real trouble registers on me when it first appears. I don't know why that happens, but I think I have the sense to understand that there is nothing to do but to face trouble with a roped control, and that any suspicion of high jinks will break me. That was where I was for the next few months — more important, for the next bad week.

The day after the visit from Fortas, I told Hammett what I was going to do. Dash rarely showed anger, but when he did, it came out in the form of staring at me. The staring would often go on for a long time, as if he were thinking over how you dealt with a crazy lady, what was the best way out. I had been through the stare periods many times in the past, but now it went longer than I could stand and I grew uneasy enough to go for a walk. When I came back we spoke of nothing more than what we would cook for dinner and I made the mistake of thinking that he had decided to say nothing, to mind his own business, which was what he usually did after the anger had passed. But I was wrong: halfway through dinner he pushed his plate away and said, "It's shit. Plain liberal shit. They are going to send you to a jail cell and for longer than usual. I don't give a damn what Mr. Fortas thinks, I do give a damn that you are ass enough to believe that those stinkers are going to pay any attention to your high-class morals. It's tough for me to believe that you haven't recovered from that crap."

"What stinkers? The Committee?"

"Not only," he said. "You know very well what I am talking about. The Committee, the press, what you think are your friends, everybody. But to hell with convincing you of anything sensible. Just re-member there are rats in jail, and tough dikes, and people who will push you hard just because they like it, and guards who won't admire you, and food you can't eat and unless you do eat it they'll put you in solitary. You're headed for a good breakdown, if not worse."

That conversation, a diary tells me, was to be re-peated with variations many times during the next week. But the next two days were the hardest for me; I was not accustomed to doing what Hammett didn't approve of and he knew it and counted on it. But on the third day, tired of no sleep, I said, "Sorry. This time I must do things my way."

There was no answer and I should have guessed there wouldn't be.

I said, "And there is more bad news. The In-ternal Revenue won't let you have any more money, I won't have any in a few years, so we'll have to sell the farm."

"O.K.," he said cheerfully, "you'll live to have another." (I haven't lived to have another and am too old now to think that I could work a farm.)

But that day there were things to do. I called Fortas to say that I had carefully decided that what he had suggested was right for me. He said well, he didn't know, he had to tell me that his partner thought the whole idea rotten and calculated to send me straight to jail.

I laughed. "Did he say it was liberal shit?"

"No," said Fortas, "he just thinks it's legal shit."

"I'd like to come to Washington, the sooner the better, and see the lawyer you spoke about."

Fortas arranged an appointment for me with Joseph Rauh for the next day. I took a night train to Washington, which was not a good idea; I still have odds and ends of notes from that rocky, no-sleep night. I should have been thinking of the House Committee, I guess, or worried about meeting Rauh. Instead I thought of the farm and how difficult it was going to be to tell Kitty, the housemaid, and Betty and Gus Benson, my farmers, that I couldn't keep the place anymore, and they had better look for new jobs. They were close to me, all three of them, and I remembered a scene only eight or nine months before that had made me know what good friends they were.

The day after Dash had gone to jail, I phoned the house to ask if there were reporters around the place. Yes, there were, the porch and lawn were filled with them. I said I wouldn't come home, I hoped they weren't too bothered, I would call again in a few days. I went to a hotel for three days and phoned again to the farm. No reporters now, nobody. I drove up from New York and asked the three of them to come and sit with me.

I said, "You know Mr. Hammett is in jail. That means it will be uncomfortable here for you, maybe more than uncomfortable. God knows what the FBI or any other government agency will decide on now, and even if they don't do anything, you have a stuffy village to face."

Gus interrupted me to say that three FBI men had already been around to ask him a great number of questions. I wanted very much to find out what questions they had asked, but I knew Gus well enough to know that when he didn't volunteer to tell me, it meant that he was embarrassed and wanted to save my feelings. So I said that was the way things would probably be from now on, ugly, possibly even danger-ous for them, and that I thought it would be better if . . . Before I could say better off in other jobs, Kitty laughed and said to Betty, "Tell Miss Hellman."

Betty said they had sent Hammett a telegram to West Street jail, congratulating him and sending him their love. Then Kitty giggled and said that in the next few days she and Betty would bake a cake and take it to him, but they were having an argument over what kind of cake, would I know what he would like? I was so moved by these nice people who had done what so many others — including the many, many people who owed Hammett money — had not dared to do that I covered my eyes.

Kitty said, "We're Irish, Miss Hellman. Jail's nothing." After a few minutes we all shook hands in a most formal manner and for a long time I could hear Kitty and Betty in the kitchen arguing about what kind of cake they would make for Hammett.

The following week they paid no attention to my warning to stay out of things, took the train to New York to deliver their coconut cake to the West Street jail. They told me on their return that they had not been allowed to see Dash, but two men said the cake would be given to him. It wasn't, but I never told them.

I LIKED RAUH. Shrewdness seldom goes with an open nature, but in his case it does and the nice, unbeautiful, rugged, crinkly face gives one confidence about the mind above it. Our first meetings were fine. About the third time we met, Joe had evidently done some research; he pointed out that the Communist Party, sometimes through the *Daily Worker,* sometimes in other publications, had attacked me. There had been, for example, the nonsense about *Watch on the Rhine*. The play, opening before the Soviet Union was invaded by Germany, was reviewed as warmongering. The movie, opening after the Soviet Union was at war with Germany, was just wonderful. And in 1948, when Tito broke with Russia, I had gone to Belgrade and written a series of sympathetic interviews with Tito which were not well received by Communists here. Joe believed that we had to point out these Communist criticisms of me because they would be useful for the Committee and for the press to prove the independence of my past. I said that I didn't want them used in my defense, that my use of their attacks on me would amount to my attacking them at a time when they were being persecuted and I would, therefore, be playing the enemy's game. This seemed to me simple and I believed it would end the discussion between us, but each time I saw Joe he returned to it as if something were nagging at him so hard that he couldn't let it go. We were, on this issue, to have our first and last sharp words: I said we were wasting time, I was not going to change my mind, and what was the matter with him? He said that James Wechsler of the *New York Post* was an old and close friend and he had talked over my case with Wechsler. I interrupted him much too sharply by saying that I had never met Wechsler, didn't like what he wrote, and wanted no advice from him. We batted all that around for so long that I said I would like Joe to stop analyzing me, it had already happened, and I didn't need another analyst, I needed a lawyer. (It has been my experience that most lawyers now consider themselves psychiatrists and should quit it.) Rauh didn't like my attack on his friend Wechsler, but when Wechsler was later called before the McCarthy Committee, I know Joe could not have liked the fact that his friend not only was a cooperative witness but had high-class pious reasons for what he did.

Rauh asked for and got a delay in my appearance before the Committee. During that time I put the farm up for sale. That pained Hammett and me deeply, of course, but we did not speak about it once we made the decision. As I moved about the house, marking things that would go on sale or go into storage, Dash would make plans for the future — the future meant to him when I came out of jail. Sometimes we would plan a holiday on a sailboat, sometimes a three-month fishing trip, often a shack on the shores of Maryland, where he came from, so cheap that maybe we could buy it after a while. Once, when I was feeling too agreeable, I even promised to go look at the Aleutian Islands if he would agree to consider a crayfish farm in the Louisiana bayous.

CLIFFORD ODETS and I started in the theatre at about the same time. We had met possibly four or five times in the years between 1935 and 1952, but I never saw him after he moved to Hollywood. During the first week of March he called me, said he was in New York, couldn't we have dinner. That seemed odd, since he had not ever called me before. I didn't much want to go, but on the third and rather insistent invitation we made a date. It was such a strange evening that I made a long entry in a diary for March 1952. I copy it here:

We met at Barbetta's, ordered a dinner I guessed right would be lousy, and a bad Italian wine. It didn't take long to get to the reason for the dinner. Clifford said, "Have you made plans for what you will do when the House Committee calls you?"

I didn't intend to tell him that the Committee had already called me. So I said, "I guess I have. But you make plans and then just hope you can carry them out, maybe, maybe not."

Clifford said something, but I couldn't hear him because the man at the next table said to two other men and a woman, "I was shaving. You know what? She was so drunk that she thought her nipple was a scar on her stomach."

"I never met her," said one of his companions.

"Easy to fix up if you don't mind 'em with nipples on their stomach," said the first man.

I laughed. That must have annoyed Clifford because his voice was sharp. "You didn't hear what I said."

"No. Sorry."

"I said that's a dangerous way to think. You better damn well know what you're going to say and do before you get there."

I didn't know how I was going to answer that, but the waiter came with our dinner. Clifford put his

629

finger to his mouth to shush me and began to whistle until the waiter went away.

"What did you mean?"

"About what?" I was stalling. I didn't like the conversation.

"About not knowing what you're going to do when the Committee calls you?"

I said I hadn't said that, you may know what you're going to do, but you can't be sure what will happen to you under pressure.

"That's a strange way to think," Clifford said, "maybe because you've never been under pressure."

"But I have been. I was in Spain during their war, at the Russian front, in London during the V-2's —"

"Didn't you know how to act then?"

"Sometimes, sometimes not. Once I screamed for a good two minutes about a V-2 and couldn't stop myself, and once in Russia I was given a pair of binoculars to look out of a dugout window at the Germans a few hundred yards away and I held the glasses smack into the light and started a barrage from the Germans."

"That wasn't smart," Clifford said.

"That's exactly what I've been saying. It wasn't smart and it almost got six of us killed. That's what I'm trying to say, how can you know how stupid you'll be until you're stupid?"

He rapped on the table. Things weren't going

well. "I'm not talking about things like that. I'm talking about political and moral convictions."

I said, "I don't like to talk about convictions. I'm never sure I'm telling the truth."

"But Hammett has convictions," he said. "I don't know much about him, but I admire him."

I wanted to say that's nice but he doesn't admire you, remembering a night long ago when we had gone to see *Awake and Sing* and Hammett, very tipsy, had kept urging me to leave and we had left simply to keep him quiet. Once outside I said I liked the play, why didn't he, and he said, "Because I don't think writers who cry about not having had a bicycle when they were kiddies are ever going to amount to much."

But I said nothing, and Odets and I talked about his art collection for a while, and then suddenly he scared the hell out of me. He pounded on the table so hard that his wineglass spilled and he yelled, "Well, I can tell you what I am going to do before those bastards on the Committee. I am going to show them the face of a radical man and tell them to go fuck themselves." I don't know which impressed me most: the violence of the gesture on the table or the brave shout that turned heads at the tables near us.

I have no other diary notes for that night. But there is an unpleasant, mysterious ending to the story. Odets, who appeared before the Committee one day before I did, apologized for his old beliefs and identified many of his old friends as Communists. There-

631

fore I don't understand that conversation in Barbetta's. It is possible that on that night he believed
what he told me. One can only guess that a few weeks
later, faced with the ruin of a Hollywood career, he
changed his mind. The old clichés were now increasingly true; the loss of a swimming pool, a tennis
court, a picture collection, future deprivation, were
powerful threats to many people, and the heads of
studios knew it and played heavy with it.

A few weeks after my dinner with Odets, Elia
Kazan, whom everybody called Gadge, told me that
Spyros Skouras had told him that unless he became
what was called a "friendly witness" for the Committee, he, Kazan, would never make another movie
in Hollywood. But before he told me anything that
simple, we had spent a strange half-hour in the Plaza
Oak Room. I couldn't understand what Gadge was
fumbling with — he is not a fumbler — so on the
excuse of having to make a phone call, I did make
one to Kermit Bloomgarden, my theatre producer and
the producer of *Death of a Salesman*, which Kazan
had directed. (Kermit and Gadge had known each
other since they were young, but I had never known
Kazan well.) I told Kermit on the phone that I didn't
know why Kazan had asked me for a drink, and I
didn't understand what he was trying to tell me.

"He is telling you that he is going to become a
friendly witness. I know because he told me this
morning."

When I returned from the phone we talked for a few minutes and I invented a pressing engagement. We stood in front of the Plaza in the rain waiting for a taxi. I didn't want to talk anymore and so we stood in silence until Kazan said, "It's O.K. for you to do what you want, I guess. You've probably spent whatever you've earned."

This puzzled me for weeks afterwards until I figured out that he was really saying what my rich grandmother used to tell her less well-heeled friends or relatives, and I had once heard her say to her chauffeur, a man whose name she had changed from Fritz to Hal, "You don't have anything to worry about. Money doesn't put heavy burdens on those who don't have it."

But the panic of movie bosses was an old story by the time Kazan and I met in the spring of 1952. It had started even earlier than their famous meeting at the Waldorf-Astoria Hotel in 1947. There they came together in a kind of sleepy hysteria, called together by forces no amount of research can positively name even today, to assure the public, in a statement of massive confusions, that they most certainly believed in the American right to dissent, but that they were not going to allow dissent if they didn't like it. It used to be said that there was nothing like a studio lawyer except another studio lawyer.

(It was probably at this Waldorf conference that what later became known in Hollywood as the

American Legion oath was decided upon. The oath was to be demanded of studio employees. It seems obvious from its name that representatives of the American Legion must have been present in some form, either in person or, more likely, by visits before and after the Waldorf conference. I have made fourteen attempts to find a sample of these famous letters that I know exist because I was asked to sign one. None of the fourteen people I asked deny the letters were demanded and complied with. But no amount of digging has turned up one letter, possibly because those who wrote them don't want to admit they did and because the present studio legal departments don't like them much anymore, may even doubt their legality. I have come up with only one fact: each studio asked its employees to write letters swearing they were not Communists, did not associate with radicals, and if they had in the past contributed to certain organizations — aid to Spanish refugees, etc. — they regretted it and would not repeat the mistake.)

I don't think the heads of movie companies, and the men they appointed to run the studios, had ever before thought of themselves as American citizens with inherited rights and obligations. Many of them had been born in foreign lands and inherited foreign fears. It would not have been possible in Russia or Poland, but it was possible here to offer the Cossacks a bowl of chicken soup. And the Cossacks in Washington were now riding so fast and hard that the soup had to have double strength and be handed up by running millionaire waiters.

But long before the studios were threatened by politicians and the American Legion, their general timidity had been a joke for writers and directors who told each other nice stories about whose twelve-year-old son, whose eighteen-year-old mistress, had said they didn't like the script, or the rough cut of a movie, and thus the script or the rough cut had to be changed about. There had been, for example, in the late 1930's, a famous crisis at Metro-Goldwyn-Mayer. They had taken one of their big musicals to San Francisco for a sneak preview. It was then as it is now the custom to hand out postcards for the audience to fill out, asking their opinion of the picture they had just seen. One postcard writer loved the picture but wrote that she was horrified that Frank Morgan, an actor in the picture, had his fly wide open during one of his scenes. The postcard caused such consternation that the picture's opening was postponed and for a week all workers in the studio, coming to the projection room in craft groups, were shown the picture several times a day, and a prize was offered to anyone who could find Mr. Morgan's open fly. It was later discovered, obviously because so great a heroine couldn't keep her mouth shut, that the postcard had been written by a discarded mistress of a Metro official.

It is well to remember what these very rich movie men were like, since I doubt they have changed. (They have, indeed, increased in number, because agents often now outstrip them in money and power.) Hollywood lived the way the Arabs are attempting to live now, and while there is nothing strange about people vying with each other for great landed estates, there is something odd about people vying with each other for better bathrooms. It is doubtful that such luxury has ever been associated with the normal acts of defecating or bathing oneself. It is even possible that feces are not pleased to be received in such grand style and thus prefer to settle in the soul.

And in those days it was heady stuff to boss around William Faulkner or Nathanael West or Aldous Huxley. Gatsby and his ambitions were peanuts next to those larger Gatsbys; they didn't want love or Daisy, they wanted power and a new Daisy every week. But the natures of Louis Mayer, Samuel Goldwyn, Harry Cohn, and so on, their advisers and lawyers, are really not very interesting; they were one man with minor variations and quirks. Certainly they had force and daring, but by the time of McCarthy they had grown older and wearier. Threats that might once have been laughed about over a gin rummy game now seemed dangerous to their fortunes. Movie producers knew full well that the Communists of Hollywood had never made a single Communist picture, but they were perfectly willing to act as dupes for those who pretended that was a danger. Thousands of letters poured into Hollywood protesting Hollywood rad-

icalism; the studios knew they were almost all faked
or written to order. But they told themselves the voice
of America was speaking, and to some extent it was.
But the tycoons were not alone in cringing before
threats that could have been investigated and forgotten. Harry Cohn told me that he was pleased at
how many writers, directors and actors had volun-
teered to help. And he was telling the truth: there was
a rush to be a helpful witness, to testify against one's
associates, to act out the dramas that the government
committees preferred.

In any case, the blacklist was not as yet completely operative in 1947 because Harry Cohn of
Columbia Pictures offered me the contract I had always wanted: to write and produce four pictures any
time I found a story I liked, and with control over the
final cut. (This was almost unheard of in those days,
and even now is seldom granted.) It was a fine contract: to write and produce without interference, at
any time during eight years that I found the material
I wanted to do. I was guaranteed almost a million
dollars and I was free to write plays or anything else,
to travel between jobs without questions asked. Harry
and I had the same lawyer, Charles Schwartz, but that
was O.K. because Charlie was an honest man. The
day the contract was ready Charlie called me, said
he was sending the copies up to Harry, would I go
round and read them with Harry?

Charlie said, "I should warn you. Harry may

have attached a new piece of paper. He had to do it and I advise you not to make a fuss. It will be required of everybody from now on."

I jumped to the conclusion that the new clause had to do with money and forgot about it.

When I got to Harry's Waldorf Towers apartment, his secretary said he'd be up in a few minutes, they were winding up the meeting downstairs. I didn't, of course, know what meeting she meant; you always wait for movie people to come from a meeting. Harry did appear about a half-hour later, greeted me warmly, went immediately to the telephone. He was still there when I came upon a paragraph attached to the contract. I skipped it in disbelief, went on reading, went back to read it again. Harry was making a new phone call when I began to pace the room. But he was watching me, and I had a feeling he was staying on the phone to avoid me, because he pointed to a desk, held up a pen, made motions about signing, and went back to the phone. When, finally, he was finished I said, "The terms are O.K., Harry, just as we agreed, but what does that new mishmash attachment mean?"

"Listen," he said, "do you think I like the two days I've wasted downstairs? I'm a loner. I don't like dictatorship. So let up on me, will you?"

I said I didn't know what he was talking about, what meeting downstairs, but we were interrupted by another telephone call and then by a waiter with a thermos of hot milk and a chicken sandwich — I

don't remember Cohn without a chicken sandwich —
and a good many anecdotes of his past, in an effort,
I thought, to avoid the present. The present didn't
please Harry much: the meeting downstairs where, he
told me, every studio head in Hollywood had come to
town to decide that every employee had to compose
and sign a version of the letter clause I had just read.
Harry did, that day, in a garble of irritation, mention the American Legion, and "men" from Washington, exhibitors, bankers and their lawyers, lawyers
from "the Committees," and many others, perhaps
correctly identified, perhaps not, in his high state of
annoyance over being dictated to and bored. (I heard
later that he had raised no protest at the meeting itself. Samuel Goldwyn was the only producer who
refused to agree with his colleagues. One would like
to think it was a vote for freedom, but most people
who knew him well, I among them, knew that he always voted against any group decision.)

As Cohn talked I read and reread the attached
piece of paper. It asked that I write a note in my own
words and "suggested" a form of the old morals
clause — my actions, my life must not embarrass
the studios — but this time it didn't mean drunken-
ness or fights or murder, it meant simply that my politics must not embarrass them or cause them any
trouble or protests. (I am making it milder than it
was; it was, in truth, a straight demand that nothing
you believed, or acted upon, or contributed to, or

associated with could be different from what the studio would allow.) I started to make a speech about constitutional rights and who the hell did they think they were, but I was exhausted by Harry's troubles: he had called room service to say the chicken sandwich stank from dryness, two obviously unimportant telephone calls had been put through, and for five minutes a pretty girl had appeared from nowhere with nothing to say. I was tired now.

I said, "You know, Harry, I live with Dashiell Hammett. I don't think he is going to stay in the attic and be taken out on a chain at night."

"Fine writer," said Harry, "wanted to hire him for years."

"Call him," I said, "skip the fine writer junk and tell him about the attic."

"Ach," he said, "you're just looking for trouble."

"And there are many other people I know, intend to go on knowing, have dinner with —"

"So have dinner in some nice little place in Santa Monica. Better and cheaper than Romanoff's or Chasen's —"

I said, "Harry, I won't write such a letter. Please stop asking for it."

"I can't do that. They'd have my tail. Write it, sign the contract and forget it."

I said, "I won't sign it and you knew I wouldn't when I came here. It's a disgrace."

As I started for the door, Harry said, "You take

things too serious. Give me a call in the morning, kid."

I was not to see Harry Cohn again for nine or ten years, and then we met on a plane flying from Los Angeles to New York. He was, of course, the first to enter the plane, followed by six or seven men. When I passed him to take my seat, we shook hands and mumbled about how many years, and he said I got younger and he got older, and things like that. When it came time for lunch, he sent back an invitation for me to join him, saying that he had brought his own food, it was much healthier than the dreck on the plane. Two of his younger employees hauled down the largest picnic hamper I have ever seen. It was filled with forty or fifty fine, thin chicken sandwiches, cold white wine, prosciutto wrapped around perfect ripe melon, homemade pickles, large peaches, wonderful walnut cookies. The hamper held enough for twenty people, and Harry and I made no noticeable dent in it. When we finished, Harry called to somebody named Lou to bring the tea bottles, and when Lou appeared to close our hamper and to present another, he leaned over to take one of the many chicken sandwiches. Harry made a fist and brought it down hard on Lou's hand.

"The chutzpah," he said to me, "plain chutzpah," and to Lou he said, "Keep yourself in line, sonny."

I don't know whether sonny ever got out of line again because that was the last time I ever saw Cohn.

I can't remember when he died, but there was a nice story at the time, attributed to George Jessel. Jessel and a friend were standing outside the funeral parlor. The line of mourners was very long.

The friend said, "I never saw such a mob at a funeral."

Jessel said, "Same old story: you give 'em what they want and they'll fill the theatre."

I⊤ ɪs ɪᴍᴘᴏssɪʙʟᴇ to write about any part of the McCarthy period in a clear-dated, annotated form; much crossed with much else, nothing obeyed a neat plan. It is plain that the producers at the Waldorf meeting, called by "them," did not know how to carry out the plans that "them" forced upon them. And most of them didn't want to know; a strict observance would have meant loss of revenue on pictures already made and still unsold to television, loss of many talented people, unwanted involvement of many of their high money-makers. If one remembers that Gary Cooper, James Cagney, Frederic March, Humphrey Bogart were all at some point variously involved, even in the most innocent way, then what new nut might appear tomorrow with what new nut charge against whom? And the most militant fighters against the

Hollywood left, the mother of Ginger Rogers, Adolphe Menjou, and such, were getting too much attention, speaking too loud for comfort. Who knew what they might say tomorrow if they spoke with God's wild eye today? Maybe producers themselves, whose private lives had been as guarded as the men in the Kremlin, might come to the attention of a Representative or a Senator; what had been a noble half-hour romance might come to light or, much more important, a strange financial maneuver. Stockholders might, with enough talk even from people who meant well, see that the often fancy accounting books attached to movies included the price of old discarded scripts, limousines, vacations, or an extra, unreported yearly bonus. And many Hollywood witnesses, even the most sympathetic to the studios, weren't always acting with sense before the committees. Gary Cooper was asked, in a most deferential and friendly manner, if he had read much Communist propaganda in the scripts submitted to him. Cooper, as a man who had not been called upon ever to speak very much, thought that one over and said no, he didn't think he had, but then he mostly read at night. This puzzling answer caused too many giggles around the country and Cooper was not a man anybody should be giggling about. (And, much later on, there were to be shudders as well as laughter when Charles Laughton, who had been a close friend of Bertolt Brecht, received a cable from the East German government inviting him to attend his old friend's memorial service. Mr. Laughton immediately phoned J. Edgar Hoover to say that he had received the wire, but after all that it wasn't his fault and shouldn't be counted against him.)

But many people who were questioned acted neither good nor bad, just puzzled. How could you know that during the war a benefit for Russian War Relief wasn't as irreproachable as Bundles for Britain? You couldn't possibly have guessed, unless you were mentally disturbed, that there would come into being such a phrase as "premature anti-Fascist." The popularity of that phrase, the fact that most of America took it seriously and even pretended to understand it, must have been the forerunner of the double-talk we were to hear in the Watergate days. We, as a people, agreed in the Fifties to swallow any nonsense that was repeated often enough, without examination of its meaning or investigation into its roots.

It is no wonder then that many "respectable," meaning friendly, witnesses were often bewildered by what was wanted of them, and that many, who were convinced by the surrounding hysterical pressures that they had something to hide, moved in a dream pavanne trying to guess what the committees wanted them to admit. They scratched around hard for dramatic revelations, inventing sins for the Inquisitor priests.

I told that to Mrs. Shipley, head of the Passport

Division of the State Department, in 1953. It was that year, after my own hearing, that I had an offer to do a movie script for the producer Alexander Korda, in London. The salary was a fifth of what I had earned before the blacklist, but we needed the money and it was no time to argue. (Korda was not the only producer who saw the chance to pick up practiced writers for little money, and the fact that he was to cheat me out of a third of the fifth that he had offered was only to come later.)

It was necessary, of course, to go to Europe to consult with Korda and to write the picture. Everybody who had appeared as an unfriendly witness had been denied a passport. Joe Rauh suggested that I go to see Mrs. Shipley. It seemed to me a useless visit, but Rauh thought I had a chance, and when I asked why, he said he'd tell me after I had seen her.

She was a severe-looking lady with a manner made more severe by its attempt not to be. We sat awkwardly in her office while a secretary was sent off for my file. I remember murmuring something about the weather and never finishing the sentence because Mrs. Shipley was staring at me. And so we sat silent for the few minutes it took the secretary to return with a fat folder. When Mrs. Shipley opened the folder I was amazed to see three large pictures of Charles Chaplin on top. I had known Chaplin, but not well, had played tennis on his court, had once listened to an endless script he wrote and never produced, had once been on a platform with him at a meeting and had been openly disapproving of his emotional, rambling speech, had once been at dinner with him and Gertrude Stein. I admired Chaplin and liked him, but to this day I do not know why his pictures were in my file. Government agencies in those wild days probably had even more misinformation than they have now, although that can always be remedied any time invention is needed again.

Mrs. Shipley did not comment on the Chaplin pictures, but began to read a list of organizations to which I had either belonged or contributed money, and a few I had never heard of. I wanted to say that I recognized the list as coming from a book called *Red Channels*, hardly a proper source for a government agency to be using. As she read down the list, there would have been no sense denying my connection with one organization and affirming the next, and so I sat silent wondering why I had sought out this degrading hour.

Mrs. Shipley had not finished the list when she looked up and said, "Tell me, Miss Hellman, do you think most of the friendly witnesses have been telling the House Un-American Committee the truth?"

It was a most surprising question. I said no, I was sure they had not, many of them had been coached to confess what they had never done and had never seen.

Mrs. Shipley said, "Edward G. Robinson, for example?"

1935: The author of The Children's Hour.

Lillian Hellman and Dashiell Hammett,
Pleasantville, the late 1940's.

Inside the Waldorf: Shostakovich and L.H. at the Cultural and Scientific Co-ference for World Peace, March 1949.

Outside the Waldorf: picketing, March 1949.

The House Committee on Un-American Activities, 1948: Chairman J. Parnell Thomas second from left, Representative Richard M. Nixon at far right.

Richard M. Nixon, Whittaker Chambers (at left) and Committee Couns
Robert Stripling, 1948.

Dashiell Hammett on the way to jail, 1951.

Senator Joseph McCarthy and Roy Cohn.

ashiell Hammett testifying before the Senate Internal Security Subcommittee, 1953.

1975: The author of Scoundrel Time.

I said I thought so, but I wasn't sure. But there were others, Martin Berkeley for example, who said that I had been at a Communist meeting in his house. I was never at his house and didn't believe I ever met him.

I said, "The kiddies have been playing games on all of you, Mrs. Shipley, and you deserve the tricks they played because you pushed them into it."

Mrs. Shipley did not seem angry. She was thoughtful as she riffled through the rest of my file, seemingly looking for something she knew was there. Then she said, "I've suspected many of them were lying. They will be punished for it."

I said, "I don't think that's the way the world is going. It's people like me who need jobs. That's why I came here, not wanting to come."

She said, "I can see that," and was close to a smile. When the near smile had been suppressed she said, "When you go to Europe do you see political people?"

I said I didn't know many, except Louis Aragon and his wife Elsa Triolet, and a few men who had fought in Spain.

She said, "Please write me a letter saying that and that you will take no part in political movements."

I thought about that for a while, not understanding it, looking for the trick. Then I said, "I've never had any part in European political movements, except

647

to be anti-Nazi and anti-Fascist. Certainly I'll write you just that. But I can't promise not to see old friends."

She rose. "Thank you." She moved toward the door. "You will be issued a limited passport. It will be sent to you this week. If you wish to stay in Europe longer because of your cinema work, you will have to apply here again."

She went out of the room. A secretary appeared and opened another door for me into the hall from which I had entered. Rauh was waiting on a bench.

He got up. "You got the passport."

"Yes."

As we left the building, he grinned. "I think you're the only unfriendly witness who has gotten one."

"Why were you so sure I would get it? Certainly I didn't think so."

"Because," he said, "one Puritan lady in power recognized another Puritan lady in trouble. Puritan ladies have to believe that other Puritan ladies don't lie."

But all that was months after I appeared before the Committee.

Two DAYS AGO, in the writing of this book, I was sitting on Gay Head beach in Martha's Vineyard, eating a sandwich, with a pile of magazines I hadn't been able to catch up on. As in all places where you've lived for a long time, I had been saying hello to people whose names I couldn't remember, and hoping they wouldn't stop long enough for them to know that I couldn't. Two middle-aged people did stop to talk, to ask me what I was writing, a question that irritates me so much that I deny I am doing anything. The man, who didn't like my answer, pointed to a copy of the *New York Review of Books* and said, "In that case you must read Lionel Trilling's piece about Whittaker Chambers. Maybe you'll want to write a history of your times."

I laughed and said I wasn't a historian. But when they had passed I did pick up the piece, which was in too old an issue to include yesterday's news that the only things that had been found in Chambers's pumpkin were five rolls of microfilm, two developed, three in metal containers, most of the frames were unreadable, none of them had anything to do with the charges against Alger Hiss. And yet one remembers Mr. Nixon holding them up for the camera, saying here was documentary evidence of the most serious series of treasonable activities which had been launched against the government in the history of America. But Nixon is a villainous liar. Lionel

649

Trilling, a distinguished critic and teacher, an early anti-Communist, the author of a novel roughly based on the career of Whittaker Chambers, is an honest man.

I suddenly wanted to go home and did, to spend the rest of the day asking myself how Diana and Lionel Trilling, old, respected friends, could have come out of the same age and time with such different political and social views from my own.

Facts are facts — and one of them is that a pumpkin, in which Chambers claimed to have hidden the damaging evidence against Hiss, deteriorates — and there never had been a chance that, as Trilling continues to claim in the *New York Review*, Chambers was a man of honor. The youthful psychotic inventions of Chambers were talked about in almost undeniable terms by those who knew him better than Trilling in Washington and New York, and later by men who had worked with him on *Time* magazine. But I told myself that Chambers was an unimportant part of an important puzzle. If facts are facts, and should not be altered, then which of us, as individuals or in groups, did the alterations and why? To many intellectuals the radicals had become the chief, perhaps the only, enemy. (There had been a history of this that preceded my generation: Eugene Debs had been hounded into jail by Woodrow Wilson, and there had been the vicious trials of the men of the International Workers of the World.) Not alone because the radical's intellectual reasons were suspect, but because his convictions would lead to a world that deprived the rest of us of what we had. Very few people are capable of admitting anything so simple: the radical had to be made into an immoral man who justified murder, prison camps, torture, any means to an end. And, in fact, he sometimes was just that. But the anti-radical camp contained the same divisions: often they were honest and thoughtful men, often they were men who turned down a dark road for dark reasons.

But radicalism or anti-radicalism should have had nothing to do with the sly, miserable methods of McCarthy, Nixon and colleagues, as they flailed at Communists, near-Communists, and nowhere-near-Communists. Lives were being ruined and few hands were raised in help. Since when do you have to agree with people to defend them from injustice? Certainly nobody in their right mind could have believed that the China experts, charged and fired by the State Department, did any more than recognize that Chiang Kai-shek was losing. Truth made you a traitor as it often does in a time of scoundrels. But there were very few who stood up to say so and there are almost none even now to remind us that one of the reasons we know so little and guess so badly about China is that we lost the only men who knew what they were talking about. Certainly the good magazines, the ones that published the most serious writers, should have come to the aid of those who were persecuted. *Partisan Review,* although through the years it has published many pieces protesting the punishment of dissidents in Eastern Europe, made no protest when people in this country were jailed or ruined. In fact, it never took an editorial position against McCarthy himself, although it did publish the results of anti-McCarthy symposiums and at least one distinguished piece by Irving Howe. *Commentary* didn't do anything. No editor or contributor ever protested against McCarthy. Indeed, Irving Kristol in that magazine wrote about McCarthy's critics, Henry Steele Commager among others, as if they were naughty children who needed Kristol to correct their innocence.

There were many thoughtful and distinguished men and women on both magazines. None of them, as far as I know, has yet found it a part of conscience to admit that their Cold War anti-Communism was perverted, possibly against their wishes, into the Vietnam War and then into the reign of Nixon, their unwanted but inevitable leader.

THAT WAS a tough spring, 1952. There were not alone the arrangements for my appearance before the Committee, there were other kinds of trouble. Hammett owed the Internal Revenue a great deal of

back taxes: two days after he went to jail they attached all income from books, radio or television,
from anything. He was, therefore, to have no income
for the remaining ten years of his life. I myself had
been badly advised about the movie sale of a play,
and although "Washington" — meaning the then director of Internal Revenue — had given his unofficial
O.K. at the time of the sale, the department now
changed its mind and claimed I owed them a hundred
and seventy-five thousand dollars. I had insisted upon
taking Hammett's conviction and prison sentence —
against his will, and without his cooperation — to
the Court of Appeals and that had cost money, a lot
of it, and certainly my own new troubles would be
expensive. And we would both now be totally banned
in Hollywood or television or radio. The money was
going, would be going faster, and I was flounder-
ing around for decisions about how to live, what to
do without, knowing that Hammett was ill and not
knowing from day to day what would be needed for
him. I don't remember whether worries like that led
to Rauh's asking for a postponement of my appearance, or whether he needed time to think about the
legal problems. I quote from a memorandum Rauh
sent me, this July, 1975. The memorandum is dated
March 26, 1952.

This morning I saw Tavenner, Chief Counsel of the House
Un-American Committee. . . . After some rather forced

pleasantries I explained the purpose of my visit. . . . I asked Tavenner what it was the Committee was particularly interested in. He said the Committee had received sworn testimony that Miss Hellman had been a member of the Communist Party and the Committee wanted to go into that subject. I said that I was not in a position to indicate whether Miss Hellman had ever been a member of the Communist Party, but I was in a position to state that she was prepared to tell the Committee about her activities in all organizations. They seemed so delighted with this that I went right on to point out the legal dilemma involved. . . . If Miss Hellman answered questions about herself she could legally be compelled to answer questions about others, and this she could not morally do. . . . They indicated sympathy but nothing more. . . . He (Tavenner) . . . mentioned that Budd Schulberg had initially refused to name anybody, but subsequently had been persuaded to change his position. He seemed to feel that Miss Hellman, too, would be persuaded. . . . [He] asked me whether I thought Miss Hellman would be more likely to name people in executive (private) session . . . indicating a willingness to talk to Miss Hellman prior to the hearing. . . . Tavenner said this was more for Miss Hellman's benefit . . . as it would make it easier for her to get her dates straight. . . . Nixon [the Committee's research director, not Richard] said they were doing the "entire entertainment field" and were particularly interested in the "literary field" to show how the Communist Party sought to control the thinking of its members. Tavenner asked me if Miss Hellman had any experience with efforts by the Communist Party to dictate her writings. I said Miss Hellman is an individualist . . . [and] I would like to point out that *Watch on the Rhine* had been written in 1940 when Communists were supposed to be pro, not anti, Nazi. They asked me how I could explain Miss Hellman writing an anti-party-line play at this time. . . . The meeting more or less broke up on the note that Miss Hellman was a maverick and they would be as nice as they could but there was no way of avoiding naming other people.

I have no memory of Joe's ever telling me of this meeting. I think I knew about it first in his letter of this July. I am sure that Rauh had to have the meeting, but it is the proof that as much as we liked each other then and now, there was a good part of me he never understood. Perhaps it is fairer to say that whenever I am making a great effort to control myself, I do act in a peculiar manner, and he is not the first who has been bewildered. But, as I have written, I did not want to use the attacks of the Communist Party on me; in my thin morality book it is plain not cricket to clear yourself by jumping on people who are themselves in trouble. Most of the Communists I had met seemed to me people who wanted to make a better world; many of them were silly people and a few of them were genuine nuts, but that doesn't make for denunciation or furnish enough reason for turning them over for punishment to men who wanted nothing more than newspaper headlines that could help their own careers. The greatest mistakes made by native Communists came from their imitation of Russians, a different breed of people with a totally different history. American Communists accepted Russian theory and practice with the enthusiasm of a lover whose mistress cannot complain because she speaks few words of his language; that may be the mistress many men dream about, but it is for bed and not for politics. Nor did they realize that as children of their time and place, they mixed idealism with the unattractive rules of the marketplace: gain, loss, fame, and a kind of comic secrecy borrowed from the directors of giant corporations. Communist-haters, particularly among intellectuals, wrote and talked a good deal about the violence they could suffer at the hands of American Communists — Whittaker Chambers sold a bill of goods on that romantic theme — but I think that was a very doubtful charge. About foreign gunmen I know only what I have read, but the American radicals I met were not violent men.

It is hard to believe, for example, that anybody could have thought of V. J. Jerome, the theoretician of the Party, as a man with a bomb or a gun. I didn't know Jerome very well, but one night, I think in the hope of convincing me that the Party had its high culture side, he insisted upon reading aloud and interpreting Shelley's *The Cenci*. During the last half I took the dog for a walk and if Jerome knew I was missing, he didn't mention it on my return. Years later, Jerome and several other Communist officials were in West Street jail at the same time Hammett was there. Hammett told me of an incident I like. There was a ping-pong table on the roof of the jail and one afternoon Hammett was playing partners with Jerome against one man who had been arrested for murdering a federal agent and one who was in for armed bank robbery. Jerome insisted the possible murderer had called a bad shot when it was really good. Hammett suggested that maybe Jerome shouldn't expect honesty from criminals. Jerome had held up the game to explain to Dash the socialist necessity to believe in the reform of all men, the duty to show them the honest way. When they resumed the game with their impatient partners, all seemed to go better until about the tenth shot, when Jerome shouted across the table that the murderer had cheated again and that he was shocked. The murderer threw his bat across the table and advanced on Jerome with a knife. Hammett said, "Mr. Jerome wishes to apologize."

Jerome said, "I do not wish to apologize. You should be ashamed of yourself for cheating a jailed comrade. You must learn —"

As the knife was thrown, Hammett pushed Jerome to the floor and held on to the murderer with repeated apologies that hinted Jerome wasn't all there in the head. Peace was restored when Hammett made Jerome buy the knife-thrower two packs of cigarettes and take an oath not to play ping-pong again. Maybe Jerome's Russian counterpart would have been dangerous, but then his Russian counterpart might also have been less silly.

The intellectuals who joined the Party, and then left it, had a right to object to the extraordinary language that the faithful used to attack them. But only literary people can confuse shouts of "renegade" or "traitor" with the damage of a gun or a bomb.

Ⅰn APRIL of 1952 I put the Pleasantville farm up for sale, and the shock of that may be the reason I have so little memory, and almost no notes, for the few weeks before my appearance before the Committee. I know, of course, that Rauh wrote a letter that I was to send to the Committee; I didn't like it much because it didn't sound like me. Then I wrote a version, he wrote another, I rewrote him, he rewrote me, and we came out with the version that I quote here.

May 19, 1952

Honorable John S. Wood
Chairman
House Committee on Un-American Activities
Room 226 Old House Office Building
Washington 25, D.C.

Dear Mr. Wood:

As you know, I am under subpoena to appear before your Committee on May 21, 1952.

I am most willing to answer all questions about myself. I have nothing to hide from your Committee and there is nothing in my life of which I am ashamed. I have been advised by counsel that under the Fifth Amendment I have a constitutional privilege to decline to answer any questions about my political opinions, activities and associations, on the grounds of self-incrimination. I do not wish to claim this privilege. I am ready and willing to testify before the representatives of our Government as to my own opinions and my own actions, regardless of any risks or consequences to myself.

But I am advised by counsel that if I answer the Committee's questions about myself, I must also answer questions about other people and that if I refuse to do so, I can be cited for contempt. My counsel tells me that if I answer questions about myself, I will have waived my rights under the Fifth Amendment and could be forced legally to answer questions about others. This is very difficult for a layman to understand. But there is one principle that I do understand: I am not willing, now or in the future, to bring bad trouble to people who, in my past association with them, were completely innocent of any talk or any action that was disloyal or subversive. I do not like subversion or disloyalty in any form and if I had ever seen any I would have considered it my duty to have reported it to the proper authorities. But to hurt innocent people whom I knew many years ago in order to save myself is, to me, inhuman and indecent and dishonorable. I cannot and will not cut my conscience to fit this year's fashions, even though I long ago came to the conclusion that I was not a political person and could have no comfortable place in any political group.

I was raised in an old-fashioned American tradition and there were certain homely things that were taught to me: to try to tell the truth, not to bear false witness, not to harm my neighbor, to be loyal to my country, and so on. In general, I respected these ideals of Christian honor and did as well with them as I knew how. It is my belief that you will agree with these simple rules of human decency and will not expect me to violate the good American tradition from which they spring. I would, therefore, like to come before you and speak of myself.

I am prepared to waive the privilege against self-incrimination and to tell you anything you wish to know about my views or actions if your Committee will agree to refrain from asking me to name other people. If the Committee is unwilling to give me this assurance, I will be forced to plead the privilege of the Fifth Amendment at the hearing.

A reply to this letter would be appreciated.

Sincerely yours,

LILLIAN HELLMAN

NOTES FROM A DIARY. May 16, 1952.

Meg maybe started it all. She jumped on my bed at five this morning. She never does this, being too proud ever to need me or anything else. I've loved this dog since I helped pull her from her mother, but now I kicked her and she went away somewhere and wouldn't eat her breakfast. Leaving the house, I bump into Maggie, who was trying to sweep the hall. She's drunk, early, as usual, but the FBI has twice examined her about me and she's drunker now than before they came.

The Shoreham Hotel, Washington. Why have I come down here this early and without telling anybody? I'll call Hammett tonight and tell him where I am. The phone will be tapped but what difference does it make. No, I won't call him. I'll go buy some magazines and order caviar and steak, and go to sleep. The steak was bad and there wasn't any caviar. I'm going to spend a lot of money on something tomorrow.

May 17th. I've just come back from looking at expensive dresses, buying nothing. I'm growing scared about money and this is the week I must not. There'll be plenty of years for that kind of thing, but this week I will pretend I don't know it. I phoned Dash and told him where I was. He said he thought he had better come down and I said he wasn't to. We've been over all this so many times before. He could do nothing but harm me here, his name, I mean, and anyway, I don't want to think about his disapproval of what I'm doing. I called Joe, didn't say I was in Washington, asked him if he needed me. He said he didn't but to keep in touch. Keep in touch is a funny phrase, I don't think I've ever said it.

May 18th. I never should have come. I haven't anything to do with myself. I'll go to the National Gallery. I hate this neighborhood: no place to walk, refined.

Night. I didn't go to the National Gallery. I went to the zoo. Nice to see living things that don't know anything about future troubles or death or Committees. I've always wanted to go to bed with an orangoutan, but I guess I never will. I now have a taxi driver who waits for me, without charge, because he says he doesn't feel cheerful. I called Dash. He said he was eating a lamb chop. I told him about me and the orangoutan and he said maybe he'd call me back after he ate his lamb chop.

May 19th. I bought a beautiful, expensive Balmain. It will make me feel better to wear it. Then I went to Harvey's for lunch and the waiter pointed out J. Edgar Hoover and Clyde Tolson and said they came to lunch every day. I bet they have an orangoutan every night. But I leave my lunch after I see them: a nasty pair. My cab driver is waiting and I decide to take a plane to New York, come back on the 20th. But halfway to the airport, I change my mind.

May 20th. In a sleepless night, I realize why I came to Washington earlier than I needed to. Five days ago I went to Lennie Bernstein's for dinner. It was a pleasant dinner with Shirley and a couple whose name I heard and forgot. After dinner Harry comes in. [Note of 1975: I have changed his name; he is an old man now, and his appearance before the Committee broke his life into poverty and ill health.] Everybody wants to hear Harry talk because two weeks ago he appeared as an unfriendly witness before the House Com. I am, of course, particularly anxious to listen, although nobody in the room knows that I will appear in the next week. Harry, of course, enjoys the attention and admiration, and I like him

662

for that. Or I like him until he says that his lawyer made him memorize the answers to twenty-five questions before his appearance. That scares me good. Rauh has coached me in nothing. Somebody asks, "How did your lawyer know what twenty-five they would ask?"

"He took the odds," said Harry, "based on what he'd seen and heard with other people."

I hear myself say, "I couldn't learn the answers to any twenty-five questions and I won't."

I feel sick and I go home. I phone Joe. "You didn't tell me I had to learn the answers to lots of questions. I can't do that and you should have told me." Joe said he didn't know what I was talking about. I told him about Harry and he asked who had been Harry's lawyer. Before I could say I didn't know, Joe said he didn't believe Harry, that maybe Harry was O.K. in other ways, but he wasn't telling the truth. Everybody had a right to make themselves a little more heroic, maybe I would do it, too; then he laughed and said no, I couldn't, the chances were the other way, get a night's sleep, there was nothing to memorize: he did have two pieces of advice to give me, nothing important, and better for the last minute.

I guess Harry was the reason I wanted to get out of New York.

One day more to go. I phoned Rauh, who is out, and left a message that I am at the Shoreham. Then I go with my taxi driver to pick up my new dress. I buy a very expensive hat and a fine pair of white kid gloves. On the way back to the hotel with my packages I ask the taxi driver if he could pick me up at eight the next morning. He says sure, it would take his mind off things. What things? His wife has cancer of the throat, but they won't do the operation before noon. That's all he said, all I said. Before I left him, I gave him a check for a hundred dollars and asked him to buy his wife a present. I'd like to think it was generous of me: it was more maybe if I'm a good girl now God will help me and stuff like that. My dress, my hat, my gloves, my gift will be the last extravagances for many years. They felt good. There were two *New York Times* in my room, one of today, one from yesterday. I hadn't wanted to read them and I was, instinctively, right: Clifford Odets had testified as a friendly witness, throwing in the names of old friends and associates. His old friend Elia Kazan had done the same thing a month before and followed it up with an advertisement in the *New York Times* that is hard to believe for its pious shit. I sat for a long time thinking about Clifford, the dinner at Barbetta's: had he meant what he told me that night or had it all been a put-on. Maybe worse — an attempt to find out what I would do or say. It is impossible to think that a grown man, intelligent, doesn't have some sense of how he will act under pressure. It's all been decided so long ago, when you are very young, all mixed up with your childhood's definition of pride or dignity.

I think this is why I don't like Joe's occasional doubts
about whether I will change my position once I am in
the Committee room; I may make an ass of myself,
but that will be all. Under special circumstances, torture, for example, people will and should break. I
remember Louis Aragon telling me, and Camus repeating it the only time I ever met him, that the
French underground during the war were given orders
to hold out against torture as long as they could, so
that others might have time to escape, but not to die
or be crippled under torture, to give in and talk.
That makes sense. But nobody here has been tortured
and I don't like the fashionable case made out for
mental torture being equal to broken arms and burned
tongues. To hell with it. I need sleep.

T HE LETTER THAT I SENT the Committee on May 19,
1952, had been refused by letter on May 20. It was,
therefore, necessary for me to do what I did not want
to do: take the Fifth Amendment. The Fifth Amendment is, of course, a wise section of the Constitution:
you cannot be forced to incriminate yourself. But the
amendment has difficulties that are hard for a layman to understand. Both Rauh and I believed that my
wartime trip to Russia, about which I have written in

another book, would be the center of the Committee's questions. In 1944 the Russians had invited me to visit the USSR as a kind of cultural representative. Both President Roosevelt and Harry Hopkins thought that was a good idea, but, understandably, did not want to endorse it as an official trip. My flight across Siberia had been arranged by the Russians, but Charles Bohlen of the State Department had evidently been instructed to get me as far as Alaska. In Moscow I had stayed for months in the embassy as the guest of Averell Harriman, who was our ambassador. Both Rauh and I believed that the Committee would ask me about that visit in their open antagonism to the Roosevelt period. The Fifth Amendment has catches: if I were asked if I knew Harriman or President Roosevelt, I would have to say yes because I could not claim that knowing them could harm me; but if I were asked if I knew Chaplin or Hammett, for example, I would have to refuse to answer because they could, in the eyes of the Committee, incriminate me. Thus, of course, one puts a finger on certain people and possibly on people about whom you know little and whose history you can only guess at. Maybe it is all legally necessary, well thought out, but it can be ugly stuff in practice.

My hearing was scheduled for eleven o'clock on the morning of May 21, 1952. Rauh had asked me to be at his office at eight-thirty. I tried to sleep, failed, tried to read, took two hot baths. Twice the phone had rung and, believing it was Hammett, I decided not to answer because I knew he would see through any pretend voice or manner. I tried during the night to find out what was going on in me — "thinking things out" was the voice of my time — and gave that up toward dawn in a kind of nasty amusement that the time for self-examination was over; calm had set in because I've known all my life that a show of temper, or even an ordinary set of jitters, once it starts, cannot be stopped and thus cannot begin. And so I had a big breakfast, and took my sad taxi driver to Joe's office. We shook hands and he said he would come and tell me about his wife. I gave him my New York address, but I never heard from him again.

Rauh was on the telephone. He nodded at me, put his hand over the phone, said he was talking to Thurman Arnold (Arnold had been an Assistant Attorney General and was now a partner of Abe Fortas). Rauh's usually cheerful face was set and stern. I picked up a newspaper, went into another room, read for a few minutes, and looked up to see Rauh standing in the doorway.

He said, "Thurman Arnold called me. He says that I am sending you straight to jail with the letter we wrote. He says he believes that we must find a way to say we have changed our mind about the letter before the hearing starts. His exact words were,

'You and Fortas are making a martyr of this woman.' I don't want to make a martyr of you. Arnold is a very fine lawyer."

I got up and went down the hall, walked up and down, tried a locked door of the ladies' room, thinking I needed to be sick. Rauh, with the best will, had upset me to the point of sickness. I cannot make quick turns, cannot even take a plane in the afternoon if I have counted on flying in the morning, cannot ever adjust fast to a new pattern, have not the mind or the nature to do one thing, maybe wiser, when I am prepared for another. I wanted to tell Rauh that I was angry with him, that the nerves I had been controlling with some kind of discipline were about to go to pieces. But when I came back into his office he looked so miserable that I could say none of that.

I said, "Please call Mr. Arnold and thank him for me. But tell him that whatever happens to me now will be better than what could happen if we start anything new. And then you stop feeling guilty because that's bad for me this morning."

Rauh, his assistant Daniel Pollitt, and I took a taxi to the Old House Office Building. I remember saying to myself, "Just make sure you come out unashamed. That will be enough."

Joe tapped me on the arm. "If things get too much for you, tell me and I'll tell the Committee you have to go to the ladies' room. You can probably do that only once, so take your time, wash your face, have a cigarette. If you don't need a rest, then keep your eye on the clock and remember that they'll take a lunch break around twelve-thirty. We may be called back, of course, but you'll have at least an hour and a half for a nap or a drink or both. Now this is more important so listen carefully: *don't make jokes.*"

"Make *jokes?* Why would I make jokes?"

"Almost everybody, when they feel insulted by the Committee, makes a joke or acts smart-aleck. It's a kind of embarrassment. Don't do it."

The Committee room was almost empty except for a few elderly, small-faced ladies sitting in the rear. They looked as if they were permanent residents and, since they occasionally spoke to each other, it was not too long a guess that they came as an organized group or club. Clerks came in and out, put papers on the rostrum, and disappeared. I said maybe we had come too early, but Joe said no, it was better that I get used to the room.

Then, I think to make the wait better for me, he said, "Well, I can tell you now that in the early days of seeing you, I was scared that what happened to my friend might happen to me."

He stopped to tell Pollitt that he didn't understand about the press — not one newspaperman had appeared.

I said, "What happened to your friend?"

"He represented a Hollywood writer who told him that he would under no circumstances be a

669

friendly witness. That was why my friend took the case. So they get here, in the same seats we are, sure of his client, and within ten minutes the writer is one of the friendliest witnesses the Committee has had the pleasure of. He throws in every name he can think of, including his college roommate, childhood friend."

I said, "No, that won't happen and for more solid reasons than your honor or even mine. I told you I can't make quick changes."

Joe told Pollitt that he thought he understood about no press and the half-empty room: the Committee had kept our appearance as quiet as they could. Joe said, "That means they're frightened of us. I don't know whether that's good or bad, but we want the press here and I don't know how to get them."

He didn't have to know. The room suddenly began to fill up behind me and the press people began to push toward their section and were still piling in when Representative Wood began to pound his gavel. I hadn't seen the Committee come in, don't think I had realized that they were to sit on a raised platform, the government having learned from the stage, or maybe the other way around. I was glad I hadn't seen them come in — they made a gloomy picture. Through the noise of the gavel I heard one of the ladies in the rear cough very loudly. She was to cough all through the hearing. Later I heard one of her friends say loudly, "Irma, take your good cough drops."

The opening questions were standard: what was

my name, where was I born, what was my occupation, what were the titles of my plays. It didn't take long to get to what really interested them: my time in Hollywood, which studios had I worked for, what periods of what years, with some mysterious emphasis on 1937. (My time in Spain, I thought, but I was wrong.)

Had I met a writer called Martin Berkeley? (I had never, still have never, met Martin Berkeley, although Hammett told me later that I had once sat at a lunch table of sixteen or seventeen people with him in the old Metro-Goldwyn-Mayer commissary.) I said I must refuse to answer that question. Mr. Tavenner said he'd like to ask me again whether I had stated I was abroad in the summer of 1937. I said yes, explained that I had been in New York for several weeks before going to Europe, and got myself ready for what I knew was coming: Martin Berkeley, one of the Committee's most lavish witnesses on the subject of Hollywood, was now going to be put to work. Mr. Tavenner read Berkeley's testimony. Perhaps he is worth quoting, the small details are nicely formed, even about his "old friend Hammett," who had no more than a bowing acquaintance with him.

MR. TAVENNER: . . . I would like you to tell the committee when and where the Hollywood section of the Communist Party was first organized.

MR. BERKELEY: Well, sir, by a very strange coincidence the section was organized in my house. . . . In June of

671

1937, the middle of June, the meeting was held in my house. My house was picked because I had a large living room and ample parking facilities. . . . And it was a pretty good meeting. We were honored by the presence of many functionaries from downtown, and the spirit was swell. . . . Well, in addition to Jerome and the others I have mentioned before, and there is no sense in me going over the list again and again. . . . Also present was Harry Carlisle, who is now in the process of being deported, for which I am very grateful. He was an English subject. After Stanley Lawrence had stolen what funds there were from the party out here, and to make amends had gone to Spain and gotten himself killed, they sent Harry Carlisle here to conduct Marxist classes. . . . Also at the meeting was Donald Ogden Stewart. His name is spelled Donald Ogden S-t-e-w-a-r-t. Dorothy Parker, also a writer. Her husband Allen Campbell, C-a-m-p-b-e-l-l; my old friend Dashiell Hammett, who is now in jail in New York for his activities; that very excellent playwright, Lillian Hellman . . .

And so on.

When this nonsense was finished, Mr. Tavenner asked me if it was true. I said that I wanted to refer to the letter I had sent, I would like the Committee to reconsider my offer in the letter.

MR. TAVENNER: In other words, you are asking the committee not to ask you any questions regarding the participation of other persons in the Communist Party activities?

I said I hadn't said that.

Mr. Wood said that in order to clarify the record Mr. Tavenner should put into the record the correspondence between me and the Committee. Mr. Tavenner did just that, and when he had finished Rauh sprang to his feet, picked up a stack of mimeographed copies of my letter, and handed them out to the press section. I was puzzled by this — I hadn't noticed he had the copies — but I did notice that Rauh was looking happy.

Mr. Tavenner was upset, far more than the printed words of my hearing show. Rauh said that Tavenner himself had put the letters in the record, and thus he thought passing out copies was proper. The polite words of each as they read on the page were not polite as spoken. I am convinced that in this section of the testimony, as in several other sections — certainly in Hammett's later testimony before the Senate Internal Security Subcommittee — either the court stenographer missed some of what was said and filled it in later, or the documents were, in part, edited. Having read many examples of the work of court stenographers, I have never once seen a completely accurate report.

Mr. Wood told Mr. Tavenner that the Committee could not be "placed in the attitude of trading with the witnesses as to what they will testify to" and that thus he thought both letters should be read aloud.

Mr. Tavenner did just this, and there was talk I couldn't hear, a kind of rustle, from the press section. Then Mr. Tavenner asked me if I had attended the meeting described by Berkeley, and one of the hardest things I ever did in my life was to swallow the words, "I don't know him, and a little investigation into the time and place would have proved to you that I could not have been at the meeting he talks about." Instead, I said that I must refuse to answer the question. The "must" in that sentence annoyed Mr. Wood — it was to annoy him again and again — and he corrected me: "You might refuse to answer, the question is asked, do you refuse?"

But Wood's correction of me, the irritation in his voice, was making me nervous, and I began to move my right hand as if I had a tic, unexpected, and couldn't stop it. I told myself that if a word irritated him, the insults would begin to come very soon. So I sat up straight, made my left hand hold my right hand, and hoped it would work. But I felt the sweat on my face and arms and knew that something was going to happen to me, something out of control, and I turned to Joe, remembering the suggested toilet intermission. But the clock said we had only been there sixteen minutes, and if it was going to come, the bad time, I had better hang on for a while.

Was I a member of the Communist Party, had I been, what year had I stopped being? How could I harm such people as Martin Berkeley by admitting I had known them, and so on. At times I couldn't follow the reasoning, at times I understood full well that in refusing to answer questions about membership in

674

the Party I had, of course, trapped myself into a seeming admission that I once had been.

But in the middle of one of the questions about my past, something so remarkable happened that I am to this day convinced that the unknown gentleman who spoke had a great deal to do with the rest of my life. A voice from the press gallery had been for at least three or four minutes louder than the other voices. (By this time, I think, the press had finished reading my letter to the Committee and were discussing it.) The loud voice had been answered by a less loud voice, but no words could be distinguished. Suddenly a clear voice said, "Thank God somebody finally had the guts to do it."

It is never wise to say that something is the best minute of your life, you must be forgetting, but I still think that unknown voice made the words that helped to save me. (I had been sure that not only did the elderly ladies in the room disapprove of me, but the press would be antagonistic.) Wood rapped his gavel and said angrily, "If that occurs again, I will clear the press from these chambers."

"You do that, sir," said the same voice.

Mr. Wood spoke to somebody over his shoulder and the somebody moved around to the press section, but that is all that happened. To this day I don't know the name of the man who spoke, but for months later, almost every day I would say to myself, I wish I could tell him that I had really wanted to say to Mr. Wood: "There is no Communist menace in this country and you know it. You have made cowards into liars, an ugly business, and you made me write a letter in which I acknowledged your power. I should have gone into your Committee room, given my name and address, and walked out." Many people have said they liked what I did, but I don't much, and if I hadn't worried about rats in jail, and such. . . . Ah, the bravery you tell yourself was possible when it's all over, the bravery of the staircase.

In the Committee room I heard Mr. Wood say, "Mr. Walter does not desire to ask the witness any further questions. Is there any reason why this witness should not be excused from further attendance before the Committee?"

Mr. Tavenner said, "No, sir."

My hearing was over an hour and seven minutes after it began. I don't think I understood that it was over, but Joe was whispering so loudly and so happily that I jumped from the noise in my ear.

He said, *"Get up. Get up.* Get out of here immediately. Pollitt will take you. Don't stop for any reason, to answer any questions from anybody. Don't run, but walk as fast as you can and just shake your head and keep moving if anybody comes near you."

I am looking at a recent letter from Daniel Pollitt, who is now a distinguished professor of law at the University of North Carolina. He doesn't comment on the run we made out of the building, the fastest I ever made since I was a child late for class. But he remembers that we went to a restaurant for a Scotch and then another and another and waited for Joe, who never came, and that he wondered how with only a dollar fifty in his pocket he could pay the check. He was saved, he said, by a friend of mine from the State Department who came by and paid the bill. But according to my diary, he has mixed that day with one that occurred a few weeks before. Rauh did join us, kissed me, patted Pollitt on the shoulder a couple of times, ordered us sandwiches and said to me, "Well, we did it."

"What did we do? I don't understand why it was over so fast."

Rauh said he didn't know whether they had made a legal mistake in reading my letter into the record, but for the first time they had been put in a spot they didn't like, maybe didn't want to tangle with. They could call me again, but they'd have to find another reason, and so he hadn't sent me to jail after all, and everything had worked just fine.*

---

* Many people through the years have asked me why the Committee did not prosecute me. I could only repeat what Rauh thought the day of the hearing. On the completion of this book, I phoned him to ask if, after all these years, there could be another explanation. He said, "There were three things they wanted. One, names which you wouldn't give. Two, a smear by accusing you of being a 'Fifth Amendment Communist.' They couldn't do that because in your letter you offered to testify about yourself. And three, a prosecution which they couldn't do because they forced us into taking the Fifth Amendment. They had sense enough to see that they were in a bad spot. We beat them, that's all."

I kept saying, "My, my," through the sandwich, too tired to understand much of what he said. And then we were back in Joe's office and Joe was calling people, and somewhere along the line somebody spoke to Arthur Krock of the *New York Times,* who said he had admired my position and thought we would find the *Times* report sympathetic. As a matter of fact the press was, in general, very good, and five days later in the *Post* Murray Kempton wrote a piece, "Portrait of a Lady," that gave me great pleasure.

I called Hammett and left a message I'd be home for dinner. I didn't want to talk to him. I didn't want to say, even by inference, "See, I was right and you were wrong," because, of course, I had not been right, if by right one means what one wanted to say, didn't say, and the fact that I got off without being prosecuted didn't prove that I had been right.

I took a late afternoon plane to New York. I felt fine until I began to vomit after the takeoff. As I washed my face, I remembered Sophronia, my nurse, saying to the cook or to anybody else who could be trapped into listening about me, "The child's got no stomach. No matter how sick she is with what, she can't throw up. She try, I try, but it ain't to be."

It was to be that night and into the next two days. I remember very little about those days except that I was always thirsty, sleepy, and saying to myself, "From now on, you make no phone calls to anybody. You will wait for them to call you. Life has changed."

Life had changed and there were many people who did not call me. But there were others, a few friends, a few half-strangers, who made a point of asking me for dinner or who sent letters. That was kind, because I knew that some of them were worried about the consequences of seeing me.

But the mishmash of those years, beginning before my congressional debut and for years after, took a heavy penalty. My belief in liberalism was mostly gone. I think I have substituted for it something private called, for want of something that should be more accurate, decency. And yet certain connecting strings have outworn many knives, perhaps because the liberal connections had been there for thirty years and that's a long time. There was nothing strange about my problem, it is native to our time; but it is painful for a nature that can no longer accept liberalism not to be able to accept radicalism. One sits uncomfortably on a too comfortable cushion. Many of us now endlessly jump from one side to another and endlessly fall in space. The American creative world is not only equal but superior in talent to their colleagues in other countries, but they have given no leadership, written no words of new theory in a country that cries out for belief and, because it has none, finds too many people acting in strange and aimless violence.

But there were other penalties in that year of 1952: life was to change sharply in ordinary ways.

We were to have enough money for a few years and then we didn't have any, and that was to last for a while, with occasional windfalls. I saw that coming the day the subpoena was first served. It was obvious, as I have said, the farm had to be sold. I knew I would now be banned from writing movies, that the theatre was as uncertain as it always had been, and I was slow and usually took two years to write a play. Hammett's radio, television and book money was gone forever. I could have broken up the farm in small pieces and made a fortune — I had had an offer that made that possible — and I might have accepted it except for Hammett, who said, "No, I won't have it that way. Let everybody else mess up the land. Why don't you and I leave it alone?", a fine sentiment with which I agree and have forever regretted listening to. More important than the sale of the farm, I knew that a time of my life had ended and the faster I put it away the easier would be an altered way of living, although I think the sale of the farm was the most painful loss of my life. It was, perhaps, more painful to Hammett, although to compare the pains of the loss of beloved land one has worked oneself, a house that fits because you have made it fit thinking you would live in it forever, is a foolish guess-game.

But something so remarkable happened five days before we moved that it turned pain into something else, something almost good, a gift that made me think maybe luck was not gone forever and past punishment might someday be of little importance.

We had always had deer on the farm, and before Westchester County forbade shooting them, Hammett would kill our allotment and we'd have splendid venison through the winter. Every now and then on a winter walk, deep in the woods or on a riding path, I would come almost face to face with a deer, or a doe with fawns. Often on a slight rustle in the distance I would immediately crouch down to wait, sometimes for a long time, and sometimes rewarded by the sight of a deer quite close to me. Deer are the most lovely of all living things to me, and once I found myself in the ridiculous position of standing deep in a snow-bank, holding out my arms to a doe and crying in shocked rejection when, startled, she fled at high speed.

Two years before we sold the farm, before there was any trouble, I had extended a large lawn into a narrow lane of fruit trees, meaning to clear an area behind them, fence it in, and have a small deer park of my own. I had planned that I would visit them only on the days when I thought I had worked hard enough, or had, in some way, earned the pleasure of them. But I had done only the work of clearing the woods when the farm had to be sold.

It was bought by a pleasant couple — there had been a number of men with strange proposals of all cash, ready with plans for subdivisions — and the agreement with the buyers was that we were to be out

within a month. The hardest of the work was over:
the tractors, the boats, the farm implements, the animals had been sold or given away.

Five days before the storage people were to come
for the furniture, I was upstairs packing something or
other in my bedroom, which was directly above a
charming workroom I had long ago made for myself.
A large terrace was off the workroom, facing the line
of fruit trees and the deer park that was never to
come, bordered on one side by a beautiful rock garden
planted by a long-dead expert before we bought the
house.

Hammett came to the foot of the stairs and in a
whisper said, "Come down. Be very quiet. When you
get to the last few steps, crouch very low so that you
can't be seen through the window." His voice was
excited and happy, and as I ran down the steps he was
standing far to the side of the large windows. He made
a down motion with his hand. I crawled the steps after
the landing, crawled across the room, and he raised
me slowly to my feet. Before me was the finest sight
of my life, so stunning, so unbelievable, that I began
making choking sounds until Hammett put his hand
over my mouth.

On the wide road from the lake at least twenty
deer, moving slowly, were joining a larger group
who were wandering up the shorter path through the
fruit trees. All of them, small and large, pale and
darker, moved without fear, stopping along the way

to nibble at the May buds. Eight of them had moved close to the terrace, were looking up at the house, but without curiosity, as if it were another kind of tree. Then a group of them went past the terrace and up into the rock garden, where they found such lovely things to eat that they were joined by six or seven others. In all, the parade from the lake road, the deer that took the fruit path, the deer in the rock garden, certainly numbered forty or fifty does, bucks, fawns, moving as I think few people have ever been allowed to see them, untroubled, not even on their usual alert for smell or rustle. Once, after about an hour, Hammett and I changed positions. Then, a long time later, he crawled across the floor, piled a small chair high with cushions, and pushed it for me to sit on, putting it a proper distance from the windows. I remember looking at my watch: it was a few minutes past four. It was after six o'clock when the deer began to disappear, in small family groups, some heading for the main road and then flying back to the rock garden, some on a new course into a large stand of pines, most of them going as they came, by the road to the lake. There were four last stragglers who stopped to examine a small dogwood immediately off the terrace, but one of our dogs barked in the distant kennels and the deer were off into the woods. Neither Hammett nor I had said a word during the hours of the deer, but I guess I made sounds once in a while, because he would laugh and pat my head.

We ate dinner without speaking. Later that evening I went into his room. He was staring at the wall, two books lying next to him.

"We had something nice. Who managed that?"

He smiled and turned his face away from me.

"Look," I said, "go back to New York. I'd rather do the last few days' packing by myself. It's O.K. now."

He didn't answer me and I went back to packing. A large part of the next morning he stood by the window and then went out into the woods, as he had for so many years, carrying a lunch sandwich in his pocket. That night he said, "Can you handle the movers by yourself?"

"Yes," I said. "We shouldn't say goodbye to this place together. It will make it bad for both of us."

He left the next morning. Kitty, the Bensons and I continued to sort and pack. It was Kitty who reminded me that we hadn't yet touched the attic. I was irritated on climbing the ladder to the attic to find that Hammett had used it for many years to hide the nutty and expensive gadgets that he liked so much and then forgot; there were a hundred feet of telephone wire; a giant unopened package which proved to be a rubber boat; a chess set that had been carefully arranged but never used; a small ice chest that had evidently been tested and was now broken; two suits of horsehide made for hunting on very cold days; a toy train, mysteriously addressed to the son of a friend but never mailed; two expensive casting rods and reels, in addition to the four that were already in use downstairs; a set of Spengler in German, a language Dash couldn't read; two pairs of fur slippers with my name on the package; an unopened extension ladder, and odds and ends of stuff that I couldn't identify. The telephone wire being the most inexplicable of the mess, I mailed it to him in New York, and for at least a year the unopened package sat in a corner and neither of us ever mentioned it.

The furniture movers were to come early on a Monday morning. On Sunday afternoon I had a telephone call from Henry Wallace asking me to come and have a farewell supper with him and Ilo, his wife. I had known Wallace very well, having been one of the people who had backed his third party presidential bid in 1948, contributed to it at a time when I should not have contributed to anything, and traveled with him on speechmaking tours. As the months went on I became more and more convinced that I had made a foolish and thoughtless move. I had seen a third party as necessary in this country — I still do — but I had not wanted all energies turned toward a presidential campaign. I had thought we would concentrate on wards, districts, even neighborhoods, building slow and small for a long future, and I disagreed that so much energy and money, all of it, in fact, was being gambled on a man about whom I had many doubts. My doubts had nothing to do with my fondness for Wallace: his rare, odd pieces of knowledge, often remarkable in their practicality, often wacky in their mysticism, interested me; he was serious about the state of America, open about his fears for the future, but there was no doubt that the powerful hand of Roosevelt had held tight rein over the conflicts in Wallace's nature and the strange digressions of his mind.

By that Sunday of June 1952, the day before I was to move, the Progressive Party had disintegrated. Wallace and I had stayed friends, in part because I had, a few years before, been willing to gamble a fair amount of money on his favorite project, the cross of the Rhode Island Red hen with the Leghorn in an attempt to get a high-laying chicken that was also a good food bird, a cross that, unlike his brilliant experiments with corn, never worked. But long before that Sunday, Wallace had turned bitter about the Progressive Party, telling people that I was the only person connected with it whom he had ever trusted. (I was never sure he said it; it didn't sound like him.)

When Wallace left Washington, and before the formation of the Progressive Party, he had bought a farm less than a half-hour from mine. We saw each other first as neighbors and then, of course, a great deal during the Progressive Party's busy days — never around Hammett, who left the room any time Henry came into it — and then less and less after the

Progressive Party campaign. I was uneasy about the rather strange statements that came from Wallace afterwards: a suspicious innocence of what had been, an unpleasant pouting quality.

During the early autumn of 1948, four or five of us were eating lunch together on the day of a large evening rally. When lunch was finished Wallace suggested that he and I take a walk. (One of us at the lunch, as always, turned back to supplement the waiter's tip: Henry never left more than five percent and there had been certain embarrassing scenes.) When we had walked for a while, he asked me if it was true that many of the people, the important people, in the Progressive Party were Communists. It was such a surprising question that I laughed and said most certainly it was true.

He said, "Then it is true, what they're saying?"

"Yes," I said. "I thought you must have known that. The hard, dirty work in the office is done by them and a good deal of the bad advice you're getting is given by the higher-ups. I don't think they mean any harm; they're stubborn men."

"I see," he said, and that was that.

But several weeks later, in a kind of policy meeting, I saw that he was restive and wary; the Communists in the room, and there were, perhaps, four of them out of the ten people in the meeting, were pushing too hard and with not much sense on an issue the particulars of which I no longer remember, but with which I disagreed. I was now convinced that my constant pleas that we turn attention and money away from the presidential campaign and put them into building small chapters around the country in the hope of a solid, modest future, not into a flashy national campaign which had no hope of working, were defeated forever. I knew I had lost the argument not only with Wallace, who wanted all money and attention for his presidential run, but with the Communist faction, who carried a great deal of weight with the non-Communist group.

That night I called a friend — I did not know if he was a member of the Party or if he was close to them — and asked if he would arrange a meeting for me and whoever he considered the two or three highest-ranking members of the Communist Party.

Two afternoons later we met in my friend's apartment. There were three men there, all high officials because I recognized their names. My friend left us alone and I said that there seemed to me to be six Communists in the Progressive Party, two of them intelligent and flexible, four of them stubborn and unwise, interested in very little except the imposition of their own will.

I said, "I think I understand Henry Wallace. He does not oppose your people because what they want fits at the minute what he wants. But when he loses, he will turn on all of you, and you will deserve it. You have a political party of your own. Why do you

want to interfere with another political party? It's
plain willful meddling and should stop because it is
going to fail. Please think about what I am saying."

I went into another room to get myself a drink
and to give them time alone. When I came back, two
of the men were gone. The one with the most important title was waiting for me.

He said, "We believe that what you have said
makes sense because we know the men you are talking about. But you have the illusion, shared by many
people, that the Communist Party is dictated to by a
few officials. The truth is that we have no control over
the men you think stubborn and willful. We will repeat to them what you have said, and I, for one, will
say that I agree with you. But don't count on any
change."

I don't know what he ever said or did, but there
was no change, and after our failure in the election
— failure to make even the number of votes I thought
we would get — Wallace withdrew in a strange humor
and, not long after, began to declare openly that he
had not known about the Communists in the Progressive Party. I, because I had told him, have to believe that he was lying, but there is a chance that so
strange a nature had put aside our conversation at a
time when it didn't suit him to hear it. He was not a
simple man.

On the Sunday night before the Monday I was to
leave the farm, I was very tired and not anxious to

make the half-hour drive to the Wallace house. But there was something kind about the supper invitation, some wish, I thought, to declare his good will. When I arrived Ilo Wallace made a pleasant picture on the porch. She said Henry was out doing something with the gladiolas, but would be back soon. He was cross-breeding gladiolas, and I remembered Hammett's remark that he'd be better off leaving things alone and cross-breeding himself. Ilo was a pretty woman, grown heavy in middle age, and a rather puzzling lady. She had told me, from time to time, stories of her past. One of them pleased me, although no amount of tactful, and then untactful, questions ever made clear whether she knew the humor of what she said, or was simply recounting something she remembered but which had not disturbed her. She told me that on the day of their marriage Henry's father, who had been Secretary of Agriculture under both Harding and Coolidge, had given them a wedding present of a new Ford. She and Henry came out of the church after the ceremony, and Henry was so pleased with the sight of the Ford that he ignored the kissers and congratulators, went immediately to the car, and drove off. It was thought odd, but people said he was testing it for her comfort until a half-hour passed, and then another. Toward late afternoon he returned, and called out from the driver's seat, "Get in, Ilo, I'd forgotten you."

She did not smile when she told the story, but

she showed no resentment, and I came to think that no deep emotion had ruled, or even entered, her life.

We chatted that Sunday evening about nothing until Henry appeared, and then Ilo said the cook was on holiday, so she, Ilo, would cook our supper.

I wanted a drink badly, but I knew that was out of the question. The talk between Henry and me was weary and worthless, the way it always is between people who would like to say things they have decided not to say. Ilo finally announced supper. The Wallace farm was an egg farm and Ilo's dinner consisted of two poached eggs for Henry put on two shredded wheat biscuits, a horrid sight, made more insulting by one egg on shredded wheat for me and one for Ilo. It was the sight of this stingy, discourteous supper that made me say I had already eaten and didn't wish anything else. I waited until they had finished, it didn't take long for such food, and while Ilo was undisturbed — what could disturb a woman who put eggs on shredded wheat? — obviously Henry had noticed my frowns. When I rose to go, he said he had a present for me. That was such an unusual event that I stood staring out in the darkness while he put something large in the luggage rack of my car. We all shook hands, said we must see each other soon.

Toward noon of the next day, in the middle of watching the movers carry out the furniture, I remembered the gift in the luggage rack. Benson and I opened it and found a fifty-pound bag of manure, a rather impractical gift for a farm that I no longer owned, not too dainty a gift for a woman. I was never to see Wallace again, although I don't think the eggs or the manure had much to do with that.

That Monday was not a happy day. People came to call for the things they had bought — the dairy cows, the ducks, the chickens, the eleven small poodles, the farm machinery, the boats, the fine butchering knives and tables, the four handsome Angus, the canning and sausage-making machinery, the hundreds of items that make a good working farm. I knew that day I would never have any of them again. But whenever I said that to myself I also said that I was lucky ever to have had them at all, and that is what I feel today, these many years later. Loss of money can take away what you like and have been good at, but in my case, I am now certain that without the trouble I would have stayed in one place, one frame too long. I am angry that corrupt and unjust men made me sell the only place that was ever right for me, but that doesn't have much to do with anything anymore, because there have been other places and they do fine. If I had stayed on the farm I would have grown old faster in its service. There are not many places or periods or scenes that you can think back upon with no rip in the pleasure. The people who worked for us must feel the same way, because each Christmas we still send each other gifts, but we do not meet because all of us fear, I think, the sad talk of a good past. Benson, my farmer, is dead, but his wife lived to raise a good son, and whenever I talk to her I remember the picture of her fat, cheerful little boy sitting on the terrace steps with Hammett, a bitter ex-Catholic, who was taking the boy through his catechism and explaining with sympathy the meaning of the ceremony.

N OTES FROM A DIARY of May 10, 1952. I called Marc Blitzstein and we met at the Russian Tea Room. I told him about my appearance before the Committee in a week or ten days and asked him not to tell anybody. I was telling him because it meant that I couldn't do the narration for *Regina* * at the concert on June 1. I should have told him before, but even though I love Marc, and we have been close friends, there are times I don't like to listen to him. I expected a lecture, I didn't know what kind, but a lecture, so I started off by saying Lennie would do as well, maybe better. Blitzstein stared at me for a while, then he said, "No. We can't call you off, and you can't call yourself off. We'd all look like cowards." I said maybe I was, I couldn't stand the idea of being hissed

* *Regina* is the opera Blitzstein wrote based on my play *The Little Foxes.*

by an audience, and that was what would happen. He said, "I don't think they will hiss you, and if they do, I won't have it. I'll just come out and say I don't want my music played before such people, and we'll give them their money back and send them home."

I laughed because I could hear him doing it, enjoying it. When we left each other he said, "You've got bigger things to worry about. Forget the concert, we'll face it the night it happens."

From a diary of June 2. So there I was last night in my Committee-Balmain dress. Marc got to the Y before I did, both of us early. He says the lobby is already full, the house will be sold out, do I know if they allow standing room. I said I didn't know anything, just fear. He said to shut up, but he is frightened, too, because he moves around so much backstage and nods at me every time he passes me. I stand in the wings. The grips are fanning themselves because it is a hot night, but I am cold. I am in much worse shape than the day I came before the Committee, maybe because this is my racket and audiences have always frightened me. A voice says, "Need a drink?" I turn to see a large Irishman with red hair. I said I sure did, but I had forgotten to bring anything. He takes his right hand from behind his back and hands me the largest shot of bourbon I've ever seen. I get it down too fast and he brings me a stool and a glass of water. Then he disappears. Marc passes again, goes down into the pit with the musicians. But the liquor makes things worse. Now I am really shaking, and in moving around on the stool I rip my stocking on the wood rungs. The young red-head reappears and says I am on the wrong side of the stage for my entrance. We cross and I stumble over a cable.

He says, "You need another drink. One is bad for the stomach."

When we get on the other side, the redhead takes his place at the lighting board, calls out something to somebody, and in a few minutes another hand gives me another bourbon. I hesitate and the redhead says: "Best thing going." I drink half of it. I see the curtain go up and remember that I am the first person on the stage. I can't get off the stool. The redhead says, "Go on. Go on fast."

I turned, I guess in full sight of the right-hand side of the audience, and said, "I wouldn't say it if I wasn't drunk, but if you're not married I hope you will consider me."

He laughs and says, "Get onstage."

I got halfway across the stage, staring straight ahead, saying something to myself, some prayer, I don't remember. Suddenly there is thunderous applause. It is so unexpected that I stop dead center in such shocked surprise that the first few rows began to laugh. Then the audience rose, applauding, and I face it, unable to move. For a second I think that the applause is meant for the musicians, but they have

risen too, and Marc tells me later that I looked behind me to see if the applause was meant for somebody else. Then I hear Marc's voice from somewhere
saying, "For Christ's sake, move to your stool." I
want very much to cry, but I moved to the stool,
opened the pages of my narrative, and couldn't believe the calm sounds that were coming out of me
about *Foxes* and what Marc had done with it in
Regina. I usually read too fast, but this time it is
just right, slow and even. At the end of one section of
my narrative the singing began — I haven't even seen
the singers come onstage — and when nobody is looking at me anymore, I reach into my pocket for a
handkerchief. I haven't any. Somebody makes a sound
to my right and I see that the redhead has crossed
backstage and is beckoning to me from the wings,
very close to me. I get off my stool. I shouldn't move,
of course, but he seems to me now the best friend
I've ever had and I wouldn't think of disobeying him.
He hands me a half-bottle of ginger ale and a paper
cup. He says, "It's bourbon. Carry it back with you."

I HAVE NO OTHER NOTES for that night. We got
through it fine, everybody says, and it was a great
success. Two days later I try to find the redhead's

name, but nobody seems to know. I call the stagehands' union, describe him, and they say they'll find
out who was working that night. But I never heard
from them, and I've never seen the redhead since.

F OR ALMOST A YEAR after my hearing before the
Committee and after the sale of the farm, I have very
little memory and only occasional diary notes. Hammett, disliking New York, had rented a small house
from friends in Katonah and made it smaller and
more miserable with the gadgets from Pleasantville
and the enormous amount of books that finally were
so piled on chairs and the floor that one moved around
the room like a snake and found only a small corner
of a couch to sit on.

I had two polyp operations on my throat that
year, and I think I remember the operations because
they came two days after the opening night of the
revival of *The Children's Hour.* I had directed the
revival, and my memory of the operations is lying in
bed thinking about my place in the theatre. Kermit
Bloomgarden, the producer, had given a pleasant
opening night party in a small Italian restaurant and,
toward midnight, our press agent phoned in the *New
York Times* review. I stood outside the phone booth

as Kermit repeated the review to me, thinking what a
fool I was to be so nervous about what anybody said
about a play written eighteen years before. The
theatre is, by necessity, often a silly business, and
that night I seemed to me the sucker of the world.

And during that year I had what could be called,
by romantic courtesy, an affair with a man I had
turned down when I was twenty-one years old. His
bastard nature, when I was young, seemed comic; but
when I was in my forties it seemed plain cruelty in
space, inflicted for the pleasure of the pain he caused
anybody who came near him. I was fair game that
year and he admitted that he had first telephoned me
thinking just that, to pay me back for a twenty-five-
year-old "insult." He did pay me back, but not for
long, and when he found out it was not for long he
followed me to Rome, put himself in a hospital, and
announced that the doctor said he had cancer. Would
I cable his children? His children did not come, but
each day when I went reluctantly to call on him we
had a farewell scene of a different variety: one day
he would be cheerful about the full life he had lived,
the pleasure his enemies would have on the news of
his death. (He said I needn't deny that and I didn't.)
Another day, in the middle of my visit, his eyes
closed in what he said were racking pains that made
death desirable. On two visits he discussed with me
the disposition of property he didn't own: all was to
go to me, he said, because his children had not re-

sponded to the cable. He left me a Picasso he had never owned and twelve Regency chairs that were in storage but he couldn't remember the name of the storage company. I did not enjoy these visits, but I cannot deny that no matter what I knew about him, I was touched by his bravery. Toward the end of the week I bumped into his doctor in the hall. The doctor was an American, so it was not language that made us not understand each other until I mentioned his patient's terrible cancer pains, was there nothing to be done? The doctor said his patient had a mild attack of colitis, he never had any need to be in a hospital, and they were putting him out that day. I went back, stuck my head in the patient's door, said all that, and he screamed, "The doctor is a liar. He told me I had cancer." I have never seen the non-cancer non-invalid since, although about eight years ago he sent me a paper parasol from Japan.

I believe that for years I have remembered this unimportant affair — far too big a term for what happened between us — because, punished by what I thought was a group of political villains, I was evidently driven to find another kind of villain and another kind of punishment. Whatever I think comic now, I did not find comic the night I stood on a dock in Palm Beach and, from a distance, watched him embrace a woman. When he saw me on the dock, he came toward me, smiling. He said, "That was my sister-in-law. My disgusting brother has left her again without a cent." It seemed more than silly to tell him that he had no brother and so I took myself back to New York to think that trouble makes trouble, and that is what is most to be feared about it. I was learning that change, loss, an altered life, is only a danger when you become devoted to disaster.

Money was beginning to go and go fast. I had gone from earning a hundred and forty thousand a year (before the movie blacklist) to fifty and then twenty and then ten, almost all of which was taken from me by the Internal Revenue Department, which had come forward with its claim on the sale of a play that the previous administration had seemingly agreed to. I didn't understand it then and I don't now; my lawyer advised a compromise. But the compromise allowed was small, and the collection very large.

The loss of money made less difference than I thought; middle-class security is a faith from which I have never recovered, but that has certain virtues. Chiefly, I was bored by the necessity of counting what could be had for dinner, what couldn't, how much housework I could do by myself, how many dresses I wanted that I couldn't have, the miserable amount that Hammett, despite my protests, would take from the safe each month, living on far too little, never buying anything for himself anymore except food and rent. That made me sad: never in the ten years since the Internal Revenue cut off his income — two days after he went to jail — did he ever buy a suit or even a tie, until the week of the opening night of *Toys in the Attic*, when he bought new dinner clothes and, I believe, had a happy evening at the play and the nice feel of a new suit. In 1960 *Toys in the Attic* was a great success and, in the money sense, the bad times were over. Hammett died a year later, but at least that year was lived in security.

I WAS IN ROME on Mrs. Shipley's temporary passport in 1953. I was working on a movie for Korda, to be directed by Max Ophuls, and had chosen to live in Rome because it was cheaper than any other place. I had a small apartment with a kitchenette in a tacky hotel in the vulgar Parioli section of the city. I had a few friends, but it was a period of not wanting to see people, wanting only to save money, doling it out on kitchenette food, walks instead of taxis, and disliking all that so much that I would go on aimless spending sprees. The spending sprees became so obsessive, so ridiculous that I finally figured out a way to deal with them: for that year and for years after, wherever I was, I gave myself the equivalent of five dollars a week to throw away. It was spent almost always in the equivalent of a ten-cent store on junk I didn't need: games, bad candy, nasty-colored lipsticks, toys that fell apart, paper books I had already read, small sewing boxes and sewing gadgets because I was teaching myself to mend and repair. My five-dollar day was always on a Monday, and it turned out I had found a good solution: once the nonsense stuff was bought, I felt better and wasn't tempted by the clothes or shoes or bags that were very pretty that year in Rome.

I was more alone than I had ever been before, but life was pleasant and I saw much of the hidden treasures of the city because I was looking for cheap restaurants or markets and thus came across many beautiful small churches and interesting buildings in sections of the city I would ordinarily have missed.

Once in a while I saw a few friends or Americans who were passing through, and sometimes I would be summoned to Korda's yacht, usually off Antibes, for a script conference or a reading of what I had written. He and Ophuls were pleased with what I had done and I would return to Rome and plug away at the adaptation of a Nancy Mitford novel that I would never have touched in the good days, hoping that I wouldn't always have to earn a living doing what I didn't like.

I have few sharp memories of those many months in Rome, except for the drama that was to happen in July. Mrs. Luce was our ambassador at the time, and that was not well considered by anybody I knew except a couple I had met years before in New York. The wife had been a radical and I had seen her around and about, and the husband, I was told, was a writer. They were friends of Mrs. Luce, often dinner guests, and that puzzled many people: why Mrs. Luce would like people with radical histories. Since I have no final proof that they were involved in what happened to me, I have here changed their names to Dick and Betty. I do have proof, however, that although he was a stringer for a newspaper service, he was also working for the CIA and, jack-of-all-trades, for the Vatican.

It has little to do with their place in my life that one night I bumped into Sam and Frances Goldwyn, and as we sat in an outdoor café we were greeted by Dick and Betty, who had with them two almost naked starlets and a man with his shirt opened to his navel and bracelets to bind both arms below the elbow. I don't think Goldwyn had ever seen a man with so much open flesh and jewelry, so his attention had wandered by the time Betty said that her friend Mrs. Luce had been affected by a mysterious poison, perhaps from falling bits of plaster from the ceiling. Goldwyn heard the word poison in his own fashion — which was not unusual — and asked how persons could fall from the ceiling, what were they doing there? And maybe he was close to the truth: Mrs. Luce did, in time, go home because she was officially ill, although many Italians believed she had been recalled for meddling too openly in their government.

But that was not yet July. One morning of that

month I woke up to read in the *Rome Daily American*
that Senator McCarthy had subpoenaed me. (He had
not subpoenaed me, but I took the newspaper headline to mean that it would be served on me in Rome
when he found that I was not in New York.) My
limited passport had only ten days to go and I had,
up to that day, taken for granted that Mrs. Shipley
would extend it for another period. But I knew that
with the news of McCarthy, and no passport, Korda
would not, could not go on employing me.

I started out for the cable office, deciding that I
would send McCarthy my Rome address, but a few
cups of coffee later I knew there was something the
matter with that kind of showing-off because most
certainly he knew that I was in Rome and where to
reach me. When I realized that it had taken me an
hour to figure that out, I knew that I had better not
rely on my own judgments. I telephoned the office of
Ercole Graziadei, a fine lawyer whom I'd met several
times, a man who had a splendid reputation as an
anti-Fascist under Mussolini. He said that although I
could not be sure of the newspaper story, it was now
certain the American consul in Rome would not issue
an extension of my passport. He also said that he
believed Rome was not a good place for me because
the Italian government often took their orders from
Mrs. Luce and they could pick me up or harass me on
an even lesser charge than evading a subpoena, or for
using a passport that had expired. I said I thought

I'd go back to New York immediately. He laughed and said he thought that was foolish: I would be giving up a job I needed, walking into trouble. Why didn't I go up to London for a few days, where the government didn't take orders from Washington, and try for an extension of my passport there? That seemed good sense and would give me a chance to phone Hammett from an untapped instrument and find out about the McCarthy story. Graziadei said his son-in-law would buy me an afternoon ticket to London. I was to go back to my apartment and do exactly whatever I did every day at that hour, take no baggage except what I could put in a shopping bag or purse, take a taxi to the Excelsior Hotel, spend ten minutes in the bar, take another taxi from the Excelsior to the airport, where his son-in-law would be waiting for me.

I did exactly what Graziadei told me. I left my hotel at two-fifteen, took a taxi to the Excelsior, bought myself a stiff drink, took another taxi to the airport. The airport was empty at that hour except for the son-in-law, who was waiting for me with my ticket. I was reading a magazine when the loudspeaker called my name, saying there was a telephone call for me. I did not move until the loudspeaker came again and then I thought I had to answer the phone because the girl at the desk who had checked me in could see me from where she was making the announcement. When I got to the desk the girl said, "The secretary

of the Contessa ——— wishes to speak with you."
I had met the elderly Contessa several times, had
once been to her palazzo for lunch, and once had
tea with her as she explained for what seemed like
many hours her English background and the pains
of being married to an Italian. Before I picked up
the phone, of course I asked myself how her secretary
could know I was at the airport. A woman spoke into
the phone in so English an accent that I began to
think it was too English. She said she was the Contessa's secretary, could I come to a small dinner
party at the end of the week when the Contessa returned to Rome? I repeated the invitation, stalling
for time and then I said yes, I would be glad to come
and I was at the airport to meet an American friend.
I telephoned Graziadei, who said he didn't believe it
was the Contessa, that he thought somebody had tried
to follow me to the airport, lost me, and was now
making sure. In any case, it was too late to worry and
to send news from London.

It was such a nervous ride to London that I was
there before I realized that I must find a hotel, certainly something cheap. But on the way to a taxi I
told myself that I was going back to Claridge's, like
the old days. I would be less nervous there and to hell
with money for a few days.

I did, indeed, feel nice in the pretty room and
was extravagant enough to order a good dinner, and
to be very glad to see the old valet I had known for

years, who said he'd be happy to wash my messy cotton dress and deliver it by eight in the morning.

At ten the next morning I was sitting on a bench in the American consul's outside office. When the lady at the desk examined my passport she said it would be necessary for me to see the consul. An hour or two later she told me he was busy and perhaps it would be better if I came back at three in the afternoon. It was obvious now that things weren't going to be easy. I took a sandwich to the National Gallery, exactly the way I had done two or three times a week during the war when Myra Hess would give lunchtime concerts. I had returned looking for the music that was no longer there, no longer needed for anybody except maybe me. I sat wondering why driving into V-2 bombs every morning as we shot a documentary on the London docks in 1944 had worried me less than my present disorder.

When I returned to the consulate, the clerk at the desk took me immediately into the consul's office. He was a pleasant, good-mannered man, and when we had finished chatting about his mother having been born in New Orleans, wasn't that a coincidence, he said that he could not renew or extend my passport, the request would have to go back to Washington and he would have to wait for an answer. I should have known that, but I heard myself say, "I can't stay here long, it's expensive and I have only one dress and it's raining." He was too good-mannered, I guess, to ask why I had come to London without a second dress. He said he would call me as soon as he heard from Washington.

I said, "Would it be possible for you to cable that unless I can have the extension this week I will lose my job?"

He smiled and said perhaps it would be best if I sent that message in another cable to Mrs. Shipley.

I didn't send it. I walked back in the rain, wondering where I could find a cheap dress and raincoat, decided not to bother, and ended up in bed.

Toward evening I remembered the pub at the next corner where I had gone so many times during the war, and afterwards, and where the charming fat lady who ran it had always been kind and friendly.

She and her middle-aged son, Oliver, were glad to see me. She had a shrewd eye because when she sat down with our beers she asked me if I was feeling sick. I said no, just troubled. We talked for a long time, she told me she was getting married again and moving to Devon, and she shouted to Oliver, who brought me a large piece of cold roast beef. I guess I had had too many beers, too much of something, because there could have been no reason to cut my right hand with the knife unless I had tried to do it. I don't know to this day if I said that out loud or if I only thought that bad luck had been sitting near that hand for a long time, and if I couldn't break the luck I would join that large army of people who know that no matter what they do it will turn out wrong, and they end up doing nothing, or doing what they shouldn't do. I know only that Oliver was over-disturbed by my cut, cleaned it, and his mother asked why I was out in such weather without a raincoat and went to get a poncho she said a customer had left behind months before and I should keep it. I never saw either of them again, although we exchanged many postcards and I had an announcement of Oliver's wedding to somebody called Poly. The pub closed down a few years later. In 1970 I had a letter from Oliver that says, "I think you want to know that Ma died ten months ago. The man would not marry, so she managed another pub and died easy in bed with my uncle not her brother, my dead father's brother. My Poly is no way sorry to see Ma go but I was and wants to thank you for wedding present."

Two days went by after my night in the pub. I couldn't make myself call anybody I knew in London. I don't any longer know what I did with those days except once I took a boat ride up the river. On the third morning a girl called from the consulate and asked me to come over at eleven. I was there at ten, for no purpose, I thought, except to make myself more nervous. At eleven o'clock I was told that the consul was in a meeting and would I come back at two. I wanted to say, "Tell him to go to hell," but I didn't, and regretted the days when I would have. But at two the consul was pleasant about the rain stopping, he liked London but the traffic was getting very naughty, and Mrs. Shipley had extended my passport for another three months.

I phoned Hammett from the London airport and made a date with him to go to a number we had long ago arranged if either one of us might be in trouble and didn't want to be phone-tapped. Then I called Graziadei with the good news and he said that was fine, there were no further Rome newspaper accounts of my subpoena, but it might be wise to stay in London. I said I couldn't do that, my dress was dirty, and he laughed and said women were women.

When I arrived back in Rome there was no mail of any importance and the clerk said nobody had asked for me. I telephoned the Contessa. Her secretary, who did not have an English accent, said the Contessa had been away from Rome for the last few weeks and would not be returning for a month.

Then I went down to the Grand Hotel and put in a call to Dash at the arranged number and time. He said there had been nothing in the New York newspapers about a subpoena for me. I said that even though I now had an extended passport, maybe I should come home and tell McCarthy I was ready when he was ready, but before I finished that sentence Dash said, "Stop the honor child stuff and stay where you are. McCarthy's going bats. Let him go bats without your help." Then I told him about the call from the Contessa at the airport and there was such a long pause that I said, "Hello, are you there?" and he said yes, I was to give him a minute to think, he wasn't a machine. I said the call at the airport had frightened me and he said that was good because it should have.

Then he said, "What's a big tip in a Wop hotel?"

"Two or three dollars."

"O.K. Give the top bellboys five dollars each. Give the same to each telephone operator. Give the desk clerks ten dollars and tell them there's ten dollars more for anybody who can tell you who followed you, or asked for you at the desk, or showed any interest the day you went to London. Then don't get your usual impatient. Let all that sink in for a few days and maybe it will turn up something and maybe it won't."

I said I thought he was awfully smart and he said, "Lilly, please stop admiring me for nothing."

The next morning I distributed the money and asked the questions. Nobody knew anything, everybody looked puzzled, everybody took the money. Two days later — I went for a walk every day around four o'clock — a middle-aged man whom I recognized as a kind of part-time relief bellboy was standing outside my grocery store as I walked down the block. He made some kind of motion to the man who owned the shop and the owner made a motion through the window for me to come inside. The store was empty, but we went into the back room and the bellboy began to talk. I could understand almost nothing of what he said, and the owner, who spoke English, said not to pay any attention, his cousin didn't talk well, something had always been the matter with him, but not too much. He said his cousin had come to him the night before to say that I was wasting my money on the tips because the hotel people were frightened to talk. He had told his cousin not to be frightened, that I would certainly pay him for what he could tell me, and would not say a word that could bring him into "the affair." I said I would certainly pay him and not bring him into "the affair," that I was in no position to make trouble and didn't want any for myself. Then the translation began and its first interruption was surprising: the owner said his cousin wanted to know if I had ever acted in the movies or was an anarchist. I said I wrote movies, didn't agree with anarchists. That was not well received because the bellboy refused to speak for a while, chewing on a thumbnail. The grocery man got impatient and pushed his cousin's hand away from his mouth. The translation for the next five minutes — it wasn't easy because the bellboy would wander off the subject and the translator would bark at him — boiled down to one of the desk clerks being a police agent, and two of the telephone operators, and it was not the first time that the man had come to ask about my movements, with whom I had gone out, what visitors, and from time to time been handed my mail. The bellboy said that one of the clerks had seen him listening, hanging around, and had told him that if he ever opened his mouth about "the gentleman" he would be deported. The store owner had evidently never heard this part before, because he grew angry and shouted that Fascism was over, and what the hell was the matter with his cousin for not telling him about the deportation shit before? He himself would go and denounce the clerk, he wanted no Fascist in his family.

There was nothing I could do but wait out the tirade. When the owner went to serve a customer I tried my bad Italian: what was the name of the man who had inquired for me so often? He did not know the name. What did he look like? He was American, past thirty, tallish, blond, always clean, losing some of his hair. When the owner came back I asked him to ask his cousin if the man's accent was like mine. No. I imitated a Westerner. No. I tried something vaguely Southern. Yes, that was nearer. Did the man give money to the clerks or phone operators? The bellboy didn't think so, the man was "official" and he thought they got their money by the month, that it came through an office. What kind of "official" did he think the man was? The grocer laughed; didn't I know that the Americans, my people, had many agencies, and all of them paid for information? After that practice had been denounced for too many minutes I gave the grocer what amounted to twenty dollars, he divided it with his cousin, and I said there would be ten more if he could call me when the man came again, or if he could find out the man's name. We all shook hands, clucked over the state of the world, and I walked for two hours trying to place the description of my caller. It fitted too many people.

But the following morning I found a note under my door. It said, in printed English letters, "The man's name is Dick ————. Put ten dollars American in envelope and leave envelope at grocery store." It was signed Sophia Sanitation, an interesting name. I did exactly that, the grocery store owner took it, nodded, and went back to work. There is a possibility that Sophia Sanitation worked in the hotel; it is more probable that the bellboy and the store owner knew the man's name the day before and saw another ten dollars in the delay.

But now I thought it best to leave Rome. I was never to hear from McCarthy or anything further about a subpoena, but Dick and Betty have frequently, in unimportant ways, crossed my life. The lady was to have an affair with a friend of mine many years later and to tell my friend that one of the reasons she wanted to leave her husband was the shame she felt about his CIA connections. When the love affair was over she went back to her husband. He evidently had a fit of nerves over the indiscretion of his wife and wrote the ex-lover that, indeed, he had once been

CIA, was no longer, but that his wife was still a valuable and highly paid agent and he hoped that would remain a secret with my friend. It didn't.

I have no idea why the CIA was interested in me in Rome, but I've always believed that Dick gave the subpoena story to the Rome newspapers with an aimless hope that he'd turn up something, have a little news to send his bosses that week. In those days, unlike these days when the level of interference is higher and more dangerous, the CIA was picking up all kinds of clowns on a piecework basis, and when you work that way the more casseroles you cook up the greater the chance one of them will taste good enough to pay off.

But nothing much was to go right that year. Korda, who had liked my script, did not like it when it was finished and refused to pay me what was due. He forgot to tell me that he couldn't pay me, that it had nothing to do with the virtues or faults of the script; he had gone bankrupt a week before.

And so I came back to New York and did nothing for a while. Then, not unexpected, we had no money left. I took a half-day job in a large department store, under another name, arranged by an old friend who worked there. I was in the grocery department and that was not unpleasant, but I kept it a secret because I knew it would worry Hammett. About six months later, an aunt I liked very much died in New Orleans, and left me a larger sum than I ever thought she could have saved in her hardworking life.

I guess I began to write again, although I can't remember what, maybe because it was just practice stuff.

Hammett and I rented a house that summer on Martha's Vineyard and the fine black lady, Helen, came back to work because now we could afford to pay her again. Nothing was as it had been, but because it had been bad, small things seemed better than ever — the occasional rental of a catboat for a day's sail, a canoe for the pond, a secondhand car, grocery bills I didn't have to worry so much about. We had a good summer.

And it was the summer of the Army-McCarthy hearings. For us, of course, they came too late to make much difference and seemed a wild mess. The boozy, hospital-patched face of McCarthy, sometimes teasing and gay as in the good days, often caught in disbelief that he was where he was, and angry. He and his boys, Roy Cohn and David Schine — the brash but less assured older brothers of Haldeman and Ehrlichman — were, indeed, a threesome: Schine's little-boy college face, Cohn plump of body, pout of sensual mouth, and McCarthy, a group breaking up before our eyes after years of a wild ride. Bonnie, Bonnie and Clyde, shooting at anything that came to hand on the King's horses that rode to battle in official bulletproof armor.

Then Mr. Stevens of the Army, a strangely un-sympathetic figure, and the lawyer Joseph Welch, certainly a Boston gentleman, remembered for that highly admired sentence, "Have you no sense of de-cency, sir?" I thought the sentence funny; had it really taken Welch so long to find that out, or was it a good actor's instinct for proper timing?

Because, of course, McCarthy was finished long before the hearings began. It wasn't because he had become too daring and taken to fooling around the sacred precincts of the Army, it was simply and plainly that most of America was sick of him and his two kiddies.

The editor and critic Philip Rahv, an early anti-Communist and then an early anti-anti-Communist, had said it a year before in one of his least decipher-able growls: "Nothing can last in America more than ten years. McCarthy will soon be finished." And that, I think, was the truth, just that and not much more. We were not shocked at the damage McCarthy had done, or the ruin he brought on many people. Nor had we been surprised or angered by Cohn and Schine playing with the law as if it were a batch of fudge they enjoyed after the pleasure of their nightly pillow fight. We were bored with them. That and nothing more.

There were many broken lives along the path the boys had bulldozed, but not so many that people needed to feel guilty if they turned their backs fast

717

enough and told each other, as we were to do again after Watergate, that American justice will always prevail no matter how careless it seems to critical outsiders.

It is not true that when the bell tolls it tolls for thee: if it were true we could not have elected, so few years later, Richard Nixon, a man who had been closely allied with McCarthy. It was no accident that Mr. Nixon brought with him a group of high-powered operators who made Cohn and Schine look like cute little rascals from grammar school. The names and faces had been changed; the stakes were higher, because the prize was the White House. And one year after a presidential scandal of a magnitude still unknown, we have almost forgotten them, too. We are a people who do not want to keep much of the past in our heads. It is considered unhealthy in America to remember mistakes, neurotic to think about them, psychotic to dwell upon them.

NOTHING MORE WAS TO HAPPEN to me. I began to write plays again and in 1958 to get movie offers that I no longer wanted; the taste had gone.

It is true, as I have said, that Hammett was never again allowed to have a nickel of his own money and that the emphysema which had started in the Aleutians was to end in cancer of the lungs. Those last years were not good for him, but he managed them fairly well, with no complaints about what had been done to him, even refusing to call the police on two occasions when people, or official people, fired shots through the window of his cottage. But none of those years were as bad as they could have been and were for many people.

I recovered, maybe even more than that, in the sense of work and money. But I have to end this book almost as I began it: I have only in part recovered from the shock that came, as I guess most shocks do, from an unexamined belief that sprang from my own nature, time, and place. I had believed in intellectuals, whether they were my teachers or my friends or strangers whose books I had read. This is inexplicable to a younger generation, who look upon the 1930's radical and the 1930's Red-baiter with equal amusement. I don't much enjoy their amusement, but they have some right to it. As I now have some right to disappointment in what the good children of the Sixties have come to.

Maybe what I still feel is best summed up in an evening I once spent in London with Richard Crossman, then an editor of the *New Statesman and Nation* and a member of Parliament. It was about a month after Hammett had gone to jail and Crossman knew nothing of my connection to Hammett. He had turned to me, as the only American in the room, to say that it was a disgrace that not one intellectual had come to Hammett's aid, that if such a case had happened in London he, and many others like him, would have protested immediately on the grounds that it is your right to believe, my obligation to stand by even in disagreement. I remember that Kingsley Martin, the intelligent, cranky editor of the *New Statesman and Nation,* very worried, was trying to tell Crossman of my relation to Hammett. He ignored Kingsley to say that it took an Englishman a long time to fight for a liberty but once he had it nobody could take it away, but that we in America fought fast for liberty and could be deprived of it in an hour.

In every civilized country people have always come forward to defend those in political trouble. (There was once even some honor in being a political prisoner.) And there were a few here who did just that, but not many, and when one reads them now the words seem slightly timid, or at best too reasonable.

And it is now sad to read the anti-Communist writers and intellectuals of those times. But sad is a fake word for me to be using; I am still angry that their reason for disagreeing with McCarthy was too often his crude methods — the standards of the board of governors of a country club. Such people would have a right to say that I, and many like me, took too long to see what was going on in the Soviet Union. But whatever our mistakes, I do not believe we did our

720

country any harm. And I think they did. They went to too many respectable conferences that turned out not to be under respectable auspices, contributed to and published too many CIA magazines. The step from such capers was straight into the Vietnam War and the days of Nixon. Many of the anti-Communists were, of course, honest men. But none of them, as far as I know, has stepped forward to admit a mistake. It is not necessary in this country; they too know that we are a people who do not remember much.

I HAVE WRITTEN HERE that I have recovered. I mean it only in a worldly sense because I do not believe in recovery. The past, with its pleasures, its rewards, its foolishness, its punishments, is there for each of us forever, and it should be.

As I finish writing about this unpleasant part of my life, I tell myself that was then, and there is now, and the years between then and now, and the then and now are one.

"Scoundrel Time" has an odd history. When it was first published two and a half years ago it got excellent reviews and sold very well indeed. I had not expected that to happen. Through the difficult decision to write it, its formation from a time of peace back to a time of crisis, the months of galleys and page proofs, I was convinced of sharp attacks for the book and failure. It was a great pleasure to find that I was wrong. All was well, particularly among young people.

When the attacks did come, strangely late, and often on shaky grounds, they caused no effect on the book except, to judge by the many letters I received and the reactions of college audiences, to make strangers more annoyed and bewildered than they made me. I had already been threatened with one bullying lawsuit, which was doomed from the beginning, and a front page publicity stunt with high-tone claims about what I had never done.

Certain people who wrote to me had memories of the time of the book, had been injured themselves or had friends who were, and they were no more surprised than I at the attacks. But it was, and is, difficult to explain to young people who know nothing of early anti-Communists, and their now middle-aged disciples, that the people who attacked the book were not necessarily personal enemies, although some of them wrote their reviews as if they were. They are mostly people for whom the view from one window, grown dusty with time, has blurred the world and who do not intend ever to move to another window.

The people who wrote to me or questioned me in a friendly way were not, of course, sympathetic to 1930's Communism. There are probably no such people in the United States and haven't been for many years, although there are various pockets that have turned toward the Chinese interpretation of Communism. I do not think that even liberalism, as a movement, survives in America, not less its radical cousins. Most of the American young, and those now in their thirties, are well on their way to a sort of shoulder-shrugging conservatism, if they even use their education to do that much thinking about the world. But they have an interesting and valuable commodity: more middle-class and well-heeled than any generation before them, they do not have much knowledge of fear. If you have only little splinters of fear or have, because of your time and background, skipped it, you may well think Tom Smith, who is your friend or maybe just somebody you heard about or read, a rather mistaken or foolish fellow, but when he refuses to allow an unjust group of men to push him around, you go down to the police station or the courthouse with him. Somewhere, somehow, convoluted and pulled from its old sources, this lack of fear has its roots in another America and maybe in eighteenth-century France or England, or wherever men of the Western world were early insisting upon freedom for dissident political opinion.

* * * * * *

It is six thirty on a bright August morning. I finished reading "Scoundrel Time" again an hour ago. I made myself a cup of coffee, carried it to the beach, and watched some minnows moving about. I do not now see as well as I once did and so, leaning over to look at them more closely, I couldn't find them again. I spilled the coffee and thought, O.K., watch yourself, sit down, be still. I don't know how long I stayed, but when I got up the memory of a small dinner party last year in San Francisco had come back and with it the reason for my occasional discomfort during last night's reading of this book.

The dinner was with a few old friends, most pleasant and easy until the host, a distinguished scientist, announced that one of my critics who also happened to be in town from New York — the crankiest, in fact — would join us. I believe that the host had really forgotten this man's strangely based, oddly personal case against the book and me. (Who can be expected to remember other people's book fights?) We were polite to each other, the new arrival and I, and I said nothing throughout his almost manic long speeches. The speeches were, in any case, not meant for me, but for a famous French visitor. When my critic left early, not because of me, but because the Frenchman was not responding with proper admiration or interest, the hostess, for her own reasons, was annoyed with me.

She said, "You must really learn to be more tolerant and forgiving."

Many people have more than a distaste for certain words. My great-uncle, who was a corrupt man, would cover his face and make a sound at the use of the word "toilet." My hostess could not be expected to know that I feel strongly about "tolerance." It is, to me, an arrogant conception. Who am I to forgive? To forget, not to punish, is one thing, but forgiveness is for God if you believe in him and maybe even if you don't. I wanted to tell my hostess that, couldn't, couldn't even say that it is not pleasant to correct people for what they haven't done.

So I said, "Yes, and that's a long story."

"No," she said, "I mean it. You do not forgive people. You must learn to forgive. The time has come in your life when you must learn to be tolerant and forgive."

Wine makes for repetition, and the fourth time she said it I was in the elevator. But I was not thinking of her, the evening or my critic. I was thinking of something else and the something else only came clear this morning on the beach.

For years before "Scoundrel Time" was written I had many offers to publish such a book. But I believed I had to wait until I could reach a view, make a "tone" that was not a jumble, not chaotic with judgments and weary storms that were meaningless to anybody but me. I was waiting for a period of what my hostess would have called "tolerance," what I called "calm." It came, I thought; I wrote the book and I misrepresented myself in the book.

725

I am, of course, sorry for that. I am not cool about those days, I am not tolerant about them and I never wish to be.

This book seemed to me last night too restrained. All those years I had waited for a view that came only because of time and recovery from pain and disorder. Or maybe I didn't have the final nerve — an accusation made by Tolstoi against Chekhov in another context, but coming out the same place here — to say that my mistakes and the political commitments of other more radical people were no excuse for the disgraceful conduct of intellectuals no matter how much they disagreed.

I believe that I am telling the truth, not the survivors' consolation, when I say that the disasters of the McCarthy period were, in many ways, good for me: I learned things, I got rid of much I didn't need. But I am angrier now than I hope I will ever be again; more disturbed now than when it all took place. I tried to avoid, when I wrote this book, what is called a moral stand. I'd like to take that stand now. I never want to live again to watch people turn into liars and cowards and others into frightened, silent collaborators. And to hell with the fancy reasons they give for what they did.

THE WIND
WILL NOT STOP

The trees want to remain quiet, but the wind will not stop.
(Despite wishing for peace, trouble is brewing)
— Chinese proverb

By Judy Carlson Hulbert

CHINESE RECONCILIATION
PROJECT FOUNDATION

塔可瑪社區協和促進會
(Publishing Division)

First printing edition 2021.

**CHINESE RECONCILIATION
PROJECT FOUNDATION**

塔可瑪社區協和促進會

CRPF Publishing Division

(with a grant from Tacoma Creates)

http://crpftacoma.org/

Library of Congress Control Number: 2021910719

Printed in the U.S.A.

Summary: A Tacoma boy in 1885 gets caught up in the conflict between

his Chinese friends and the town that wants them gone.

ISBN: 978-1-7373039-0-9 (Paperback) 978-1-7373039-1-6 (e-book)
Washington state—History-1885—Juvenile History [1. USA history—
Fiction. 2. Washington state history—Fiction. 3. Race relations—Fic-
tion. 4. 19th Century history—Fiction. 5. Chinese in America—Fiction]
Front cover image by Joni Joachims
Book design by Rebecca Young